Research Journeys into Ways of Knowing

Jennifer Markides and Laura Forsythe (Eds.)

ISBN 978-1-64504-010-1 (Hardback)
ISBN 978-1-64504-009-5 (Paperback)
ISBN 978-1-64504-011-8 (E-Book)

Printed on acid-free paper

© DIO Press Inc, New York
https://www.diopress.com

All Rights Reserved

No part of this work may be reproduced, stored in a retrieval system, or transmitted in any form or by any means, electronic, mechanical, photocopying, microfilming, recording or otherwise, without written permission from the Publisher, with the exception of any material supplied specifically for the purpose of being entered and executed on a computer system, for exclusive use by the purchaser of the work.

This book is part of the *Critical Pedagogies* Series
Series Editor: Shirley R. Steinberg

Dedication

It is with a heavy heart that we acknowledge the passing of contributor, Chuck Bourgeois.

When we requested permission to include his work in the publication posthumously, Chuck's wife Tina Munroe (personal communication, November 14, 2018) wrote:

> You are most welcome to include this piece. I remember the day when Chuck finished writing it. He picked me up from work for lunch and brought flowers. He was so very excited to share it with me and he was so very proud of having completed it. He dug very deep inside when he was working on this and came out with these words. He wasn't sure if he would be able to finish it in time for the deadline, but he fought tooth and nail for every word he put into it. Many knew his strength in writing, but where he went with his mind and words in his journey of self-exploration in finding his own "way of being" was beyond what I or anyone could possibly comprehend. He was most humbled by the opportunity to share a panel with his Métis relations and to co-write a piece with his co-presenters. Thank you for including his piece. He was a proud St. Pierre Métis and I trust that inclusion of his work will add some context to contemporary explorations of identity.

She also included the following picture taken at the *Rising Up: A Graduate Students Conference on Indigenous Knowledge and Research* in March of 2018, featuring Chuck Bourgeois with the Métis relations mentioned above.

From left to right: Jason Surkan, Victoria Bouvier, Angie Tucker, and Chuck Bourgeois

We are grateful to Tina Munroe for her generosity. Thank you for allowing us to honour and remember Chuck Bourgeois in this way. *All Our Relations.*

Table of Contents

Foreword   xi
Niigaan Sinclair

Introduction   xvii
A Decolonizing Approach to Publication
Jennifer Markides

Knowing Self and Learning in Community: Teachings Shared Towards Advocacy and Understanding

En el Centro de Este Fuego – In the Center of the Fire: 1
Indigenous Women's Storytelling as Decolonial Resistance
Sarah María Acosta Ahmad

Barriers to Indigenous Athletes' Athletic Development in   9
Canada: An Analysis Framed by Daniels' Ingredients of Success, Part I
Nickolas J. Kosmenko

Who has the Right? A Reflection on Indigenous Research as a   19
Chinese Anthropology Student Researcher
Xiao Zheng

Rooted in Place: Métis Identity and Connections to Geographic   31
and Temporal Landscapes
Angie Tucker

The Indigenous Dick Joke: A Thorough yet Noninvasive   41
Examination of Our Most Famous Tribal Member
Waylon Lenk

Unsettling Colonial Effects and Returning to Indigenous Ways

Constricting Self-Determination: Colonial Racism and Sexism in   51
the Lives of Indigenous Women in Canada's West
Jessica Martin

Raising the Voices of Survivors and Collaborators Confronting   63
Sex Trafficking and Exploitation of Indigenous Women and
Girls in Manitoba, Canada
Robert Chrismas

Is "Harm Reduction" Indigenous?   73
Aura Lavallée

Working in Circles – Indigenous Methodology Restoring our   83
Wellness, Restoring our Roles, Indigenous Women and Birth
Stephanie Sinclair

The Duojár: An Agent of the Symbolic Repatriation of Sámi   93
Cultural Heritage
Liisa-Rávná Finbog

The Unavoidable Alienation of Indigenous Artists in our Mass-   103
Produced Society: Lattimer Gallery and Pacific Northwest
Coast Art
Laura Forsythe

Respecting Language and Ways of Knowing While Troubling Colonial Images of Indigeneity

Bridging Gaps: Intercultural Education as a Tool for   115
Revitalization
Monica Morales-Good

Language, Storytelling, and Intergenerational Learning Among   125
the Abam People of South-Eastern Nigeria
Uwakwe Kalu

Han—Korean—Ontology: Similarities and Differences from   135
Indigenous Ontologies
JuSung Kim

Application of Malthusian Theory in Colonization Schemes in   147
Canada
Kseniya Zaika

Anishinaabe Mino-Bimaadiziwin in Margaret Atwood's *MaddAddam*   155
Bryn Skibo-Birney

IResidential School Photography: From Photographic Propaganda to Empowering Pictures   165
Melanie Braith

Indigitalgames.com and Representations of Indigenous Peoples in Video Games   175
Naithan Lagace

Expanding Métis Curriculum   185
Chantal Fiola

Honouring Identity and Strengthening Community Through Resistance and Personal Narratives

Honouring our Relations: Exploring a Wider Acumen of Métis Spaces   199
Victoria Bouvier, Angie Tucker, Jason Surkan, and Chuck Bourgeois

I am told I was Fierce: A Personal Narrative on Decolonization Through Written and Spoken Word   217
Liberty Emkeit

Decolonization? What is it? Does anyone know what it is? Let's find out!   225
Patricia Siniikwe Pajunen

Indigenous Student Experience in an Indigenizing Institution: Preliminary Results from a Canadian University   235
Iloradanon Efimoff

Beyond Indigenization: Indigenous Collaboration and Imagining our own Academy   245
Adam Gaudry

Indigenizing Protocols and Decolonizing Practices in Research and Teaching

The Honourable Harvest: *An Indigenous Research Protocol* 263
Silvina Antunes, Kara Passey, Jordan Tabobondung, and Erika Vas

Striving for Authenticity: Embracing a Decolonizing Approach 275
to Research with Indigenous Athletes
Shara R. Johnson, Jennifer Poudrier, Heather Foulds, and Leah J. Ferguson

Miýo-Pimātisiwin: Decolonizing Self Through Culturally 287
Responsive Pedagogy (CRP)
Obianuju Juliet Bushi

Decolonizing/Indigenizing: (Re)Imagining Educational Systems, 295
even those Mathematical
Shana Graham

Research, Technology, and Neocolonialism 307
Orest Kinasevych

Decolonizing Through Counter-Narratives: Working to Disrupt Colonizing Systems and Structures

"In this war of words": Canada 150 and the (re)Telling of 319
History
Wanda Hounslow

Deconstruction of Barriers in Anti-Racist/Decolonization 331
Discussions Through the Education of Canadians Vis-à-vis
DiAngelo's Theory: "White Fragility"
Belinda (Wandering Spirit) Nicholson

Reframing Catholicism: Agency and Resistance in Mi'kmaw 339
Stories
Micheline Hughes

A Colonial Institution with Colonial Voices and Values: *351*
Exposing Daniels v. Canada's Tribute to the Colonizers
Karine Martel

Indigenous Schools in Brazil and Canada: A Call to Action for   *363*
Sovereignty
Eduardo Vergolino

Indigenous Self-government, Land Management and Taxation   *373*
Powers
Esteban Vallejo-Toledo

Reconciling Diversity: Acknowledging the Challenges   *385*
Paul D. Hansen

Foreword

Niigaan Sinclair

Creating Our Own: A Call out for Indigenous Word Warriors

> If our struggle is anything, it is the struggle for sovereignty, and if sovereignty is anything, it is a way of life. That way of life is not a matter of defining a political ideology or having a detached discussion about the unifying structures and essences of American Indian traditions. It is a decision – a decision we make in our minds, in our hearts, and in our bodies – to be sovereign and to find out what that means in the process.[1]
>
> Robert Warrior

Indigenous scholarship is a critical site where Indigenous politics, identity, and nationhood are envisioned and enacted in some of its fullest articulations. This is not a new site; scholarship has been taking place in lodges and homes and educational spaces on Turtle Island for millennia. And, while intellectual work is by no means the only place where Indigenous life is lived and practiced, thoughts, ideas, and visions – and the dissemination and publication of them – are some of the most robust ways in which self-determination and "sovereignty" – physical, intellectual, and otherwise – is proven as possible. It is in work by Indigenous creative and critical voices, I assert, where our nations, families and communities are grown, restored and activated for the future. It is here, to use a phrase from the brilliant Acoma Pueblo poet and theorist Simon Ortiz, "there is something more than survival and saving ourselves: it is continuance."[2]

This collection of Indigenous scholarship embodies Muskogee Creek critic Craig Womack's vision of "young Native critics" in his essay "The Integrity of American Indian Claims (Or, How I Learned to Stop Worrying and Love My Hybridity)" in which he argues that Indigenous critics and allies of Indigenous communities cannot sit idly by and watch while Native communities endure political, legal, and scholarly attacks. Womack reminds us that "activism nor criticism should be a mutually exclusive endeavor."³ As Indigenous critics and allies of Indigenous communities, we have a responsibility, Womack asserts, to engage in the real-life intellectual and political acts of resistance and nation-building occurring amongst our relatives and in our communities. This is particularly true if only for the fact that it is these peoples and places that will nurture and support our work, sacrifice and fight for us, and practice and protect the very values we draw upon to produce our scholarship. Simply, it is due to Indigenous peoples and communities that we are here and we must return this gift. Indigenous scholars must take up this responsibility to give back for "we have to tend to ourselves."⁴

Perhaps more forcefully, Cherokee-Quapaw-Chickasaw critic Geary Hobson – who supervised Womack when he was a PhD student at the University of Oklahoma – points out that Native scholars must adopt the same kinds of interests in sovereignty as practiced by their nations. In his contribution to Cherokee-Choctaw-Creek scholar Kimberly Roppolo's "Wisdom of the Elders" series (who he also supervised), she asked him how "aspiring young Native American scholars" can "take part in the dominant culture [academic] discourse surrounding Native American cultural productions and still preserve their allegiance to their Native American community." Hobson responded by stating:

> Indian academics must stop allowing our friends to speak for us. This happens all too frequently. Despite the most sincere wishes of our non-Indian friends that Indian voices be heard, this will generally not deter them from speaking for us, or standing-in for us in the often important deliberations affecting Indian people. Whenever this happens, you no longer, of course, have an Indian viewpoint... I mean no disrespect to all our White colleagues by saying these things, but the bottom line for me is, damnit to the White Man's Hell, let Indian people speak for Indian people."⁵

Although perhaps hard to discern from Hobson's fiery rhetoric, what Hobson really means, Roppolo writes, is that "no matter how much lip service there may be in the academy toward making a space for American Indian voices, that in truth, the American Indian voice is generally unwelcome."⁶ Indigenous scholars simply cannot wait for others to give space to advocate for Indigenous communities and our principles and ideas; we must create our own.

Importantly, these sovereign spaces, like Indigenous nations, can also include non-Native scholars. In his essay "Splitting the Earth: First Utterances and Pluralist Separatism," Cherokee scholar Jace Weaver points out that Indigenous critics speaking with and for our communities must not deter non-Native allies.⁷ Allies are badly needed in this effort.

Responding to charges that Indigenous literary critics working with and in the interests of Indigenous communities promotes a naïve separatism, he points out that culture- and nation-centred criticism does not mean that "non-Natives should not do Native American Studies, much less the study of Native American literature" for "[t]he survival of Native authors, if not Native people in general, depends on it. But we do not need modern literary colonizers. We only ask that non-Natives who study and write about Native peoples do so with respect and a responsibility to Native community. The same applies to Native scholars. We ask no more than we ask of ourselves, but neither do we expect less."[8] This means that non-Indigenous peoples can – and indeed, must – participate in the creation of Indigenous scholarship.

In Dale Turner's book *This is Not a Peace Pipe: Towards a Critical Indigenous Philosophy*, an academic, sovereign, Indigenous space is envisioned and given purpose. In it, Turner describes how Indigenous intellectuals can work with their communities while fulfilling the equally-important role of protecting, fostering, and honouring the knowledge systems they emerge from. As he argues, Indigenous scholars "must be more cautious about what they do with their ways of knowing the world, and especially with how they develop legal and political strategies for asserting, defending, and protecting the rights, sovereignty, and nationhood that they still believe they possess."[9] As Turner suggests, Indigenous ways of knowing too often get interpreted by mainstream Amer-European governments and intellectuals and co-opted on their political terms – resulting in bastardized representations of Indigenous knowledges and knowledge systems, and equally disasterously-devised and delivered policies and programs. To deal with this, what Turner prescribes is:

> a community of indigenous intellectuals – word warriors – [that] ought to assert and defend the integrity of indigenous rights and nationhood *and* protect indigenous ways of knowing within the existing legal and political practices of the dominant culture. However, their intellectual labour must be guided by indigenous philosophies; that is, indigenous philosophies – the wisdom of the elders – must inform and shape the strategies word warriors use to engage European intellectual discourses.[10]

These "word warriors" (a term Turner borrows from Anishinaabe critic Gerald Vizenor) must bravely take up the dual responsibility of advocacy and action in their scholarly pursuits and practices, for:

> our survival as sui generis political nations depends on it. Aboriginal law and politics is quickly evolving into a highly sophisticated overlapping set of discourses. Gaining expertise in Aboriginal legal and political issues

> necessarily involves learning complex legal, political, historical, and philosophical discourse. Word warriors must critically engage these discourses but must do so in accordance with indigenous ways of knowing the world. The difficult problem is to make better sense out of what we mean by 'acting in accordance' with indigenous ways of knowing. Furthermore, by making their way into the agonic intellectual community of the dominant culture – a community driven by non-Aboriginal institutions, interests, and methodologies – word warriors will be able to create stronger and more vibrant Aboriginal intellectual communities. Hopefully, in time, these people will help forge the necessary legal and political spaces that will allow indigenous forms of government – and consequently indigenous ways of being – to thrive within a more inclusive Canadian democratic state.[11]

While Turner, I believe, is describing the "wisdom of the elders" as being the words and actions of grassroots peoples in Indigenous communities, I assert that this definition can also be interpreted as including those speaking to us in written texts too. And, barely needing saying: word warriors can be allies as well. Indigenous communities adopt newcomers, human and non, all the time.

So, just as Hobson calls out his two students Womack and Roppollo to become the kind of "word warriors" of Turner's vision and Weaver encourages allies of Indigenous communities to join them, I extend this to the writers and critics in this anthology. Some in this book I have taught and have had the honour of working with in the Native Studies Department here at the University of Manitoba. Here we are creating scholars doing ground-breaking work, researching with and advocating for Indigenous communities while evoking a world in which Indigenous pedagogy and continuance is possible. It is in this space where our graduate students came together to found the annual international Indigenous graduate scholar forum called *Rising Up: A Graduate Students Conference on Indigenous Knowledge and Research* – a conference that continues to expand and blow me away as I see brave, vigorous research emerging that expands Indigenous futures. The book, *Research Journeys in/to Multiple Ways of Knowing*, is an extension of the relationships and collaborations arising from the conference. I hope you enjoy the critical and creative gifts here and witness and participate in the vibrancy, dynamism, and beauty of Indigenous scholarship.

As Indigenous professors it is always our job, first and foremost, to create space for our future visionaries, traditionalists, and, yes, scholars. This is what we have always done and what we create when we walk the halls of the lodge, raise our children, or travel the hallways of universities today. It is my hope that I have contributed in some small way to these voices in a similar way that it had been done for me too. I went to the University of Oklahoma. Dr. Womack was my supervisor and Dr. Roppolo, Dr. Weaver, Dr. Turner, and Dr. Warrior were influential voices in my life (and all continue to be). I even spent a few lunches visiting with Dr. Hobson. This foreword is my attempt to acknowledge their gifts to me and show how I too have been created by generous and brave visionaries along the way. This is our praxis as Indigenous scholars: to create our future. Indigenous scholarship is Indigenous continuance.

I am so honoured to be asked to contribute this small piece to this ground-breaking book and offer miigwech to everyone involved, especially Laura Forsythe and Jennifer Markides who showed incredible resilience in getting this completed.

Miigwech indinawemaganidog.

Dr. Niigaan Sinclair is Anishinaabe (Little Peguis/Peguis First Nation) and is an Associate Professor in the Department of Native Studies at the University of Manitoba.

notes

[1] Warrior, Robert. *Tribal Secrets: Recovering American Indian Intellectual Traditions*. Minneapolis: U of Minnesota Press, 1995. 123.

[2] Ortiz, Simon. *Woven Stone*. Tucson: U of Arizona P, 1992. 32.

[3] Womack, Craig. ""The Integrity of American Indian Claims (Or, How I Learned to Stop Worrying and Love My Hybridity)." *American Indian Literary Nationalism*. Eds. Weaver, Jace, Craig S. Womack and Robert Warrior. Albuquerque: U of New Mexico P, 2006. 172.

[4] Ibid. 168.

[5] Roppolo, Kimberly. "Wisdom of the Elder: Geary Hobson, P. Jane Hafen, Jeane Breinig, Clifford E. Trafzer, Carol Miller, Louis Owens and Vine Deloria." *Paradoxa* 15 (2001): 275-8. 279.

[6] Ibid. 276.

[7] For two excellent recent examples of this kind of scholarship, see James Cox's *Muting White Noise: Native American and European American Novel Traditions* (Norman: U of Oklahoma Press, 2006) and Sam McKegney's *Magic Weapons: Aboriginal Writers Remaking Community after Residential School* (Winnipeg: U of Manitoba Press, 2007).

[8] Weaver, Jace. "Splitting the Earth: First Utterances of Pluralist Separatism." *American Indian Literary Nationalism*. Eds. Jace Weaver, Robert Warrior, and Craig Womack. Albuquerque: U of New Mexico P, 2006. 1-89. 11-12.

[9] Turner, Dale. *This is Not a Peace Pipe: Towards a Critical Indigenous Philosophy*. Toronto: U of Toronto P, 2006. 73.

[10] Ibid. 74.

[11] Ibid. 74-75.

Introduction

A Decolonizing Approach to Publication

Jennifer Markides

About the Book

Research Journeys in/to Multiple Ways of Knowing brings together the research and writing of Indigenous and non-Indigenous scholars from a variety of disciplines. The research featured in this book, focuses on Indigenous perspectives, addressing colonial legacies and decolonization work in proactive ways. The Indigenous groups and perspectives are diverse, representing knowledge and experiences of specific communities from across North America and around the world. The work is being done in good ways, honouring traditions, amplifying voices, and respecting commitments. The book is multifaceted and reflects the complexity and breadth of issues resulting from colonization and hundreds of years of oppression. Some authors point out systemic racism and injustice, while others explore humour and stories. Some groups share frameworks and successes, while others discuss identity and personal struggles. Some chapters share teachings that have been passed on to the researchers through relationships built on trust and respect. Other chapters represent learning that has come from deep study and analysis of existing literatures. The teachings that each author has been gifted—from community, Creator, or other relations—are honoured here. We are grateful to the Elders, Knowledge Keepers, and community members who have generously contributed to the learning. We are grateful to the scholars who have come before us; they have made the academic ground less treacherous for us along their way. We are grateful to our teachers who come in many forms: human, more-than-human, spiritual, and beyond.

This book represents a holistic approach to publication, pushing back against Western systems that would see the disciplines as separate rather

J. Markides, and L. Forsythe (Eds.), Research Journeys in/to Multiple Ways of Knowing, xix–xxxii.
© 2019 DIO Press Inc. All rights reserved.

than interrelated—the topics as disparate rather than connected. When subject areas, ideas, and arguments are partitioned off from each other, it becomes more challenging to see the bigger picture. Indigenous peoples and communities have been studied more than any other group of people in the world (Tuhiwai Smith, 2012); yet many people have little understanding of the life experiences, historic events, systematic oppression, and systemic racism that Indigenous people have faced since colonization. The history of colonization has long been told by the colonizers. These narratives have been pervasive and tacitly understood as truths. As a result, many people do not understand or empathise with the realities of colonial legacies, intergenerational traumas, or continued oppressive forces that are constantly at work in the lives of Indigenous people. Add to this taken-for-granted telling of history, the media's narratives of Indigenous people: receiving government handouts; demanding more rights and greater say in governmental decisions; protesting pipelines; perpetrating acts of violence; engaging in substance abuse; and more. It becomes understandable why public perception of Indigenous people is so bleak. People feel justified in making off-the-cuff comments that are blatantly racist in nature. Now, more than ever, Indigenous scholarship needs to be speaking back in public forums and presenting counter-narratives in all areas of discussion. In this volume, the voices from many disciplines come together to present ideas and spark discussions that readers might not otherwise be having. Like the many points of intersection in a "spider web" of relations (Leroy Little Bear, 2000), the chapters and have points of intersection—and present ideas that are in relationship. By acknowledging and lifting up *multiple ways of knowing*, the book may help readers to see the world in new ways, to have greater understanding of the multiple influences and perspectives of a variety of Indigenous voices, and to recognize the strength in communities coming together in knowledge sharing.

I have made some bold claims about public perceptions of Indigenous people. I have criticized the colonial influences in the education systems, the telling of history, the government's policies and agendas, the media, and anyone else perpetuating racist ideologies for political or financial gain, or out of ignorance. I have done so without citations and evidence, because I believe that my assertions are commonplace truths of our current relational climate.

While I make the above claims, which may be taken as harsh and pejorative, I see that change is happening too. Indigenous people are gaining and claiming more and more allies all of the time. Systems, that have long been entrenched in colonial and colonizing ways, are making

INTRODUCTION

conscious efforts to address gaps and shortcomings when it comes to knowledge and treatment of Indigenous people, topics, policies, and more. Many universities across Canada are requiring Indigenous content to be embedded in courses and programs in all specializations. Education curriculums are being redrafted to include more meaningful and sustained engagement with Indigenous-related learning outcomes. Government run services—from health care to law enforcement—are providing professional learning for staff at all levels to increase cultural knowledge, understanding, and responsiveness. Some political leaders are making efforts to prioritize and act upon reconciliatory promises, despite instances of public backlash that may affect their chances for re-election. Some media outlets are making concerted efforts to change their portrayals of Indigenous people and stories. Some progress is being made.

As an educator, I see the changes as ongoing. The efforts need to be sustained, supported, and open. Each person is at a different place in their learning journey, and the people working to see change need to be persistent, courageous, and patient. Teaching pre-service teachers, I can see how the work of changing people's deeply-entrenched beliefs and perceptions can be very taxing: mentally, emotionally, physically, and spiritually—the work is never done. I can also see how some people might become discouraged and frustrated, seeing progress with some students and then expecting others to have done the same work and to hold similar knowledge—wide-spread change is slow. Hopefully this type of publication will be useful in continuing to make change; to increase the reader's knowledge of topics and issues; to increase interest and awareness; and to promote greater understanding of interrelated discourses. It is again hoped that the readers will carry the conversation forward in their own lives.

About the Editors

Both Laura Forsythe and myself, Jennifer Markides, are strong and proud Métis. We met at the 2nd annual *Rising Up: A Graduate Students Conference on Indigenous Knowledge and Research* in 2017. Laura was on the organizing committee; she appeared to be doing the work of ten people, as is what I have come to know of her in all respects. We are both graduate students working towards PhDs. Laura studies at the University of Manitoba. I am in the Werklund School of Education at the University of Calgary. We have young families who understand and support our often ambitions goals. We are both active in our communities, volunteering on committees and advocating for Indigenous peoples' rights and representation in many circles. It is important for us that we form community, especially in academic settings, and lift each other up. We are humbled to be trusted as the editors of this book and honoured to get to know and work with such strong contributors. We are proud to bring the chapters together and lift up the voices of the talented scholars. We are grateful to work with a creative and knowledgeable series editor, Shirley Steinberg, and a flexible and supportive publisher, DIO Press. While Indigenous research publications are becoming increasingly common, it takes a visionary publisher to trust and embrace the alternative format that we proposed here. Marsii.

About the Editing

Due to the inter-disciplinary nature of the edited collection, the referencing, formatting, and style of the texts vary from chapter to chapter. Each contributor has been asked to stay true to the style that is germane to their academic field, the one notable exception being that all footnotes have been changed to endnotes. While the referencing and styles may be unfamiliar or different than the reader may be used to seeing, I hope that they can push through any discomfort to celebrate and enjoy the diversity of the work that has been brought together.

Additionally, I would like to note that I have learned a lot about editing from my experience working on this book and a previous edited collection. One contributor that I had the pleasure of working with in 2017-2018, Kāshā Julie A. Morris, taught me an important lesson about the pitfalls of editing from a Western academic lens. I noted that the phrasing on her interview subheadings felt awkward, so I reworded her headings (e.g. Mary's interview, etc.). Later, Morris taught me a valuable and humbling lesson. Her (2018) chapter about Tahltan language nests, honours Tāɬtān itself, which as it turns out does not have or use possessive terminology. What I interpreted as awkward phrasing, turned out to be aligned with the language system and Tahltan worldview. With this new knowledge, I try to read works differently now. I am mindful of my shortcomings and my ignorance to the nuances of other cultural perspectives and knowledge systems. I am learning from the contributors. Laura and I consult each other about our uncertainties before requesting significant changes or greater clarification. In a short time, I have learned

INTRODUCTION

to approach the work of editing with a tentative hand, an open mind, and a humble heart.

I would like to share two examples of the shift in my editing that appear in the Research Journeys text. In Kim's chapter, *Han—Korean—Ontology: Similarities and Differences from Indigenous Ontologies*, he uses the term "vitalogy". Up until the point of editing his chapter, I had only ever heard the word "Vitalogy" as the title of a Pearl Jam album from 1994. Kim explained that he had chosen this term intentionally and that he wanted to attach new meaning to the word as he used it in his piece. From this exchange, I now see the use of vitalogy as Kim's prerogative as a writer, rather than an error to be edited. Similarly, I paused when I read the word "invisiblizes" in Hounslow's chapter, *"In this war of words": Canada 150 and the (re)Telling of History*. After some discussion, I learned that "invisiblizes" is a widely used term in Hounslow's field of study. While some editors might have asked that the term be replaced—labelling the word as subject-specific *jargon*—I have chosen to embrace the word choice as a learning opportunity that again expands the way we might think and what we might come to know from listening to voices of authors from diverse disciplines. These are just two minor examples, but there are many more throughout the text Sometimes the differences are in word choice, other differences are in writing style. Editing the chapters often made me question *how* the authors were discussing Indigenous people, terminology, and related topics. My discomfort often signalled a difference in the norms from one specialization to another. *In education, we frame things differently than they do in law, history, philosophy, etc.* I had to remind myself that different does not mean wrong. I hope that readers will use the experiences of questioning and potential unrest to reflect on their own misgivings towards increased understanding of other ways of engaging in scholarship.

About the Contributors

Many of the chapters come from graduate students. There are also chapters by established scholars, associate and assistant professors. The editors of this book, Laura Forsythe and myself, see the scholarship and voices of graduate students as a strength. The contributors bring perspectives and view research with fresh eyes, gathering references from established sources and wrestling with ideas that the readers might be questioning too. Some authors are sharing the findings from their graduate research, contributing to the broader discourse of their fields.

About the Weaving Together of Disciplines

There are many ways these chapters could have been arranged. It would have been possible to put all of the Métis chapters together; or group the chapters related to Indigenous athletes, legal matters, exploitation of Indigenous women, etc. As previously stated, the points of intersection are many. Some contributors working in different disciplines drew on similar bodies of literature or themes. This spoke to me. So instead of putting like disciplines together, I took inspiration from the symbolism of the spiral, as a path journeying outward/inward in a continuous relationship: beginning with self and identity, moving to community, and spreading out into larger societal systems. I anticipate that readers will draw their own connections, seeing points of intersection that speak to them. The points of affinity will be different for all.

I am excited about the possible uses, reach, and impacts of this publications. I could imagine using the book as course texts in undergraduate classes: requiring the students to read 1-2 chapters prior to a class; asking them to find examples that support the dominant discourse on the subjects; requesting that they look for counter-narratives beyond the chapters themselves; and engaging in dialogue, sharing, and debate. Imagine the possibilities.

Inspired by Carl Leggo's "Sensational Sentences (*found poem*)" (2018, p. x), I would like to share some of the statements that moved me as I read through the contributors' offerings in weaving the book together.

Research Journeys

(found narrative/poem)

Niigaan Sinclair

Indigenous scholarship is a critical site where Indigenous politics, identity, and nationhood are envisioned and enacted in some of its fullest articulations.

INTRODUCTION

In/to Multiple Ways of Knowing

Sarah María Acosta Ahmad

Complicated lives require complicated analyses. Through this, we begin to expand our reach in dismantling oppressive forces both infrastructurally as well as in our colonized minds.

Nickolas J. Kosmenko

We never experienced systemic racism during my upbringing, racism that, for too many people in Canada, is a concern that takes precedence over athletic aspirations. In that way, I was lucky, but I was nevertheless angry.

Xiao Zheng

I have regularly witnessed people's astonishment — "You're from China, and you're interested in our culture?" or "You're doing research on powwows?" followed with "Why are you interested in our culture?" or "Why are you interested in powwows?"

Angie Tucker

I had never considered how differing land ontologies could have affected Métis people. Is it possible that both physical and temporal detachments from land could be responsible for the complexities of identity that often arise within contemporary Métis bodies?

Waylon Lenk

Let none of this imply that fun is not a centrally important element of Indigenous dick jokes. I have heard a ton of these things since word got out that I was engaging in this research, and generally they're good-natured, healthy (if not wholesome) fun.

Jessica Martin

A gendered analysis makes clear that decades of colonial nation-building policies implemented by the Canadian government have created social, economic, and political environments in which Indigenous women are oppressed on two axis: race and sex.

Robert Chrismas

While it is no surprise that Indigenous women are overrepresented in Canada's sex industry, the degree of disparity and disproportionate marginalization and victimization should be shocking to all Canadians.

Aura Lavallée

Each week the Indigenous Elder would come into the overdose prevention site and smudge the space and offer it to anyone who was interested whether or not they were injecting, already under the influence, or working on-site.... medicines were utilized to support those who wanted it but often felt that they could not go near ceremonial practices due to their use.

Stephanie Sinclair

There is a responsibility when working with First Nations to situate the research in the larger historical, political, and cultural context to influence change in colonial policies and practices that continue to impact the well-being of First Nation women.

Liisa-Rávná Finbog

In an effort to safeguard the material culture in question, museums all over the world began collecting the "vanishing objects" of the cultures doomed to extinction.... to this day, important ritual, social and jucidial objects in large numbers are still held in museum collections outside of source communities reach.

Laura Forsythe

The ceremonial creation and motivation to carve or produce regalia is an honoured tradition bastardized by the re-creation of six-inch mass-produced totem poles and dolls wearing button blankets once revered for their symbolism.

Monica Morales-Good

Many Indigenous peoples who find themselves facing the legal institutions prefer to speak the little Spanish they know.... just to avoid the negative effects of colonialism, even if this disadvantages their case; in addition,

INTRODUCTION　　　　　　　　　　　　　　　　　　　　　　　　xxvii

Indigenous attorneys, cultural brokers, and Indigenous judges are rarely requested within the courtroom.

Uwakwe Kalu

Before the interruption of storytelling traditions of Abam by the colonialists, Abam had a rich cultural heritage. The oral narrative was one of the live wires of the Abam cultural heritage.

JuSung Kim

Given the importance of oneness through harmony and balance, an atma of collective spirit is another hallmark of Han ontology. An embodiment of collective spirit would not be possible without taking into account the equation of harmony and balance within samjae.

Kseniya Zaika

The Conquest of North America unlocked an array of employment opportunities for the British. …the new products found in North America and exported to Europe, such as potatoes and sugar, …contributed to the gradual increase in the life expectancy of the colonizers.

Bryn Skibo-Birney

Atwood's conclusion is troubling for its reiteration of the "Native-as-Nature" stereotype.... However, her [work brings] … Indigenous philosophies into more mainstream Euro-American [consciousness, therefore] … despite Atwood's troubled/troubling relationship with Indigeneity, reading her novel in terms of Anishinaabe worldviews would have a variety of benefits.

Melanie Braith

Photographs of children in residential schools were taken in extremely coercive contexts and emerged from asymmetrical power relations. Often, the pictures were staged with the goal to create propaganda for settler society and children were forced to perform as the objects of successful assimilationist endeavours.

Naithan Lagace

A dominant contributing trope continuing to restrict representations of Indigenous cultures, communities, and traditions is through mystical and Wendigo tropes. These tropes share similar relationships with the "savage" or "noble savage" tropes as their representations other and limit mystical or traditional ties of Indigenous communities to their past.

Chantal Fiola

Too often Indigenous content is included in curriculum in a tokenistic way. The focus is usually on First Nations rather than Métis; this is true from early years through to post-secondary education including within Indigenous Studies departments.

Victoria Bouvier, Angie Tucker, Jason Surkan, and Chuck Bourgeois

Looking at the diversity within Métis consciousness, both historically and contemporarily, the discussions that envelop Métis self and collective understandings are complex and multidimensional.

Victoria Bouvier

Framing settler-colonialism as benevolent (re)traumatizes individuals and communities by continuing to erase Indigenous presence.

Angie Tucker

Having a distant Indigenous relative does not give access to claiming Métis as part of your identity - which is confusing, because what non-Indigenous society has learned, is that this *mixedness* is exactly what determines 'being' Métis.

Jason Surkan

The Métis have built and continue to build spaces across the prairie provinces that respond to each local environment in ingenious, sustainable, egalitarian, and resourceful ways. This Métis vernacular architecture is the physical manifestation that developed when the lived consequences were too severe to make error.

INTRODUCTION   xxix

Chuck Bourgeois

Being a Métis person in Manitoba today is much different than it was for my ancestors in the nineteenth century. For them, being Métis did not entail a process of rediscovery, or sifting through stacks of dusty archives; nor did they require federal recognition to be who they were. They were brought up in the world *as* Métis people.

Liberty Emkeit

In an oppressive and unequal colonialist society, I wonder, how many women, especially Indigenous women does this happen to? Fierce little girls transformed into muted shadows?

Patricia Siniikwe Pajunen

Decolonization starts with rejecting internalized hatred and reconnecting with who we are as Anishinaabeg. All the colonial lies told about Anishinaabeg need to be purged from our own beliefs about ourselves.

Iloradanon Efimoff

Indigenization manifests itself in many ways – on the very surface level, this includes paintings on walls, artifacts in glass boxes displayed for the White onlooker, and on a more in-depth level, changes in policies and curriculum to equally value Indigenous ways of knowing with those of the White world.

Adam Gaudry

Where at one time public discussion of indigenization was so novel as to elicit optimism, now the same language is increasingly viewed with skepticism where action does not accompany a rhetorical shift.

Silvina Antunes, Kara Passey, Jordan Tabobondung, and Erika Vas

The research relationship should be formed much like any other - how do our interests align? Are our intentions honourable? How willing are we to protect and nurture this relationship?

Shara R. Johnson, Jennifer Poudrier, Heather Foulds, and Leah J. Ferguson

As researchers partnering with Indigenous peoples, it was imperative that the methodological framework we chose would respectfully and ethically illustrate the Indigenous participants' experiences in culturally responsive ways.

Obianuju Juliet Bushi

The effects of colonization have had a profound negative effect on generations of Indigenous people. Unequal and inequitable access to social institutions and services have impacted Indigenous peoples and children especially.

Shana Graham

It was time… to develop policy and actions rather than lip service to the idea of Indigenization…. without access to Indigenous worldviews, cultures and languages, the notion of Indigenization would likely never become anything more than token.

Orest Kinasevych

[Neocolonialism] is insidious and happens without boats or invading armies but through transnational bureaucracies and processes. This new form of colonialism is an incursion that, like a second wave, washes over societies while they still endure an earlier colonization which had never receded.

Wanda Hounslow

The rhetoric of reconciliation and its (re)telling of history, relegates colonial violence, if remembered at all, to the past and, by omission, justifies present colonial harms such as those experienced by Indigenous children who have been separated from their families and placed in the child welfare system.

Belinda (Wandering Spirit) Nicholson

White Fragility acts as a barrier to appropriate discussions, and until this concept is better understood and dealt with – progress towards decolonization in North American society will continue to face obstacles.

INTRODUCTION

Micheline Hughes

Mi'kmaw Catholicism is a distinct religious tradition that does not exist elsewhere. It incorporates elements of Mi'kmaw tradition with Catholicism... The creation of this tradition allowed, and continues to allow, Mi'kmaq Peoples to maintain their own identity, agency, and permits them to define the world for themselves.

Karine Martel

In the modern-day, Canada should be using its jurisdiction to engage with Indigenous peoples on a nation-to-nation basis, to promote Indigenous peoples' rights, and to work towards reconciliation.

Eduardo Vergolino

Indigenous people are sovereign people and they have the right to decide how [their] schools should be, and what content the children should learn.

Esteban Vallejo-Toledo

Indigenous communities are not only political entities; they are economic actors who, unfortunately, have been deprived of development opportunities by an inadequate institutional framework. Suggesting that reserves should not participate in a regional and national system of governance and economic interaction could displace them even more.

Paul D. Hansen

Canadian governments have historically tended to treat reconciliation as a project rather than a process—something that can be done once ... ticked off a political 'to do' list and forgotten. ... [Reconciliation]... requires the courage and political will of all parties to move forward towards an environment based on equality, dignity, and respect for the culture and traditions of the Indigenous and settler peoples of Canada and the potential it holds for all.

References

Little Bear, L. (2000). Jagged worldviews colliding. In M. Battiste (Ed.), *Reclaiming Indigenous voice and vision* (pp. 77-85). Vancouver, BC: UBC Press.

Morris, Kāshā J. A. (2018) Using language nests to promote the intergenerational transmission of Tāłtān. In J. Markides & L. Forsythe (Eds.), *Looking back and living forward: Indigenous research rising up*. Leiden, NL: Brill | Sense.

Tuhiwai Smith, L. (2012). *Decolonizing methodologies: Research and Indigenous peoples* (2nd ed.). New York, NY: Zed Books.

Leggo, C. (2018). Foreword: Searching rumination. In E. R. Lyle (Ed.) *Fostering a relational pedagogy: Self-study as transformative praxis*. Leiden, NL: Brill | Sense.

Knowing Self and Learning in Community

Teachings Shared Towards Advocacy and Understanding

Chapter One

En el Centro de Este Fuego

In the Center of the Fire: Indigenous Women's Storytelling as Decolonial Resistance

Sarah María Acosta Ahmad

> Decolonizing your existence is a radical act.
>
> It means loving the seeds that your ancestors planted,
>
> that grew roots as long as your hair,
>
> and as thick as your thighs.
>
> The same roots that intertwine with the ones of fellow comrades,
>
> that together are stronger,
>
> growing up the sides of buildings that once kept us out,
>
> and tearing down bridges we were never meant to cross,
>
> but did. (Acosta Ahmad, 2017).

Complicated lives require complicated analyses. Through this, we begin to expand our reach in dismantling oppressive forces both infrastructurally as well as in our colonized minds. The borders put up around us, as Indigenous peoples, not only exist on occupied lands, but in our heads. We are socialized to see separation as a constant force in our lives whether through race, class or gender, without questioning it. Generations upon generations of our people assimilated to Anglo/European/Western society. Today, we honor their *raíces* and recognize that through the trickle down of ancestral knowledge, we are still resisting.

The purpose of this research is to identify and share the ways in which Indigenous women and femmes are resisting colonial and imperialist forces through their cultural knowledge and traditions. In making visible their existence as a multifaceted form of resistance and their struggles, these women are making a bold statement against colonialism, imperialism, westernization and patriarchal violent forces that are a threat to their communities. This theory simultaneously rests on a critical understanding of colonialism as not just an encounter or moment, but rather a historical process that produced certain privileged epistemic positions as well as exuberant amounts of mass violence. Through this dialectic relationship of feminist, indigenous theory and colonial history, this paper is able to trace the lineages of colonial violence to its impact on contemporary Indigenous communities. This work is centered around decolonization stories and the process of shedding the traumas of colonial violence in communities of color *en la lucha*. The purpose of this project is to collect and share narratives of the women in the Kalpulli Tekpatl Mexika Nation women's moondance circle. Through the documentation of narratives of otherness, I seek to share intergenerational genealogies and reflections on decolonization. The aim is to include these notions of de-coloniality, cultural visibility, and occupying space to construct a praxis in which decolonial thought opens up new ways of researching and reading Indigenous histories. There is very little theoretical work on this type of feminist analysis and methodological production. Thus, the following seeks to bridge a gap between auto-biographic narrative collection and theory to reclaim storytelling as an academically legitimate method of historical investigation.

Native feminist theorists have reclaimed ways of thinking about settler colonialism and how feminist praxis can reimagine different modes of knowledge production to radically decolonize themselves (Maile, Tuck, Eve, Morrill, 2013). The rejection of colonial knowledge through ethnographic ways of representation in theoretical work is just one way of doing this. Telling these stories of resistance and learning from them under the guise of decolonization through cultural visibility, dance, song, and smudging, are acts of community resistance and preservation will seek to disrupt and deconstruct the multifaceted ways in which Indigenous women and femmes exist and take up space.

Academic liberatory theories speak of resistance as only what your physical body can do to make noise, however we never include simply existing as revolutionary. There is rarely any simplicity in an existence that was founded and structured in resisting violent forces; these forms of resistance are complex and rooted in survival. And in this is overdetermination of oppression is where I position the decolonial turn away from postcolonial theory, as I hope to read resistance into the histories of colonialism and, thus, into contemporary modes of Indigenous living. The process of shedding white settler colonialism and the heteropatriarchy are in the bloodlines of Indigenous women who are fighting and healing within the roots of restorative justice. Thus, this paper not only uncovers divergent methods of decolonial resistance, but also highlights non-Western manifestations of resisting through cultural expression and visibility.

Positionality is crucial to this work. As a theorist of resistance, this work seeks to address the stereotypes made about Indigenous people and what modernized and imperialist structures deem as authentically Indigenous and/or Native (Lugones, 2012. As the first generation living off my ancestral land to reclaim my language and ceremony, I understand that not everyone has the ability to re-learn through the guidance of elders. I hope to reject Western, European and Anglo colonial tools through language and how they can manifest in violence for communities of color. Further, I reject imposed eurocentric ways of knowledge production, assimilationist politics and respectability. These shared narratives are unapologetic and unaltered, as they are to serve as historicized stories and epistemic histories of othered bodies.

The goal of colonialism is to erase people of their Indigeneity. It is a geopolitical diaspora, and every time we deny our ancestral roots, we let colonialism win. We let it erase us from history and from this occupied land. Chicanx feminist, Gloria Anzaldúa says that, "colonization may have destroyed our Indigenous civilizations but colonization could not eliminate the evolution of an Indigenous psyche" (Anzaldua, 1987). Colonization has taken shape differently in the lives of Indigenous peoples, but we have been removed nonetheless. Removed from our land, our homes, our families and our spiritual selves. The refusal to cooperate with our dehumanization begins with reclaiming our own power. I am weaving together the stories of our ancestors and our knowledge. These narratives are hand stitched like the colors of the four directions we wear on our ceremonial *huipiles*. Red for the blood our ancestors shed, Yellow like the fires that we sing around, White like vapours in the *temazkal*, and Black like the night sky we dance under. Together we join to share our stories, our struggles, our resistance. A Mexika woman, without her community, is alone in a world that seeks to erase her *poder* and claim it no longer exists. The struggle, *la lucha*, lies in finding self, finding community, and once doing so, loving it with all energy. It begins with discovering our truest self in the smoke of sage, or the aroma of lingering *copal*. All of this is tied together in long and thick black braids trailing down our backs.

Under the Potlatch Ban, Indigenous ceremonies and rituals of First Nation people were banned from 1867 until the late 1960s, leaving nearly 75 years of ceremony and Indigenous knowledge left to the women to maintain and the children to keep secret (Joseph, 2012). Causing ceremonies to go underground and pushed into the private sphere, Abuela Celia Perez-Booth, my ceremonial grandmother, reflects on what is was like to be raised around this cultural conflict and of being lost without ceremony. In her own search to uncover her *raíces*, she learned that the community will teach you and show you. "After everything was taken away from us, the moondance helped us balance our energies and connect with our power," she reflects. In preserving cultural ceremonies and treasures, we are learning our own medicines and reclaiming our own power. "If you forget your ancestors, that's when they really die," she says, thin silver hair falling past her waist. Historical trauma is at the root of our struggle and survival as Indigenous women. Decolonization comes in the energies we reconnect to. The wind is the breath of our ancestors, the stones are their bodies, burning in remembrance, gaining *fuerza* with the fire, we are the water poured over them, together our steam fills and cleanses. "We have been brainwashed, what they [colonizers] did to one, they did to all of us" and so, reconnecting to our ancestors is in fact resistance (Abuela Celia Interview, 2017).

There is an old saying, '*ni de aqui ni de alla, pero siento por los dos*,' meaning, not from here nor there, but feeling for both. Thus, we are not at home where we live, nor where our parents are from, and at times, not even in our own bodies. "What are you?" is a question we are all too familiar with. It means we do not belong, and that even though race and ethnicity manifest themselves differently, people know we are not the norm. "Indigeneity is based on intention, not assertion of your identity," says Sandra Gonzales, a scholar, mother, and moondancer in the Kalpulli Tekpatl (Gonzalez Interview, 2017). We are constantly changing our language, habits and lives in order to acculturate to the Western world.

Living in the United States, Indigenous youth carry the generational struggles of our ancestors, while facing assimilation and marginalization in both our native country and the one we live in. The United States is a name to a land that is not its own. 'America' does not exist without the inclusion of Latin America, yet that jagged and exotified part of the continent is overlooked much like the people living there. This exclusion is part of our lived experience as women of color in the United States with Indigenous ties that have been uprooted and thrown into dry sand that cannot sustain the growth of our minds and cultures. We are suppressed

CHAPTER ONE

from the day we are born, spanked, the first breath of air, we cry because this is not our homeland, but we cannot yet find it.

Through understanding and theorizing, we begin to learn that the complexities of our lives have reason and meaning. The romanticization of revolution is present and real, but revolution is not sexy; you cannot take it out, sleep with it, touch it. Revolution is what keeps you awake at night, tossing and turning, but it is hard to tell if it is here when marginalized bodies have been losing sleep for ages. "The revolution begins at home" (Anzaldua, Moraga, 1987, p. 70). Indigenous peoples follow in the footsteps of our ancestors, but this time digging our feet further in the dirt. They are overlooked, overworked and hungry for a revolution that can sustain Indigenous communities for generations. White feminism has valued reform over revolution, but today, our visibility, our existence, is a revolution. Anzaldúa describes this as survival, to "ayudar a las mujeres que todavía viven en la jaula a dar nuevos pasos y a romper barreras antiguas. To help women who still live in cages to take new steps, and to break old barriers" (Anzaldua, 1987, p.82). Collectively, Indigenous peoples may come from different marginalized identities, but uniting in the struggle, we must break down the boundaries of academia and theory, and hold people accountable in sharing our own stories.

Our resistance is constant, even though we fight in different ways than our ancestors. We, Indigenous mujeres and warriors, act with intentions. We put intentions into the fire, into the soil, and into our words. We are seeds planted in revolution that sprout and grow, twisting up towards the sun, drying out, blowing away in the wind to new places, we are as alive as the leaves on the great *ceiba* tree. This notion of decolonization is not a metaphor, but a reclaiming of your agency and body within the constructs of the clothes you wear, spaces you take up, food you eat, people who you are intimate with, and even communities you are surrounded by (Tuck and Yang, 2012).

It is important that as this develops, one keeps in mind that the ultimate goal of colonialism is to erase the existence of Native peoples. It is geopolitical terrorism and violence that we still feel to this day as our bodies are condemned and policed. Indigenous people have been resisting since the 15th century; they move and uproot themselves to escape violence; that is why we have diasporic communities. It is also why some of our own histories are torn apart and slowly being pieced back together.

Here are some questions to keep in mind as this moves forward:

Did you agree to be colonized?

Did your ancestors agree to be colonized?

Did you agree to have your body regulated by the state?

Did you consent to any of it?

We live in power structures we did not consent to. So either we resist or comply.

Indigenous people have been taught that this is just a means of survival instead of a way of resistance. Without decolonizing our minds, our bodies, the ways we occupy space, the ways we dress, eat, love, and make love, then we are going to move towards a revolution where people do not know what to do afterwards. After these white supremacist and heteropatriarchal systems are dismantled, and they will be dismantled, we are going to be left with no answers, and all the questions. It is here that we must go back in order to move forward. People tend to not see the overlap between social justice and indigeneity, but Indigenous peoples have been doing social justice work for more than 500 years. The fact that we see our faces, challenges the ways in which we are still alive and fighting to survive.

Healing ourselves and our communities also heals the spirits of our ancestors. The vision for the future lies in the community and their ability to rise up and take power, share it, and know what to do with it. It is known to us, that springtime comes with the awakening of the earth. With tobacco and intentions, we thank the earth for providing us with what we need for our ceremonies and our lives. This awakening is one of the spirit and mind to recreate methods of healing and or learning. If I am to move forward with this work, I must also realize that there is no answer to the questions I am asking, rather a series of revelations and revolutions that sizzle like copal on hot charcoal. What I do know, is that this revolution will be built on the backs of Indigenous peoples, much like this land was. Looking forward, there is still so much to do and learn about our Indigenous roots and how to build this revolution more inclusively. We must continue learning and fighting.

Sin lucha, no avanzamos.

And so we call out, Mexika Tiahui!

References

Abuela Celia. In-Person Interview. April 2017.
Acosta, Sarah María Ahmad. *Raíces*. La Liga Zine. 2017.
Anzaldúa, Gloria. *Borderlands: La Nueva Mestiza*. Aunt Lute Books. 1987.
Arvin, Maile and Tuck, Eve and Morrill, Angie. *Decolonizing Feminism: Challenging*

CHAPTER ONE

Connections between Settler Colonialism and Heteropatriarchy. Feminist Formations. 2013. p. 9.
Joseph, Bob. *Potlatch Ban: Abolishment of First Nation Ceremonies*. Indigenous Corporate Training Inc. 2012.
Lugones, María. *Toward a Decolonial Feminism*. Hypatia. 2010. p. 746.
Sandra Gonzales. In-Person Interview. April 2017.
Tuck and Yang. *Decolonization is not a metaphor*. Pub. 2012.

Chapter Two

Barriers to Indigenous Athletes' Athletic Development in Canada

An Analysis Framed by Daniels' Ingredients of Success, Part I

Nickolas J. Kosmenko

It was around 6:00am on a Wednesday in mid-January. The location was a small town in northern Manitoba that was home to only 600- or so people, situated in the boreal forest and nestled among the lakes, swamps, and rock outcrops of the Canadian Shield. The morning sky was dark and clear, speckled with a million stars and a touch of aurora-borealis some people wait their whole lives to see. My breath turned to frost before my eyes, and my nose felt that familiar, bittersweet greeting only a minus 34-degree Celsius morning could bring as I walked out the door and looked up at the beauty the Creator had painted above me. For a moment I felt at peace, and I felt privileged to live where I did. Then I went for a run.

As a competitive runner, I knew not all runs are fun, and that there is very little glamour in the world of distance running, a fact that was epitomized in my stride that morning. My feet slipped with each step on the ice beneath the four inches of snow that had fallen overnight, splaying out to the sides as I ran, and there was already a slimy, white trail of mucus trickling from my left nostril down to the corner of my mouth… not exactly the breakfast I had in mind. Luckily for me, however, there was no chilling wind to add to the sting of winter on this morning, nor were there any cars or people to worry about. It was just me, the sound of my footsteps, and that familiar voice in my head that would often ask that same, redundant question: "Why do I do this?"

Winter provided some freedom, however, when it came to running in the wee morning hours. This freedom was, in part, a product of *Ursus americanus'* tendency to sleep during most of the snowy season. I could drop my guard in winter while the bears slumbered, and I didn't have to worry about bugs during that time of year, either. Mosquitoes would keep my running pace honest in the warm months, as they could only swarm me if I stopped. The horseflies, however, could keep up with even the likes of the great Billy Mills in his prime, and during their peak periods in the months of July and August, they would fly circles around me as if to point out the athletic inferiority of humans, landing on me periodically to bite chunks out of my skin.

There were few animals to worry about on this day in January, save for the million- or so stray dogs in the community. There was one in particular that would nip at me when I ran. He was only playing, but his antics would become annoying after a while. He also liked to bark from time to time, which would initiate a chorus of off-key labs, huskies, mutts, and the like as we covered ground through town. I'm sure the sleeping townspeople appreciated that.

The point of these anecdotes, to which I could add extensively, is that running in the north is difficult, which I reckon is a reason few great runners come from northern Manitoba. My upbringing in the north and experience training in the south has made me aware of the differences between resources available to athletes (runners, in particular) in small northern- versus large southern locations in Manitoba. Yet although I was immersed in an environment unconducive to training for distance running, the life I was born into, although not storybook, was still fairly accommodating to my athletic aspirations. My parents are hard-working, middle class people and, despite a hint of Ojibwe on my mom's side, are mainly of Euro-Canadian descent. We never experienced systemic racism during my upbringing, racism that, for too many people in Canada, is a concern that takes precedence over athletic aspirations. In that way, I was lucky, but I was nevertheless angry. Coming from a town surrounded by reserve communities, as well as having graduated from a high school with a mainly Indigenous student composition, I was well aware of the consequences of hundreds of years of oppression.

With the Truth and Reconciliation Commission's (TRC, 2015) call for an elite athlete development program for Indigenous athletes in mind (call #90, part ii), the purpose of this chapter is to discuss some obstacles facing Indigenous athletes in pursuit of sport, particularly in northern communities in Canada that are geographically isolated from large, urban centres. Historic and contemporary systemic racism challenges Indigenous people and affects many areas of life, including access to sport. Although it is beyond the scope of this paper to describe the distorted history (Green, 1995) through which Indigenous people have persevered, yet by which colonization continues, I emphasize the crucial role reflexivity plays in discussions pertaining to colonization, and I encourage readers to wonder why/how colonization, including the racism inherent within it (Memmi, 1965), still continues; in short, to exercise their critical social consciousness (Ladson-Billings, 1995) by seeking deeper understanding. Lastly, I remind readers that Indigenous people are often over-generalized and that, although I discuss issues that affect many Indigenous athletes, I recognize individuals and their situations vary.

On with Business...

Being a running nerd, I use Daniels' (2014) Ingredients of Success as a framework to guide my discussion. Daniels has been a coach of elite and sub-elite distance runners for decades. He holds a Ph.D. in exercise physiology and is an Olympic medalist in modern pentathlon. His Ingredients of Success include inherent ability, intrinsic motivation, opportunity, and direction. Extensive discussions could be had regarding most of these ingredients and how they are withheld from Indigenous athletes in northern communities. It is my contention that inherent ability can be found anywhere there are people, however, so perhaps this ingredient is an exception. Whatever the case, due to the significant depth to which one could delve with respect to at least three of these ingredients, I have chosen to focus this chapter on only one: opportunity. This ingredient, or the lack of it, is obvious in many northern communities, and by writing about opportunity in Part 1 of this (potentially) three-part series, I believe I am addressing what is the "elephant in the room" in terms of barriers to athletic success that should have been dealt with long ago. Subtler, yet more sensitive elephants will be discussed in Parts 2 and 3, if I ever get that far.

Opportunity. Daniels' (2014) wrote about opportunity in terms of factors such as weather, facilities, competition, teammates, money to pay for travel and equipment, and exposure to sport (through watching sports). Although he was transparent about the need for adequate opportunity, he also recognized the benefits of resourcefulness when opportunities are lacking. However, in isolated communities in Canada, it is questionable how far one can go in sport simply by being resourceful due to the numerous barriers that exist. In some ways, too, opportunities can still be relatively limited for Indigenous athletes who move to urban areas, and even when they are not, the foundations built (or not built, due to the "numerous barriers" eluded to earlier) during developmental years may be critical to success later on (Athletics Canada, n.d.). As such, much of this discussion is focused on barriers existing at early stages of athletic development. Let us delve into these issues.

An obvious place to begin is Canadian Heritage's (2005) *Sport Canada's policy on Aboriginal peoples' participation in sport*. The barriers identified in this document relating to opportunity include: financial challenges such as team fees, equipment costs, and funding for travel; distance from programs, facilities, people with expertise (coaches, athletic therapists, etc.), and competition; and lack of sport infrastructure. In fact, reserve communities have been long underfunded by the federal government in relation to other communities in Canada (Milloy, 2008), which has limited the infrastructure that can be built and maintained. The importance of sport infrastructure is highlighted by the harsh climate in many areas of Canada, which often prevents athletes from safely and effectively training outside. Indeed, some sports, particularly those relying on speed and power, require indoor facilities for at least part of the year. Alas, for many young Indigenous athletes, even though the motivation to pursue sport may be there, the environment is not always on their side and, unfortunately, neither is the government. As such, researchers have sought solutions to overcome opportunity-related barriers.

For instance, Blodgett et al. (2008) highlighted the importance of parents, stating they play key roles in guiding youth to sport and providing opportunities such as travel, financial support, etc. Extended families and role models were also identified as important resources, as they provide support and examples for aspiring athletes to follow. Further, involving the community in sport initiatives is valuable because members can often help provide equipment, finances, and program delivery. In fact, a passionate volunteer base was a suggestion that arose in a follow-up study (Blodgett et al., 2010). Finally, Blodgett et al.'s (2008) research highlighted the importance of educating Indigenous youth about sport opportunities off reserves, as well as the importance of being persistent in the face of challenges. Indeed, relocating to pursue sport may entail an arduous acculturation process (Blodgett et al., 2014) through which one must persevere in order to be successful.

In addition to barriers that affect sport in a direct sense, there are also barriers that affect sport indirectly through its close tie with education, making discussion of barriers to Indigenous students' education relevant here. Halas, McRae, and Carpenter (2013) argued that culturally relevant physical education (PE) can contribute to success in sport for Indigenous participants by helping affirm cultural identities and facilitating physical literacy. They used Whitehead's (2001) idea of physical literacy, which defined this concept largely in terms of one's ability to survey environments and physically respond in appropriate ways, with imagination, intelligence, and confidence, by drawing upon a set of movements from a larger repertoire. Halas et al. mentioned PE is often the first introduction to sport for many Canadian children. Through affirming identities, facilitating physical literacy, and introducing children to sport, PE plays an important role in early athletic development.

Halas et al. (2013) referred to Côté, Baker, and Abernethy's (2007) developmental model of sport participation, which highlights sport sampling as an early stage of one possible pathway to the elite level. By providing exposure to a variety of sports, PE can help in the sampling process, which youth may use as an opportunity to assess which types of sports they prefer, and which align best with their baseline talents. Early sampling may encourage prolonged engagement in sport, and it does not hinder athletes' pathways to elite levels (Côté, Murphy-Mills, & Abernethy, 2012). In fact, some physiological adaptations are transferable across sports (Côté et al., 2012), so early sampling may increase opportunities with respect to the sports in which one may be able to successfully specialize later on.

Unfortunately, there are numerous challenges affecting PE opportunities for Indigenous youth. Halas et al. (2013) emphasized the need to understand that Indigenous students' PE experiences are contingent upon the colonial contexts shaping their educational experiences in general. The researchers demonstrated how the systematic underfunding of federally- (i.e., First Nations) relative to provincially-funded schools results in insufficient facilities, equipment, and instruction in PE settings. In addition, the authors discussed reduced opportunities for sport participation and competition in schools with fewer students, challenges of geographic isolation such as financing trips to other communities, teacher turnover in remote areas, the discomfort imparted on students by change room atmospheres, substitute teachers with little knowledge of PE, lack of Indigenous teaching staff, the need for teachers to try to fit into the culture of Indigenous communities and develop a critical consciousness with respect to colonization, and culturally irrelevant curriculum.

Some of these issues resonate with my own experiences, as do some of the solutions Halas et al. (2013) suggested. Although I never participated in Frontier Games, which is an annual, multi-day event in which students from Frontier School Division (FSD) in Manitoba take part in a variety of sports and cultural activities (snowshoeing, trap setting), from what I observed as a student in FSD, I agree with what Halas et al. indicated: it is quite a successful program. The organizers are resourceful, as is needed when holding large events in small towns. For instance, during my primary years of education, I noticed that classrooms would be set aside as sleeping quarters for athletes during the games. A similar type of resourcefulness was emphasized by Halas et al., who suggested using community facilities, such as hockey rinks, as well the land for PE classes. For example, they cited van Ingen and Halas (2006) who discussed how one First Nations school made use of a trapline in its community. In fact, the high school I attended has its own trapline for students to use. Conversations with a counselor at this school, however, have suggested there are few staff willing to supervise students as they make use of the trapline, thus reducing an otherwise prime opportunity for students to engage in land-based, culturally relevant physical activity that may help develop physical literacy.

Staff play significant roles in school proceedings, and as Halas et al. (2013) suggested, they must be willing to integrate into the culture of the community in order to facilitate cultural relevance in school settings. Drawing on work by Ladson-Billings (1995), Halas et al. summarized culturally relevant pedagogy as having three main goals, with four steps to reach those goals. The three goals described by Ladson-Billings are: 1) academic success, which necessitates the need for teachers to be cognizant of students' strengths and know how to translate those strengths to success in the classroom; 2) cultural competence, by allowing the cultures of students to be vehicles for learning in classroom settings, encouraging students to "be themselves" (Ladson-Billings, p. 161); and 3) critical consciousness, which encourages one to question societal norms and their implications. The four steps summarized by Halas et al. include: 1) meaningful and relevant curriculum, 2) teacher as ally, 3) understanding students' day-to-day cultural landscapes, and 4) supportive learning climates. Assessing these goals and steps, one may argue that serving as a fundamental basis of culturally relevant pedagogy is relationship building, as teachers need to be able to understand the backgrounds of their students in order to implement the four steps appropriately and, eventually, achieve the three goals. Hence the need for staff (including coaches) to integrate into the culture of the community (i.e., in the case of my high school, go trapping).

Although the solutions conveyed here may be helpful, it is also important to recognize that for some Indigenous athletes, getting through primary and secondary school is only the beginning of their educational journeys. University-level sport may be a pathway to elite sport because it can provide elite-level coaches, access to state-of-the-art facilities, sport psychology services, and athletic therapy. Yet as with primary and secondary education, there are many barriers to Indigenous peoples' post-secondary education. Kirkness and Barnhardt (1991) differentiated between coming and going to the university, wherein the latter entails an acceptance of the student as he/she is, but the former requires the student to adjust to the dominant culture. Similarly, the need to make education culturally relevant for Indigenous students was echoed by Preston (2008) in her discussion of historical obstacles to education. Within the same paper, she also discussed obstacles at the educational level, at social, economic, and geographical levels, at cultural and pedagogical levels, and at the financial level.

For obstacles at the educational level, Preston (2008) highlighted how primary and secondary schools in remote communities struggle to prepare students for university, which is understandable considering the lack of funding these schools receive, as discussed earlier. Other issues discussed include lack of academic counsellors, few role models, and not enough Indigenous teaching staff. Preston also highlighted one of the many problems of using grade-point average (GPA) as a criteria for entry to university, stating, "[p]ostsecondary acceptance which is wholly dependent upon a grade-point average captures neither the intellect nor the experience of many Aboriginal students" (p. 59), and she suggested schools should accept Indigenous cultural knowledge as legitimate. Finally, she recommended universities provide support for Indigenous students, as well as show greater presence in Indigenous communities during recruitment campaigns. All of these areas present opportunities for improvements with respect to the number of Indigenous athletes reaching the university level.

At the social, economic, and geographical levels, Preston (2008) briefly discussed the effects colonization has had on many Indigenous people, such as poverty, compromised health, increased rates of suicide, and derelict housing. She also explained that Indigenous people in smaller communities often have to move great distances to pursue university education which, for students with children, may necessitate the need to find childcare providers in the new location. Preston emphasized the need for support in the form of housing, transportation for dependents, on-campus daycares, and counselling (e.g., elders). As a solution, she suggested bringing post-secondary education to rural communities, and she stressed that credits received at these locations should be transferrable to other institutions. However, despite being a step in the right direction, for students interested in athletics, these schools might not provide the same levels of athletic resources as larger universities.

As for obstacles at pedagogical and cultural levels, similar to Halas et al. (2013), Preston (2008) highlighted the need for cultural relevance. She also discussed how Western education is more competition-driven and individual-focused, whereas traditional Indigenous pedagogy focuses on communalism, experimental learning, and being transformative and wholistic. She suggested universities use culturally relevant content in courses, and that they incorporate Indigenous styles of learning (group work, reflections, story-telling, field trips, work-placements, etc.). As Blodgett et al. (2014) found, significant challenges may arise when Indigenous athletes relocate to pursue sport in mainstream contexts. Including culturally relevant practices into the university environment may help Indigenous university athletes feel more welcome and comfortable.

Finally, with respect to financial obstacles, Preston (2008) explained that students who move to attend university are at a disadvantage financially compared to students who go to school in the communities in which they already live. Preston also emphasized that it can be difficult for Indigenous students to obtain band funding to attend school, as these funds are not widely available, and she suggested that, due to increasing enrolment of Indigenous students at universities, competition for band funding is increasing. As solutions to financial issues, Preston suggested more contributions from provincial and federal governments to help alleviate financial burdens experienced by Indigenous institutes, and she highlighted the need for more scholarship and bursary opportunities for Indigenous students. Perhaps scholarships specifically for Indigenous athletes would help, at least to some extent. Whatever the scholarship type, I think Preston's suggestion that application procedures become less bureaucratic should be strongly considered (Preston, citing the Assembly of First Nations, 2005).

Conclusion

An elite athlete development program for Indigenous athletes was one call developed by the TRC (2015). I believe anyone who has experienced the satisfaction that comes with completing a difficult workout, or the comradery and feelings of acceptance common to a team atmosphere, or the empowering feelings that arise when one overcomes defeat to meet a challenge, should be able to see that this call is an important one. In addition, sport provides young athletes with role models, aspirations, and dreams. It presents challenges that can bring out the best in people, it teaches life lessons, and it facilitates friendships that can last a lifetime. For these reasons, all people should be allowed to pursue sport, and for those who find meaning in competitive sport and wish to fulfill their athletic potentials, athletic development should be promoted, and the barriers to it minimized.

Yet there are many barriers to Indigenous athletes' athletic development in Canada. This chapter focused solely on barriers relating to opportunity. I have shown that many Indigenous athletes have higher hurdles to jump than many non-Indigenous athletes in terms of this Ingredient of Success (Daniels, 2014). I have also provided some suggestions for improvements in this area. In short, at the very least, I believe this chapter works to help affirm in the minds of readers that being an Indigenous athlete often entails overcoming far more obstacles than many non-Indigenous athletes ever have to overcome or even think about. In addition, I hope I have conveyed the significant amount of work that remains if we are to level the playing field a bit, providing Indigenous athletes the same opportunities by which many non-Indigenous athletes are privileged.

References

Assembly of First Nations. (2005, April). First Nations early learning and child care action plan.

Athletics Canada. (n.d.). Athletics Canada Long Term Athlete Development. Retrieved from http://athletics.ca/wp-content/uploads/2015/01/LTAD_EN.pdf.

Blodgett, A. T., Schinke, R. J., Fisher, L. A., Wassengeso George, C., Peltier, D., Ritchie, S., & Pickard, P. (2008). From practice to praxis: Community-based strategies for Aboriginal youth sport. Journal of sport and social issues, 32(4), 393-414.

Blodgett, A. T., Schinke, R. J., Fisher, L. A., Yungblut, H. E., Recollet-Saikkonen, D., Peltier, D., ... & Pickard, P. (2010). Praxis and community-level sport programming strategies in a Canadian aboriginal reserve. International journal of sport and exercise psychology, 8(3), 262-283.

Blodgett, A. T., Schinke, R. J., McGannon, K. R., Coholic, D. A., Enosse, L., Peltier, D., & Pheasant, C. (2014). Navigating the insider-outsider hyphen: A qualitative exploration of the acculturation challenges of Aboriginal athletes pursuing sport in Euro-Canadian contexts. Psychology of Sport and Exercise, 15(4), 345-355.

Canadian Heritage. (2005). Sport Canada's policy on Aboriginal peoples' participation in sport. Minister of Public Works and Government Services Canada. Retrieved from https://www.canada.ca/content/dam/pch/documents/services/sport-policies-acts-regulations/aborignial_v4-eng.pdf

Côté, J., Baker, J., & Abernethy, B. (2007). Practice and play in development of sport expertise. In Eklund, R., & Tenenbaum, G. (Eds.), Handbook of sport psychology, third edition. (pp. 184-202). Hoboken, NJ: Wiley.

Côté, J., Murphy-Mills, J., Abernethy, B. (2012). The development of skill in sport. In Hodges, N. J., & Williams, A. M. (Eds.), Skill acquisition in sport: research, theory and practice (pp. 269-286). Abingdon, Oxon, UK: Routledge.

Daniels, J. (2014). Daniels' running formula, third edition. Champaign, IL: Human Kinetics.

Green, J. (1995). Towards a détente with history: Confronting Canada's colonial legacy. International Journal of Canadian Studies, 12, 85-105.

Halas, J., McRae, H., & Carpenter, A. (2013). Quality and cultural relevance of physical education for youth. In Forsyth, J., & Giles, A. R. (Eds.), Aboriginal peoples & sport in Canada: Historical foundations and contemporary issues (pp. 182-205). Vancouver, BC: UBC Press.

Kirkness, V. J., & Barnhardt, R. (1991). First Nations and higher education: The four R's—Respect, relevance, reciprocity, responsibility. Journal of American Indian Education, 1-15.

Ladson-Billings, G. (1995). But that's just good teaching! The case for culturally relevant pedagogy. Theory into practice, 34(3), 159-165.

Memmi, A. (1965). The colonizer and the colonized (H. Greenfeld, Trans.). London, UK: Earthscan Publications Ltd.

Milloy, J. S. (2008). Indian Act colonialism: A century of dishonour, 1869-1969. National Centre for First Nations Governance. Retrieved from http://fngovernance.org/ncfng_research/milloy.pdf

Preston, J. P. (2008). Overcoming the obstacles: Postsecondary education and Aboriginal peoples. Brock Education: a Journal of Educational Research and Practice, 18(1), 57-63.

Truth and Reconciliation Commission of Canada. (2015). Truth and Reconciliation Commission of Canada: calls to action. Winnipeg, MB. Retrieved from http://www.trc.ca/websites/trcinstitution/File/2015/Findings/Calls_to_Action_English2.pdf

van Ingen, C., & Halas, J. (2006). Claiming space: Aboriginal students within school landscapes. Children's Geographies, 4(3), 379-398.

Whitehead, M. (2001). The concept of physical literacy. European Journal of Physical Education, 6(2), 127-136.

Chapter Three

Who has the Right?

A Reflection on Indigenous Research as a Chinese Anthropology Student Researcher

Xiao Zheng

Introduction

One day in the course **Community-Based Research Methods,** while we were discussing the ideas of "study up" and "study down" (Nader 1972: 284-311), I suddenly realized the significance of my own identity as an anthropology student researcher who comes from China. When I brought up my research on powwow, the professor replied, "I think your position is really special. You are a young, female, student researcher. And you are from China, not white or Indigenous…" Her comments lingered in my mind for a long time, as I had never considered that people would perceive me that way, and thus had not considered how those perceptions had influenced my research. In an ethnographic experience, Lévi-Strauss states that "Clearly, he [the anthropologist] must learn to know himself, to obtain, from a *self* who reveals himself as *another* to the *I* who uses him, an evaluation which will become an integral part of the observation of other selves" (Lévi-Strauss 1976: 36). With the development of reflexive anthropology since the early 1970s, anthropologists are now strongly encouraged to reflect on their identities and how their identities influence their research projects. Therefore, in this chapter I will begin by explaining why I became interested in Indigenous cultures and chose powwow as my research topic; then while talking about the methodologies I adopted, I will reflect on how my identity as a Chinese anthropology student interacted with my fieldwork.

Indigenous Culture is Beautiful: Sources of my Research Interest

Since entering my field and beginning this research I have regularly witnessed people's astonishment — "You're from China, and you're interested in our culture?" or "You're doing research on powwows?" followed with "Why are you interested in our culture?" or "Why are you interested in powwows?" To be frank, even after finishing my fieldwork there was a period where I could not figure out why, among so many options, I chose to step into the world of Indigenous cultures and powwows: it was probably the most challenging area I could have selected as a Chinese anthropology student who had been in Canada for only one year. If my own interest and curiosity is an appropriate reason, then that is the answer. But what other factors were an influence?

To begin with, I must give the credit to the field of anthropology, where I have been training for more than six years. I was enrolled in the Department of Ethnography and Anthropology at the Xiamen University, which is one of the best anthropology departments in China. There, in addition to learning the anthropological research on Chinese culture, I was constantly exposed to the theories come up with by, such as Franz Boas and his students. That was where my knowledge and interest in the North American Indigenous cultures began. Then, in a reading course on Indigenous cultures and museum studies in the first term of my graduate program, my supervisor Dr. Jean DeBernardi assigned me several related reading materials. This furthered my fascination and deepened my understanding of Indigenous studies in current North America. For example, it was through the book *This is Our Life: Haida Material Heritage and Changing Museum Practice* that I engaged with the concept of repatriation for the first time, realizing the discrepancy between the western and Indigenous philosophy about objects. Most importantly, my anthropological education has helped me develop a mindset of paying attention to cultures different from my own home culture, and promoting cultural diversity. Therefore, when I was given the opportunity for direct contact with the Indigenous cultures that I was interested in for a long time, I decided that I wanted to make this the focus of my MA thesis research.

In addition, the notice of the similarities between Indigenous cultures and the Chinese culture has been a further motivator in my work. For example, when reading *The Way of the Masks* by Lévi-Strauss, I was attracted by his argument about the relations between the cylinder eyes and the earthquake (Lévi-Strauss 1982: 123-134); because, surprisingly, a Chinese Bronze mask with the protruding eyes — the most well-known mask in Chinese history—was also excavated in an earthquake-prone region, Sichuan Province. Further, without knowing each other, Franz Boas describes "split representation" (Boas 1955: 43-44), a dominant decorative pattern among the Northwest Coast Indigenous cultures, in an almost identical way with sinologist H.G. Creel's depiction of a commonplace decorative method existing in the Chinese Shang Dynasty (Creel 1935: 64). During my fieldwork, at my first powwow practice, I was told that due to the idea of keeping balance, it was important to do the same movements in both the left and right sides. Surprisingly again, "balance" is also one of the most crucial notices which is widely applied to almost everything, such as physical conditions, mental health, and life styles, etc. in Chinese culture.

My decision to conduct research on powwow culture began out of personal fascination. In the summer of 2016, I got an email from the University of Alberta, which contained the information about the 35th Bent Calf Robe Traditional Powwow, so I decided to go. Even though I had no idea about powwows at that time, what I witnessed was so compelling that I even stamped along to the drumbeat. Moreover, similar with the situation in Canada, there are many ethnic groups in China[12], and similar with the Indigenous people in North America, singing and dancing is also one of the most significant part of many of them and hold sacred connotations. However, when I traveled in China to the minority groups' regions, basically all the performances of dancing and singing I had seen served the main purpose of attracting tourists. I am not indicating the traditional and authentic ceremonies and activities do not exist any more in China, but neither the commercial performance nor the traditional gatherings enjoys the similar popularity or influence as the powwow does in North America. Therefore, I became interested in powwow culture out of my own admiration for its success. Also, when I went to meet Dr. Kisha Supernant, a Métis archeologist in my department to discuss my prospective research idea, she brought up the topic of powwows and told me that it was probably a good option to know the Indigenous cultures.

Before finally making my decision, I wrote a term paper for the course *Anthropology of Modernity* to discuss the resilience of the Indigenous cultures with powwow as a main example. In the process of doing my literature review, I gained more understanding of the powwow culture, and realized that it is not only a result of "warrior society dances, reservation-era intertribal dance, Wild West shows and other exhibitions, and postwar homecoming celebrations" (Browner 2002: 19) but also an agency which plays a crucial part in "social, cultural, political, and material affairs" influencing "every corner of life" (Ellis 2003: 29). As a result of this — and because the powwow is open to the public — I believed that conducting research on it could be a meaningful great and relatively easy starting point for me to enter Indigenous cultures as an outside researcher.

Nevertheless, if it is not too inappropriate to make some emotional statements, I would like to acknowledge that the real reason I decided to explore powwow was my deep fascination with it. When discussing the preference to objectivity in the dominant research paradigm, Eber Hampton, an Indigenous scholar, states:

One thing I want to say about research is that there is a motive. I believe the reason is emotional because we feel. We feel because we are hungry, cold afraid, brave, loving, or hateful. We do what we do for reasons, emotional reasons. That is the engine that drives us. That is the gift of the Creator of Life. Life feels...... Feelings is connected to our intellect and we ignore, hide from, disguise, and suppress that feeling at out peril and at the peril of those around us. Emotionless, passionless, abstract, intellectual research is a goddam lie, it does not exist. It is a lie to ourselves and a lie to other people. Humans— feelings, living, breathing, thinking humans — do research. When we try to cut ourselves off at the neck and pretend an objectivity that does not exist in the human world, we become dangerous, to ourselves first, and then to the people around us (1995: 52).

This best describes my approach to research and my interest in Indigenous cultures and powwow.

It is Confusing: Anthropological Methodology and Indigenous Methodology

With respect to methodologies, I adopted the methods of participant observation and interview from anthropology, and simultaneously drew on Indigenous methodology in my study. Participant observation has been one of the most important methods in anthropological research since the late 19th century. It requires anthropologists to stay with "a group of people for extended periods, often over the course of a year or more, in order to document an interpret their distinctive way of life, and the beliefs and values integral to it" (Hammersley and Atkinson 2007: 1). Traditionally, the main purpose of the anthropologist in participant observations was to study other cultures and collect objective data. In writings as well, in order to reach the goal of objectivity, a third-person authoritative voice was preferred, and the information was presented as the meaningful data from the objects of study by removing all traces of the observer (Tedlock 1991:72). Therefore, as Stephen Tyler once noted, "ethnography is a genre that discredits or discourage narrative, subjectivity, confessional, personal anecdote, or accounts of the ethnographer's or anyone else's experience" (1987: 92).

However, the situation has changed with the movement of reflexive anthropology. Generally speaking, reflexivity indicates "the constant awareness, assessment, and reassessment by the researcher of the researcher's own contribution/influence/shaping of intersubjectivity research and the consequent research finding" (Salzman 2002: 806). In anthropology, reflexivity suggests "the public examination of the anthropologist's response to the field situation, the inclusion of methodology, and the participation in constructing the final report" (Myerhoff and Ruby 1982: 19). In this vein, as the primary instrument of the data generation, anthropologists started to realize the roles that their identities, such as gender, social status, cultural backgrounds, behaviors, and basic assumptions played in the fieldwork.

As a result, the method of participant observation has been changing towards 'observation of the participation' (Tedlock 1991) by incorporating the researcher and their relationships into the investigation. Under this circumstance, anthropologists are switching from being objective to "appear[ing] to be more personal, subjective, biased, involved, and culture bound", sometimes people even hold the opinion that *the more scientific anthropologists try to be by revealing their methods, the less scientific they appear to be*" (Myerhoff and Ruby 1982: 26). In ethnographic writings, it is noteworthy that reflexive anthropology does not mean putting the focus on researchers themselves. Instead, by disclosing "the character and process of the ethnographic dialogue or encounter", it provides readers the opportunities and possibilities to "identify the consciousness which has selected and shaped the experiences within the text" (Tedlock 1991: 78).

Around the same time as the shift within the field towards reflexive anthropology, Indigenous studies were becoming more prevalent within the academy. More and more Indigenous scholars were sharply criticizing dominant western perspectives and bringing forward Indigenous perspectives as part of a greater anti-colonial project. For instance, in her "anti-research book" (Smith 1999: 16) *Decolonizing Methodologies*, Maori scholar Linda Tuhiwai Smith puts forward "an agenda for Indigenous research" and "ethical research protocols" (115-122), which "challenge western methods and western focused researchers who have studied Aboriginal people" (Wilson 2008: 53). Additionally, Wilson, in his book *Research Is Ceremony: Indigenous Research Method*, addresses the expected paradigm in Indigenous research with exploring the Indigenous meanings of the terms ontology, epistemology, axiology, and methodology (2008). In the *Handbook of Critical and Indigenous Methodologies*, a number of the contributors support the use of "critical indigenous pedagogy" as a strategy to decolonize western methodologies (Denzin, Lincoln, Smith 2008).

In retrospect, it was only when I finished my fieldwork and had been inspired by these other works, that I could speak to how my research has been influenced by my identity as a Chinese anthropology student. First of all, different from many anthropologists who already had the connections with the people with whom they would work, I entered my field alone and as a complete outsider. For the purpose of building relationships with the powwow participants and powwow communities, I went to the powwow practice and powwow fitness workshops organized by the Canadian Native Friendship Center (CNFC) in Edmonton. There I became a close friend with a jingle dancer, and I made other friends with whom I sometimes traveled to powwows. However, my relationship with the powwow communities were not solid enough, especially in the initial phase. Therefore, I had to spend much more time observing than participating and interviewing, even though I did dance the inter-tribal together with friends and occasionally acted as a water girl for the dancers.

When it came to conducting interviews, it was almost impossible to conduct formal interviews at powwows since people were busy with performing and socializing. Fortunately, the presentations made by the emcees and Elders at powwows, as well as the small discussions I had with spectators and dancers, were of great help in my understanding not only of powwow culture but also of Indigenous worldviews. In addition, considering the idea that "Indigenous knowledge are born of relational knowing" (Kovach 2009: 57), even in the formal interviews, I, in like manner, preferred to both ask questions about powwows and other aspects of their cultures. In some cases, if they were interested, I would share my own life experience as well. Acknowledging the "principles of native oral traditions" (Kovach 2009:124), I intended to design my interviews in less structured ways, as open-ended conversations.

As a non-native English speaker, conducting interviews have been particularly challenging, especially when recording is unwanted. Occasionally I had to ask the same question in different ways or repeat my understanding to the interviewees to make sure I did not misunderstand what I was told. Worse, having to give my whole attention to communication had usually meant that I did not have time to take detailed notes. Hence, usually at the moment of the interview was over, I would have to run into my vehicle and start writing down everything that I recalled. Although embarrassing, I admit that the language barrier must damage the depth and thoroughness of information I have collected, which is probably the greatest weakness of my research.

In this anthropological research, I have to be confronted with the intense relationship between Indigenous cultures and anthropology. Before my fieldwork, I was told that it would be a strenuous and sensitive direction to take, not because I am an international student but more because I am doing anthropological research. Fortunately and not as predicted, except for some expected ignorance, I did not encounter any hostility due to my anthropology background during my field work. My hypothesis about my positive experience is that if the strain between Indigenous cultures and anthropology is true, then it is highly possible that being a Chinese female student weakened my role as an anthropological researcher. Most of the time, the (stereotypical) public image of an anthropologist is more like how Charles L. Briggs describes himself:

> By occupying a high status position that is not localized within any of the foregoing locations, I was able to treat all of them as fieldwork sites. By

> virtue of my status as a faculty member at prestigious academic institutions in the United States, I possessed the sorts of cultural capital (Bourdieu 1977) and connections needed to obtain research grants that have provided me with the time and financial resources to pursue a number of research projects in Venezuela......Having an adequate budget allocated in U.S. dollars during a period of profound economic crisis provided me with a tremendous advantage in terms of my ability to travel anywhere in Venezuela where discourse related to this project was being produced and received (1996: 456).

Obviously, this is not what I am. On the contrary, during my presence at powwow, instead of being interested in what my research is about, people were more curious about, for instance, which part of China I come from, am I the only child in my family, and why I came to Canada, etc.

Nevertheless, when entering the literature world, the situation started changing. There is little, if any, literature available on how a graduate student should conduct research with Indigenous cultures, and even less on how a Chinese student is supposed to behave. I have been "pushed" to pay extra attention to my anthropological identity, and hence the relationship between anthropology and Indigenous cultures stands out. In particular, with the development of the Indigenous studies, "questions about the appropriateness of ethnographic research being conducted into Aboriginal issues of ethnographic researchers" (Dyck 2006: 86) has become more and more poignant.

Anthropology and anthropologists in the Indigenous writings are the most frequently referenced examples of colonialism. On the one hand, the voices from Indigenous scholars are of great significance, as they benefit the scholars interested in Indigenous cultures by putting forward ethical methodologies and point out the expectations of Indigenous people. But on the other hand, I cannot help feeling guilty as an anthropological researcher, even though I have had nothing to do with the colonial history of anthropology, and do not comply with the public image of an anthropologist in a traditional sense. Most importantly, I believe anthropology has been changing for the better.

In my research, the feeling of guilt was transformed into self-doubt, uncertainty, and overcompensation. I endeavored to follow Indigenous methodology and protocols, but I never knew if I was on the right track. The consequence of this complex feeling is that conducting ethical research became extremely important and created a lot of pressure. Before I started my fieldwork, I consulted with some professors in my department who had experience with Indigenous cultures, the Elder in the Aboriginal Students Services center at the University of Alberta, as well as some of my Indigenous friends. Following their advice, I, for instance, always brought tobacco and small gifts to people who shared their knowledge with me. Also, I never touched the powwow regalia without permission, or went across the dancing grounds.

Although I believe that I have made my best effort, I am still concerned that what I have done is not enough. For example, reciprocity or giving back, a term used more often in Indigenous literatures, is a significant protocol in Indigenous research. However, as a graduate student, I could not afford to hire a local research assistant, as some anthropologists do. Also, since my research was more concentrated on sociocultural aspects of Indigenous cultures, it might not directly benefit the communities and people I was working with, at least not in the short term. Therefore, I would like to seize every opportunity to volunteer with Indigenous institutions and for Indigenous activities to make contributions however I can, regardless of whether they are related to powwows.

Conclusion

As a Chinese researcher, my interest in Indigenous culture and the powwow grows out of my anthropological education and curiosity about the similarities between Indigenous cultures and Chinese cultures. In turn, my Chinese and anthropology backgrounds impact my powwow research. As one of my Indigenous friends has said, "we have lots of things in common." Being Chinese, I wonder if people might temporarily forget that I am an anthropological researcher. My encounters with reflexive anthropology and Indigenous studies have forced me to confront my own role in the relationship between anthropology and Indigenous cultures, bringing lots of confusion. Furthermore, as a student who had little research experience with on Indigenous cultures previously, I have always doubted whether my research was ethical enough, and anthropologically professional enough.

Navigating my complex identity, I once felt lost in this powwow research; and at times, I still do. I am left wondering if non-Indigenous researchers should develop interests in Indigenous cultures and be involved in Indigenous studies? Is being Indigenous key for conducting research with Indigenous groups? If not, are the projects ethical? And is there any difference in protocols for Indigenous researchers and non-Indigenous researchers? Who has the right to conduct Indigenous research? I do not have these answers, but I hope to find an appropriate position for myself in Indigenous studies as a Chinese anthropology (student) researcher.

References

Boas, Franz. 1955. "Primitive Art", in *Anthropology of Art: a reader*, edited by Howard Morphy and Morgan Perkins in 2006. Malden, MA: Blackwell Pub.

Browner, Tara. 2002. *Heartbeat of the People: Music and Dance of the Northern Powwow.* Urbana and Chicago: University of Illinois Press.

Briggs, Charles L. 1996. "The Politics of Discursive Authority in Research on 'Invention of Tradition'". in *Cultural Anthropology*, 1996, 11(4): 435-469.

Creel, Herrlee Glessner. 1935. "On the Origins of the Manufacture and Decoration of Bronze in the Shang Period", in *Monumenta Serica*, 1935, 1(1): 36-69.

Denzin, Norman K; Lincoln, Yvonna S; Smith, Linda Tuhiwai. 2008. *Handbook of Critical and Indigenous Methodologies.* Los Angeles: Sage.

Dyck, Noel. 2006. "Canadian Anthropology and the Ethnography of 'Indian Administration'". in *Historicizing Canada Anthropology*, edited by Julia Harrison and Regna Darnell. Vancouver: UBC Press.

Ellis, Clyde. 2003. "The Sound of the Drum Will Revive Them and Make Them Happy: Nineteenth Century Plains Society Dances and the Roots of the Powwow." in *A Dancing People: Powwow Culture on the Southern Plains*. Lawrence, Kan: University Press of Kansas.

Hammersley, Martyn and Paul Atkinson. 1983(2007). *Ethnography: principles in practice.* London: Routledge.

Hampton, Eber. 1995. "Memory Comes Before Knowledge: Research May Improve If Researchers Remember Their Motives." in *Canadian Journal of Native Education*, 1995, 21(supplement): 46-54.

Honigmann, John J. 1976. "The Personal Approach in Cultural Anthropological Research." in *Current Anthropology*, 1976, 6(17): 234-250.

Kovach, Margaret. 2009. *Indigenous Methodologies: Characteristics, Conversations, and Context*. Toronto Buffalo London: University of Toronto Press.

Krmpotich, Cara Ann, and Laura Peers. 2013. *This is Our Life: Haida material heritage and changing museum practice*. Vancouver: UBC Press.

Levi-Strauss, Claude.

1976. "Jean-Jacques Rousseau, Founder of the Sciences of Man". In *Structural Anthropology: volume II*, 1976: 33-43, translated from the French by Monique Layton. New York: Basic Books.

1982. *The Way of Masks*. Translated from the French by Sylvia Modelski. Seattle: University of Washington Press.

Myerhoff, Barbara and Ruby, Jay. 1982. "Introduction" in *A Crack in the Mirror: Reflexive Perspectives in Anthropology*, edited by Jay Ruby, 1982: 1:35. Philadelphia: University of Pennsylvania Press.

Nader, Laura. 1972. "Up the anthropologist: perspectives gained from studying up," in *Reinventing Anthropology*, edited by Hymes, Dell H., 284-311. New York: Pantheon Books.

Salzman, Philip Carl. 2002. "On Reflexivity". in *American Anthropologist*, 2002, 104(3): 805-813.

Smith, Linda Tuhiwai.1999. *Decolonizing Methodologies: Research and Indigenous Peoples*. London: Zed Books.

Tedlock, Barbara. 1991. "From Participant Observation to the Observation of Participation: the Emergence of Narrative Ethnography." in *Journal of Anthropological Research*, 1991, 47(1): 69-94.

Tyler, Stephen A. 1987. *The Unspeakable: Discourse, Dialogue, and Rhetoric in the Postmodern World*. Madison Wisconsin: Universit of Wisconsin Press.

Wilson, Shawn. 2008. Research is Ceremony: Indigenous Research Methods. Nova Scotia: Fernwood Publishing.

notes

[12] There are Han group—the biggest and main ethnic group— and fifty-five minority groups in China. The relationship between Han group and the other fifty-fie minority group in history was different from the Indigenous peoples and the rest of the Canadian/White Society; there was no colonization involved among different groups. However, the Han group is sometimes called as the main group, and Han society the main society, because the population of Han people is much more than even the sum of number of the people of all the fifty-five minority groups. Also, each group of people has their own specific costumes, traditions, and for some groups languages as well. In addition, even though urban minority group people is really common, all the minority groups have their own specific living districts, the scale of which depends on the population of the certain group people and varies from a small town to a whole province. Nevertheless, even in a province which is named as a minority group province, such as the Inner Mongolia Autonomous Region, there are more Han people than Inner Mongolians and sometimes people from other minority groups.

Chapter Four

Rooted in Place

Métis Identity and Connections to Geographic and Temporal Landscapes

Angie Tucker

Both sides of my family have deep roots in the province that is now called Manitoba. There are very few hamlets, trees, or farmhouses that are not recognizable to me in either place or name in southern Manitoba. There is a comfort when I return home from Alberta. Despite living away from Manitoba, my body seems to fall into its place when I am in it. In Manitoba, I am 'home.' My body embraces the familiarity of its landscape, the connections to my family; both past and present, and the ties to the events that I have within it. Where I am from, and who I am from has shaped who I am, and has been responsible for a large part of my identity. However, identities are complex. Identities can change in context or the phases of your life. Identities are personal. Identities can shift depending on the relationships that you have with another person, and sometimes your identity is determined by those other people. Parts of your identity can be hidden from sight or pulled out into the open, depending on what you choose to share with others. But identity is most importantly, almost always, collective. Who you are today has been shaped by your ancestors and is continued through your family. Over time, I have recognized that despite the many memories that have persisted about my family and my home in Manitoba, others have been silenced. Parts of my paternal family's identity have been shut out of their history, which in turn, has been shut out of my mine. However today, there is a persistence to no longer privilege these silences, and to reclaim the identities that have been either refused or intended to be erased.

My Dad never talked about his background. If asked, he would state that he was Scottish or English, but that we were now Canadian, because our family had been in Canada *for a long time*. So long, that I could have been the 'Princess of Manitobah,' he joked when I was young. Dad used to tell me that we were related to Thomas Spence (1832-1900). Spence, a Scot, was a man who had petitioned the early British Government from the small town of Portage la Prairie, west of Winnipeg, for a legally constituted administration called New Caledonia. New Caledonia would later become the "Republic of Manitobah." This arrangement however, was never recognized, and Spence quickly lost his position. Thomas Spence was eventually arrested by Louis Riel, but later became an English delegate for St. Peters to the Provisional Government's Convention of Forty (Goldsborough 2014, par. 2). My father's true great-grandfather, David Charles Spence, also sat on the Convention of Forty[13], but alongside George Dunn in the parish of St.Annes, near Poplar Point, where he is today buried. The confusion began in our family because both Thomas and David had histories of political involvement within the same general region of Assiniboia. However, we have no relation to Thomas Spence in our genealogy. Therefore, when Dad and Grandma used to say that were "part-Indian, you know," we took it with a grain of salt. We never talked about it, and never really questioned it. "Part-Indian" was void of any real meaning other than possibly having a distant Indigenous relative from years prior. However, nobody ever attempted to uncover more information. There were never any photographs of my grandmother's parents or grandparents on the walls of our homes, and there were certainly never any stories shared about who they were or where they came from.

A number of years ago, I set out to provide my father with a more accurate geneaological record. While looking through old census records at the Manitoba Provincial Archives, I began to easily uncover that my father's family was not simply the Scottish/English family that they presented themselves to be. His mother was Métis. We have been connected to ancestral land and community at Red River, and genealogically attached to a strong line of Métis ancestors for many generations. However, my memories and attachments are not recognizable to me as Métis in any way because this history was hidden. My father's family potentially fabricated a familial attachment to a Scottish man with no Indigenous roots rather than align themselves to their Métis ancestry. It seems that over time, my father's family erased their Indigenous past in favour of silencing and existing in a non-Indigenous present.

I have since spent my years in academia unpacking and working to understand the reasons for my family's silences – why or how was this part of my family's identity contained or denied? I have realized that my family's denial is far from an isolated experience. I have considered many

CHAPTER FOUR

possibilities that lay in the gray area between what was and what is, and have recognized that the colonial experience continues to be responsible for restricting Métis bodies today through the definitions and misunderstandings of both epistemology and identities. I have particularly contemplated the impact of the actions of others who have influenced Métis identities over time. I have continued to recognize how the Canadian colonial state has not only perpetrated these crimes, but have also contributed to destructive silences and misunderstandings. I have concluded that the historical and continued control over Métis people has resulted in only fragments of traditional culture being shared due to the severing and removal of Métis people from their traditional spaces, relations, and communities.

I have concluded that the refusal to admit membership to a Métis community does not abolish your lineage, genealogy, and ancestors. It is necessary to consider how the systemic structures of racial and legal thinking in Canada contributed to the notion that being an Indigenous person was objectionable. I argue that colonial structures reinforced the desire of my family, specifically, to reject their Indigenous heritage to protect themselves within a society that is more often discriminatory of Indigenous people. These refusals were neither spontaneous or natural. Rather than these refusals being accepted and reproduced, I insist they must be questioned in order to recognize the complexities of independent Métis identities today.

Over the summer of 2017, I lived at Buffalo Lake Métis Settlement in Northern Alberta. Initially, I approached the Settlement because I assumed that a collective land-based community could be a catalyst for understanding or decolonizing Métis identity, including my own. However, while engaging with the community, I began to recognize the diversity of experience within its population. Some of the members have lost their language and practices, while many others have kept a strong sense of themselves as Métis. I recognized that people living within its boundaries have, in many ways, had their own complex experiences with identity and of inclusion. I learned that over time, attachments and relationships to land and our relations have become diverse. I further took away that the ways in which people continue to 'be' Métis is multifaceted, generational, and spatial. I began to recognize that even today, colonial frameworks were not only responsible for how I have come to know myself, but that they continue to restrict or deny other Métis people as well.

While at the Settlement, I asked Métis Elder, Elmer Ghostkeeper, how he continued to use the land today. "No, no," he said, "you think like *moniyaw*.[14] You need to think about living with the land. Not living off of it.

Métis are connected to the earth, and we are connected to each other. We are connected to all of the plants and animals, the blades of grass, trees and waterways." Ghostkeeper's master's thesis, *Spirit Gifting: The Concept of Spiritual Exchange* (1995), works to balance Métis traditional worldviews with Western scientific knowledge in order to provide a model for self-realization and discovery. "Because Métis people view themselves as part of the land of living beings, Spirit Gifting or *mekiachahkwewin*," Ghostkeeper writes, "is when one makes a living with the land using the spiritual gifts of plants and animals for food and medicinal purposes" (Ghostkeeper 2007, 4). Therefore, he recognizes the spiritual connections that Métis have to the land, and how this worldview can provide a guiding methodology for group revitalization. Ghostkeeper's text was able to provide a framework to think through how Métis have become separated from the land, and how regaining the relationship to the land could help to reconnect the Métis Nation. I had never considered how differing land ontologies could have affected Métis people. Is it possible that both physical and temporal detachments from land could be responsible for the complexities of identity that often arise within contemporary Métis bodies? How have these detachments to land contributed to the loss that we feel to a connected community? Many Métis have become estranged from the relations and traditional teachings that occurred on this land that once informed our ancestors.

I began to consider the role of the early Canadian government during Confederation and their role in land acquisition. After all, the colonial government was responsible for driving so many Métis away from their homelands in the prairies in multiple ways – fundamentally altering their connection to specific places of knowing. Furthermore, the colonial government was responsible for impressing their own discourse and understanding of land into policy - rejecting Indigenous knowledge systems. I questioned if the physical and temporal disconnections from the land may have contributed to my family's silence.

I began this chapter by geographically placing myself inside modern-day Manitoba because I recognize that my identity relies on the connections that I have to that land and to that place. It is where I feel 'at home.' It is the place where I can continue to return to both physically and temporally – travelling the roads in my mind until I have arrived back home, or to my grandmother's house; passing the familiar towns, signs, open fields, and trees. It is in that place where I gain my strength because I know that my ancestors helped to shape the landscape. Today, the ancestors continue to live with our relations in the prairie grass and atop the slow waves that meet the shoreline at Lake Manitoba. This place continues to bind me to the memories that I have of not only growing up but to the memories of the family who collectively shaped me. My grandmother, my parents, my aunts and uncles all contributed to my identity in that place.

Elmer Ghostkeeper drove me to consider how the loss of this connection to the land and to my ancestors could affect my identity. What if the town names in Manitoba were no longer recognizable to me? What if the rivers, forests, and fields were altered? If this place became unrecognizable to me in both name and layout, if I no longer knew the people living within it, and if I became restricted from using the space in the ways that I recognized, I would quickly become estranged not only to this place but from myself. If my connections to place and actions within it were deemed uncivilized or wasteful, or if I were critiqued for my backwardness or halfness, it could alter how I self-identified. I questioned how colonial definitions of land and of the notions of home have overshadowed Métis ontologies.

The land is of legal importance to Métis identity. However, I argue that the notions of locality and identity in policy are couched solely in British understandings of territory, and are perpetuated in the definitions of who can claim Métis identity. Métis are legally validated by the Canadian government as those with "distinctive collective identity *living together* in the same *geographic area* while sharing a *common way of life*" (Section 12, R. v. Powley, [2003] 2 S.C.R. 207, 2003 SCC43). Therefore, the colonial understanding of land is fused into the government definitions of Métis identity. This pressure to define ourselves through their definitions of recognition is a restrictive category that overlooks the history of land acquisition and the bias of British ontologies in understanding land and land use. I am highly critical of how the Canadian government has collectively defined Métis groups using non-Indigenous ontologies, particularly when the aims of colonialism were not only to define, attain, and appropriate land but to restrict and assimilate Indigenous people in Canada. Because of this fact, the legal requirements of both connections to the ancestral community in the past, and membership within a community in the present is difficult to navigate.

The objectives of early British colonizers were to assert dominance over territories and the people living within them in order to exploit resources and attain capital. The perceived belief that British ways of knowing were superior and progressive created a landscape in which Indigenous people would find themselves bound as both uncivilized and backwards (Stark 2016). The British, specifically relevant in the Canadian context, had a unique approach to land, land-use and ownership. John Locke's 1713 work, *Two Treatises of Property*, offers a glimpse into the

British ideological framework for settling the 'New' World. Locke established a central theory of colonial property-making that is fundamental to understanding the underlying differences in land ontologies between British and Indigenous people. For individual property to exist, Locke believes there must be a means for individuals to appropriate the things around them. He recognizes that the innate property of an individual is their own body and that labour is, in fact, an action of one's body (Locke 1988, 292). The land is therefore transformed through labour. Generally, this labour is thought to 'improve' the land and is manifested through both the work of cultivation and through the building of homes and fences that enclose land, trees, waterways, and plants within it. Fencing and enclosing the land makes it accessible only to those living within it, and inaccessible to those who do not. John Locke's work presents an ideological problem. The understanding of bounded and improved territory created difficulty in contextualizing not only Indigenous but Métis culture. The act of property accumulation, cultivating, building, and fencing of private property, further created borders within which Métis people were in many instances, unable to sustain traditional land-use activities.

The historical understanding of the 'New' World by British colonizers as an uncultivated wasteland and as an unoccupied *terra nullius* clearly differed from the realities and knowledges of existing Indigenous groups and their connections to land and practices. Although many Métis people had defined properties and homesteads in the prairies, Métis also had, and continue to have, non-cartographic attachments to place: one defined by cognitive, symbolic relationships to place that extends beyond the realm of territorial maps and quantifiable geography. Métis relationships to land include relating to their landscapes through oral stories and songs, linking their relationships to specific locations and relationships, and naming the locations on the landscape that they have occupied. Étienne Rivard defines this as "oral geography" (Rivard 2012, 144). Rivard explains that the "concept of oral geography can be defined as oral history, but also the connection between spatial structures – the material, political, and symbolic orderings of space – and social structures inherent to oral cultures" (Rivard 2012, 156). Rivard is describing an alternate way of engaging with the territory. Landmarks and geographical knowledge, oral tradition and sharing are fundamental to Métis for recognizing and engaging with spaces. The knowledge and framing of space were also reliant on the seasons and the presence of animals and medicines during specific times of the year. James C. Scott writes in *Seeing Like a State*, "it was the orderly succession of say, the skunk cabbage appearing, the willows beginning to leaf, the red-wing blackbird returning, and the first hatch of the mayfly that provided a readily observable calendar of spring. Indigenous knowledge is vernacular and local, keyed to common features of a *local* ecosystem: it inquires about oak leaves *in this place*" (Scott 1998, 311-312). Scott has realized that Indigenous people have local knowledge of the plants and animals that inhabit their traditional spaces, and that their inclusion or absence determine not only land engagements but the familiarity of the landscape. Elmer Ghostkeeper further taught me that land offers a partnership with Métis people, one that relies on respect, harmony, and equality in the same ways as a personal relationship. Land is not just something that you live on, but live with.

The government, however, as a political actor, is unable, or perhaps *unwilling* to understand identities that do not align with their knowledge of the place and of territory. James C. Scott's *Seeing Like a State* describes how the modern State, over time, got a handle on its subjects and environments. "The government" Scott begins, "took exceptionally complex, illegible and local social practices, such as land tenure customs or naming customs and created a standard grid whereby it could be centrally recorded and monitored" (Scott 1998, 2). Scott, therefore, suggests that despite deeply rooted traditional customs that existed prior to colonial advancement, the government chose to simplify territorial understandings and naming of spaces into a mapped system that made sense only to themselves, thus denying the knowledges and customs of the original people (Scott 1998, 2).

The destruction and recreation of space as bounded territory were both disruptive to the people living within it because this scientific and modernist ideology restricted Indigenous engagement with their territories in both physical and temporal ways. "Formal order is always, and to some considerable degree, parasitic on informal processes, which the formal scheme does not recognize" (Scott 1998, 312). Scott has uncovered that the formality of the state in defining spaces, privatizing land, making 'improvements' and eliminating resources has been privileged and therefore continues to perpetuate the ignorance of informal systems. Métis people were restricted from fully engaging with their spaces because their interactions on the land were more often considered backward (Rivard 2012; Stark 2016). Métis movement and engagement with their spaces were ideologically different from those of the British colonizer. The continued privilege of the colonial discourse of land and land use in Canada can only contribute to the fracturing of traditional knowledge of Métis people. Because standardization, homogenization, and grid making have become central to the way that contemporary levels of government in Canada continues to know and define people *within* its spaces, Indigenous people continue to be recognized, qualified, and quantified based on their original geographic locations.

Therefore, I would like to propose that the connection that is presumed by colonizers to be natural between bounded land and identity is problematic. These ideologies act only to restrict and oppress Métis epistemologies and have contributed to the social, political and economic experiences of Métis people. The loss of mobility and connection to traditional landscapes has altered the basis of cultural reproduction, and the loss of traditional culture has affected contemporary Indigenous identities. There is a continued loss of Métis agency in the contemporary landscape through the history of the colonial denial of Indigenous epistemologies.

In *Time & The Other*, Johannes Fabian writes that the Indigenous subject is rarely associated with modernity, but rather defined by passivity and an ahistorical 'unmodern' landscape (2014), and Patricia Seed projects in American Pentimento, that the denial of Indigenous epistemologies continues to be embedded in language, popular culture, and within legal systems (2001). Today, Indigenous people are still largely portrayed stereotypically as hunters, warriors, environmental guardians and spirit guides, not as landowners. These representations further define the codes of economic conduct to which we must adhere. Identity has been created and maintained by the government through paternalistic law and structure, is viewed negatively as the antithesis to British, and is reflective of the ideologies behind the historical land acquisition. This misrecognition contributes to the belief that Indigenous people are either lazy due to their assumed inability to 'use' their land or that they stand in the way of economic advancement. These stereotypes continue to be evident in cases involving contemporary land-claims, resistance to resource exploitation, and protection of water and sacred spaces.

Throughout this chapter, I have suggested that contemporary definitions of Métis identity rely not only on the rhetoric of non-Indigenous policy but also on the reproduction of colonial silence. I have further projected that by way of the colonial legal understanding of the land, colonizers were able to transform the landscape into bounded territory; removing Métis groups from their traditional homelands. The loss of mobility and connection to the landscape, therefore, has altered the basis of cultural reproduction, and the loss of shared traditional culture has affected contemporary Métis identities. I have also asserted that the recognition of 'being' Métis rests not within the Métis body, rather through the continuation of definitions that were born from the unequal power relations in Canada, rendering a continuation of paternalistic relationships that is often forgetful or passive of the historical treatment of Indigenous groups in Canada. I would also like to suggest that colonialism is economically motivated and culturally embedded in our society, and continues to negate and suppress Indigenous knowledge.

Federal and provincial decisions, therefore, cannot possibly, nor should, provide a unified definition of Métis identity. These definitions collectively define Indigenous groups using non-Indigenous ontologies. We have repeatedly learned that the Canadian state continues to create and define Metis identities for its own specific use, and we are guilty of attempting to fit ourselves and others into these narrow qualifying definitions. Métis identities must be disentangled and decolonized from static legal and social definitions by recognizing the colonial role of the Canadian state in contemporary Métis understanding and how this, in turn, has created fluidity in both the recognition of and recognition within Métis bodies. The dispossession of Métis land has created and perpetuated institutionalized inequalities between the colonizer and the colonized, and this fact continues to predicate the relationships in which Metis have with the state, in society, within us, and even sometimes with each other.

References

Daniels v. Canada (Indian Affairs and Northern Development). [2016] 1 S.C.R. 99, 2016 SCC12.

Fabian, Johannes. 2014. *Time and the Other: How Anthropology Makes its Object*. New York: Columbia University Press.

Ghostkeeper, Elmer. 2007. *Spirit Gifting: The Concept of Spiritual Exchange*. Alberta: writing on Stone Press.

Goldsborough, Gordon. 2014. "Memorable Manitobans: Thomas Spence (1832-1900)." *Manitoba Historical Society*. Accessed April 10, 2018. http://www.mhs.mb.ca/docs/people/spence_t.shtml. January 25, 2014.

Hall, D.J. 2015. *From Treaties to Reserves: The Federal Government and Native Peoples in Territorial Alberta*. Canada: Queen's University Press.

Hall, Norma J. n.d. "The Convention of Forty/La Grande Convention." *Provisional Government of Assiniboia*. Accessed April 12, 2018. https://hallnjean2.wordpress.com/chronology-the-resistance-during-1870/the-convention-of-fortyla-grande-convention/.

Locke, John. 1713. *Two Treatises of Government*. London: Churchill.

Macdougall, Brenda. 2010. *One of the Family: Métis Culture in Nineteenth-Century Northwestern Saskatchewan*. Vancouver: UBC Press.

Macdougall, Brenda, Carolyn Podruchny, and Nicole St-Onge. 2012. "Cultural Mobility and the Contours of Difference." In *Contours of a People: Métis Family, Mobility and History*, 3-21 edited by Nicole St-Onge, Carolyn Podruchny & Brenda Macdougall. University of Oklahoma Press.

Rivard, Étienne. 2012. ""Le Fond De L'Ouest: Territoriality, Oral Geographies, and the Métis in the Nineteenth-Century Northwest." In *Contours of a People: Métis Family, Mobility and History*, 143-168, edited by Nicole St-Onge, Carolyn Podruchny & Brenda Macdougall. University of Oklahoma Press.

R. v. Powley, [2003] 2 S.C.R. 207, 2003 SCC 43, Section 12.

Scott, James C. 1998. *Seeing Like a State: How Certain Schemes to Improve the Human Condition Have Failed*. New York: Yale University Press.

Seed, Patricia. 2001. *American Pentimento: The Invention of Indians and the Pursuit of Riches*. Minnesota: University of Minnesota Press.

Stark, Heidi. 2016. *Criminal Empire: The Making of the Savage in a Lawless Land*. Johns Hopkins University Press.

notes

[13] The Convention of Forty were a collection of both French and English speaking settlers and Indigenous people of the Red River Settlement led by Louis Riel. This group worked to ensure that Métis rights and their claims to the land would be recognized during the transfer of Rupert's Land to Canada (Hall n.d., par. 1).

[14] *Moniyaw* is a term used in "Y"-Cree dialect to refer to a 'white person'.

Chapter Five

The Indigenous Dick Joke
A Thorough Yet Noninvasive Examination of Our Most Famous Tribal Member

Waylon Lenk

This project started with a joke that I almost didn't hear. I was flying out of Oregon in the morning at six AM to research a defunct Indian boarding school in Nebraska for a wholly different project, and I thought getting to bed early might be in order. But then a good-looking friend of mine texted to see if I was going to see the 1491s perform at Southern Oregon University that evening. "Are you going?" I texted back. She was, so I did too. The 1491s were performing for an academic crowd, so they had a question and answer period after they showed their videos and told their jokes. I don't know why – they knew the questions would be academic and obtuse, and that they were mostly just interested in telling dick jokes.

But dick jokes aren't just about fun and showing off, they insisted. As an example, they told an Iktomi story. As I recall it, Iktomi happened upon a young woman swimming out on a lake. He sent his dick out across the water like a piece of seaweed to penetrate her without her permission. Luckily, her grandma was sitting on the beach and hits it with her knife. In all the stories after that, everyone laughs at Iktomi because he's only got half a dick. Imagine being a young man who grows up hearing stories like this one. It becomes normal to you to consider consent any time you take your dick out. This story taps not only into deep-seated male fears of castration as a punishment for being irresponsible with one's penis, but also threatens misbehaving men with being treated as fools. Compare that to the lessons learned by young men growing up in a time when men who brag about preying upon women can get elected president.

This chapter is my own response to the 1491s' attempt at academic legitimacy (and the title is an amalgamation of ideas of Ryan Red Corn's). I engage with Indigenous responses to feminist theory (Child 2012, Deer

2015, Jacob 2013, Jagodinsky 2016, Simpson 2014) to explore the ways in which Indigenous dick jokes constitute a form of social control that normalize the recognition by men of female corporeal sovereignty. After working through the theory, I apply it to a pair of texts: a joke that exists in Karuk discursive repertoire, and Randy Reinholz's play *Off the Rails*.

Thinking hard about dick jokes

One of the central themes, I'll argue, of Indigenous dick jokes – and the Iktomi story is a good example – is that men need to put women first. So, with that in mind, it makes sense to start this investigation of dicks with Katrina Jagodinsky's theories on the corporeal sovereignty of Indian women. "A central assumption" of her book *Legal Codes and Talking Trees* is that "stories constitute a form of 'case law' that makes up the legal traditions of Indigenous people." She centers her legal research "on the efforts of Indian women to achieve corporeal sovereignty – authority over their own bodies and progeny." (3) Her notion of "case law" is cited wholesale from James W. Zion's theories on "Indian common law". Zion theorizes a family of tribally specific legal codes which he names after British common law, somewhat tentatively, because the tribal legalisms in the U. S. and Canada by necessity exist in close relationship with the progeny of British common law that the U. S. and Canada practice. (Zion 123) The short version, for Zion, is that "Indian government, law and daily life are founded upon long-standing and strong customs, and since the stated rationale for the English Common Law is that it is a product of custom, that approach may be used for Indian law as well." Jagodinsky uses the stories of six Indian women to orient discussions of tribal sovereignty onto these women's struggle for corporeal sovereignty. As part of her project, she focuses on "the tribal philosophies that such women drew from in order to make cultural and gendered claims to protect their bodies, progeny, and lands threatened under imperial legal regimes." (4) Her second argument is a prescient critique of President Trump: "the project of American conquest and settler-colonialism depended upon newcomers' abilities to claim and control Indigenous women's productive and reproductive labors and access to land in addition to the use of legal and military violence to incarcerate or incorporate Indigenous men…" It's my position that Indian dick jokes, at least in part, teach men how to respect women and teach women what to expect from men. Since both Jagodinsky and Zion's theories are foundational to my own, I think it's useful to take a look at how they treat dick jokes.

CHAPTER FIVE

Jagodinsky, in her story of Nora Jewell, describes that Salish woman's legal fight for restitution from her white American rapist. That she followed through with legal proceedings, instead of cowering in hopelessness and fear, Jagodinsky attributes to her acculturation with Coyote stories:

> Understanding Nora's sexual assault in these contexts helps to explain why she felt empowered to report Smith's crime in an imperial court when so few women achieved justice in similar instances. Like the women in Salish stories about sexual assault, Nora and her Salish aunt applied their own understanding of legal principles and reported Smith's misbehaviors, no doubt expecting their community to punish him. What they might not have expected is that territorial jurists had built a system that assumed female consent, while the Salish system had assumed Coyote guilt. (83)

Zion describes an event in which humor was successfully directed at a man who strayed outside of his community's sexual norms,

> One recent case from the Rocky Boy's Reservation in Montana, involved the conduct of a tribal councilor who liked women much older than he. One day an elderly man came before the full council and asked to be heard. He said: 'Please tell this man (indicating the councilor with a sign) to return my wife who he borrowed from me; I want her back now.' The council collapsed in laughter and ordered the council member to return the wife. The story is now told and retold on the reservation (as it will be for many years) because it is not only case law showing the foolishness of taking another man's wife, but case law illustrating the foolishness of being attracted to a much older woman. (132)

Both of these stories demonstrate the importance of listening to Indian dick jokes from the point of view of Indian common law; that is, how do they normalize certain behaviors with regards to penises.

Jagodinsky writes from the shoulders of a body of literature stretching back at least to the 1990s. One of her citations is Miroslava Chávez-Garcia's book *Negotiating Conquest: Gender and Power in California, 1770s to 1880s*. Chávez-Garcia engaged in a project that in many ways directly presages Jagodinsky's. While not specifically focused on Native women, Chávez-Garcia traces a history of female engagement, negotiation with, and oppression by colonial legal structures. While Jagodinsky and Chávez-Garcia focus on individual women and their relationships with the law, a larger body of both academic and artistic work has emerged – predominantly by Native women – that centers discussions of sovereignty on Native women. Some of these are tribally specific – I mention in passing Jacob's *Yakama Rising* and Simpson's *Mohawk Interruptus*, and I'll return in more detail to Brenda Child's *Holding Our World Together*. Other works focus on how American interventions into tribal legal processes puts Native women at pointed risk – on the academic side, Sarah Deer's *The Beginning and End of Rape* is emerging as a seminal work, and artistically both Louise Erdrich in her *Round House* and Mary Kathryn Nagle in her *Sliver of a Full Moon* deal with problems incumbent to limited or absent tribal jurisdiction over major crimes, including rape. Speaking of my primary discipline, theater (*Sliver* is a play), Yvette Nolan has been particularly productive with regards to investigating how Indian men often implicate ourselves in violence against Indian women in her plays *Annie Mae's Movement* and *The Death of a Chief*.

Why men don't do close weave

I'm building this project primarily on the basis of Jagodinsky's work – specifically, how dick jokes operate as "Indian common law" to normalize healthy behavior by men towards women. One of the key elements of Zion's notion of Indian common law is that it forms "...in the mind of the adult Indian, a body of law which he or she may be hard-pressed to articulate in terms of actual rules, but which are in the mind. This is why Indians, and only Indians, can truly have a comprehensive knowledge of their law." (129) I'd like to take it one step further and claim that only a Karuk can have comprehensive knowledge of Karuk law, that only a Métis can have comprehensive knowledge of Métis law, and so on and so forth. So here I'd like to take a look at a joke that I heard growing up.

My mother is a traditional basketweaver, and so I spent a good deal of my youth around Karuk, Yurok, Hupa weavers. In fact, I did a little weaving myself – but only open weave, where you can see through the sticks. Close weave was and is reserved for women. As these older ladies told me, if a man does it his sîish would fall off.

I'm fine though. I never risked it.

This dick joke's social function is to entrench gendered labor amongst Karuk, Yurok and Hupa communities. Brenda Child, in *Holding Our World Together* makes the importance of gendered labor in combatting overwhelming patriarchy clear. In her chapter on "Nett Lake: Wild Rice and the Great Depression", she demonstrates that the masculinization of rice harvesting at Nett Lake. That masculinization was the outcome of settler-colonial interventions into Ojibwe economics during the swelling of public employment during the American New Deal. During the Great

Depression, the United States federal government invested in emergency relief work programs like the Civilian Conservation Corps and the Works Progress Administration, which were major employers of Ojibwe men during the 1930s. (Child 112) This regendering of rice harvesting reflected American labor norms in which agriculture was primarily male work. As always, with settler-colonialism comes settlers. Masculinization of rice harvesting was an intermediary step between the labor as a site of female production and unsustainable harvesting by settler speculators which had an ultimately negative impact on Ojibwe food supply. (Child 115) Maintaining close weave basketweaving as a female endeavor insulates this economic endeavor from similar devastation (although a closer parallel might be our inability to protect salmon runs in the face of New Deal-era dam building). Close weave baskets are a form of wealth, and while Karuk notions of wealth are different from American notions, the two are transmutable enough for basketweaving to emerge as a major economic endeavor for Karuk, Yurok and Hupa women during the first half of the 20th century. Weaving baskets implies gathering materials, which in turn implies stewardship of gathering spots. Maintaining it as a female endeavor insulated it from the change that occurred with our men when we started wearing pants, which was a moment of change within Karuk masculinity, according late elder Violet Super. Pants imply buying, which implies dollars, which implies male engagement in American economic structures. Story is, our men changed when we started wearing pants. Since we were engaging in an economic structure that privileges male labor, apparently, we got to feeling ourselves and trying to imitate white masculinity, which carries with it exploitive relationships with the land.

Laughing to keep from crying

Let none of this imply that fun is not a centrally important element of Indigenous dick jokes. I have heard a ton of these things since word got out that I was engaging in this research, and generally they're good-natured, healthy (if not wholesome) fun. For this final section, I would like to turn to a play on which I had the privilege to work as dramaturg for its world premiere at the Oregon Shakespeare Festival – *Off the Rails*, Randy Reinholz's adaptation of Shakespeare's *Measure for Measure*, but set in Genoa, Nebraska, home of the Genoa Industrial Indian School. (This is where I was going the day after I went to the 1491s' show).

Reinholz made a point of writing a comedy about the boarding schools, and he apparently was met with a load of skepticism from the elders with whom Native Voices at the Autry works. (Reinholz is the Artistic

Director at Native Voices where *Off the Rails* was first developed). The reason why he felt so strongly about it is that he could not expect an audience to sit through 90 to 120 minutes of child-torture – they would just check out and an important story would be lost. In this way, Reinholz deploys a familiar strategy of comic relief also deployed by Erdrich in *The Round House*. In that book, when the boys have found the gas can and things are super heavy, Erdrich breaks the tension by having them discuss the relative merits of having a Darth Vader versus an Emperor – a circumcised versus uncircumcised penis. (Erdrich 70) And, trust me, the tension needs to be broken in *Off the Rails*. The first time I have heard an audience legitimately hiss a stage character is about halfway through that play. Angelo has sentenced Pawnee boarding school student Momaday to death for impregnating a white woman (it was consensual by Momaday and Caitlin, but Angelo still considers it rape). Momaday's older sister, Isabel, comes home to Genoa to plead for her brother's life. Angelo takes a shine to her and offers her a deal: if she'll "give him love" he'll set her brother free. Isabel retorts, "You sign a pardon for my brother now, / Or with an outstretched throat I'll tell the world / The Kind of man you are." (69) In probably the most chilling line of the play, Angelo replies

> Who will believe you, Isabel?
>
> My unsoiled name, and you an Indian.
>
> My word against yours, my station in town,
>
> Will so outweigh your accusation,
>
> That you shall choke in your own report,
>
> Reeking of squalor and be the squaw you are.
>
> Now I give my superior race the rein:
>
> Fit your consent to my sharp appetite;
>
> To redeem your brother, there by
>
> Yielding your body up to my will;
>
> Or by your unkindness his death will draw out
>
> To lingering sufferance. You'll answer me today,
>
> Or, by the passion that now guides me most,
>
> I'll torture that boy to make the Sand Creek Massacre
>
> Look like a Sunday picnic. As for you,
>
> Say what you can, my false outweighs your true." (70)

CHAPTER FIVE

A few scenes later Isabel and Madame Overdone, the Lakota proprietor of the Stewed Prunes Saloon, have concocted a bed trick to save Isabel from rape and Momaday from execution. Isabel is walking Overdone and Daisy, a Paiute sex worker at the saloon, through the plan. Isabel has convinced Angelo that she has indeed consented, and so they have arranged

> …to liaison and couple, behind the school.
>
> He has arranged for us to link in the corn crib
>
> That little shack behind the chicken coop,
>
> Fenced with a wooden gate, which this big key opens.
>
> This tiny key opens a little door out front…
>
> DAISY
>
> That's a little key.
>
> OVERDONE
>
> Must be Angelo's. (93)

Like in the Iktomi story and in the warning about men doing close weave, emasculation is both a punishment and a joke. Angelo has set himself up as the most powerful person in the play. The effort to undermine his authority includes discursive castration.

Later in the play, Overdone's white male sidekick Pryor wakes up in prison after a drunk and disorderly. He notes that he recognizes clients from the brothel in prison. There's

> Slick Eyed Slim, who sold rabbit shine, only to prove the hair of the hare that bit you still won't get you drunk. Then there's "Dynamite Dick" Dawson, whose buckle bunny almost lost an eye, and George "Goose the Sheep" Shepard – ya'll know what his offense was. Kid was baaaad." (110)

Stephen Michael Spencer, who played Pryor at OSF, went out into the audience for this monologue and picked on individual men in the first few rows. It was all in good fun, and he didn't make anybody cry. It was also, in a way, subversive. Men who can afford seats in the first few rows of the Angus Bowmer Theater tend to have plenty of social capital – which means they tend to be white. Whether or not they are predators, they have enough power that the option for them to act as Angelo exists. In this monologue, a fellow white man makes jokes about them using their penises in irresponsible ways.

These are two of Randy Reinholz's superfluity of dick jokes, and the two that stand out the most clearly for me. The humor in the play anticipates the ending with the ultimate castigation of Angelo, a new social order in which Native women Isabel and Overdone and Black man Sherriff Shadrach have markedly more influence, and the ultimate round dance with the cast and members of the audience.

Conclusions

Like I mentioned, there are far more types of indigenous dick jokes than I have time to analyze here. For this paper, I selected jokes that strike me as 1) being in current use, and 2) having a definite antipatriarchal lesson for men. The Iktomi story is about men keeping their penises to themselves. The Karuk joke is about maintaining female-gendered economic autonomy. And the dick jokes in *Off the Rails* are about Native women taking social control away from white men (particularly the more Trump-ish white men). They all operate from a modicum of fun. The work from the assumption that people learn better when they're laughing, and that men have plenty to learn if we are to act in a way that facilitates female autonomy and sovereignty.

References

Chavez-Garcia, Miroslava. Negotiating Conquest: Gender and Power in California, 1770s to 1880s. University of Arizona Press, 2006.
Child, Brenda J. Holding Our World Together: Ojibwe Women and the Survival of Community. Viking Penguin, 2012.
Deer, Sarah. The Beginning and End of Rape: Confronting Sexual Violence in Native America. University of Minnesota Press, 2015.
Erdrich, Louise. The Round House. Kindle, HarperCollins Publishers, 2012.
Jacob, Michelle M. Yakama Rising: Indigenous Cultural Revitalization, Activism, and Healing. University of Arizona Press, 2013.
Jagodinsky, Katrina. Legal Codes and Talking Trees: Indigenous Women's Sovereignty in the Sonoran and Puget Sound Borderlands, 1854-1946. Yale University Press, 2016.
Nagle, Mary Kathryn. Sliver of a Full Moon. 3 May 2017.
Nolan, Yvette. Annie Mae's Movement. Playwrights Canada Press, 1998.
Nolan, Yvette, and Kennedy Cathy MacKinnon. "Death of a Chief." The Shakespeare's Mine: Adapting Shakespeare in Anglophone Canada, edited by Ric Knowles, Playwrights Canada Press, 2009, pp. 379–427.
Reinholz, Randy. Off the Rails. Oregon Shakespeare Festival, 2017.
Simpson, Audra. Mohawk Interruptus: Political Life Across the Borders of Settler States. Duke University Press, 2014.
Zion, James W. "Searching for Indian Common Law." Indigenous Law and the State, edited by Bradford W. Morse and Gordon R. Woodman, Foris, 1988.

Unsettling Colonial Effects and Returning to Indigenous Ways

Chapter Six

Constricting Self-Determination

Colonial Racism and Sexism in the Lives of Indigenous Women in Canada's West

Jessica Martin

During the economic and social restructuring of Canada's west[15] that occurred following the annexation of Rupert's Land, the Canadian government began a process of devaluing, segregating, and reconstructing Indigenous women as *others* as part of broader nation-building goals in the region. The result of such efforts was the marginalization of Indigenous women on the two axis of sex and race, thereby creating a unique duality that they continue to experience in contemporary contexts. This duality constricts Indigenous women's self-determination within their families and communities, which is perhaps most potently represented in the staggering statistics regarding gendered violence committed against them.[16] This chapter provides a brief analysis of the constriction of Indigenous women's self-determination in Canada's west throughout vital nation-building decades in order to examine how such constriction continues to impact them with specific regards to gendered violence. Further, it seeks to assert the importance of adopting an Indigenous feminist approach when developing approaches to gendered violence against Indigenous women and Indigenous self-determination.

I. Colonial Nation-Building Strategies for the Dual Oppression of Indigenous Women in Canada's West

Rashmi Goel argues that colonial policies that promoted the evolution of domestic violence in Indigenous communities can be classified within a three-part framework:

First, those policies aimed at assimilating Aboriginal peoples. Second, policies that upset the flow of traditional values and teachings from one generation to the next by separating and dislocating each generation. Third, policies designed to diminish the status and power of women or to establish and entrench male dominance.[17]

The following examples of nation-building strategies utilized by the Canadian government in Canada's west can be conceptualized within this framework, as they each sought to accomplish one or more of the goals through the creation and imposition of racism and sexism against Indigenous women. Such forces constricted and continue to constrict Indigenous women's self-determination and contribute to high rates of gendered violence within Indigenous communities.

a. Indian Act, 1876

Representing all three dimensions of Goel's framework, the first strategy under discussion is the *Indian Act*, 1876, which worked to impose Western patrilineality in Indigenous communities. Joanne Barker argues that the *Act* initiated a process of normalization and internalization of sexism and other colonial logics in Indigenous communities that worked to devalue women's positions while elevating those of men, a comparatively new colonial setting characterized by heteronormativity, racism, and sexism.[18] For example, section 12(1)(b), the infamous "marrying out"[19] rule, worked to devalue Indigenous women within their families and communities by attempting to eliminate women from roles of authority and giving responsibility for the communities' well-being largely to male members. This, Barker argues, has led Indigenous men to gain a sense of entitlement to band rights and authority over Indigenous women.[20] Such patriarchy and entitlement was demonstrated by the resistance of many Indigenous men to calls for and amendments to the *Act* made in the 1980s—i.e., Bill C-31—that worked to partially reverse the strictly patrilineal structure of Indigenous communities as outlined in the *Act*.[21] Indigenous women calling for such amendments were often accused of resorting to colonial methods for achieving their goals—such as adopting feminist rhetoric and pursuing their emancipation via legal channels—and were therefore largely dismissed.[22] Such resistance demonstrates the extent to which nationalist rhetoric trumps feminist discourse in patriarchy, as it is assumed that "what is good for the nation is good for women."[23] The *Indian Act* has played a substantial role in the internalization and normalization of patriarchal values, and, therefore, in the oppression of Indigenous women and the constriction of their self-determination.

b. Residential Schools

Demonstrating all three aspects of Goel's framework, the residential school system was one of the most powerful strategies applied with regards to assimilating Indigenous peoples within the broader nation-building context. As part of the system's mandate "to 'civilize' and Christianize Aboriginal peoples[,]"[24] the government and school administrators implemented a series of formal and informal policies that worked to reconstruct students' conceptions of sex and gender in order to assimilate them to British-Canadian standards for gender and associated roles.[25] Educating Indigenous students in residential schools not only furthered their racial segregation as *others* in Canada's west, but the mechanisms in place within the schools also worked to entrench patriarchal sexism amongst students. Indigenous women were devalued, and their roles redefined, effectively altering their place in their families and communities, encouraging patriarchal values in these settings, and, ultimately, constricting Indigenous women's self-determination.

c. Manipulation of Cultural Imagery

Demonstrating the first and third aspects of Goel's policy framework, another strategy was the manipulation of cultural imagery regarding Indigenous women—meaning the way that Indigenous women were constructed via colonial discourse and popular culture.[26] During the latter half of the nineteenth century, Indigenous women were portrayed as threats to the new utopian order of British-Canadian settlement and capitalism that the federal government sought to create. For example, while white women were increasingly depicted as "the civilizer and the reproducer of the race,"[27] Indigenous women were portrayed as the opposite: particularly following the North-West resistance led by the Métis in 1885, Indigenous peoples were described as instigators of violence, and as "agents of destruction of the moral and cultural health of the new community."[28] This manipulation of cultural imagery allowed the government to create a utopian narrative of Canada's west as a moral haven for settlers and establish an anti-narrative of what Canadian western ideals and lifestyle rejected. It also acted as a method of legitimization for the expanding influence of Canadian authority and law.[29] Reduced opportunity in economic pursuits and other areas of socio-economic life for Indigenous women in the expanding sphere of government influence in Canada's west were a direct result of the manipulation of popular rhetoric that actively worked to devalue Indigenous women and constrict their self-determination based on their position as Indigenous and as women.

Moreover, such stereotypes of Indigenous women as "hypersexual and amoral" have long provided spurious invitations for violence and injustices against them.[30] Many of these stereotyped portrayals were further entrenched through their codification in the *Indian Act*, and continue to impact Indigenous women's treatment in contemporary settings, including law enforcement and justice.[31]

d. Imposition of Colonial Marriage Ideals

Representing the first and third dimensions of Goel's framework, yet another nation-building strategy was the manipulation and regulation of marriages to abide by a hetero-patriarchal model largely constructed by the Canadian government. Several values represented in this model of marriage were imposed on Indigenous women and worked to devalue their traditionally-revered positions within their families and communities by encouraging their departure from public and political life and embodying a purely domestic role. This strictly intraracial model of marriage was also a conscious attempt to further segregate Indigenous and non-Indigenous peoples: it represented a method through which to "maintain settlers' social and sexual distance from Indigenous peoples."[32] The adoption of such a model of marriage has greatly contributed to the entrenchment of colonial racial assumptions regarding Indigenous peoples and to the internalization of patriarchal values within Indigenous families and communities, and therefore to the constriction of Indigenous women's self-determination.[33]

II. Indigenous Women's Confrontation with Gendered Violence and Constricted Self-Determination

a. Framework

While racist ideologies and practices by the Canadian government and other colonial actors have largely characterized the experiences of Indigenous peoples in Canada's west over the last century and a half, the "differential impacts"[34] of colonization on men and women become clear as the oppressive force of sexism is highlighted.[35] Racism and sexism, while largely interconnected in the way in which they shape the experiences of Indigenous women, are conceptually distinct. This divergence is significant in that it ensures an understanding that does not conflate or equate the two, or imply that violence against Indigenous women is simply "just another manifestation of racism" and therefore "a consequence of discrimination against men."[36] If such a conceptualization is accepted, then it could be argued that gendered violence is a result of minority men's inability to exert their perceived rightful power as men in broader society due to the racism they experience; therefore, in order to reduce gendered violence, these men must obtain greater power in broader society.[37] As such, while it is argued here that racism and sexism intersect and interact within the context of colonialism to create a unique duality in which Indigenous women are more likely to experience gendered violence and constriction of self-determination, it is also acknowledged that they are distinct forces that operate within separate, if overlapping, spheres.

b. Gendered Violence and Self-Determination

Several scholars have examined the role of socioeconomic risk factors such as age, education, and employment status on the elevated risk of Indigenous women being victims of gendered forms of violence. However, such risk factors do not entirely explain the differences in rates of gendered violence between Indigenous and non-Indigenous women. As such, colonization theory, which argues that the impact of colonization has created unique experiences for Indigenous women that make them more likely to experience, in this context, gendered violence, is often applied as an explanation for these differences.[38]

In a comparison of Sámi communities in Scandinavia and Indigenous communities in Canada, Rauna Kuokkanen similarly found that socioeconomic factors do not appear to have a significant role in determining the risk of violence against women in Sámi communities.[39] Therefore, highlighting the extent to which colonization and patriarchy have affected the lives of Indigenous women in a comparative global context, she argues that the internalization of colonial and patriarchal values has shaped the attitudes and practices of community members for both groups, thereby increasing their risk of gendered violence: "[w]hether it is relatively well-off Sámi women or low-income, and impoverished Aboriginal women, the violence they face in their own communities is regularly silenced or dismissed."[40] As Kuokkanen argues, in Indigenous communities entrenched with patriarchal colonial values, the communities often demand "cultural authenticity and affiliation," and, as such, "women who experience violence may feel pressured not to report abuse for fear of being labelled as engaging in 'culturally inappropriate behaviour' and hence being disciplined for speaking out."[41] Such pressure exerted by patriarchal values and attitudes within Indigenous communities in Canada's west in this context is directly related to Indigenous women's self-determination not only in that they experience increased levels of gendered violence, but also in that they may not have the means or opportunity to seek out help to address gendered violence, and, even if they do, their calls for help may not necessarily receive appropriate responses.[42] Many may also be hesitant to seek help and assert their right to safety outside of their communities, as race continues to shape their experiences within the mainstream Canadian justice system.[43] Internalized patriarchal values also work to depoliticize domestic violence in that it reduces it to a private family matter, thereby further devaluing Indigenous women's position within their own families and communities.[44] Therefore, the entrenchment of racism against Indigenous peoples and sexism specifically against Indigenous women has not only devalued the latter's status and rights within their families and communities by way of increasing rates of gendered violence as a result of internalized patriarchy, but it also continues to oppress Indigenous women as their specific needs are often disregarded for the sake of broader collective issues. This is a direct demonstration of the extent to which Indigenous women's right and ability to be self-determining continues to be constricted as a result of internalized and normalized colonial patriarchy.

III: A Case for Indigenous Feminism in Understanding and Approaching Self-Determination and Gendered Violence

Violence maintains a ubiquitous presence in the lives of many Indigenous women in Canada's west; such unfortunate and unjust realities arise largely from the differentiated impacts of colonization and the internalization of patriarchy and are a major driving force behind Indigenous women's calls for increased and inclusive self-determination.[45] However, Indigenous women's concerns regarding self-determination have long faced resistance and criticisms, as they have been conceptualized as dichotomous to collective self-determination processes.[46] Brenda L. Gunn refutes such a dichotomization as antithetical to collective Indigenous self-determination processes, particularly given that such processes are foundational to other individual and collective rights and are considered to be detrimental to actualizing decolonization.[47] As such, she argues that self-determination, as a collective right, "necessitates the inclusion of Indigenous women, as they are an important component of the collective."[48] Further, she argues that addressing the differentiated gendered impacts of colonization and including Indigenous women are absolutely necessary for ensuring legitimate Indigenous self-determination processes.[49] Andrea Smith, too, negates the spurious dichotomy of individual versus collective Indigenous rights and argues that adopting an Indigenous feminist approach is a given in order to actualize decolonization as "it has been precisely through gendered violence that [Indigenous peoples] have lost [their] lands in the first place."[50]

Further, exclusively antiracist or feminist agendas for change within Indigenous communities often result in what Kimberle Crenshaw has described as "political intersectionality," in that each agenda alone often fails to recognize the unique experiences and challenges that the other faces.[51] Therefore, placing antiracist strategies and rhetoric above those of feminism creates an intra-community dynamic in which issues such as gendered violence are disregarded or underestimated, thereby reducing the likelihood that a victim-survivor will come forward about her experiences with violence;[52] such is evident in Kuokkanen's examination of the experiences of Sámi women and Indigenous women in what is now Canada. Indigenous agendas that are focused on antiracism and collective self-determination at the expense of feminist agendas disregard the intersectionality of race and sex, focusing instead on the impact of history and racism against the communities. As such, Kuokkanen argues that Indigenous women become the canary in the coal mine: "[r]ather than victims of gendered violence in their own right, Indigenous women become simply the means by which discrimination against Indigenous communities at large can be recognized."[53] It is thus of vital importance that both feminist and anti-racist ideologies and strategies be applied when addressing gendered violence in Indigenous communities in Canada's west. Joyce Green argues that both of these issues are addressed within Indigenous feminist theory, which relies on feminist and anti-colonial critiques to work in tandem, taking into consideration how and the extent to which Indigenous women occupy a space in which they are oppressed by both sexist and racist ideologies and practices.[54]

A gendered analysis makes clear that decades of colonial nation-building policies implemented by the Canadian government have created social, economic, and political environments in which Indigenous women are oppressed on two axis: race and sex. The resulting devaluation of Indigenous women and constriction of their self-determination within their families and communities, as largely reflected in rates of gendered violence and responses to it, demonstrates this unique dualistic oppression against Indigenous women. Approaches and solutions to the pervasive issues of constricted self-determination and gendered violence in Indigenous communities must, therefore, account for both race and sex as defining features in contemporary Indigenous women's experience.

References

Barker, Joanne. "Gender, Sovereignty, Rights: Native Women's Activism Against Social Inequality and Violence in Canada." American Quarterly 60, no. 2 (2008): 259-266. https://www.jstor.org/stable/40068533?seq=1#page_scan_tab_contents (accessed August 9, 2018).

Bradbury, Bettina. "Colonial Comparisons: Rethinking Marriage, Civilization and Nation in Nineteenth-Century White-Settler Societies." In Rediscovering the British World. Edited by Phillip Bucker and R. Douglas Francis. Calgary: University of Calgary Press, 2005. http://www.deslibris.ca/ID/402860 (accessed August 9, 2018).

Brownridge, Douglas A. "Male Partner Violence Against Aboriginal Women in Canada: An Empirical Analysis." Journal of Interpersonal Violence 18, no. 2 (2003): 65-83. http://journals.sagepub.com/doi/pdf/10.1177/0886260502238541 (accessed August 9, 2018).

Carter, Sarah. Capturing Women: The Manipulation of Cultural Imagery in Canada's Prairie West. Edited by Bruce G. Trigger. McGill-Queen's Native and Northern Series. Montreal and Kingston: McGill-Queen's University Press, 1997.

---. The Importance of Being Monogamous: Marriage and Nation Building in Western Canada to 1915. Edmonton: The University of Alberta Press; Athabasca: Athabasca University Press, 2008.

Crenshaw, Kimberle. "Mapping the Margins: Intersectionality, Identity Politics, and Violence Against Women of Color." Stanford Law Review 43, no. 6 (1991): 1241-1299. https://www.jstor.org/stable/1229039?seq=1#page_scan_tab_contents (accessed August 9, 2018).

Daoud, Nihaya, Janet Smylie, Marcelo Urquia, Billie Allan, and Patricia O'Campo. "The Contribution of Socio-Economic Position to the Excesses of Violence and Intimate Partner Violence Among Aboriginal Versus Non-Aboriginal Women in Canada." Canadian Journal of Public Health/Revue Canadienne de Santé Publique 104, no. 4 (2013): e278-e283. http://journal.cpha.ca/index.php/cjph/article/view/3724/2842 (accessed August 9, 2018).

Dylan, Arielle, Cheryl Regehr, and Ramona Alaggia. "And Justice or All? Aboriginal Victims of Sexual Violence." Violence Against Women 14, no. 6 (2008): 678-696. http://journals.sagepub.com/doi/10.1177/1077801208317291 (accessed August 9, 2018).

Eberts, Mary. "Being an Indigenous Woman is a 'High-Risk Lifestyle'." In Making Space for Indigenous Feminism. 2nd ed. Edited by Joyce Green. Halifax and Winnipeg: Fernwood Publishing, 2017.

Fiske, Jo-Anne. "The Womb is to the Nation as the Heart is to the Body: Ethnopolitical Discourses of the Canadian Indigenous Women's Movement." Studies in Political Economy 51 (1996): 65-95. https://spe.library.utoronto.ca/index.php/spe/article/%20view/6877/3858 (accessed August 9, 2018).

Goel, Rashmi. "No Women at the Center: The Use of the Canadian Sentencing Circle in Domestic Violence Cases." Wisconsin Women's Law Journal 15, no.293 (2000): 293-334. https://papers.ssrn.com/sol3/papers.cfm?abstract_id=2657644 (accessed August 9, 2018).

Green, Joyce. "Taking Account of Aboriginal Feminism." In Making Space for Indigenous Feminism. Edited by Joyce Green. Black Point: Fernwood Publishing, 2007.

---. "Taking More Account of Indigenous Feminism: An Introduction." In Making Space for Indigenous Feminism. 2nd ed. Edited by Joyce Green. Halifax and Winnipeg: Fernwood Publishing, 2017.

Gunn, Brenda L. "Self-Determination and Indigenous Women: Increasing Legitimacy Through Inclusion." Canadian Journal of Women and the Law 26, no.2 (2014): 241-275. https://muse.jhu.edu/article/564330/pdf (accessed August 9, 2018).

Indigenous Foundations. "Bill C-31." The University of British Columbia: First Nations and Indigenous Studies. https://indigenous foundations.arts.ubc.ca/bill_c-31/ (accessed August 9, 2018).

Kuokkanen, Rauna. "Gendered Violence and Politics in Indigenous communities: The Cases of Aboriginal People in Canada and the Sámi in Scandinavia." International Feminist Journal of Politics 17, issue 2 (2015): 271-288. https://www.tandfonline.com/doi/abs/10.1080/14616742.2014.901816 (accessed August 9, 2018).

Miller, J.R. Shingwuak's Vision: A History of Native Residential Schools. Toronto: University of Toronto Press, 2012.
Perreault, Samuel. "Criminal victimization in Canada, 2014." Statistics Canada: Jursistat, Catalogue no. 85-002-X (2015): 1-43. https://www150.statcan.gc.ca/n1/en/pub/85-002-x/2015001/article/14241-eng.pdf?st=dcUrz0OK (accessed August 9, 2018).
Smith, Andrea. "Native American Feminism, Sovereignty and Social Change." In Making Space for Indigenous Feminism. Edited by Joyce Green. Black Point: Fernwood Publishing, 2007.
Stark, Heidi Kiiwetinepinesiik. "Criminal Empire: The Making of the Savage in a Lawless Land." Theory & Event 19, issue 4 (2016): 48 para. https://muse.jhu.edu/article/633282 (accessed August 9, 2018).
Truth and Reconciliation Commission of Canada. Canada's Residential Schools: The history, Part 1, Origins to 1939—The Final Report of the Truth and Reconciliation Commission of Canada. Vol. 1. Montreal and Kingston: McGill-Queen's University Press, 2015. http://www.myrobust.com/websites/trcinstitution/File/Reports/Volume_1_History_Part_1_English_Web.pdf (accessed August 9, 2018).

notes

[15] I have specifically chosen to apply the term "Canada's west" in this chapter as its paternalistic implication is representative of colonial ideology and rhetoric at a time of active nation building in what are now known as the prairie provinces. When the capitalized term "West" is used, this is referring to the ideological West that largely informed colonial rhetoric.

[16] For example, whereas the rate of sexual assault against non-indigenous women in 2014 was 35 incidents per 1000, indigenous women recorded a much higher rate of 115 per 1000. Samuel Perreault, "Criminal Victimization in Canada, 2014," Statistics Canada: Juristat, catalogue no. 85-002-X (2015): 17, https://www150. statcan.gc.ca/n1/en/pub/85-002-x/2015001/article/14241-eng.pdf?st=dcUrz0OK (accessed August 9, 2018).

[17] Rashmi Goel, "No Women at the Center: The Use of the Canadian Sentencing Circle in Domestic Violence Cases," Wisconsin Women's Law Journal 15, no. 293 (2000): 302, https://papers.ssrn.com/sol3/papers.cfm?abstract_id=2657644 (accessed August 9, 2018).

[18] Joanne Barker, "Gender, Sovereignty, Rights: Native Women's Activism Against Social Inequality and Violence in Canada," American Quarterly 60, no. 2 (2008): 262, https://www.jstor.org/stable/40068533?seq=1#page_scan_tab_contents (accessed August 9, 2018).

[19] Indigenous Foundations, "Bill C-31," The University of British Columbia: First Nations and Indigenous Studies, https://indigenousfoundations.arts.ubc.ca/bill_c-31/ (accessed August 9, 2018).

[20] Barker, supra note 4 at 259.

[21] Ibid. 259-260; Also see Joyce Green, "Taking Account of Aboriginal Feminism," in Making Space for Indigenous feminism, ed. Joyce Green (Black Point: Fernwood Publishing, 2007), 28-30.

[22] Barker, supra note 4 at 260.

[23] Jo-Anne Fiske, "The Womb is to the Nation as the Heart is to the Body: Ethnopolitical Discourses of the Canadian Indigenous Women's Movement," Studies in Political Economy 51 (1996): 69, https://spe.library.utoronto.ca/index.php/spe/article/%20view/6877/3858 (accessed August 9, 2018).

[24] Truth and Reconciliation Commission of Canada (TRC), Canada's Residential Schools: The History, Part 1, Origins to 1939—The Final Report of the Truth and Reconciliation Commission of Canada (Montreal & Kingston: McGill-Queen's University Press, 2015), 1:83, http://www.myrobust.com/websites/trcinstitution/File/Reports/Volume_1_History_Part_1_English_Web.pdf (accessed August 9, 2018).

[25] For example, see J.R. Miller, Shingwuak's Vision: A History of Native Residential Schools (Toronto: University of Toronto Press, 2012), 219-223; TRC, supra note 10 at 511, 644, and 648.

[26] Sarah Carter, Capturing Women: The Manipulation of Cultural Imagery in Canada's Prairie West, ed. Bruce G. Trigger, McGill-Queen's Native and Northern Series (Montreal and Kingston: McGill-Queen's University Press, 1997), xiv.

[27] Ibid. 8.
[28] Ibid. 9.
[29] Heidi Kiiwetinepinesiik Stark, "Criminal Empire: The Making of the Savage in the Lawless Land," *Theory & Event* 19, issue 4 (2016): para. 32, https://muse.jhu.edu/article/633282 (accessed August 9, 2018).
[30] Joyce Green, "Taking More Account of Indigenous Feminism: An Introduction," in *Making Space for Indigenous Feminism*, 2nd ed., ed. Joyce Green (Halifax and Winnipeg: Fernwood Publishing, 2017): 10; also see Mary Eberts, "Being an Indigenous Woman is a 'High-Risk Lifestyle'," in *Making Space for Indigenous Feminism*, 2nd ed., ed. Joyce Green (Halifax and Winnipeg: Fernwood Publishing, 2017): 69-102.
[31] Eberts, *supra* note 15 at 70-71.
[32] Bettina Bradbury, "Colonial Comparisons: Rethinking Marriage, Civilization and Nation in Nineteenth-Century White-Settler Societies," in *Rediscovering the British world*, eds. Phillip Buckner and R. Douglas Francis (Calgary: University of Calgary Press, 2005), 136, http://www.deslibris.ca/ID/402860 (accessed August 9, 2018).
[33] For an in-depth examination of the Canadian government's imposition of the hetero-patriarchal model of marriage in the west, see Sarah Carter, *The Importance of Being Monogamous: Marriage and Nation Building in Western Canada to 1915* (Edmonton: The University of Alberta Press; Athabasca: Athabasca University Press, 2008).
[34] Brenda L. Gunn, "Self-Determination and Indigenous Women: Increasing Legitimacy Through Inclusion," *Canadian Journal of Women and the Law* 26, no. 2 (2014): 243, https://muse.jhu.edu/article/564330/pdf (accessed August 9, 2018).
[35] Barker, *supra* note 4 at 263.
[36] Kimberle Crenshaw, "Mapping the Margins: Intersectionality, Identity Politics, and Violence Against Women of Color," *Stanford Law Review* 40, no. 6 (July 1991): 1257, https://www.jstor.org/stable/1229039?seq=1#page_scan_tab_contents (accessed August 9, 2018).
[37] Ibid. 1257-1258.
[38] For example, see Douglas A. Brownridge, "Male Partner Violence Against Aboriginal Women in Canada: An Empirical Analysis," *Journal of Interpersonal Violence* 18, no. 1 (2003): 65-83, http://journals.sagepub.com/doi/pdf/10.1177/0886260502238541 (accessed August 9, 2018); and, Nihaya Daoud et al., "The Contribution of Socio-Economic Position to the Excesses of Violence and Intimate Partner Violence Among Aboriginal Versus Non-Aboriginal Women in Canada," *Canadian Journal of Public Health/Revue Canadienne de Santé Publique* 104, no. 4 (July/August 2013): e278-e283 http://journal.cpha.ca/index.php/cjph/article/view/3724/2842 (accessed August 9, 2018).
[39] Rauna Kuokkanen, "Gendered Violence and Politics in Indigenous Communities: The Cases of Aboriginal People in Canada and the Sámi in Scandinavia," *International Feminist Journal of Politics* 17, issue 2 (2015): 282-283, https://www.tandfonline.com/doi/abs/10.1080/ 14616742. 2014.901816 (accessed August 9, 2018).
[40] Ibid. 280-283.
[41] Ibid. 276.
[42] Ibid. 276-277.
[43] For example, see Arielle Dylan, Cheryl Regehr, and Ramona Alaggia, "And Justice For All? Aboriginal Victims of Sexual Violence," *Violence Against Women* 14, no. 6 (2008): 678-696, http://journals.sagepub.com/doi/10.1177/1077801208317291 (accessed August 9, 2018); also see Eberts, *supra* note 19 at 73-76; Gunn, *supra* note 19 at 254-255.
[44] Kuokkanen, *supra* note 24 at 277.
[45] Gunn, *supra* note 19 at 254.
[46] Ibid. 242; also see 250-253.
[47] Ibid. 260, 265-269.
[48] Ibid. 253, 254, 259, and 271; also see 266-267.
[49] Ibid. 265-274.
[50] Andrea Smith, "Native American Feminism, Sovereignty and Social Change," in *Making Space for Indigenous Feminism*, ed. Joyce Green (Black Point: Fernwood Publishing, 2007): 97-98.

[51] Crenshaw, *supra* note 21 at 1245, 1251-1252, and 1256.
[52] Ibid. 1256-1257.
[53] Kuokkanen, *supra* note 24 at 272.
[54] Green, *supra* note 15 at 12.

Chapter Seven

Raising the Voices of Survivors and Collaborators Confronting Sex Trafficking and Exploitation of Indigenous Women and Girls in Manitoba, Canada

Robert Chrismas

Violence Against Indigenous Women and Girls in Canada

This exploratory case study shares insights and stories of experts, stakeholders and survivors about sex trafficking and sexual exploitation in Manitoba, and how we, as a society, can better address this growing social scourge. Here is one survivor's story;

> **MARIE**: (a survivor with Indigenous heritage): Me and my friends we all came from poor backgrounds; we all lived in the North End, my mom had severe addictions issues so a lot of the times there wasn't the basic needs at home so, when I found out my friends were doing it just seemed to happen I guess. For me I think it was a lot easier for me because my dad was a pedophile so I already had that experience of being with older men so when I made the, well I didn't really make a decision when I was put into the sex it just seemed right at the moment because there is no other way to support myself. I wasn't old enough for welfare so that was my only means of obtaining clothing and stuff.

Marie is one of the survivors who graciously gave me an interview for the research conducted for my Ph.D. in Peace and Conflict Studies at the University of Manitoba (Chrismas, 2017). Her comment at the head of this chapter, is consistent with my findings of the violence that so many Indigenous women, endure, in general, and in the sex trafficking and exploitation industry. Indigenous women and girls are overrepresented in Manitoba's sex industry, despite the province having one of the most well-funded provincial counter-exploitation strategies in Canada. In Manitoba, Indigenous women and girls make up well over 70 percent of those who are sexually exploited and oppressed.

My research takes advantage of over 1,000 years of collective experience, amplifying the voices of the broad spectrum of stakeholders, including police, social workers, Indigenous community leaders, politicians and lawmakers, numerous non-government organizations and survivors (Chrismas, 2017). It broadens the net from previous research that often has left out some of these important perspectives. This chapter explores my findings specifically with respect to the impact of the sex industry on Indigenous women and girls in Canada, and Manitoba.

The context of this research is Manitoba, but it is a worldwide problem.

Sexual exploitation and trafficking affects people in, "virtually every country in every region of the world," with Worldwide profits in the sex industry estimated at over $99 billion (USD), and in most regions, is continually getting worse (UNODC, 2014; Canadian Women's Foundation, 2014). Substantial previous research has continually reaffirmed that Indigenous communities in Canada are still suffering the negative impacts of colonization, and will for decades to come (Mandel, 2016). Now, in 2018, Canada's Indigenous people are still suffering, and the social expression of these previous moral settlement injustices includes significantly high incarceration rates, lower employment, and overall poor education completion in comparison with Canada's majority, mainstream, population (Hallett, Thornton & Stewart, 2006). My research confirms that this marginalization also includes a substantially higher incidence of oppression and victimization of Indigenous women through sex trafficking and exploitation (Chrismas, 2017).

The social phenomenon and movement around missing and murdered Indigenous women have highlighted the historical and present systemic oppression of Indigenous Canadian women (Welch, 2014). The challenge of having over 10,000 children in the care of Manitoba's child protection agencies (Puxley, 2014), and the fact that children continue to be exploited and harmed- is compelling change, albeit slowly. In many ways, Manitoba and British Columbia have been ground zero for Canada's Missing and Murdered Indigenous Women movement (MMIW). The disappearance of 63 women from Vancouver between 1990 and 2004, later linked to a serial killer, Robert Pickton, and the subsequent Oppal Inquiry, sent shock waves through Canada's justice community, causing police agencies to examine and focus on how missing person cases are handled (Oppal, 2012; Cool, 2004).

Tina Fontaine's murder, in Winnipeg, and the similar circumstances around several previous Manitoba homicide cases have fueled the fire (Paperney, 2009). In 2009, The Native Women's' Association of Canada (NWAC) identified 520 cases of missing or murdered Indigenous women and girls in Canada, 24 percent identified as missing and 67 percent "having died as a result of homicide or negligence" (NWAC, 2009). In 2016 NWAC reported more than 1,000 missing or murdered Indigenous women in Canada, raising awareness around the marginalization of Indigenous women and girls.

The MMIW movement has also raised awareness of the "Highway of Tears" in British Columbia. It is believed that between 1989 and 2006 nine women were murdered, or missing and believed murdered, along a 700-kilometre stretch of Highway 16 in the interior of British Columbia (Highway of Tears, 2016). Presenters at a seminar I once attended, described how the Highway of Tears threads through the impoverished neighborhoods that are inhabited by Indigenous people in the rotted cores of most Canadian cities.

In 2013 the RCMP reported on their examination of case files gathered from police agencies across Canada, that between 1980 and 2012 there were 20,313 homicides across Canada. They found that of 6,551 female homicide victims (32 percent), 1,017 (16 percent) were Indigenous. The number of Indigenous female victims climbed from eight percent in 1984 to 23 percent in 2012, while the number of non-Indigenous female victims remained constant (ibid.). Indigenous victims were found more likely to be involved in illegal activities for financial support (18 percent for Indigenous vs. 8 percent for non-Indigenous); more likely to be unemployed (12 percent for Indigenous vs. 8 percent for non-Indigenous), to be on social assistance or disability insurance (23 percent for Indigenous vs. 9 percent for non-Indigenous), to have substance abuse problems and to be under the influence of intoxicants at the time they were murdered (63 percent for Indigenous vs. 20 percent of non-Indigenous); 12 percent of female homicide victims had known involvement in the sex industry (RCMP, 2013).

Research by Farley et al. (2003) found that 52 percent of women in the sex industry in Vancouver were Indigenous. The proportion is much higher in some areas including Manitoba. Cook and Courchene (2006) found that 70 percent of sexually exploited children and youth in Manitoba had Indigenous ancestry, a massive overrepresentation—considering they make up about four percent of Canada's population (McCracken & Mitchell, 2006).

My research method was qualitative, emphasizing the subjective interpretations of my research subjects (Palys & Atchison, 2008). Mac Ginty and Williams (2009) have described how this approach can better capture "local voices and Indigenous solutions" (p. 8). It was clear from the start that women and children in the sex industry face numerous intersectional challenges. Scholars have suggested that qualitative research is ideal for the study of intersectionality because it allows us to explore and capture the rich, multidimensional nature of humanity and people in their unique contexts (Hunting, 2014). My research explores intersectional challenges that women and youth face in the sex industry in Manitoba, looking for the insights that only those directly involved can provide (Mac Ginty & Williams, 2009, p. 8).

My findings included the following eight salient and significant findings with respect to the violent reality that Canadian Indigenous women and children live with.

First, the majority of trafficking survivors in Manitoba are Indigenous. My respondents report the percentage of people exploited in the sex industry in Manitoba are higher than previous studies that estimate it at 70 percent (see Cook & Courchene, 2006). My subjects report as many as 90 percent of trafficking and sexual exploitation victims in Manitoba are Indigenous, although the growing newcomer population and increasing use of the Internet are both difficult to measure and need future research.

Second, Indigenous Manitobans are significantly marginalized. My interviews reveal that poverty and the lack of educational and employment opportunities are more salient among Indigenous people. Systemic marginalization and impoverishment of Indigenous women in Canada is well documented (Mandel, 2016). While it is no surprise that Indigenous women are overrepresented in Canada's sex industry, the degree of disparity and disproportionate marginalization and victimization should be shocking to all Canadians. A key to eradicating sex trafficking and exploitation in the sex industry lies in improving standards of living and reducing disparity among our most disadvantaged and penurious populations, through improved income and better access to education and employment (Chrismas, 2017).

Third, the rural to urban trafficking pipeline must be interrupted. A real and immediate threat to the safety of Indigenous youth in Manitoba is the perils they encounter when they travel to larger urban centers, out of necessity, for education and employment. Kaitlin, a survivor, described how rural girls are often vulnerable when they come into the city.

KAITLIN: There are a lot of girls that come in from the reserve, and they're naïve. They don't know how the city is. They come in, and right away they get sucked in.

I've had a couple of friends who went missing and murdered all because of one girl that got them started. The one girl that got me started got them started. And suddenly they are gone. I'm proud to say that, I've never introduced anyone, never got anyone hooked on crack.

Traffickers are aware and target youth for grooming when they reach the age of 13, knowing they will have to move to large city centers such as Winnipeg in the South and Thompson in the North because there is no high school in their home reserve. Some practitioners are trying to raise awareness among Indigenous youth and their families to make them more resistant to sexual predators, yet this is a threat that is still growing and must be addressed in Manitoba.

Fourth, cultural programming needs improvement. My research participants expressed mixed opinions about whether existing addiction, medical, educational, and other counselling programs offered to sex industry survivors are culturally suitable. Most agreed that overall cultural appropriateness in the system at large has improved over the past decade. Some participants said that there is a great deal of cultural sensitivity and some even opined that there is too much. Others described some agencies as having a false visage, for example, putting a medicine wheel on their stationery, solely to gain funding for having Indigenous programming, without real substance in the services they provide to Indigenous people.

Most study participants felt that there are pockets of good cultural programming, yet it is sporadic and not always available in the right programs. For example, several subjects highlighted that survivors often have addictions and multiple layered issues that all need to be addressed simultaneously. Some of those support programs, per my interviewees, have better cultural services than others. Kelly Holmes, Executive Director of Resource Assistance for Youth (RAY), proposed that there should be a cultural hub that all agencies could access to provide a range of services from elders to cultural training.

KELLY HOLMES: We could always improve on being culturally sensitive. There's s much to know and I feel like, I've been around for a long time, 35 years, and all working on the streets with marginalized communities, and I'm still learning about cultural stuff. And I think I always will learn, there's so much to know. But could we do it in a more organized way? I tend to have the reputation of getting shit done. That's sort of my claim to fame. And if I were in charge, I would have The Thunderbird House being used and funded more readily. So, Thunderbird House becomes sort of the education hub for all of us non-Indigenous types where schools can access it, police can access it, you know, a number of the unrelated sector communities can access it.

Ms. Holmes proposed that agencies and individuals that want cultural resources, training, and advice, could access it through the shared resource hub.

Fifth, cultural programming must fit the person. People are often not matched with the appropriate cultural programming as part of their survivor-oriented trauma care. For example, survivors and practitioners advised me that a youth who looks Indigenous in appearance might have been raised Christian and might not wish to have anything to do with traditional healing. Or, that a person might later wish to have traditional healing and it should be made available to her/him when s/he is ready for it. This flexibility of choices and the ability for service recipients (the survivors) to move from one program to another is currently lacking and could be improved.

Another finding was the diversity that exists within the Metis and Indigenous communities. There are multiple languages, cultures and intra-group traditions among the various Indigenous groups in Manitoba. It is important not to categorize people. Gabriel Simard, the RCMP provincial Human Trafficking Coordinator, described how predators identify and target youth before they even leave the reserve, knowing they will soon be forced to leave their community and normal support structures for school. Simard described his role, travelling to rural communities to educate people on justice issues, and how diverse people are. Simard stressed that the same community could have within its people, multiple languages and religious beliefs, some are Christian (Catholic or Protestant) and others non-Christian. Moreover, there are numerous different paths, some are more orthodox, and others are more relaxed within the traditional Indigenous ways. Several of my participants described an "Indigenous" resource pool that could be tailored to fit individual wishes of people from different Indigenous backgrounds.

Sixth, Indigenous programming needs improvement. Kim Trossell works with sex industry survivors at the Dream Catcher program at Klinic Community Health. She describes how cultural sensitivity in her agency has come a long way in recent years, yet she feels that it must still improve.

KIM TROSSELL: Culturally sensitive? Considering people don't even acknowledge the fact that a lot of the sex trade, especially here in Manitoba, is a direct result of colonization and long-term effects of that. So, if people can't even come to the table and agree on that, that is an issue. It's hard for them to be culturally sensitive. I mean our agency made huge changes since Dream Catcher became a part of the programming here. You know, we now have a space that is considered culturally friendly, where we have smudging available for all clients, not just clients of our program but Indigenous within our agency. So, there has been a huge movement within our own agency. I don't know as far as the outside world and being culturally sensitive. I don't think that that is even a reality. You know, 80 percent of our street population in the street sex trade is of Indigenous decent. That was identified over 12, 15 years ago. But it's still working toward a language that is appropriate, and practicing and, like, the ceremonies that we've attended. Our elders have talked to us about the importance of bringing the teachings back to the Indigenous community that was stripped of these things, originally. So just rebuilding what was taken away, creating space for it to happen is so essential.

Ms. Trossell finds that over 80 percent of people in the sex industry are Indigenous youth and it is crucial to be more culturally sensitive in terms of understanding the emotional trauma that many carry as a result of colonial impacts, despite great strides having been achieved in that area. She raises the point that after many years, the appropriate language around cultural sensitivity has still not been defined. Perhaps this points to the difficulties involved in defining what culturally appropriate or sensitive programming is.

Seventh, we need more flexibility in the system of supports. People need choices in their treatments, so that appropriate treatment are accessible to them at the time they are required. My participants described the current state of the system of resources in Manitoba as diverse, fragmented, and inflexible. They observed that there should be greater flexibility in the system with regards to cultural sensitivity and other programming dynamics so that people get the services they need when they need them. My research participants emphasized that sex industry survivors need to have some choice and a sense of control over what programs they participate in. This provision of choice often lacks in the current treatment resource system. For example, Chelsea Jarosiewicz works with high-risk youth at Marymound; she mentioned that sometimes people are restricted to services within Marymound or counselling programs within MacDonald Youth Services, but the two generally do not mix well together. This problem should be addressed so that survivors can access an appropriate placement within one system while also accessing needed resources within other agencies. NGOs compete for limited resources within a fixed pie.

Eighth, Indigenous people need more control over their own healing. Indigenous people need more control over their participation in programs and healing. Some Indigenous practitioners and leaders that I interviewed expressed a sense of paternalistic control by government agencies specific to funding. For example, Chief Ron Evans of Norway House, a leader in Manitoba's counter sexual exploitation planning, describes poor housing as the main issue that leads to all manner of social ills, including the exploitation of youth in the sex industry.

RON EVANS: At a young age, teenagers, that's when there needs to be family supports.

There used to be access to education and training and recreational opportunities, strong family support and family unit health, and social stability. Now those are words that are too easy to say.

Now I've been in leadership for 26 consecutive years. I first became a leader back in 1980, which would be 36 years ago, so I've seen it you know. I've seen the challenges. I've seen governments. I've seen how things were.

There's been progress, but I've seen where there isn't. If there was true progress, the numbers would have declined, you know, from the number of people in jails, the number of murdered and missing women, the number of, you know, how people that are impacted by the healthcare system.

And so, governments over the years have made every effort to say, "Okay education is the key. Education is the key so that you can get yourself out of poverty." Or, "education is the key so that you can you know make a contribution to your community, to society." Or, they'll throw money at economic development so that you can have jobs, you know, and begin to make your life better. Or they'll throw money at social programs. They'll throw money to the front-line workers.

But nobody is dealing with the root cause. The root cause is, as you have probably read in the paper now last week, where Manitoba needs $1.9 billion for housing. In my community alone we have 8,000 people and we have a birth rate of 200 a year, and so in the last eight years we have not been able to build a house for that 1,600. We've grown by 1,600. So, where do people live when there is no housing? We've not been able to build a house.

But we've been able to build other infrastructure like an entertainment center, and we're going to build a baseball field. We've got other economic initiatives because we've partnered with others so our community grows in that regard.

So, then we talk about the number of inmates. You know, the jails are bursting at the seams. The healthcare system, the healthcare cost and future [costs] rise because of the illnesses—whether it's illness caused by mold in the home or there's just not enough services to meet the needs.

And, many of the patients that come to the clinic or to the hospital is a result of violence through the social problems that overcrowding creates. So, overcrowding and shortage of housing that is the absolute root problem in First Nation communities.

Chief Evans highlights that vulnerability to being sexually exploited is a symptom of larger problems, including lack of resilience due to poverty and lack of opportunities.

This research contributes insights into Indigenous and Metis perspectives and the choices that must be created for people trying to avoid or exit the sex industry. Indigenous and Metis people should be engaged in developing future services and treatments, and service agencies require greater flexibility so that people can choose and access elements when they are ready for them. My research also confirms the theory that trauma is passed forward trans-generationally as young Indigenous people cope with the impacts of colonialism (see Volkan, 1997).

Chief Ron Evans described how persisting social ills in the Indigenous community are tied to poverty, consistent with Galtung (1996) who stressed that self-reliance and resilience are significant determinants of one's ability to escape structural violence. It is clear from my interviews that young people are in jeopardy of being trafficked in the sex industry, due to being born a female, being born Indigenous, and/or born into poverty.

This exploratory case study shares insights and stories of experts, stakeholders and survivors of sex trafficking. The visions of this reality are disturbing, yet at the same time hopeful for the future. It is auspicious because it sheds light on the fact that Indigenous people are overrepresented in our prison and child welfare systems, and that those people who are oppressed in the sex industry have hopes and dreams, just like the rest of us, and they deserve to experience the same basic human rights and standard. It is also promising as well because it exposes the compassion and respect for humanity that resides among the people working in the broad range of frontline services to restore and protect the dignity of some of society's most marginalized and vulnerable people. This chapter intends to help raise those voices.

References

Canadian Women's Foundation. (2014). "Stories and Strategies to end Sex Trafficking in Canada." http://www.canadianwomen.org/sites/canadianwomen.org.

Cook, R. & D. Courchene. (2006). "Preventing and eradicating the abuse of our children and youth: Regional team development." The Manitoba Association of Friendship Centers.

Chrismas, R. (2017). *Modern Day Slavery and the Sex Industry: Raising the Voices of Survivors and Collaborators While Confronting Sex Trafficking and Exploitation in Manitoba, Canada.* Published at MSpace, University of Manitoba.

Cool, J. (2004). "Prostitution in Canada: An Overview." Library of Parliament.

Farley, M. (2003). *Prostitution, Trafficking, and Traumatic Stress.* Binghamton, NY: Haworth.

Galtung, J. (1996). *Peace by Peaceful Means: Peace and Conflict, Development and Civilization.* Thousand Oaks, CA: Sage.

Hallett, B., N. Thornton & D. Stewart. (2006). "Indigenous People in Manitoba." Manitoba Indigenous Affairs Secretariat, Her Majesty the Queen in Right of Canada.

Highway of Tears website. (2016). http://highwayoftearsfilm.com.

Hunting, G. (2014). "Intersectionality-informed Qualitative Research: A Primer." *The Institute for Intersectionality Research & Policy.* Public Health Agency of Canada.

Mac Ginty, R. & A. Williams. (2009). *Conflict and development.* New York, NY: Routledge.

Mandel, C. (2016, 8 March) "Indigenous girls face tough hurdles, new report on women in Canada states." *National Observer.*

McCracken, M. & C. Michell. (2006). "Literature Review of Post-Secondary Education Skills Training and Aboriginal People in Manitoba." Canadian Center for Policy Alternatives, Manitoba.

Native Women's Association of Canada. (2010). "Sisters in spirit: 2010 research findings." NWAC website. https://www.nwac.ca.

Oppal, W. (2012). "Forsaken: The Report of the Missing Women Commission of Inquiry." Library and Archives Canada Cataloguing in Publication, British Columbia.

Palys, T. S. & C. Atchison. (2008). *Research decisions: Quantitative and Qualitative Perspectives.* Toronto, ON: Thomson Nelson.

Paperney, A. M. (2009, 27 August). "Latest deaths of native women may be linked to crack-for-sex case." *Globe and Mail.*

Puxley, C. (2014, 18 November). "Manitoba wants fewer kids in care put up in hotels." *The Canadian Press.*

RCMP. (2014). "Human Trafficking National Co-ordination Center. Statistics: Human Trafficking in Canada" (March) http://www.rcmp-grc.gc.ca/ht-tp/index-eng.htm.

RCMP. (2013). "Missing and Murdered Indigenous Women: A National Operational Overview." http://www.rcmp-grc.gc.ca/pubs/mmaw.

UNODC. (2014). "Global Report on Trafficking in Persons 2014." United Nations.

Volkan, V.D. (1997). *Bloodlines: From Ethnic Pride to Ethnic Terrorism.* New York, NY: Farrar, Strauss and Giroux.

Welch, M. A. (2014, 24 January). "New database lists 824 murdered, missing native women in Canada." *Winnipeg Free Press.*

Chapter Eight

IS "HARM REDUCTION" INDIGENOUS?

Aura Lavallée

Introduction

The purpose of this research is aimed at exploring the interconnection of substance use, harm reduction, and cultural inclusion with respect to Indigenous peoples who are actively using licit and illicit substances. For the purpose of this paper, I will be utilizing the term Indigenous in place of the distinct groups: Métis, First Nations, and Inuit. This paper will address the conceptualization of harm reduction; the treatments that are available, including supervised sites and programs that are now being utilized through parts of Canada; community impact and roles, and finally addressing how it is applicable to Indigenous people with respect to cultural inclusion.

What is Harm Reduction?

The Winnipeg Regional Health Authority (WRHA) report published in December 2016 a definition of harm reduction by stating, "Harm Reduction is a perspective that focuses on reducing the adverse health, social, and economic consequences of psychoactive drug use, and its principles can be equally applied to other stigmatized and/or criminalized practices and behaviours related to substance use" (p.3). The driving force behind funding a harm reduction approach is often administered by health authorities, which are geared towards reducing the spread of communicable diseases and reducing the need for services from the health authorities. Although there is a growing awareness of the necessity to reduce stigma and create a non-judgmental space; "therefore focuses not only on client services but extends to considering the social and structural factors that create the conditions for harm" (WRHA, 2016, p.3). Harm reduction must be adaptable due to the complexity of using and intersectional lives that people experience while in addictions. "Harm Reduction is as much an attitude and way of being as it is a set of policies and methods" (Maté, 2008, p.318). It should also be noted that "[t]here is also no contradiction between harm reduction and abstinence. The two objectives are incompatible only if we imagine that we can set the agenda for someone else's life regardless of what [they] may choose" (p.317). For the objective of this paper, harm reduction is recognized as supporting substances of licit drugs, illicit drugs, potable and non-potable alcohol. Harm reduction is a recognized practice through means of supplies distribution are often organized through the health authorities, giving out supplies for injection, smoking materials and overdose prevention. Injection materials include needles, ties (tourniquet), sterile water, cookers (preparation spoon), ascorbic acid (vitamin c), cotton balls, and alcohol swabs. Common smoking materials are glass stems, bubble pipes, screens, and push sticks. Additional supplies include naloxone kits that are used for an opioid overdose response. The legal distribution of substances and potable alcohol beverages through services can only be found in certain locations in Canada and is not considered common practice nationally at this point in time.

Harm Reduction Treatments

Opioid Replacement Treatments (ORT)

ORT's are available for the purpose of harm reduction practice, as well as, the practicality of the treatments for its intended service users. ORT allows people to maintain their use through a consistently recognized source, regulated drug potency and unintentional withdrawal symptoms. The availability of these treatments depends on the geographical location, philosophy of practice in the health care sectors, the subjectivity of the physician's philosophies, ethical and moral practice, as well as the hurdles to getting the actual treatment.

The treatments that are often used for opioid replacement are methadone, buprenorphine (Suboxone), and hydromorphone (Dilaudid). It should be noted that most of these treatments have been available for a

CHAPTER EIGHT

while but have only recently taken a frontline approach in supporting people through their addictions due to the opioid crisis, some have changed the language to opioid poisoning due to fatality rate among those who use substances and the fatigue among service workers in relationship with the concept of crisis. The change in language is subjective to the position taken in support or understanding of substance use. It should also be considered that there are other substance replacing treatments available; however, Methadone and Suboxone are the treatments that are actively promoted.

ORT's are used in the health care system to help individuals maintain their dependence to opioids without the use of illicit substances. For some people who are actively trying to stop their addiction, and want to pursue daily activities without the following stressors of where they can inject, smoke or inhale, experiencing withdrawals, and finding a supplier, this could be a support program for those individuals. This is only accommodating for a small population of people who use, as the programs that were developed with the intent to discourage using behaviours can be restrictive and patronizing. It creates restrictions on the methods of distribution and methods of consumption. Depending on the physician, individuals can be subjected to a urine test or have their prescriptions revoked due to 'misuse.' This approach to practice is not meeting the low barrier needs of the using community and negates the importance of using rituals and community that surround substance use. This non-peer focus of treatment although good for some has also been identified as dissatisfactory, reinforcing stigma, and has led to the discontinuation of the program (McNeil, Kerr, Anderson, Maher, Keewatin, Milloy, Wood, Small, 2015, p.169).

Managed Alcohol Program (MAP)

When discussing the importance of treatment plans, managed alcohol programs are paramount to the discussion of harm reduction. As a number of factors can dictate the substance of choice between potable and non-potable alcohol including accessibility, socio-economic status, and community influence. With regards to the managed alcohol program, there are well-established programs throughout Canada that cater to this area of harm reduction.

> Managed alcohol programs (MAPs) take this approach a step further by providing beverage alcohol of known quality to program participants at regular intervals to stabilize drinking patterns and to replace more hazardous non-beverage alcohol. We are aware of at least ten MAP programs in Canada that offer some form of alcohol administration for

those who have been unsuccessful in maintaining housing even when alcohol use is tolerated on-site. The first Canadian MAP, Toronto's Seaton House, opened in 1997 after an inquiry into three tragic deaths on the streets of Toronto during the winter months (Pauly, Gray, Perkin, Chow, Vallance, Krysowaty, and Stockwell, 2016, p. 2).

The importance of these programs can be understood through the means of providing a substance that would be taken regardless of external pressures to quit; by ensuring that people have space and are not turned away because of their use, an element of dignity is offered, which has too often been taken away from people due to their choice of substances or the level of consumption.

"The program generally uses 12% alcohol by volume white wine, and clients may receive up to one 6 oz, i.e., 20.46 mL or 16.14 g of ethanol hourly between the hours of 8 am and 11 pm. To receive a dose, participants must not be overly intoxicated and must have been present at the facility for at least 60 min prior. Drinking outside the program is discouraged, and participants are not allowed to store their alcohol on-site for later consumption" (Pauly, Gray, Perkin, Chow, Vallance, Krysowaty, and Stockwell, 2016, p. 2).

The problem with discouraging outside drinking is that it presents a level of disapproval on the individuals potential using rituals and community network.

Overdose Prevention Sites (OPS)/ Safe Consumption Sites (SCS)

What is an Overdose Prevention Site versus a Safe Consumption Sites? The reason for the difference in language was developed due to the status of permanency. Overdose preventions sites were developed throughout British Columbia and in response to the overdose crisis. British Columbia's Coroner's Service Reported on Illicit Overdose Deaths from 2008 to 2018:

Year	Fatalities
2008	183
2009	201
2010	211
2011	294
2012	269
2013	333
2014	368

2015	518
2016	995
2017	1436
2018 (Jan)	125

Posting Date March 6th, 2018. p.4

Safe Consumption sites would be classified as a fixed site, such as the long-standing InSite located in Vancouver. Along with other more recently opened sites such as Victoria's Harbour SCS, British Columbia. The purpose of these sites: to allow individuals a physical location to safely use, the opportunity to use in a clean environment, the option to not rush the injection, reduce the response time when someone does overdose which reduces the time that someone goes without oxygen, thereby significantly decreasing the chance of a fatal overdose. Although there is more to a Safe Consumption Site than just medical support, it is also about creating a safe space that gives people a place to use without fear of being arrested, stigmatized and provides cultural inclusion in a using-sense.

> An OPS [Overdose Prevention Sites] provides a space for people to inject their previously-obtained illegal substances with sterile equipment in a setting where staff can observe and intervene to prevent overdoses. The sites were not implemented as an alternative to Health Canada sanctioned SCS. Rather, the province described the response as a temporary measure that would save lives without breaching the Controlled Drugs and Substances Act while waiting for Health Canada approval of supervised consumption services. These OPS are a significant part of the overdose response across BC. By September 2017, there were over 400,000 visits, 2,000 non-fatal overdoses, and no overdose deaths recorded at overdose prevention sites in British Columbia (Wallace, Pagan, & Pauly, 2017, p.3).

Ritual using. When considering methods of treatment of individuals using, the personal ritual of using should be considered and supported if the individual desires it. It should be noted that not all people want to maintain the ritual of using but for those that are more comfortable with their ritual than this should take a serious acknowledgement when providing medical treatment plans. Treatment plans that do not consider who is using the treatment and how it will meet the needs of the individual is not a supportive treatment plan but add an additional barrier that develops further survival practice of deception by the individual to get by. In general, medical practice injection methods of use by medical practice is considered to be a more effective method of treatment for a patient. So why can injection not be considered when people are looking to use in a safe capacity? Both Methadone and Suboxone are prescribed through oral consumption to move away from injection use and are designed to deter other substance use.

Suboxone has a combination of Buprenorphine (opioid modulator) and Naloxone (opioid antagonist). Hydromorphone, on the other hand, can be taken in by injection and through pill forms. The injection method is the hardest to be prescribed, and often those who use have to have exhausted all other treatment options before being considered for hydromorphone. Some practitioners require injections to be done on-site and must be done within a reasonable timeframe. In theory, this is a better fit for someone who is actively using, although this ensures social isolation from the rest of the community who use substance and dictates the individual's schedule. For proper support to take place in ORT plans, it is imperative for rituals to be understood and supported, as well as establishing flexibility for multi-substance use, reducing the social isolation of use, and incorporating the community in using, and utilizing peer critiques of treatment methods and programs.

Community Impact and Influences

At a community level, the perspectives and influences on those who are using can have detrimental effects if supportive services are not serious about operationalizing a 'non-judgmental' approach both at a service providers level and at a community members level. This is where harm reduction encompasses more than simply handing out supplies and cleaning up needles or pipes. It includes the language used, the power dynamics by services providers and community members assert an element of control over those who are using. Understanding the power and control is key when giving support at both an individual of communication and at a services provider level when creating rules and regulations.

Services Providers

In an article by Landry, Veilleux, Arseneault, Abboud, Barrieau, Bélanger (2016) about a methadone maintenance program with an Aboriginal community the main issue is that while this article appears to discuss the importance of incorporation of culturally appropriate practice and offer cultural supports for users of the methadone program in the Indigenous community and spiritual practice, the contradiction is in their introduction. The authors state, "Illicit drug use and dependence continues to plague populations worldwide and contribute to the global burden of disease" (2016, E431). Our practice cannot truly be transparent until we stop viewing substance use as a 'burden/plague' on our society. This way of thinking suggests that the individual may only be accepted by society if they fit within society's values and once they stop using and maintain abstinence. The concept and application of the Methadone Maintenance Treatment (MMT) program cannot claim to be a harm reduction focus of practice until this idea of these individuals being a burden is removed. The object of this article was "[t]o improve our understanding of how methadone maintenance treatment programs may be received in Aboriginal communities, the main objective of this qualitative study was to determine the perceptions of members of the Elsipogtog First Nation on the Elsipogtog treatment program and the impact of its implementation on the community" (2016, E432). This is an inconsistency expectation. These authors are looking to identifying how Indigenous people can change their views of the methadone program without asking themselves to change their own views and values around addictions.

Community Members

Community members play a key role in how successful people are with their individual goals of wellness. Within Indigenous contexts, the need for community involvement in healing has remained a focus of discussion and an important connection that must not be broken. Removing people from their contact with community and limiting their sense of attachment leads to "cultural dislocation [which has] created a situation in which the opportunities for a self-sufficient, healthy and autonomous life for First Nations people on individual and collective bases are extremely limited" (Alfred, 2009, p.42). Community members have the power to utilize the language of inclusion, but it required personal accountability on the roles of support and transparency between all involved. The risk to dismissive language from the role of the community member is that it creates a gap of greater isolation and leads to unnecessary physical, emotional, and mental risk from said isolation.

Does Harm Reduction fit Indigenous Healing?

The overarching question of this paper has been to identify if harm reduction is Indigenous in values and ways of being? The practice of treatment and programs have been addressed, as well as the need for creating safe spaces for using. Indigenous peoples have been impacted by addictions in ways that require reflection on Indigenous methods and utilizing our traditional knowledges for the communities that we are connected to.

According to the First Nations Health Authority (FNHA) "Harm reduction is an approach used to address substance use and is consistent with FNHA's vision of holistic wellness. It is based on respecting where an individual is located on their health and wellness journey and providing a continuum of options to assist the individual, their family, and their community on their path to sustaining or improving their health and wellness without judgment or shame" (FNHA, 2017, p.5). And according to the National Native Alcohol and Drug Abuse Program General Review (NNADAP), "Culture is Treatment" is the foundation of the work carried out locally, regionally and nationally (1998, p.43). The desire for cultural and community inclusion is evidently being presented through some First Nations authorities and programs.

This is a value of inclusion by incorporating health and spiritual wellness together, although, this is still a controversial perspective that I hope to explore in my thesis research. I addressed the levels of attainment of cultural inclusion with Elder, Don Beacham from Norway House, Manitoba. He and I worked at the same non-profit where he demonstrated an example of cultural inclusion. Each week the Indigenous Elder would come into the overdose prevention site and smudge the space and offer personal smudging to anyone who was interested whether or not they were injecting, already under the influence, or working on-site. Of course, it should be noted that smudging was a part of his practice, not to be confused with an overall practice done by Elders, in general, as some of the First Nations do not follow this practice. Clients always had the option not to participate. The result was that many of the clients expressed a sense of relief while they were using and often explained that they had an easier time injecting after smudging. The Indigenous medicines were utilized to support those who wanted it but often felt that they could not go near ceremonial practices due to their use. Elder, Ovide Caribou is paraphrased in the following statement, *"Ceremony isn't the reward for getting clean but the work that you do to further your healing."*

With that being said, it should be noted that not everyone is ready to participate or have an interest in ceremony and/or traditional medicines. This is where the practice of non-interference is considered and meeting people where they are. In Thunderbird Partnership Foundation guiding principles they state a 'Clients First' approach, "The interest of clients must always be paramount, with all other considerations being secondary" (TBF, 2017).

Conclusion

In closing, the methods of harm reduction must consider the motive of the practice and the aim of who is being supported in this approach. Indigenous services and community members should be critical of the ways that addictions have been addressed, as the root of the addictions has been from colonization and the methods to recovery have been constructed by societal visions of sobriety, rather than Indigenous values of community.

References

Alfred, T. (2009). Colonialism and State Dependency. In *Journal of Aboriginal Health*. November 42-60.

Ministry of Public Safety & Solicitor General. (2018). British Columbia Coroners Service: Illicit Drug Overdose Deaths in BC. January 1, 2008 – January 31, 2018. 1-20.

Ovide Caribou. (2017). (Elder oral teaching).

Don Beacham. (2017). (Elder oral teaching/ Professional Practice).

First Nations Health Authority. (July 2017). Overdose Data and First Nations in BC: Preliminary Findings. Retrieved from www.fnha.ca (Media Release) (August 3rd, 2017).

Landry, M., Veilleux, N., Arseneault, J.-E., Abboud, S., Barrieau, A., & Bélanger, M. (2016). Impact of a methadone maintenance program on an Aboriginal community: a qualitative study. *CMAJ Open*, 4(3), E431–E435. http://doi.org/10.9778/cmajo.20150076

Maté, G. (2008). *In the realm of hungry ghosts: Close encounters with addiction*. Toronto: Knopf Canada.

McNeil, R., Kerr, T., Anderson, S., Mahar, L., Keewatin, C., Milloy, M.J., Wood, E., Small, W. (2015). Negotiating structural vulnerability following regulatory changes to a provincial methadone program in Vancouver, Canada: A qualitative study. *Elsevier Ltd*. http://dx.doi.org/10.1016/j.socscimed.2015.04.008

National Native Alcohol and Drug Abuse Program General Review. (1998). Retrieved from https://www.canada.ca/content/dam/hc-sc/migration/hc-sc/fniah-spnia/alt_formats/fnihb-dgspni/pdf/pubs/ads/1998_rpt-nnadap-pnlaada-eng.pdf

Pauly, B., Gray, E., Perkin, K., Chow, C., Vallance, K., Krysowaty, B., Stockwell, T. (2016). Finding safety: a pilot study of managed alcohol program participants' perceptions of housing and quality of life. *Harm Reduction Journal*, where is the rest of the reference? DOI 10.1186/s12954-016-0102-5

Wallace, B., Pagan, F., Pauly, B (November 2017). Mitigating Risk Environments: Analysis of Overdose Prevention Sites in Victoria, British Columbia. Victoria, British Columbia: Canadian Institute for Substance Use Research.

Winnipeg Regional Health Authority: Position Statement on Harm Reduction. (December 2016). Retrieved from http://www.wrha.mb.ca/community/publichealth/files/position-statements/HarmReduction.pdf

Thunderbird Partnership Foundation. (2017). Untitled. Retrieved from http://thunderbirdpf.org

Chapter Nine

Working in Circles

Indigenous Methodology Restoring our Wellness, Restoring our Roles, Indigenous Women and Birth

Stephanie Sinclair

The Indigenous birth helper research project originated through a partnership between Wiijii'idiwag Ikwewag, Nanaandawewigamig, First Nation communities, and the University of Winnipeg. The partnership started with a ceremony where participants were instructed by the grandmother to honor the spirit of the work through hosting community feasts and giveaways throughout the duration of the research. The partnership was created because all three partners have similar goals of working towards restoring Indigenous ways of knowing and creating supports for healthy families. The overall research project is designed to measure the impact of having an Indigenous birth helper on the health and wellness of First Nation women who travel for birth. The principle investigator for the overall project is Dr. Jaime Cidro from the University of Winnipeg. The Indigenous birth helper training was developed by four Indigenous women: Kathleen Bluesky, Melissa Brown, Jolene Mercer and Candace Newman with consultation of community members including families, health professionals with the direction of grandmothers. The birth helper training is a five-day comprehensive certification that includes learning about both western and Indigenous methods of supporting mothers through pregnancy and birth.

This paper will discuss the methodology of working with First Nations to develop a project that is respectful and relevant. The paper will also review how the project implemented the ethics of reciprocity and responsibility. I am an Ojibway mother of two children. I am the research coordinator for the research project and I am work for Nanaandawewigamig, the First Nation Health and Social Secretariat of

Manitoba. I am a single mother and have benefited from having a strong circle of support. My relationship to the research project is to assist other women to have a strong circle of support to assist in developing healthy families. My role in the research project is to coordinate the activities and maintain the relationships and partnerships.

The research project is based on Indigenous methodology which engaged communities from the onset and honored the spirit and intent of the work. Indigenous research methods originate with Indigenous ways of knowing by Indigenous theoretical perspectives (Kovach, 2009). "Indigenous ways of knowing arise from interrelationships with the human world, the spirit, and the inanimate entities of the ecosystems" (Battiste & Henderson, 2000). The project has acknowledged and invited spiritual helpers to guide the work, through the incorporation of ceremony and knowledge keepers.

The goal of the research partnership is to Honour the sacred relationships and birth traditions of nations to promote connection and wellness. The project will work with First Nation communities to incorporate their specific teachings, history and cultural ways of knowing into the training. Local women will be trained and supported to be birth helpers to women in their community.

The project will utilize both qualitative and quantitative methods to examine the relationship between the renewal of the traditional role of birth helpers and the holistic health of the birth helpers. The Indigenous birth helpers will be rooted in Indigenous ways of knowing through cultural teachings, spiritual connections and traditions as they help families in the community throughout their pregnancy and birth. The birth helper is to be a support for the mother and her family and to provide information and teachings which support healthy child development and Indigenous identity.

One of the First Nation communities was invited to participate during the application for funding phase as they had identified returning birth and supporting mothers as one of their priorities. There was an open call to all Manitoba First Nations to express interest in partnering on the project. Two more communities signed on to the project in 2018. Each community added required a letter of support or band council resolution to obtain the community free prior informed consent, this usually entails conversations, community visits, and development of briefing note or summary documents to share with the leadership. Once the community consent is obtained, the research team works with the health director to set up a community advisory circle who will lead the implementation of the project in their community. The community advisory circles have included those that are selected by community leadership and typically include those that work with mothers and families in the community, grandmothers and Knowledge Keepers, and leadership from health.

The initial meeting serves as a discussion to locate oneself within the research project, the advisory circle connected to the research project and defined their roles and responsibilities. The main discussion questions were: What would we like to get out of their research project in terms of data? Findings? support for our community's long-term goals? What can this project help us to address? The discussions guided the purpose and meaning for each advisory circle member as to why they would be involved in the project.

Additional meetings with the community advisory circle were used to begin planning the implementation of the project. At these meetings the advisory circle reviewed the piloted curriculum and the proposed research questions and survey tools and brainstormed what was needed to meet the objectives of the community. The advisory circle also developed a community specific selection process for identifying people in the community that will be trained and serve the community as birth helpers. The training curriculum was adapted to meet the needs of each community and new materials were designed by the advisory circle as requested. The community also selected local data collectors that were hired and training by the Nanaandawesigamig in data collection, OCAP, informed consent and survey collection.

The advisory circle selected 12 individuals to be trained as birth helpers in each community. The Indigenous birth helper training is a five-day intensive training that is based on Indigenous knowledge. The training covers the following information, building the lodge (first trimester), nurturing our bundles (second trimester) nurturing our home fires (third trimester) nurturing new life (post partum), protecting the sacred circle. The women also go through personal healing ceremonies and learn about other ceremonies and traditional medicines used for birth. The women who are trained will be supported and offered additional continuing education opportunities and mentorship throughout the project. The project has now trained a total 24 birth helpers in two First Nations who will be working with families.

The trained birth helpers will participate in focus groups within 6 months of working with families, to reflect on the process, suggest improvements and discuss the impact it has had on their own lives. After one year of providing services as a birth helper, the women will be interviewed to assess the impact of restoring their roles as guiding the transition from the spiritual world to the physical world.

The project will continue to work to ensure the research is relevant, respectful, responsible, and reciprocal (4Rs) (Kirkness & Barnhardt, 2001). Potts and Brown (2005) state that making research relevant includes "clarity as to whom the research is going to benefit, recognizes the implication and accepts responsibilities of the knowledge that one is constructing" (as cited in Kovach, 2009, p.130). Following the cultural protocols when developing the research questions and implementation plan. The focus of the research was determined by the local advisory circle, that is they determined what data or questions are necessary to benefit their community. The local advisory circle also selected the data collector and the women who will be trained as birth helpers. Once the data is collected the local advisory circle will be involved in the making meaning from the data.

The community advisory circles will also determine how the data will be used and disseminated. As distinct and independent First Nation possess the inherent rights to self-determination. These inherent rights were not endowed by any state or Nation, but passed on through birthright, care collective, and flow from the connection to the Creator and the lands. They cannot be taken away. Self-determination means First Nations freely and independently determine and exercise their own political, economic, social, and cultural systems without any external interference. In other words, First Nations have jurisdiction over all aspects of their lives. Therefore, the jurisdiction over data rests with the community, and each autonomous First Nation has the right to determine how jurisdiction is interpreted and enforced. First Nations have always recognized, and respected protocols pertaining to the collection, use, and sharing of community information.

Due to the history, politics, and ongoing colonial practices, a focus on First Nation self-determination is required in the research methodology. Kovach (2009) quoted Maurice Squires "All problems must be solved within the context of the culture – otherwise you are just creating another form of assimilation" (p. 75). Focusing on the priorities of the communities who want to bring birth back, we are respecting self-determination. Looking at how colonization has impacted the ceremony of birth and what can be done in the current context to restore the ceremony of birth for mothers and their families.

The project will honour the responsibility to the nations by using First Nation ethics, based on the community protocols and practices, work with the community to ensure the data is compliant with OCAP, the project will have a direct benefit to the First Nations, and both the community and individuals will have free prior informed consent. In terms of maintaining ethical space, the project team will build and maintain trust by following through on decisions made by the advisory circle, use clear communications, transparency on overall project and communicate in writing the foundation of the relationship in a research agreement document. The project will be approved by the ethical bodies of the university, the First Nation Health Information Governance Committee or the local Community Research Ethics body. The project partners also signed a Memorandum of Understanding to clearly define the roles and responsibilities of each partner.

The project will adhere to the principles of OCAP, Ownership, Control, Access and Possession of the data. First Nation data governance is First Nation inherent right to use data and information to improve the lives of First Nation people. Data governance is the ownership, collection, control, analysis, and use of the data (The Data Governance Institute, 2015). Wende (2007) states that data governance is "a framework for decision rights and accountabilities to encourage desirable behavior in the use of the data" (p.419). Data governance is an important tool for self-determining nations to advance First Nations aspirations for collective and individual well-being. There are many successful examples of researchers partnering with communities to form relationships based on respect to develop a mutually beneficial project as Caldwell and Maloney (2008) state... "Communities have the solutions" (p. 4).

OCAP stands for ownership, control, access, and possession and was developed in 1998 and trademarked in 2015 by the First Nation Governance Centre to help guide the development of the First Nations Regional Health Survey (FNRHS) and to be used as a framework to negotiate research relationships where First Nations rights to their own data are protected. OCAP is rooted in a commitment to First Nation self-determination and the community's right to make "decisions regarding why, how and by whom information is collected, used, and shared" (FNIGC, 2007; Schnarch, 2004). In addition, research that has used OCAP as the basis for establishing a relationship and developing the research question is high quality research that is useful to First Nations.

OCAP assert that First Nations have control over data collection processed in their communities and that they own and control how this information will be used. First Nations require control over their data, as it is their inherent right to self-determination, and is supported by UNDRIP which Canada dully endorsed in 2016.

The research project will be helpful to the community as it will assist them in bringing birth back to the community by training people interested in supporting women through pregnancy and birth. The advisory circle created a dialogue and support around the project from community partners and programs, knowledge keepers and families. The methods will be respectful to the community protocols by working with the advisory circle which is appointed form the community to develop the implementation plan, the advisory circle is invaluable in working through how to do things in the best way possible to ensure that the community is actively involved. The use of the language is important "Language is a central system of how culture, code, create and transmit meaning, values and honor the relationship" (Kovach, 2009). Since people speak Cree in the communities we will be working with, the curriculum will be customized to include Cree language and teachings, the data collector in both communities are fluent Cree speakers and will translate the questions as required during the interview, she also reviewed the questions to ensure they could be translated. We will also strive to include the language and teachings in each of the communities that partner on the project.

Giving back to the community will also be done through training, hiring and paying for the Indigenous birth helpers to work in the First Nation for 3 years, hiring a local data collector for 3 years to interview the mothers and doulas, working with the families of the mothers to share knowledge, creating opportunities for further learning of the doulas and networking opportunities.

The study will contribute to the existing literature base on the critical necessity of using Indigenous ways of knowing as the basis for health and wellness promotion and intervention. The work is guided by Indigenous scholars that have stated the importance of Indigenous Knowledge as the foundation for healing form the ongoing trauma of colonization and for improving health and wellness of Indigenous people (Duran, 2006; Hart, 2002; Linklater, 2014). These scholars have called for the inclusion of culture in mental health interventions. In agreement with these calls the First Nation Mental Wellness Continuum Framework – jointly developed by the First Nations Inuit Health Branch of Health Canada and the Assembly of First Nations with Indigenous mental health leaders from First Nations across Canada highlights culture and the use of culturally specific holistic interventions incorporating Indigenous knowledge as the foundation to wellness.

Green (2010) states that culture must be recognized as an effective treatment along with specific rituals, customs, and meanings related to healing. It is important to recognize that all cultures evolve and culture as the foundation for wellness must be understood as interventions of the Indigenous people responding to their current situation. In recent years, scholarship has demonstrated the effectiveness of Indigenous Ways of Knowing as effective treatment for addictions (Rowan et al., 2014). A study examining drug misuse among urban Indigenous adults living in Edmonton, reported that enculturation defined as the "degree to which Indigenous peoples identify with, feel a sense of pride for, and integrate the values and norms of their Indigenous heritage culture" was associated with reduced illicit and prescription drug problems (Currie et al., 2013).

Furthermore, these scholars have established the importance of recognizing the impact of historical trauma (Braveheart & DeBruyn, 1995; Gone, 2013; Kirmayer et al, 2003) specifically, Indian Residential Schools (Bombay, 2014) on wellness. There is a responsibility when working with First Nations to situate the research in the larger historical, political, and cultural context to influence change in colonial policies and practices that continue to impact the well-being of First Nation women. Building the knowledge base around how Indigenous Ways of Knowing can support wellness is critical to obtain proper resources.

Thus, the research project has strived to embody the 4Rs of research (Kirkness & Barnhardt, 2001) through utilizing Indigenous ways of knowing in all stages of the research project. For example, the use of ceremony to develop and maintain respectful relationships and partnerships embodies the 4R's of research. The project also adheres to community protocols that ensure the research is relevant, respectful, responsible and reciprocal. The key for this project is to respect the autonomy and self determination of each community and form partnerships based on the shared goals of restoring Indigenous ways of knowing and supporting the development of healthy families.

References

Anderson, K. (2009). Leading by action: Female chiefs and the political landscape. In G.G. Valaskakis, M. Dion Stout, and E. Guimond, eds., *Restoring the Balance: First Nations Women, Community and Culture*. Winnipeg: University of Manitoba Press, pp. 99–123.

Anderson, K. (2011). *Life Stages of Native Women: Memory, Teachings, and Story Medicine*. University of Manitoba Press, Winnipeg MB.

Battiste, M. (2002). *Indigenous knowledge and pedagogy in First Nations educations: A literature review with recommendations*.

Battiste, M. & Henderson, J. Y. (2000). *Protecting Indigenous Knowledge and Heritage: A Global Challenge.* Saskatoon, Saskatchewan, Purich Publishing Ltd.

Bombay, A. Matheson, K, & Anisman, H. (2014). The intergenerational effects of Indian Residential Schools: Implications for the concept of historical trauma. *Transcultural Psychiatry, 51*(3), 320-338.

Brandy, M. (1995). Culture is treatment, culture as treatment. A critical appraisal of developments in addictions programs for Indigenous North Americans and Australians. *Social Sciences & Medicine, 41*, 1487-1498.

Brant Castellano, M. (2009). Heart of the Nations: Women's contribution to community healing. In G.G. Valaskakis, M. Dion Stout, and E. Guimond, eds., *Restoring the Balance: First Nations Women, Community and Culture.* Winnipeg: University of Manitoba Press, pp. 203–235.

Brave Heart-Jordan M. Y. H., DeBruyn L.(1995) So she may walk in balance: Integrating the impact of historical trauma in the treatment of Native American Indian women. In: Adelman J., Enguidanos G. (eds) *Racism in the lives of women: Testimony theory and guides to anti-racist practice*, New York, NY: Haworth, pp. 345–368.

Boksa, P., Joober, R., Kirmayer, L. J. (2015). Mental wellness in Canada's Aboriginal communities: striving toward reconciliation. Journal of Psychiatry Neuroscience, 40(6), 363-365.

Bombay, A., Matheson, K., Anisman, H. (2011). The impact of stressors on second generation Indian Residential School survivors. *Transcultural Psychiatry, 51*, 299-319.

Bombay, A., Matheson, K., Anisman, H. (2014). The intergenerational effects of Indian Residential schools: implications for the concept of historical trauma. *Transcultural Psychiatry, 51*, 320-338.

Brown, L. & Strega, S. (2008). *Research as Resistance: Critical, Indigenous, and Anti-Oppressive Approaches.* Canadian Scholars Press.

Caldwell, D. & Maloney, A. (2008). It started over coffee: The Aboriginal Community Youth Resilience Network (ACYRN) in Mi'kmaq and Maliseet Communities of Atlantic Canada, *Pimatisiwin, 6*(2), 129-143.

Cardinal, H. & Hildebrandt, L. (2000). *Treaty Elders of Saskatchewan: Our Dream is that Our Peoples will one day be clearly recognized as nations.* Calgary: University of Calgary Press.

Chandler, M.J. & Lalonde, C.E. (1998). Cultural Continuity as a hedge against suicide in Canada's First Nations. *Transcultural Psychiatry, 35*, 191-219.

Couchie, C. & Sanderson, S. (2007). A report on best practices for returning birth to rural and remote Aboriginal communities. *Journal of Obstetricians and Gynaecologists of Canada, 29*(3), 250–254.

Currie, C. L., Wild, T. C., Schopflocher, D. P., Laing, L., & Veugelers, P. (2013). Ilicit and prescription drug problems among urban Aboriginal adults in Canada: The role of traditional culture in protection and resilience. *Social Sciences & Medicine, 88*, 1-9.

Doyle, M., Carter, S., Shaw, J., & Dolan, M. (2012). Predicting community violence from patients discharged from acute mental health units in England. *Social Psychiatry and Psychiatric Epidemiology, 47*, 627– 637.

Duran E. (2006) *Healing the soul wound: Counseling with American Indians and other Native peoples*, New York, NY: Teacher's College.

Duran, E. & Duran, B. (1995). *Native American Postcolonial psychology.* Albany, NY: State University of New York Press.

Elias, B., Mignone, J., Hall, M., Hong, S. P., Hart, L., & Sareen, J. (2012). Trauma and suicide behaviour histories among a Canadian indigenous population: an empirical exploration of the potential role of Canada's residential school system. *Social Science and Medicine, 74*(10), 1560–1569.

Evans-Campbell, T. (2008). Historical Trauma in American Indian/Native Alaska Communities A Multilevel Framework for Exploring Impacts on Individuals, Families, and Communities. *Journal of Interpersonal Violence,23*(3), 316-338.

Fabrega, H. Jr. (2004). Culture and the origins of psychopathology. In U.P. Gielen, J.M. Fish, & J. G. Draguns (Eds.), *Handbook of culture, therapy and healing* (pp.15-36). Mahwah, NJ: Erlbaum.

Firestone, E., & Stirbys, C. (2017. Indigenous Birth in Canada: Reconciliation and Reproductive Justice in the Settler State in J. Cidro and H.T. Neufeld *Indigenous Experiences of Birth and Pregnancy.* Bradford, Ontario, Demeter Press.

First Nation Information Governance Centre (FNIGC). (2007). *First Nation Regional Longitudinal Health Survey: Our voice, our survey, our reality. Selected results from RHS Phase I (2002/03)*. Ottawa, ON: Author.

Gone, J. (2004). Keeping culture in mind. In D.A. Mihesuah & A.C. Wilson (Eds.), *Indigenizing the academy: Transforming scholarship and empowering communities* (pp. 124-142). Lincoln: University of Nebraska Press.

Gone, J. P. (2013). Redressing first nations historical trauma: Theorizing mechanisms for Indigenous culture as mental health treatment. *Transcultural Psychiatry, 50*, 683–706.

Green, B. L. (2010). Culture is Treatment: Considering Pedagogy in the Care of Aboriginal People. *Journal of Psychosocial Nursing, 48(7)*, 27-34.

Grace, S. L. (2003). A Review of Aboriginal Women's Physical and Mental Health Status in Ontario. *Canadian Journal of Public Health*.

Hart, M. A. (2002). *Seeking Mino-Pimatisiwin: An Aboriginal approach to helping*. Halifax, NS: Fernwood Publishing.

Health Canada & Assembly of First Nations (2014), *First Nation Mental Wellness Continuum Framework*, Ottawa: Ontario.

Jasen, P. (1997). Race, culture, and the colonization of childbirth in northern Canada. *The Society for the Social History of Medicine, 10(3)*, 383–400.

Jilek, W. G. (1994). Traditional healing in the prevention and treatment of alcohol and drug abuse. *Transcultural Psychiatry, 31*, 219-258.

Kirkness, V. J. and R. Barnhardt (2001). First Nations and Higher Education: The Four R's - Respect, Relevance, Reciprocity, Responsibility. In Knowledge Across Cultures: A Contribution to Dialogue Among Civilizations. R. Hayoe and J. Pan. Hong Kong, eds., Comparative Education Research Centre, The University of Hong Kong.

Kirmayer, L. J. (2004). The cultural diversity of healing: Meaning, metaphor and mechanism. *British Medical Bulletin, 69*, 33-48.

Kirmayer L., Simpson C., Cargo M. (2003) Healing traditions: Culture, community and mental health promotion with Canadian Aboriginal peoples. *Australasian Psychiatry 11(Supplement)*: S15–S23.

Kirmayer, L. J. & Valaskakis, G. G. (2009). *Healing Traditions: e Mental Health of Aboriginal Peoples in Canada*. Vancouver: UBC Press.

Kornelsen, J., Kotaska, A., Waterfall, P., Willie, L., & Wilson, D. (2010). The geography of belonging: The experience of birthing at home for First Nations women. *Health & Place, 16(4)*, 638-645.

Kovach, M. (2010). *Indigenous Methodologies: Characteristics, Conversations, and Contexts*. Toronto, U of Toronto Press.

Linklater, R. (2014). *Decolonizing Trauma Work: Indigenous Stories and Strategies*. Halifax, NS: Fernwood Publishing.

Maranzan, K. A., Sabourin, A., & Simard-Chicago, C. (2013). A community-based leadership development program for First Nation women: Revaluing and Honoring Women's Strengths. *The International Indigenous Policy Journal, 4(2)*, 1-12.

Mitchinson, W. (2002). *Giving Birth in Canada 1900–1950*. Toronto: University of Toronto Press.

Monture-Angus, P. (1995). *Thunder in my Soul: A Mohawk Woman Speaks*. Halifax, NS: Fernwood Publishing.

Mosby, I. (2013). Administering colonial science: Nutrition research and human biomedical experimentation in Aboriginal communities and residential schools, 1942-1952. *Social History, 46(91)*, 145-172.

O'Donnell, V. & Wallace, S. (2011). First Nations, Metis, and Inuit Women. In *Women in Canada: A gender –based statistical report* (6th ed.). Ottawa: Statistics Canada.

Olsen Harper, A. (2009). Sisters in spirit. In G.G. Valaskakis, M. Dion Stout, and E. Guimond, eds., *Restoring the Balance: First Nations Women, Community and Culture*. Winnipeg: University of Manitoba Press, pp. 175–199.

Regnier, R. (1994). The sacred circle: A process pedagogy of healing. *Interchange, 25*, 129-144.

Rowan, M., Poole, N., Shea, B., Gone, J. P., Mykota, D., Farag, M. & Dell, C. A. (2014). Cultural interventions to treat addictions in Indigenous populations: Findings from a scoping study. *Substance Abuse, Treatment, Prevention, and Policy*, 9(34).

Scharch, B. (2004). Ownership, control, access, and possession (OCAP®) or self-determination applied to research: A critical analysis of contemporary Frist Nations research and some options for First Nation communities. *Journal of Aboriginal Health*, 1, 80-95.

Smith, L. T. (2012). *Decolonizing Methodologies: Research and Indigenous Peoples*. Zed Books.

Stewart, S. L. (2008). Promoting Indigenous mental health: Cultural perspectives on healing from native counsellors in Canada. International Journal of Health Promotion & Education, 46(2), 12-19.

Tobobondung, R. (2017). Revitalizing Traditional Indigenous Birth Knowledge in J. Cidro and H.T. Neufeld Indigenous Experiences of Birth and Pregnancy. Bradford, Ontario, Demeter Press.

Wesley-Esquiaux C. C. (2003). Trauma to Resilience: Notes on Decolonization in G.G. Valaskakis, M. D. Stout, & E. Guimond *Restoring the Balance: First Nations women, community and culture.* Winnipeg, Manitoba, University of Manitoba Press.

Chapter Ten

The Duojár

An Agent of the Symbolic Repatriation of Sámi Cultural Heritage

Liisa-Rávná Finbog

Introduction

Within a museological context, repatriation is for the most part associated with the return of the dead and/or objects (e.g. Turnbull & Pickering 2010, Svestad 2013). And yet the complexities of repatriation also touch upon abstract ideas of cosmological belief (Krmpotich 2011), ritual practices (Peers, Reinius & Shannon 2017), symbolic values (Olli & Harliin 2014) and human actions. In recent years Indigenous artisans and craftspeople working to reclaim and revitalize their cultural heritage from museums have been afforded considerable attention (Olli & Harliin 2014; Varutti 2015).The effect of their actions in processes of repatriation have nonetheless been grossly under-communicated. The following chapter is my attempt to highlight one possible way in which artisans and craftsmen may make a difference in Indigenous source communities[55] efforts to repatriate while at the same time discuss repatriation from an Indigenous point-of-view. To do so I will examine how Sámi duojárs –skilled practitioners of Sámi customary craftmanship (duodji) – in Norway reproduce objects from museum collections, and I suggest that by doing this they engage in *symbolic repatriation* – that is a return of cultural heritage but without an actual return of material objects. To begin with, however, I will provide the reader with some context for understanding the practice of repatriation.

From a historical perspective, the relationship between Indigenous source communities and museums have almost certainly been founded on asymmetrical relations of power that heavily favour the latter over the former (e.g. Clifford 1997:191-2). By and large, this is due to the colonial pasts of museums. During the advance of colonialism, Indigenous people were thought to be evolutionary dead ends and their material culture was thus expected to disappear with time (Bennett 2004:51-2, Lonetree 2012:9-11). In an effort to safeguard the material culture in question, museums all over the world began collecting the "vanishing objects" of the cultures doomed to extinction. This self-appointed task was however, not always carried out with the blessings or even the knowledge of the cultures in question (Westman 2002, Krmpotich 2011). The end result being that to this day, important ritual, social and jucidial objects in large numbers are still held in museum collections outside of source communities reach.

Collecting and removing Indigenous material culture from source communities was the status quo until the middle of the 20th century, when the question of Indigenous peoples' rights took centre stage (Colchester 2002) and extending from this, source communities all over the world made demands for the return of their cultural heritage (Clavir 2002, Turnbull & Pickering 2010). Successful attempts aside (e.g. Merill, J. Lass & Ferguson 1993), calls for repatriation of cultural heritage were and are sometimes hampered. At times difficulties arise from museums insufficient will to return objects that have, at one point, been appropriated from the source communities in question (Clavis 2002, Mulk 2009). Other times it is simply a question of lack of funds to ensure the continued preservation of the returned objects by building suitable facilities or hiring professional staff in community museums (Hammer 2017). Even if the balance of power is slowly shifting (See Erikson 1999, Harth 1999 Kreps 2003, Fienup-Riordan 2010, Buijs 2016), most older Indigenous cultural heritage objects are still under the ownership of museums both physically and spiritually removed from their source communities (Olli and Harliin 2014:65). This atleast is the experience of the Sámi, a people indigenous to northern Fenno-Scandinavia and the Kola Peninsula in the Russian federation (Harliin 2008).

Despite a repatriation-project promising the return of cultural heritage being launched in Norway[56] (Pareli et al. 2012), lack of government funding toward suitable storage from the government has led to the project being put on what appears to be indefinite hold (Hammer 2017). For the time being the greater part of all older Sámi objects are stored in museums outside of the Sámi communities. It should be noted that as of the year 2000 the general practice of museums in Norway has been to make Sámi collections accessible to the entirety of the Sámi population by granting the Sámi rights to view and study the collections (NMU 2000).

Prior to this, Sámi collections were rarely on full display, and rarer still were they made available for study outside of the museums. Consequently, before 2000 the Sámi people had little to no access to the lions share of older Sámi heritage objects. I say "little to no" because there were some exceptions. Here I refer to the times when duojárs in the 1980s and 1990s were given provisional access to study and/or reproduce the form, decoration or production of traditional Sámi objects (as seen in Inga et al. 1986, Fors and Enoksen 1991, Dunfjeld 1999). In the following chapter, I take a closer look at one of these early exceptions by examining how duojárs in the past have used Sámi traditional objects from museum collections as templates for the making of replicas. In particular, I look at the *riebangolleavvi* – Sámi belts decorated with mica minerals. Before going into detail on this matter, however, I will first provide some context concerning the importance of repatriation from a Sámi perspective.

Repatriation – a call for autonomy?

The idea of personal autonomy – the capacity to decide for one's self – is an indisputable fact of human life, but the right to personal autonomy has not always been afforded to Indigenous peoples. In fact until very recently Indigenous communities lacked any true legal ownership of their land, history, language, culture and identity – and in some extreme cases, even their dead (Hilden 2000, Henare 2005, Cubillo 2010, Krmpotich 2011, Smith [1997]2012). This lack of ownership may be explained by either nationalistic or colonial agendas (see Hesjedal 2000 for a discussion related to the Sámi, also see Henare 2005 for a more general discussion), and museums have often taken an active part in executing these agendas (Bennett 2004). While one might wonder how, the fact of the matter is that one way of symbolizing conquest, at least in the case of colonization, is by collecting the material culture of those conquered (Hooper-Greenhill 2000:18-9). The logic is as follows by controlling the dissemination of a culture and its people, one inadvertently also holds power to name and represent that culture and, furthermore, how it is included or excluded from national and official narratives (Hooper-Greenhill 2000, Reid 2002, Rinta-Porkkunen & Ylitalo 2003, Han 2013). By taking ownership of a Peoples' cultural heritage you also take away their power to name and define. This means that it is no longer the source communities themselves that decide how they are presented to the world (Webb 2006). As custodians of innumerable collections from colonized cultures, museums have been greatly influential in determining how source communities are perceived by the general public. It is from understanding this logic that one may begin to see why repatriation matters to Indigenous Peoples.

Initially, it is the source communities that give value to their objects, but when the objects are relocated to museums other meanings are attributed – and they often supercede the original ones (Phillips & Steiner 1999:3, Cameron 2007:54, Deidre 2007:57). The result is that the object is made unrecognizable to its source community, and in a worst case scenario is alienated from its originators (e.g. Olli 2013:87, Buijs 2016:539). For many Indigenous source communities repatriation becomes a way of addressing and correcting this alienation by allowing for the recovery of a healthy emotional relationship between people and objects (Peers 2013).[57] More importantly, when repatriating Indigenous cultural heritage, the ownership of that heritage is restored to the source communities. Restoring ownership allows Indigenous people to take back the power of definition and with it the re-appropriation of their autonomy. However, as I initially stated, repatriation is not always a possibility. When repatriation seems impossible, what options are there for the source communities to regain autonomy? In the following I argue that in these situations, artisans and/or craftspeople can initiate a process of symbolic repatriation.

Symbolic repatriation and the role of the duojár.

In the past, both colonial (Gjestrum 1995:102) and nationalistic (Hesjedal 2000:22) motives helped shape how the Sámi were perceived and treated. In 1851 the Norwegian government even adopted an official policy of assimilation intended to force the Sámi to abandon their language and culture (Minde 2005). The long-term consequences of this assimilation is discussed elsewhere (Eidheim 1961, 1971, Hesjedal 2000, Minde 2005, Eypórsson 2008), but in short Sámi culture and language was ridiculed, suppressed and subjugated to such a degree that many Sámi felt it necessary to hide their ethnicity from the world at large and even from future Sámi generations. Sámi cultural heritage was at best put aside, but in many cases forgotten. In particular this holds true for the Sámi communities on the coast of Norway (Minde 2005, e.g. Eidheim 161:38, 1971:50-6, Eypórsson 2008:11-20). The program was repealed in the 1950s, but by that point, assimilation had done enough damage to ensure that entire Sámi communities had seen the loss of both their tangible and intangible cultural heritage (Fors & Enoksen 1996:16).

With the aforementioned progress of Indigenous rights in the the 1970s and 1980s however, something changed and the Sámi in Norway began a process of revitalization (Gaup 2006:91, Josefsen 2006:16-7, Olsen [1986]2007:36). Very often this effort was linked with the practice of duodji (e.g. Inga et al. 1986). This link is unsurprising given that duodji has an important place in Sámi society, having been credited with a positive influence on the preservation of both Sámi languages and cultures (Lehtola 2006). It follows that those practicing duodji, the duojárs, play an equally significant part in realizing that preservation. Trained as they were in the material culture of the Sámi the duojárs, in the early years of revitalization, were particularly aware of the objects and/or knowledge lost through assimilation.[58] Being cognizant of the fact that Sámi objects at the time of assimilation had been highly sought after by private collectors many of whom later bequeathed their collections to various museums (Gjestrum 1995:103), they began a search of said institutions.[59] Ove Pettersen, who at this time worked at the Norwegian Museum of Cultural History, home to the largest and oldest collection of Sámi artefacts in Norway, recalls many visits from duojárs asking for the opportunity to study Sámi material culture.[60] In particular, he recalls that old clothes and accessories were a favoured object of study – including the riebangolleavvi.

Riebangolli, also known as "poor mans silver", is a mix of minerals with a tendency to glitter, or shimmer, when hit by light. It is thought that using riebangolli to decorate clothes or accessories is an old Sámi technique in the Norwegian coastal areas, and written sources dating to the 18th century seem to confirm this as being the case (Gjessing & Gjessing 1940:23-4). The true nature of its function is not known, but it is likely that riebangolli was used as an alternative to the far more expensive silver (Inga et al. 1986:45), perhaps as protection against malevolent powers or spirits (Turi [1910]1987:158). Regardless of its exact function, there is little doubt in the minds of duojárs that the riebangolleavvi of old was related to what in Sami society is known as árbediehtu, or traditional knowledge (For more on this concept see Guttorm 2011).[61] Sadly the use of riebangolli, and its associated árbediehtu, gradually disappeared during the years of assimilation [Larsen [1950]1979:12), and by the 1930s it had largely been forgotten (Løkvold 2017:4).

This would change in the 1980s and 1990s with the initiation of a large-scale revitalization project set in the municipalities of Kåfjord and Kvænangen in the county of Troms and the municipality of Loppa in the county of Finnmark (Fors & Enoksen 1991). During one of their visits to the Norwegian Museum of Cultural History, the duojárs in said project involved rediscovered the riebangolleavvi. After meticulously documenting every discernable detail of several belts, the duojárs began making reproductions to relearn how the riebangolleavvi had been made in the past and the techniques of decorating with mica. The intent was to reclaim the riebangolleavvi for contemporary use in their source communities.[62] One duojár has suggested that as repatriation of the historical riebangolleavvi, though desirable, was at the time thought to be impossible, at least by reproducing the riebangolleavvi they would be able to take both the cultural heritage and the knowledge of its making back home to its source communities.[63] It is based on this view that I would argue that the duojárs working on the riebangolleavvi in the early years of the revitalization were working to repatriate Sámi culture without actually changing the physical location of the objects in question. The practive I have here described is similar, if not equal, to visual repatriation as discussed by Cunera Bujis (2016), the curator of the Arctic collection of Museum Volkenkunde in Leiden, Netherlands. By digitalizing pictures of Native Greenlanders, the Inuit, and giving their source communities access, she argues that the images are visually repatriated and thus there is no need to return ownership of the actual pictures to the people in them or their descendants (Buijs 2016:548). Of course, there are some key differences between the Inuit and Sámi cases. In the case discussed by Buijs the intent to repatriate comes from the Museum, while the duojárs of the early revitalization were the sole agents in promoting repatriation – and in a way, these duojárs did achieve their objective, albeit in a symbolic manner. Despite the original riebangolleavvi still being owned by a Norwegian museum, their replicas are today in extensive use throughout the Sami coastal communities in Norway[64]. Some form of árbediehtu has even been recovered: when looking at the templates in the museums and cross-referencing with written sources and old pictures, the duojárs have been able to determine that belts decorated with separated elements of decor are meant to be worn by females. When the decoration continues all around the belt, it is meant to be worn by men.[65] With this example of symbolic repatriation in mind, I will lay out my conclusions below.

In closing.

In the early years of Sámi revitalization in Norway, reclaiming the cultural heritage that had been aquisitioned by museums during the years of assimilation seemed an impossible dream to Sámi communities. The Sámi communities as a result had to redefine what repatriation or return would come to mean. For the Sámi duojárs, this redefinition lay in crafting and duodji. Denied legal ownership of their material culture, the duojárs bypassed any conventional understanding of repatriation and chose to reclaim what was theirs by making reproductions of the museum-owned objects. In short, the duojárs re-appropriated something taken from their ancestors – objects, autonomy and power of definition – by taking advantage of the very tools of that removal.

When restoring their sense of ownership, the Sámi duojárs, denied conventional repatriation, were forced to find alternate ways of returning cultural heritage to the Sámi communities. They did so by engaging in a symbolic form of repatriation. The symbolic repatriation allowed for a shift in the definition of ownership so that Sámi cultural heritage was no longer the exclusive property of museums, but equally belonged to their source communities. Though not named as such in the relevant literature, the process that this chapter defines as *symbolic repatriation* happens frequently – just as in the case I have discussed here – and often it involves the actions of Indigenous artisans and craftspeople that are making efforts to de-colonize the material expressions of their culture. To conclude I argue that the enactment of repatriation is always multifaceted. It happens on many, and varied levels depending on needs and context. Within these complexities, it is clear that artisans and craftsmen have a vital role to play.

References

Bennett, Tony. 2004. Past beyond memory: evolution, museums, colonialism. London: Routledge.

Buijs, C. 2016. "Museum collection decolonization and indigenous cultural heritage in an island community: East Greenland and the 'Roots 2 Share' Photo Project." Island Studies Journal 11 (2):537-560.

Cameron, Fiona. 2007. "Beyond the Cult of the Replicant: Museums and Historical Digital Objects - Traditional Concerns, New Discourses." In Theorizing digital cultural heritage : a critical discourse, edited by Sarah Kenderdine and Fiona Cameron, 49-75. Cambridge, Mass: MIT Press.

Clifford, James. 1997. Routes: travel and translation in the late twentieth century. Cambridge, Mass: Harvard University Press.

Clavir, Miriam. 2002. Preserving what is valued: museums, conservation, and First Nations, UBC Museum of Anthropology Research publication. Vancouver, B.C: UBC Press.

Colchester, Marcus. 2002. "Indigenous rights and the collective conscious." Anthropology Today Vol. 18, No. 1, pp. 1-3.

Cubillo, Franchesca. 2010. "Repatriating Our Ancestors: Who Will Speak for the Dead." In The long way home: the meanings and values of repatriation edited by Paul Turnbull and Michael Pickering, 20-26. New York: Berghahn.

Deidre, Brown. 2007. "Te Ahua Hiko: Digital Cultural Heritage and Indigenous Objects, People, and Environment." In Theorizing digital cultural heritage: a critical discourse, edited by Sarah Kenderdine and Fiona Cameron. Cambridge, Mass: MIT Press.

Dunfjeld, Maja. 1999. "Åarjel-saemien gapta, gåptoe - sørsamekofta." In Dräkt - rapport från seminarium vid Ájtte, edited by Inga-Maria Mulk, 51-59. Jokkmokk: Ájtte.

Eidheim, Harald. 1961. "Samane - nokre aktuelle problem." Sámi ællin : Sámi særvi jakkigir'ji ... = Sameliv: Samisk selskaps årbok ... Nr. 4 (1959/1960):34-47.

Eidheim, Harald. 1971. Aspects of the Lappish minority situation, Scandinavian university books. Oslo: Universitetsforlaget.
Erikson, Patricia Pierce. 1999. "A-Whaling We Will Go: Encounters of Knowledge and Memory at the Makah Cultural and Research Center." Cultural Anthropology 14 (4):556-583.
Eyþórsson, Einar. 2008. Sjøsamene og kampen om ressursene. Karasjok: ČállidLágádus.
Fienup-Riordan, Ann 2010. "From Consultation to Collaboration." In Sharing Knowledge and Cultural Heritage: First Nations of the Americas. Studies in Collaboration with Indigenous Peoples from Greenlandm North and South America, edited by Laura van Broekhoven, Cunera Buijs & Pieter Hovens, 1 - 5. Leiden: Sidestone Press.
Fors, Gry, and Ragnhild Enoksen. 1991. Vår folkedrakt - sjøsamiske klestradisjoner, Sámi Instituhtta. Karasjok: Davvi Girjii.
Gaup, Káren Elle. 2006. "Historie, minne og myte i moderne samisk identitetsbygging." Samisk identitet / Vigdis Stordahl (red.):85-98.
Gjessing, Gjertrud, and Gutorm Gjessing. 1940. Lappedrakten: en skisse av dens opphav. Vol. 4:2, Instituttet for sammenlignende kulturforskning (trykt utg.). Oslo.
Gjestrum, John Aage. 1995. "Utstilling av levende mennesker: ei historie om samisk kultur og fremmede blikk." Dugnad Vol. 21, nr. 1 (1995):93-108.
Guttorm, Gunvor. 2011. "Árbediehtu (Sami traditional knowledge) - as a concept and in practice." Working with traditional knowledge / edited by Jelena Porsanger, Gunvor Guttorm: [59]-76.
Hammer, Sara Hegna. 2017. "Dårlige bevaringsforhold ved samiske museer bremser tilbakeføring av samisk kulturarv: Flyttelass satt på vent." Klassekampen, 07.11.2017.
Han, Le. 2013. "Our Home Is Here: History, Memory, and Identity in the Museum of Chinese in America." Communication, Culture & Critique Vol. 6, No. 1, pp. 61-178.
Harliin, Eeva-Kristiina. 2008. Recalling Ancestral Voices. Repatriation of Sámi Cultural Heritage. In Projektets Interreg IIIA slutrapport: Ájtte, Várjjat & Sámi Musea Siida.
Harth, Marjorie L. 1999. "Learning from Museums with Indigenous Collections: Beyond Repatriation." Curator: The Museum Journal 42 (4):274-284. doi: 10.1111/j.2151-6952.1999.tb01149.x.
Henare, Amiria J. M. 2005. Museums, anthropology and imperial exchange. Cambridge: Cambridge University Press.
Hesjedal, Anders. 2000. "Samisk forhistorie i norsk arkeologi 1900-2000."Phd-dissertation, Archaeology, Universitetet i Tromsø.
Hilden, Patricia Penn. 2000. "Race for Sale: Narratives of Possession in Two 'Ethnic' Museums." TDR: The Drama Review: A Journal of Performance Studies 44 (3 [T167]):11-36. doi:
Hooper-Greenhill, Eilean. 2000. Museums and the interpretation of visual culture. Vol. 4, Museum meanings. London: Routledge.
Inga, Torbjørg A., Lise Gjesdal Thelle, Ardis Ronte Eriksen, and Elrun Ronte Eriksen. 1986. Samisk kofteburk: i Ofoten og Sør-Troms. Tromsø: Universitetsforlaget.
Josefsen, Eva. 2006. Selvopplevd diskrimminering blant samer i Norge. Alta: Norut NIBR Finnmark.
Karp, Ivan, and Steven D. Lavine. 1991. Exhibiting cultures: the poetics and politics of museum display. Washington: Smithsonian Institution Press.
Kreps, Christina F. 2003. Liberating culture: cross-cultural perspectives on museums, curation, and heritage preservation, Museum meanings. London: Routledge.
Krmpotich, Cara. 2011. "Repatriation and the generation of material culture." Mortality Vol. 16 No. 2, pp. 145-160.
Larsen, Anders. [1950]1979. Mærrasámiid birra. Vol. 16, Om sjøsamene. Tromsø: Tromsø museum.
Lehtola, Jorma 2006. Sámi Duodji - Sámi duodjesearvvi 30-jagi ávvudančájáhuskataloga. . edited by Sami Siida Museum.
Lonetree, Amy. 2012. Decolonizing museums: representing native America in national and tribal museums. Chapel Hill, N.C: University of North Carolina Press.
Løkvold, Jorunn. 2017. Duodji - samisk håndverk: Sjøsamiske koftebelter med kråkesølvdekor - riebangolleherven. In Stipendiaters årsrapport ved Norsk Håndverkinstitutt, Senter for Immateriell Kulturarv.

Merrill, William L.and T. J., Edmund J. Ladd, and T.J. Ferguson. 1993. "The Return of the Ahayu: Da: Lessons for Repatriation from Zuni Pueblo and the Smithsonian Institution " Current Anthropology 34 (5):523-567.
Minde, Henry 2005. "Fornorskina av samene - hvorfor, hvordan og hvilke følger." Gáldu čála - tidsskrift for urfolks rettigheter (3).
Mulk, Inga-Maria. 2009. "Conflicts Over the Repatriation of Sami Cultural Heritage in Sweden." Acta Borealia 26 (2):194-215. doi: 10.1080/08003830903372092.
NMU, Nasjonalt utvalg for universitetsmuseene. 2000. Utlån og avhending av materiale fra museenes samlinger. Edited by Jon Birger Østby. Vol. 5:2000, Norsk museumsutvikling (trykt utg.). Oslo: Norsk museumsutvikling.
Olli, Anne May. 2013. "Pesticider i samisk gjenstandsmateriale." Master Master, Institutt for arkeologi, konservering og historie, Universitetet i Oslo.
Olli, Anne May, and Eeva-Kristiina Harliin. 2014. "Repatriation: Political Will and Museum Facilities." In Museums and restitution: new practices, new approaches, edited by Louise Tythacott and Kostas Arvanitis, 55-70. Farnham: Ashgate.
Olsen, Bjørnar. [1986]2007. "Norwegian archaeology and the people without (pre-)history : or how to create a myth of a uniform past." Critical concepts in heritage:9-25.
Pareli, Leif, Sissel Ann Mikkelsen, Anne May Olli, and Stein Storsul. 2012. Bååstede - tilbakeføring av samisk kulturarv. Norsk Folkemuseum, Sametinget, Norsk Kulturhistorisk Museum.
Peers, Laura & Alison K. Brown. 2003. "Introduction", In Museums and Source Communities: A Routledge Reader edited by Peers, Laura & Alison K. Brown, 1-16, New York: Routledge
Peers, Laura, Lotten Gustaffson Reinius & Jennifer Shannon. 2017. "Introduction: Repatriation and Ritual, Repatriation as Ritual." In Museum Worlds Vol. 5, No. 1, pp. 1 - 8.
Peers, Laura. 2013. "'Ceremonies of Renewal': Visits, Relationships, and Healing in the Museum Space." Museum Worlds 1 (1).
Phillips, Ruth B., and Christopher B. Steiner. 1999. "Art, Authenticity, and the Baggage of Cultural Encounter." In Unpacking Culture: Art and Commodity in Colonial and Postcolonial Worlds, edited by Ruth B. Phillips and Christopher B. Steiner, 3-19. Berkeley: University of California Press.
Reid, Donald Malcolm. 2002. Whose pharaohs? : archaeology, museums, and Egyptian national identity from Napoleon to World War I. Berkeley: University of California Press.
Rinta-Porkkunen, Nina, and Saija Ylitalo. 2003. "If we do not know our past, we have no future: the importance of a museum and a home district for local identity." Nordisk museologi (trykt utg.). 2003, nr 1:111-128.
Smith, Linda Tuhiwai. [1997]2012. Decolonizing Methodologies: Research and Indigenous Peoples. New York: Zed.
Svestad, Asgeir. 2013. "What Happened in Neiden? On the Question of Reburial Ethics." Norwegian Archaeological Review:1-49. doi: 10.1080/00293652.2013.839575.
Turi, Johan. [1910]1987. Muitalus sámiid birra. [Ny utg.]. ed. Jokkmokk: Sámi Girjjit. Original edition, 1910.
Turnbull, Paul, and Michael Pickering. 2010. The Long way home: the meanings and values of repatriation. Vol. vol. 2, Museums and collections. New York: Berghahn.
Webb, Sharon. 2006. "Making museums, making people: the representation of the Sámi through material culture." Public archaeology (trykt utg.). 5(2006) No. 3:167-183.
Westmann, Anna. 2002. "Samiska trummor, vilken är deras betydelse i dag?". In Vem äger kuturarvet? Anföranden vid konferens om återföringsfrågor vid Ájtte Svenskt Fjäll- och Samemuseum 6 – 8 juni 2000. 55-59, Jokkmokk: Ájtte
Varutti, Marzia. 2015. "Crafting heritage: artisans and the making of Indigenous heritage in contemporary Taiwan". International Journal of Heritage Studies. pp.1-14.

notes

[55] Source community refers to the communities, cultures and peoples' from which a museum collection originate (Brown & Peers 2003:2)

[56] Discussions of repatriation in Sweden have been broached, but as of yet no final plans have been made. In Russia there is neither action nor talks. In Finland however, sámi collections have already been repatriated.

[57] Interview with "Áile", 05.01.2018, Interview with "Sara" 10.03.2018.

[58] Interview with "Elle", 24.01.2018.

[59] Interview with "Raste", 30.05.2018.

[60] Personal communication from 08.09.2017.

[61] Interview with "Áile", 05.01.2018

[62] Interview with "Inga", 15.01.2018

[63] Interwiev with "Aile", 05.01.2018

[64] Interview with "Elle", 24.01.2018.

[65] Interview with "Aile", 05.01.2018

Chapter Eleven

The Unavoidable Alienation of Indigenous Artists in our Mass-Produced Society

Lattimer Gallery and Pacific Northwest Coast Art

Laura Forsythe

Unsolicited and unanswered the following request to assist the commodification of Indigenous art is a constant reminder of the pervasiveness of capitalism in the lives of Indigenous people today;

> Laura, I had a conversation earlier today in which it was recommended to me that I reach out to you. I am currently conducting a search for a Sales/Account Manager for a rapidly growing international retailer of Indigenous products and promoter of the Indigenous culture. They are ideally in search of someone of Aboriginal descent with a customer service background and a go-getter attitude to develop as a sales professional working with their clients across Canada and into the US, and attending trade shows on their behalf. It is a truly unique opportunity to develop a sales career with a positive culture that is second to none. If you would know of anyone that comes to mind for the role, please let me know. I can be reached at 204-926-3508. I look forward to hearing from you. Thanks in advance, Maurice Cadieux Senior Recruitment Consultant | Pinnacle (Linked in Messaging, 2017)

Companies such as Northwest Coast Gifts, Native Northwest and Aya Northwest create the capitalistic marketplace that requires Indigenous people's involvement in the alienation of labour, thereby jeopardizing authenticity in the Indigenous Arts. Through an analysis of the company Northwest Coast Gifts established in 1986 by two non-Indigenous business owners, the exploration of the commodification of Indigenous art in the province of British Columbia will be highlighted using the works of Karl Marx, Frederic Jameson, and Walter Benjamin.

Northwest Coast Gifts employs individuals that are not necessarily Indigenous to create works to stock the shelves of its Gallery located on Granville Island, a trendy Vancouver shopping destination, the Vancouver National Airport location and their website with "convenient 24/7 opening hours to meet all of your shopping needs" (Lattimer Gallery, 2017a) shipping worldwide. The gallery was created to foster the relationships that Leona and David Lattimer formed during their time travelling in British Columbia and meeting with Northwest Coast artists according to the Lattimer Gallery website (2017b). Upon inheriting the business in 2001 their grandson Peter Lattimer, eager to uphold the legacy built by his grandparents, has commented on the importance of Northwest Coast artists being represented in the Indigenous art market (Lattimer Gallery, 2017a). Although potentially revered in both in the art world and the Indigenous artist collective within the Province of British Columbia, Peter Lattimer and his gallery are the underpinnings of commodification and a catalyst for the fetishization of Indigenous art in the modern world.

Alienation of Labour

Within the gallery, there are two distinct types of produced art; handcrafted and mass-produced depending on market and price point. To begin a discussion on the alienation of the artist from their labour one acknowledges that although there are two distinct types, they both alienate the artist in the same manner. Marx argued that workers, in this case artists, are alienated from not only the product created but their labour, the results of their labour, the wealth they create and their individuality (Marx, 1844). Artists that provide handcrafted jewellery, carvings and paintings to the Lattimer Gallery are alienated due to the nature of the relationship they have with the art piece they intend to sell or commission it to the gallery. With the increase of artists in British Columbia willing to sell their art in galleries such as Lattimer Gallery, the artists become a cheaper commodity; the more art pieces they create, according to the Estranged Labour theories expressed by Marx (1844), the more they are alienating themselves from their creations. One must consider the relationship between the artist and the production of their piece due to the estrangement, for those working for the gallery create objects of ritualistic beauty that allow for the expansion of the gallery locations and profits for the owner but the artist produces "privation" (Marx, 1844, p.4). Due to this privation, the artist is no longer fulfilled; their pieces are not of them but rather outside of them. Disassociated from their production they become a commodity. Furthering the concept of the alienation of their labour that once commissioned to create pieces for the gallery, there is now a new pressure to continue to create pieces; therefore, the art is not voluntary and according to Marx (1844) becomes "coerced; forced labour" (p.4).

The alienation from their labour results in a labour product, the art piece, which then becomes material and can be expressed according to Marx's (1844) theories of the "objectification of labour" (p.2). This process degrades artist's insightful, cultural and personal expression to the status of mere objects isolated from the artist and prepared for profit. Marx's (1884) theory suggests the art piece "exists outside of" (p.3) the artist, the piece now possesses power as it now controls the destiny and trajectory of the artists' fame and ultimate earning power, thus alienating the artist from their labour. Through the theory of primitive accumulation, Marx (1867) discusses the "historical process of divorcing the producer from the means of production" (p.2) and indicates that the business practice of Lattimer Gallery is based in a historical capitalistic fashion of separating the artist from their creation. The gallery then becomes an "alien person" (Marx, 1844, p.11) to which the artist relinquishes the object or art piece. By commissioning the art for the Gallery, the labour is quite literally the property of another, other than the worker, as Marx (1844) suggests the artist is alienated from the wealth they have created (p.8). Compensation received for their work in the form of a wage implies fairness in a wage economy. However, the gallery in standard practice will set the selling price of the item at a significant profit, increasing the margin on the piece, often greater than the artist could afford to purchase. The owners of the Lattimer Gallery according to Marx's (1867) Theory of Primitive Accumulation are "the owners of money, means of production, means of subsistence, who are eager to increase the sum of values they possess, by buying other people's labour power" (p.2).

Marx's (1867) description of primitive accumulation speaks to the perception of Indigenous artists and the value placed on their work. In revelling in the historical Marx (1867) describes "two sorts of people; one, the diligent, intelligent, and above all, frugal elite: the other, lazy rascals, spending their substance, and more, in riotous living" (p.1). The belief that these two sorts exist in the political economy is illustrated by the perceptions of art collectors and consumers on Granville Island. Within the Lattimer Gallery, there are carvings made by authentic artists, exhibited in a manner which inspires the consumer to put an exchange value based on the socially constructed quantum of socially necessary labour as well as the perceived exchange value which the art gallery places on it. A carved paddle created by Ross Henderson of the Kwakwaka'wakw ranges from two hundred to six hundred dollars, the gallery website features a bio along with other works sold by the carver (Lattimer Gallery). As an accomplished artist, Henderson's work has a high exchange value. One cannot deny that a street artist on Granville Island with their pieces displayed on a blanket would not command the same exchange value despite knowing that the two paddles would be in the same tradition. It appears that for an artist to be successful at earning a wage from their labour they must sell it to another; for in the current system, their fate, if they do not, is to be undervalued and impoverished.

Alienation of the artist life's work or gift merely occurs by losing the passion for the ability to create through the process of capitalism. An artist is driven to produce as a pastime between working hours in another profession, uses art as the escape from the reality of wage working, and subsequently begins to see the value of their art in the marketplace. Begins to create wealth from selling a few pieces to friends and family encouraged to seek further opportunities they then start to create not for release but profit. Alienation begins as the person becomes a self-employed artist for they have now become their position in the act of alienation from human identity. According to Peter Kulchyski (January 11, 2017) the reality in society that a person is what he/she does, therefore, becoming estranged from their source of identity and life purpose. According to Marx (1844), "the animal is immediately one with its life activity. It does not distinguish itself from it", seen in the promotion of the Lattimer Gallery artist of Bill Helin. Descriptions of Helin state "Designed by First Nations Tsimshian artist Bill Helin" (Lattimer, 2017c). Not only attaching the occupation to their name but leading with their nation to signify the importance of his Indigenous authenticity nation, followed by his occupation and ending with their name.

The artist is alienated from their life and individuality, to be competitive in the art world one must be celebrated and considered a best-selling artist. Pieces featured in the Lattimer Gallery are considered traditional art which in itself has limitations as an artistic expression for it must meet the parameters placed on it by community members and art collectors. To facilitate becoming featured at the Lattimer Gallery artists create pieces that tourists and art collectors prefer. Jameson (1936) speaks to the fact that in the postmodern era art forms have "gradually been colonized and extinguished by commodification and the market system" (p. 63) to appease the mass-culture. The success of the commissioned artists at the Lattimer Gallery is evident in the history of the gallery expanding over the past thirty-two years to a global online business with multiple locations. The artist compromised to produce a profit by replicating at any scale, jeopardizing their creativity, mystery, and genius according to Benjamin (1936).

Jeopardizing Authenticity

Two practices at the Lattimer Gallery jeopardize the authenticity of Indigenous art; participation in the new program Authentic Indigenous initiated by Aboriginal Tourism and their mass-produced products. The handcrafted masks, house-posts and paintings featured in the gallery provide for its patrons a sense of legitimacy and authenticity which are shrouded in a cloud of the doubt due to the participation of the Gallery in the Authentic Indigenous Arts Resurgence Campaign three-tier system;

> Tier 1 products are designed, produced and distributed by Indigenous artists or businesses.
>
> Tier 2 products are designed, approved and distributed by Indigenous artists but may be produced by non-Indigenous people or businesses.
>
> Tier 3 products bear the artwork of an Indigenous artist who has been fairly compensated for their work and has also approved of the final design. The producer and/or distributor need not be of Indigenous ancestry. (Authentic Indigenous, 2017)

Items throughout the Gallery and their Northwest Coast Gifts website feature tags indicating to the consumer the level of 'authenticity,' marketed as an opportunity to be an informed purchaser. Unfortunately, from a theoretical perspective, the tagging system allows the Gallery and the consumer to be a complicit accomplice in the devaluing Indigenous art while placating their ethical consciousness. Within the Authentic Indigenous three-tiered system only tier-one features Indigenous artists or businesses on all three levels of design, production, and distribution. Although it states they are Indigenous, it does not stipulate the act of production as handcrafted, but merely the production was arranged by an Indigenous business or person which raises a question in regards to authenticity from a production perspective. Analyzing both tier two and three they indicate to the consumer that a non-Indigenous person or company has replicated the art form or a particular piece for distribution and production. Benjamin (1936) argues that "The presence of the original is the prerequisite to the concept of authenticity" (p.3), however also acknowledges that "its manual reproduction, which is usually branded as a forgery" (p.3) and claims that "reproduction is more independent of the original" (p.3). Furthering Marx's (1844) Theory of Alienation of the results of labour for the artist while defining that these replications created by non-Indigenous producers are no longer authentic for they no longer embody the essence of the artist.

Regarding the technical aspect of mass-producing pieces whether they are prints, engraved leathers or screened scarves prepared for gifts whose price point is affordable to the average consumer there is a challenge to its authenticity; mechanical reproduction. Benjamin (1936) asserts that "mechanical reproduction of art changes the reaction of the masses towards art" (p.13). The Work of Art in the Age of Mechanical Reproduction speaks to the phenomenon of detaching the art from tradition as an Indigenous Art form targeting its authenticity at a theoretical level (Benjamin, 1936). The causing of an erosion of the authenticity heralded by the owner of the Lattimer Gallery quoted in the Vancouver Sun (Griffen, 2014) stating "Our customers have the confidence in us that the question of authenticity is not a huge question for us." This "confidence" is an illusion, and an incredible marketing ploy for the items produced regardless of the distributor not being authentically Indigenous for they have simply been appropriated ethically from an Indigenous artist. Controversially, the definition of appropriation according to Oxford Dictionary (2017) includes "deliberate reworking of images and styles from earlier, well-known works of art" and "dishonest appropriation of property." Arguably, the artists have approved the design and therefore relinquished any call of appropriation to their works. However, the artists are commissioned to their ability to use traditional images and methods used by Northwest Coast communities, and this calls into question their ability to approve designs for mass production. Benjamin (1936) theorizes that "The authenticity of thing is the essence of all that is transmissible from its beginning, ranging from its substantive duration to its testimony to the history which it has experienced" (p.2). Contemplating this understanding of authenticity, one must consider the history of the art form and images used in pieces along with the communities and cultural groups from which they are derived.

Considering authenticity, one must also contemplate its effect on value. Benjamin (1936) argues "Works of art are received and valued on two different planes. Two polar types stand out; with one, accent is on the cult value; with the other on the exhibition value of the work" (p.5). An exploration of this assertion lends itself to the discussion of authenticity in the world of Indigenous art. Within the Indigenous community and protocol of the Northwest Coast, there are unspoken and spoken truths in regards to the commodification and sharing of Indigenous culture. Benjamin (1936) speaks to the cult value and demands that specific works of art should remain in a community hidden from the world (p.5). A viewpoint shared by many in the Northwest Coast culture where images and art forms belong to family lines and individuals making them unavailable for reproduction. Over time the exhibition value has appeared tempting to artists along with the reclaiming of their ability to produce regalia, carving masks, and totem poles which had been outlawed in Canada from 1884 to 1951. The ceremonial creation and motivation to carve or produce regalia is an honoured tradition bastardized by the recreation of six-inch mass-produced totem poles and dolls wearing button blankets once revered for their symbolism. Benjamin (1936) speaks to the relationship both cult, and exhibition value has as polarized views replicated in the dichotomy of community members clinging to their heritage and others excited to display their treasures in their living rooms. Arguably Benjamin (1936) states "the unique value of the 'authentic' work of art has its basis in ritual, the location of its original use value" (p.3), furthering the theory to include the beauty of the reproductions stem from "the cult of beauty" (p.4). Heralding the reproduction as the emancipator from its dependence on Indigenous ritual or ceremony making it anew (Benjamin, 1936, p.4). The piece is then removed from its cult status and becomes a mere object for consumption.

Northwest Coast gifts mass production of an object have lessened the social significance of the art form creating uncritically enjoyed and predetermined attitudes in pieces carried throughout Canada unchallenged (Benjamin, 1936). Despite sales in territories that Indigenous people do not practice the Northwest Coast art style, the art is marketed to the consumers as authentic Indigenous art in situ. The mass production of the art to facilitate the pan-Indian effect that Northwest Coast Gifts is having on the Indigenous Art world is demonstrated in their pieces being the only Indigenous art showcased in Museums and art galleries such as the Manitoba Museum and the National Art Gallery. The products available are Tier 3 mass produced, created in China and at a low price point. Marx (1867) in The Commodity speaks to this when stating "If one succeeds in converting coal into diamonds with little labour, then the value of diamonds sink beneath that of paving stones" (p.4).

By mass producing their artistic and traditional expression, the artists have relinquished their pieces to become a cheap commodity. By allowing the mass production of their art, it has been devalued. Arguably, this practice drives the original piece's value to increase. One must also consider the perception of exchange value placed on it by collectors and tourists. Values are driven by the collector's perception of "the quantum of socially necessary labour" (Marx, 1867, p.3) which in our society is often minimized to devalue the art for the collector's benefit. By allowing this perception, we are encouraging the relation of labour to equate value according to Marx (1867). Ultimately, making the mass production of an artist's vision from a capitalistic view more profitable and therefore, the online business of Northwest Coast Gifts is very successful.

Success not only stems from a perceived price point but also from the gallery and the artist's ability to brand items such as coffee mugs, fridge magnets, and countless other household items with traditional Indigenous art through mechanical mass production. Jameson (1936) explains that;

"the frantic economic urgency of producing fresh waves of ever more novel-seeming goods (from clothing to airplanes), at ever greater rates of turnover, now assigns an increasingly essential structural function and position to aesthetic innovation and experimentation" (p.4).

The traditional art forms in this new postmodern marketplace connect to The Cultural Logic of Late Capitalism for they possess "a new kind of flatness or depthlessness, a kind of superficiality in the most literal sense" (Jameson, 1936, p.8) for they have now been reduced to an oven mitt.

Fetishization

The creation of superficial and material goods brandishing traditional Indigenous art forms vilifies the gallery and the artists neglecting the true culprit, our collective involvement in capitalism. Marx (1857) theorizes in *Grundrisse*:

> Production creates the objects which correspond to the given needs; divides them up according to the social laws; exchange further parcels out the already divided shares in accord with individual needs; and finally, in consumption, the product steps outside this social movement and becomes a direct object and servant of individual need, and satisfies it in being consumed (p.5)

In the case of the production, distribution, and consumption of the mass-produced Indigenous art seen at Northwest Coasts Gifts one cannot critique those who produce without considering those that distribute or consume. Marx (1857) outlines that "without production, no consumption; but also, without consumption, no production; since production would then be purposefulness" (p.7) highlighting the issue of all parties role in jeopardizing authenticity and alienating artists.

Marx's (1867) theories on commodity fetishism explain the social relationship derived from the artist's labour. The artists fail to see their ability to produce art profitably without the gallery and its ability to use technology to mass produce their art. By allowing the Lattimer Gallery to use their technology to produce it increases the fetishism and decreases the wage to the artist seen in their profit per unit sold.

Benjamin (1936) argues that "the unique value of the 'authentic' work of art has its basis in ritual, the location of its original use value" (p.4), his theories grounded in Marx (1867) commodities theories of value which state "the smaller the productive power of labour, the greater is the labour-time necessary for the production of an article, and the greater its value is" (p.4). An artist handcrafting items value it substantially higher at the Lattimer Gallery than the mass-produced items found on the Northwest Coast Gifts website. The exchange values were seen at the Lattimer Gallery align with Marx (1867) assertions of the "quantum of simple labour" and that an object or art pieces use value or good only has a value because labour is objectified or materialized in it" (p.3). Counterproductively to be competitive, the artists devalue their art-based relationship with the Gallery to continue in the wage economy. An action supported by Marx (1867) theory of the role society plays in the value of Indigenous art as consumers the "quantum of socially necessary labour" (p.3) or hours socially perceived to create the piece determine the quantity of the value.

The role of social perception in the fetishization of Indigenous art as a commodity includes the direction the art takes and what is produced outlined in Marx (1867) explanation that states "if it useless, then the labour contained is also useless" (p.3), the exchange value of a piece of art that is undesirable actualizes to a price point of zero. The artist placed into the delicate position of creating a relationship with the Gallery to continue in the wage economy relying on their expertise in dictating the exchange value acceptable to most collectors and tourists. Due to the social construct of their relationship the artist's pieces are now a fetishized commodity.

Conclusion

Undoubtedly a successful business the Lattimer Gallery provides space for artists in British Columbia to create wealth and art collectors to increase the value of their collections. With its mass-produced product, it also provides accessibility for others to obtain works that in their original form would be unattainable due to price. Vilifying the gallery, their patrons or their artists is not the intention of this paper. However, the process of alienation currently experienced by Indigenous artists is often unchallenged or discussed due to Indigenous peoples struggle to be a part of our fetishized society. An exploration of the Lattimer Gallery and their business practices speaks to the exploitation of artists under the guise of capitalism. According to the theories of Karl Marx, Frederic Jameson, and Walter Benjamin, the Lattimer Gallery has successfully alienated and completed the commodification of Indigenous artists in British Columbia. Significantly, this changes the nature of the actual artwork itself!

Artists alienated from themselves, their creations and their labour to satisfy consumers and producers. Artists jeopardize authenticity. Artists strive to become successful in the fetishized society seeking a relationship based on their labour hoping to exploit themselves and their culture to earn a wage. Success equals becoming the unavoidable commodity. All facilitated by the Lattimer Gallery business model which seeks to commodify Indigenous art and be the catalyst for fetishization for profit.

References

Benjamin, W., (1936) The work of Art in the Age of Mechanical Reproduction. Schocken/Random House, ed. by Hannah Arendt Translated Harry Zohn

Griffen, K., (2014, October 7) Authentic Indigenous: new program helps ensure artists are fairly paid (with video). Vancouver Sun. Retrieved from http://vancouversun.com/news/staff-blogs/authentic-indigenous-new-program-helps-ensure-artists-are-fairly-paid

Griffen, K., (2015, December, 23). Hand-crafted First Nations art lands at Vancouver International Airport. Vancouver Sun. Retrieved from
http://www.vancouversun.com/news/metro/hand+crafted+first+nations+lands+vancouver+internationa l/11610600/story.html

Jameson, F., (1936). Postmodernism, or, the cultural logic of late capitalism. Durham: Duke University Press.

Kulchyski, P., (January 11, 2017) Estranged Labour Lecture. Critical Theory and Native Studies.

Lattimer Gallery., (2017a). Northwest Coast Gifts: About Us. Retrieved from https://northwestcoastgifts.com/pages/about-us

Lattimer Gallery., (2017b) Lattimer Gallery: About the Gallery Retrieved from https://www.lattimergallery.com/pages/about-us

Lattimer Gallery., (2017c) Lattimer Gallery: 100% Silk Raven Scarf. Retrieved from https://northwestcoastgifts.com/collections/recent/products/100-silk-raven-scarf

Marx, K., (1844) Economic and Philosophical Manuscripts of 1844: Estranged Labour Retrieved from https://universityofmanitoba.desire2learn.com/d2l/home

Mark, K., (1857) Grundrisse. Retrieved from https://universityofmanitoba.desire2learn.com/d2l/home

Marx, K., (1867) Capital. A Critique of Political Economy. Volume 1. Book One: The Process of Production of Capital Retrieved from https://universityofmanitoba.desire2learn.com/d2l/home

Oxford Dictionary., (2017). English Oxford Living Dictionaries; Definition of appropriation in English. Retrieved from https://en.oxforddictionaries.com/definition/appropriation

Respecting Language and Ways of Knowing While Troubling Colonial Images of Indigeneity

Chapter Twelve

Bridging Gaps

Intercultural Education as a Tool for Revitalization

Monica Morales-Good

Introduction

Today, in Mexico alone, *thousands* of Indigenous peoples are in jail, not knowing the charges they face due to a language barrier. The State's failure to integrate the Indigenous population into the legal sphere and provide appropriate interpretation has been cited as one of the primary reasons for the many disadvantages to which Indigenous peoples are subjected, among them linguistic and cultural prejudice (Berk-Seligson 11-6); this, in spite of Mexico's Law on Linguistic Rights. In Mexico, there are important matters yet to be resolved to deal with the implementation and recognition of the human rights granted to the Indigenous communities. An example of this is the lack of consultation and integration of Indigenous authorities, the participation of the community at the State level and the absence of Indigenous presence in the design of the criminal justice system.

These junctures are addressed in the present article. It will be shown that in order to gain access to justice for Indigenous peoples, the Mexican institutions require an important structural transformation. This transformation must recognize Indigenous jurisdiction and ways of knowing and will generate a better alignment between two systems -- the State and the Indigenous jurisdiction -- in order to secure the human rights guaranteed to all Mexican subjects (Ley General de Derechos Linguisticos; Mexican Constitution article 2b).

In order to achieve better communication among the State legal system and the Indigenous jurisdiction, the present essay proposes Intercultural

Education as a method to breach gaps. For this purpose, we take the specific case of Mexico, more specifically Oaxaca. We trace the efforts of a grassroots organization pursuing intercultural education and trying to include it within the present legal system. Lastly, we take into consideration a case that took place in the State of Oaxaca where the Indigenous authorities were allowed to solve a federal case.

Mexico — A Pluralistic State?

As of 2015, Mexico has registered 7,382,785 people who speak an Indigenous language. This represents 6.5% of the national population. Mexican states showing the largest population of Indigenous peoples are Oaxaca, Chiapas, and Veracruz. The number of people who *only* speak an Indigenous language is approximately 959,762 (INEGI). The Indigenous peoples in Latin America continue to endure the long-lasting effects of colonialism such as linguistic racism ethnic discrimination (Diaz-Polanco 84-8; Sierra, 15-26) and the neverending removal of their ancestral territories due to land exploitation.

Access to justice and public services continue to be one of the biggest challenges faced by the Indigenous communities. Every year many Indigenous people are arrested and prosecuted without access to appropriate interpretation services. Article 8, Part A, of the American Convention on Human Rights—to which Mexico signed adherence in 1981—grants defendants the right of free access to a translator or interpreter to ensure a fair trial (Multilateral Treaties); moreover, Mexico has its own Law of Linguistic rights, a no-less important piece of legislation protecting Indigenous peoples' rights to language and self-determination. Yet interpreters who speak an Indigenous language are very limited throughout the Republic. This leaves Indigenous monolinguals defenceless, as qualified interpreters in their language might not be available within a reasonable distance or may simply not exist (Betancourt 53-59; Kleinert and Stallaert 235-254; Sierra 287-314). Additionally, the right to speak through an interpreter is contingent on the officer's impression of whether this service is needed, the State's funding to cover the cost of an interpreter, and whether a qualified interpreter is available in the area (Escobar 198-204).

Oaxaca - A Living Example of Indigenous Pluralism

The State of Oaxaca has around 3,506,821 inhabitants; of these, 1.7 million speak an Indigenous language (INEGI). The state is home to fifteen constitutionally recognized Indigenous tribes and five linguistic families of which approximately 176 linguistic variables derivate (CNLI-INALI). Oaxaca ranks number one in the Indigenous population in Mexico. Amazingly, it is also worth noting that besides being home of Mexico's largest Indigenous populations, Oaxaca also shows the worst indexes of poverty within the country (Quinto-Cortés et al. 409-432; Hoobler 441-460). According to official numbers, Chiapas, Oaxaca, and Guerrero suffer from extreme poverty where the population is not able to secure enough income to cover the expenses of the basic food basket. About 24.2% of Mexican households suffer nutritional poverty (Diagnostico 1-224).

Along with Chiapas, after the Zapatista movement, Oaxaca has experienced an era of grassroots movements for local autonomy – especially regarding education – among teachers and unionists (Norget 96-127; Favela 63-72). Through this movement, the Indigenous population has been able to utilize their ethnicity, linguistics, and cultural commonalities as a tool for revitalization. They seek the right to use their ancestral language and traditional knowledge, as well as fair participation in the justice system. In an effort to gain greater autonomy in a variety of sociopolitical spheres of life, while challenging Mexico's dominant culture (Muñoz 585-610). Indigenous people have attempted to transform their political situation and coexist in the national arena (García 78). Through this struggle, the people of Oaxaca are in a constant fight to recover their Indigenous identities, their land, their education rights, and their ancestral languages (Hoobler, 441-460), while the government of Oaxaca is constantly engaged in efforts to silence these intentions. Through continuous radars and demonstration shutdowns, the State has not sought to recognize or accommodate its vast diversity, but to eliminate it through cultural assimilation – trying to erase the 'Indigenous problem' by creating a homogeneous Mexican identity (Muñoz 585-610).

Additionally, the State will protect its own interest at the expense of Indigenous peoples. For instance, the lucrative tourism industry in Oaxaca means that the State is especially motivated to stop protests, mobilization and resistance movements that could potentially turn away tourists and their investments. Sadly, while trying to achieve land rights, and appropriate education, Indigenous peoples fall into the gaps of the legal system (Norget 96-127). Katya Salazar, Executive Director of the Due Process of Law Foundation (DPLF), reports that many Indigenous protest movements are terminated when the State sends presumed suspects to jail for long periods of time, sometimes without evidence. She states that one of the most serious problems regarding human rights for Indigenous communities in Oaxaca is the tendency for the government to utilize laws and the judicial system to penalize and criminalize Indigenous peoples who pursue their constitutional rights (Salazar 40-41; Betancourt 59).

Rodolfo Stavenhagen reports that most of the trials involving Indigenous peoples are full of irregularities. This is not only because of the lack of interpreters and defence counsels who are trained and accustomed to Indigenous traditions but also because of the police officers, defence attorney offices and judges who choose to ignore Indigenous perspectives and law practices. Further, he notes that the Indigenous peoples' situation in Mexican prisons is alarming (Stavenhagen 11).

Many Indigenous peoples who find themselves facing the legal institutions prefer to speak the little Spanish they know, even if this means to respond to questions with the monosyllables "sí" or "no." Some would admit to Spanish proficiency just to avoid the negative effects of colonialism, even if this disadvantages their case; in addition, Indigenous attorneys, cultural brokers, and Indigenous judges are rarely requested within the courtroom.

Why is Intercultural Education Needed?

The Indigenous Professional Center for Legal Counsel, Defense, and Translation Civil Association (CEPIADET per its acronym in Spanish) is a civil organization arising from the need of Indigenous speakers to exercise their linguistic rights in the legal field. Along with many other initiatives, CEPIADET promotes talks and workshops between the State officials and the Indigenous Jurisdiction in the State of Oaxaca. The organization emerged in 2005 in response to the need of Indigenous peoples to exercise their linguistic rights in the field of justice. Some of their principal objectives are 1) Evaluate the manner in which the institutions address the individual and collective problems of Indigenous societies and, with an educated view, generate proposals for public policies to include the cultural and linguistic relevance needed; 2) Follow and implement processes that allow the Indigenous communities to see themselves as the only ones responsible for their living conditions (thus changing their actions), promoting knowledge about their rights and making sure they have full access to them (CEPIADET).

Indeed, education can be the bridge to solve gaps between cultures and languages. In her influential essay "The Experience of Colonization Around the World," Erica Daes refers to an antidote, such antidote is education, travel, discovery of other ways of knowing "the rebuilding of old alliances and kinships across borders, and the discovery of like-minded peoples in other parts of the globe. In other words, the antidote is the discovery of other colonized peoples who share the same experiences and feelings" (Battiste, 7). Daes explains that oppression, slavery, discrimination, genocide has been felt universally around the world. For her, the agents have to be made aware of the role they play within their society (e.g. oppressor versus oppressed). She points out that once a person has portrayed a part for so long, there comes a time when it is difficult to overcome reality. For example, a person who lives and grows with the oppressive pattern may not fully appreciate the damage done to the people around him; for him, that specific behavior is normal; whereas the oppressed have been so accustomed to an oppressive treatment that it becomes tough for them to believe that self-government and self-determination is a tangible option. In fact, after people who have endured oppression for lengthy periods of time, they become numb and don't believe they are worthy of love. Their experience becomes internalized as a result of their limitation of freedom (Battiste 3-8).

Cultivating a Two-Sided Road Towards Inclusive Participation

Indigenous peoples in Mexico have been victims of oppression in a never-ending circular pattern, which is visible in the states of Chiapas and Oaxaca. The Mexican Constitution (Article 2) and the General-Law of Linguistics Rights (Articles 2-7) shed light on the influence and importance of Indigenous cultures and their significance to the present day State. However, there exists a systematical lack of resources to attend the needs of the Indigenous communities. In its Constitution, Mexico recognizes itself as a pluricultural nation, one that *is* ancestrally based through its Indigenous peoples (descendants of the great empires inhabiting the land before colonization) and preserves Indigenous social, economic, and political institutions.

Article 2 of the constitution is very explicit about Indigenous peoples' rights to self-determination and normative systems. Per the Mexican legal frame, Indigenous peoples should be able to:
— Decide and enforce their internal forms of coexistence and protect their social, economic, political, and cultural organization.
— Apply their own normative systems to regulate and solve their internal conflicts; however, this clause imposes constraints to Indigenous communities, limiting them to only solving cases of domestic violence, farm animal theft, land distribution, and youth vandalism. Historically,

the Indigenous communities had the power to solve criminal- and State-level cases. Nowadays, the constitution has delimited the lines over what can be solved with Indigenous knowledge and what should be State-mandated. Thus, the Indigenous judges' knowledge is hardly ever sought to solve cases in which Indigenous defendants are involved (CEPIADET)(Caso Quiavicusas).
- To elect their authorities according to their traditional rules, procedures and customs.
- "To preserve and enrich their languages, knowledge and *all elements that constitute their culture and identity* (Article 2, part 4 - my emphasis)."
- Finally, and most importantly, Indigenous peoples should enjoy full access to State jurisdiction. Specifically, it is stated that "in order to protect this right, in *all trials and proceedings that involve natives*, individually or collectively, their customs and cultural practices *must* be taken into account, respecting the provisions established in [the] Constitution. Indigenous peoples have, *at all times*, the right to be assisted by interpreters and counsels, who are familiar with their language and culture." (Article 2, part 8 - my emphasis).

Indeed, from the legal standpoint, the Constitution seems to promote equal opportunities for Indigenous peoples and, at the same time, strives towards eliminating discriminatory practices. In reality the case is so severely disproportionate that Indigenous peoples suffer torture and abuse and are usually unable to understand the case being made against them because of a language barrier (Salazar 40-41).

Considering multiple events disadvantaging the Indigenous communities, CEPIADET promotes dialogues between the State and Indigenous Justices (La Voz del Sur). Tomás López-Sarabia, CEPIADET's executive director, refers to these meetings as knowledgeable dialogues that help breakdown misinterpretation and misunderstanding amid the two systems, and educate both sides about processes and the implementation of legal, social, public policies (Personal Interview); thus trying to alleviate the rhetoric of "You cannot be the doctor if you are the disease" (Daes on Batisste, 4). CEPIADET promotes research and intercultural dialogue participating in the creation and execution of training projects aimed to include justice servants as well as Indigenous authorities. Ultimately coordination and dialogue among justices will avoid the invasion of competencies, subordination of systems, double judging, among other aspects contrary to the law.

In this fashion, it is clear that the Mexican institutions require a deep transformation in order to 1) Guarantee access to justice for the

Indigenous communities so that the Indigenous jurisdiction can be given the importance it deserves; 2) Create stronger ties and collaboration between the two systems and 3) Guarantee the human rights aimed toward Indigenous peoples (linguistic and culturally speaking). The first and foremost challenge is for the justice system and public servants to recognize that Mexico's Indigenous diversity is not a problem to fix but an integral part of Mexican society to with which to collaborate (Hernández Andrés y Martínez Ortega, 141-143).

CEPIADET initiative to promote intercultural education during the Dialogues among Justices progresses slowly, but surely, as more State officials become aware of the competences suitable for the Indigenous communities. Maria Teresa Sierra (CIESAS-Mexico) also brings attention to new forms of justice that are going beyond the official legal frameworks to put into practice autonomous Indigenous jurisdictions that confront the State, as is the case of the Community Police of Guerrero, Puebla, and Michoacan (17). Sierra makes reference specifically to the case of Puebla, where the Superior Court of Justice built an Indigenous Court in 2003 giving the Indigenous officials the opportunity to contend Indigenous justice to that of the State. She mentions the patience and negotiating-style characteristics of the Nahuatl authorities allow them to see and to act accordingly, *with the support of the national system* that to a point, defines the scopes and modalities of Indigenous justice (Sierra,20). For Sierra, one of the most notorious signs of progress is the active participation of Indigenous women in the justice system. This breaks previous role models that prevent women from taking part in social and justice roles. Though it has definitely not reached its full potential, Indigenous women continue an arduous fight to gain voice.

For me, the most relevant example of Indigenous capability to solve complicated cases is definitely the Quiavicusas case in the State of Oaxaca, where a State official declined its competence to solve the case, thus allowing the Indigenous court of Quiavicusas to solve a federal offense case.

Quiavicusas, an Example to Follow.

In September 2012, an Indigenous man who was a native of the community known as Santiago Quiavicusas, a Zapotec community, was asked to transport a group of people in exchange for a non-specified payment, that was also not made. His vehicle was later detained by immigration officers who identified the passengers as illegal Guatemalans.

The driver was detained and sentenced later for "violation to the immigration law" with the legal hypothesis that the driver was transporting people in national territory hoping to attain remuneration by avoiding immigrating checkpoints. He was sentenced to eight years without the right to conditional condemnation or to the substitutes of the imposed imprisonment, nor the benefit of the conditional sentence. He was also fined with five thousand days (323,800.00 MXP), the suspension of his political and civil rights and confiscation of the vehicle. He was then made aware that he had five days to file an appeal (Muñiz-Diaz 61-63; Martinez Ortega).

When the Indigenous person presented his appeal, the State officials recognized that he was self-ascribed as Indigenous Zapotec and made the necessary arrangements to have an Indigenous defender with Zapotec culture and language knowledge, but couldn't find such a defender. The Constitution guarantees just and fair trial for Indigenous defendants. In this case, however, the State was not in the position to guarantee its obligations pertaining human rights. The court then declined its competency to judge the Indigenous driver and assigned the case to the Indigenous jurisdiction of Santiago Quiavicusas so that the matter was judged according to their normative systems, with decision making and sanctions according to the use and customs (Usos y Costumbres) of the community to which the defendant belonged. Gerardo Martinez Ortega (member of CEPIADET) refers to the importance of this case, as it was the very first case in which a Mexican judge admitted the State's flaws to judge the case fairly and requested Indigenous expertise. This, of course, made evident the Indigenous systems, norms and procedures. Gerardo points out that there are always two sides to one coin. For the State officials, transporting a group of illegal peoples from one place to another (it is worth noting that the driver was not made aware of the people's precedence until the arrest) is an immigration offence –a federal offense. In the community, however, transportation service is not an offence; and in a case like this involving migrants, it is even expected and encouraged to lend a hand and to help as much as possible. In the Indigenous communities it is habitual and a cultural practice to help those in need; for without solidarity, migrant's survival across the Mexican Republic would be rather difficult. The Quiavicusas community absolved the driver under the principle of "Solidarity," but he was reprimanded for wanting to obtain a monetary good; for that he was assigned to haul 300 bags of sand (Martinez Ortega).

The above makes visible that once the State and Indigenous officers know their competencies, they are more qualified to discern who would assess the case fairly. Though the Quiavicusas case happened in 2012-3, it definitely showed that intercultural education between the two justices is needed in order to understand cases from different angles and according to Indigenous customs (Usos y Costumbres).

In 2017 the Mexican attorney general's office finally admitted a mistake when accusing three Indigenous women of kidnapping six police officers. Eleven years went by before the mistake was admitted and the women (who were unjustly processed) were recognized as innocent and a public apology offered (La Jornada). Obviously, more education is still needed. The collaboration between the State and the Indigenous jurisdiction is vital, at present times more than ever, as social leaders and Indigenous activists, whose only offense is to seek for better living conditions, are being murdered. Indigenous peoples will continue to pursue collaborations that will allow for fair proceedings and that will permit the active participation of Indigenous peoples within the national arena "until justice becomes a customary act of human kind (La Jornada)."

References

Angelelli, Claudia. Revisiting the Interpreter's Role: A Study of Conference, Court, and Medical Interpreters in Canada, Mexico, and the United States. 55 Vol. John Benjamins Publishing, 2004. Print.

Battiste, Marie. Reclaiming Indigenous Voice and Vision. UBC Press, 2011. Print

Berk-Seligson, Susan. "Judicial Systems in Contact Access to Justice and the Right to Interpreting/Translating Services among the Quichua of Ecuador." Interpreting 10.1 (2008): 9-33. Print.

Betancourt, Yuri Escalante. "Zonas Del Silencio: La Supresión De La Alteridad Lingüística En Los Procesos Judiciales." Boletín de Antropología Americana.35 (1999): 53-9. Print.

Carranza, Ariel Vazquez. "Linguistic Rights in Mexico." RAEL: Revista Electrónica de Lingüística Aplicada 8 (2009): 199-210.

Constitution of the United Mexican States, 1917 (as Amended). Washington: Pan American Union, 1961. Print.

Cossío, José Ramón. "Oaxaca y el derecho indígena." Nexos: Sociedad Ciencia Literatura, May 1998, p.10+. Literature Resource Center, http://link.galegroup.com/apps/doc/A20849284/LitRC?u=ubcolumbia&sid=LitRC&xid=f1fb7c50. Accessed 2 June 2018.

De León Pasquel, Lourdes. Costumbres, Leyes y Movimiento Indio En Oaxaca y Chiapas. Miguel Angel Porrua, 2001. Print.

"Diagnóstico Sobre La Situación De Los Derechos Humanos En México." Oficina del Alto Comisionado de las Naciones Unidas para los Derechos Humanos en México (2003): 1-224. Print.

Escobar, Sidney Ernestina Marcos. "El Derecho De Los Indígenas a Una Defensa Adecuada En El Nuevo Sistema De Justicia Penal En México." Revista legislativa de estudios sociales y de opinión pública 5.9 (2012): 181-207. Print.

Favela, Alejandra. "Lasting Lessons from Oaxaca: Teachers as Luchadores Sociales: An Inside Account of the Historic 2006 Oaxacan Teachers' Movement and Why it is Still Relevant Today." Radical Teacher 88.1 (2010): 63-72. Print.

García, Carlos Ochoa. Derecho Consuetudinario y Pluralismo Jurídico. Cholsamaj Fundacion, 2002. Print.

Hoobler, Ellen. "" to Take their Heritage in their Hands": Indigenous Self-Representation and Decolonization in the Community Museums of Oaxaca, Mexico." The American Indian Quarterly 30.3 (2006): 441-60. Print.

"Informe sobre el estado que guardan los derechos lingüísticos de los pueblos y comunidades indígenas en el Sistema de procuración y administración de justicia en Oaxaca." *Http://fundar.org.mx/mexico/pdf/informecepiadet.pdf*. CEPIADET, Dec. 2010. Web. 3 Mar. 2017

Kleinert, Cristina V., and Christiane Stallaert. "La Formación De Intérpretes De Lenguas Indígenas Para La Justicia En México. Sociología De Las Ausencias y Agencia Decolonial." Sendebar 26 (2015): 235-54. Print.

Ley General de Derechos Lingüísticos de los Pueblos Indígenas, 2009. http://www/diputados.gob.mx/LeyesBiblio/pdf/257.pdf

Lopez, Francisco Barcenas. "Hasta Que La Dignidad Se Haga Costumbre." La Jornada, 23 Feb. 2017, www.jornada.unam.mx/2017/02/23/opinion/021a1pol.

Martinez, Gerardo Ortega. "Declinación de competencia: Caso Quiavicuzas I. Oaxaca.quadrin.com.mx/Declinacon-De-Competencia-Caso-Quiavicuzas-I/ Agencia Quadratín. Quadratin Oaxaca, 9 Sept. 2015, Oaxaca.quadratin.com.mx/Declinacion-de-competencia-casp-Quiavicuzas-I/.

Martinez, Gerardo Ortega y Violeta Hernández Andrés,."Derechos Indígenas en el Sistema Penal: Caso Oaxaca." ENSAYOS SOBRE LA IMPLEMENTACIÓN DE LA REFORMA PENAL EN MÉXICO: 141.

".:: Multilateral Treaties Department of International Law OAS ::." :: Multilateral Treaties Department of International Law OAS ::. Organization of American States. Web. 15 Aug. 2015.

Muñiz Díaz, Carlos, & Vicente Marín Martínez. "La jurisdicción constitucional indígena en Oaxaca." Prospectiva Jurídica [En línea], 7.14 (2016): 61-90. Web. 20 jun. 2018

Muñoz, Alejandro Anaya. "The Emergence and Development of the Politics of Recognition of Cultural Diversity and Indigenous Peoples' Rights in Mexico: Chiapas and Oaxaca in Comparative Perspective." Journal of Latin American Studies 37.03 (2005): 585-610. Print.

Norget, Kristin. "The Politics of Liberation: The Popular Church, Indigenous Theology, and Grassroots Mobilization in Oaxaca, Mexico." Latin American Perspectives 24.5 (1997): 96-127. Print.

"Organiza Fiscalía General Diálogo Entre Justicias, En La Mixteca." La Voz Del Sur, 1 Mar. 2018, vozdelsur.com.mx/blog/2018/03/01/organiza-fiscalia-general-dialogo-entre-justicias-en-la-misteca/.

Perfil Sociodemográfico De La Población Que Habla Lengua Indígena. Mexico City: INEGI, 2009. Print.

Quinto-Cortés, Consuelo D., et al. "Genetic Characterization of Indigenous Peoples from Oaxaca, Mexico, and its Relation to Linguistic and Geographic Isolation." Human biology (2010): 409-32. Print.

Salazar, Katya, and Daniel Cerqueira. "Due Process of Law Foundation (DPLF)." Inter-AmericanPrint.

Sierra, María Teresa. "Mujeres indígenas, justicia y derechos: los retos de una justicia intercultural." (2008).

Sierra, María Teresa. "Indian Rights and Customary Law in Mexico: A Study of the Nahuas in the Sierra De Puebla." Law and Society Review (1995): 227-54. Print.

Stavenhagen, Rodolfo. "Derechos Indígenas y Derechos Culturales De Los Pueblos Indígenas." Lo propio y lo ajeno. Interculturalidad y sociedad multicultural, Ciudad de México: Plaza y Valdés/Asociación Alemana para la Educación de Adultos/Instituto de la Cooperación Internacional (1996): 71-94. Print.

Stavenhagen, Rodolfo. "Report of the Special Rapporteur on the Situation of Human Rights and Fundamental Freedoms of Indigenous People." Engaging the UN special rapporteur on indigenous people: Opportunities and challenges. Baguio City, Philippines: TEBTEBBA Foundation (2003) Print.

Chapter Thirteen

Language, Storytelling, and Intergenerational Learning Among the Abam People of South-Eastern Nigeria

Uwakwe Kalu

Introduction

My paper emerged from my research which investigated the storytelling traditions and intergenerational learning among Abam (Indigenous people of south-eastern Nigeria). My interest in this research developed from my experience with the people of Abam on their concern over complete extirpation of their storytelling traditions and intergenerational learning. Postcolonial theories by Frantz Fanon and Paulo Freire guided the research. The study discovered that people's language is the vehicle through which oral traditions could be preserved and transmitted from generation to generation. Language facilitates learning and enhances the relationship that exists within a language community. Indigenous people's language also constitutes their identity. They use their language to communicate their rich cultural heritage such as stories, songs and dance. Indigenous people communicate their norms through oral stories. Oral stories also remind them of their historical origin and help to inculcate discipline and good morals to their children. The study discovered that globalization which is seen here as a continuation of colonial legacies had dealt a deadly blow on Indigenous people's language vis-à-vis oral storytelling traditions of Abam people. The study design was qualitative, while the research method applied key informant interview and focus group discussion (FGD). Seven males and seven females were involved in two FGD groups respectively. While one person each was selected from the two different FGD groups for the key participant interviews, the study suffered some limitations which includes time constraints, the absence of baseline information, and language issues. Also, the study recommends ways of revitalizing Abam language and Igbo language in general through the pedagogies of storytelling.

The Abam People

The Abam clan was discovered by a man called Onyerubi Atitakpo. Onyerubi, the founding father of Abam was a blood brother of Ezema Atita Akpo, the founding father of Ohafia all in South-eastern Nigeria. History indicates that Onyerubi Atitakpo and his brother Ezema Atitakpo were originally from a community called Owan (other history said they were from Ndoni, Benin) from where they migrated to Abam and Ohafia respectively (Obuba, 2008; Onyejieke, 2010). Abam and Ohafia are Igbo speaking communities of South-eastern Nigeria, although their Igbo version/dialect are slightly different from 'Igbo Izugbe' (central Igbo language).

Abam is one of the clans that make up the Arochukwu local government area of Abia State in Nigeria. Other clans in the local government area are Arochukwu, Ihechiowa, Isu and Ututu. The Abam and Arochukwu have the highest population among the five clans. It was perceived that Abam first encountered the Europeans during the colonial era in this part of Nigeria (Achebe, 1958). This contact with the Europeans was made possible because the two clans were surrounded by *igwu* (river) from where the Europeans could gain access to Abam from Calabar river of Sou-south Nigeria. The Europeans proceeded to the hinterland from Abam community. During this colonial period, the major means of transportation was by the *kenu* (boat).

According to the data provided by the National Population Commission (NPC) (2011), the Arochukwu local government had a population of 193,820 and occupied a land area of 524km^2. As the largest clan in Arochukwu local government area (LGA), the population of Abam is estimated at between 45,000-50,000 according to the 2011 NPC projection.

Abam People and Storytelling Traditions

Storytelling remains a global phenomenon. It is not peculiar to people of Abam or Igbo land or Africa in general; however, different cultural groups may have different ways of telling their stories. Emeagwali and Sefa Dei (2014) reason that what is vital for Indigenous storytelling are recollections of the past inherited from earlier generations and contemporaries and transmitted into diverse forms of verbal testimonies, including the following: oral narratives, poetry, songs, legends, proverbs, interviews, and so on. The transmission process may have involved public performances or may have been embedded in popular culture. These oral narratives continue to supplement other historical sources of information. In some cases, they have been more valuable than written documents. According to Emeagwali and Sefa, the goal of oral narratives may be the celebration of success and conquest of doubts, fears, and uncertainties; testimonies about trials, tribulations, and heroic deeds in the past, historical mythology.

Emeagwali and Sefa Dei (2014) further add that oral storytelling may collectively reveal local or family accounts or the history of lineages, family privileges and inheritance, migration of specific people or extended families and communities to where there are located, inspirational stories to guide generations, popular cultural belief system, or local fauna, and ecology. I am totally in support of Emeagwali and Sefa Dei views on oral storytelling traditions. Before the interruption of storytelling traditions of Abam by the colonialists, Abam had a rich cultural heritage. The oral narrative was one of the live wires of the Abam cultural heritage. Traditional storytelling in Igbo land and Abam refers to tales told in the home by the fireside, 'usekwu' sitting room 'obi,' and in the wider community. Stories were incorporated in the Abam dances such as Abam war dance, and women dance. These dances, especially Abam war dance reminded the Abam people of their historical origin.

There is no gainsaying that storytelling is part of life for Indigenous people as their existence is perceived to be incomplete without these stories. The Abam and Igbo tribe in general, believe strongly in oral narratives transmitted from one generation to another, using Indigenous language and cultural symbols as the vehicle of transmission of these narratives. Oral narratives are "the means by which knowledge is reproduced, preserved and convey cultural heritage from generation to generation" (Hulan & Eigenbrod, 2008, p. 7). Of course, oral tradition is not possible without oral communication through language.

Language and Storytelling Traditions

Hornberger and Mckay (2010) stated that "If we subscribe to the position that linguistic communities are not homogeneous and consensual but often heterogeneous and conflicted, we need to understand power relations between individuals, communities, and nations" (p. 350). Bourdieu (1977) notes that the value ascribed to speech in communicating people's idea through storytelling or otherwise cannot be understood apart from the person who speaks and the person who speaks cannot be understood apart from the larger network of people who share the same language. In their essay on oral traditions of Kumeyaay community of Baja California Norte, Mexico, Field and Cuero (2012) observed that for many Indigenous communities, the language in which a story is conveyed is just as valuable to the community as the content of the story, and both require the careful attention of the researcher of such language community. This position reflects the true nature of the Indigenous communities of the world, where local dialects are important emblems of cultural and group identity.

Most Indigenous stories are written with a different language, not in the language in which the story was originally told. This may discredit or alter the original intention of the story and exclude the majority of audiences the story was meant for because they may not understand the written language. In a study conducted by Gudhlanga and Makaudze (2012) regarding Indigenous languages in Zimbabwe, the study participants pointed out the following:

> Opportunity to enjoy some degree of flexibility: Conversation in an Indigenous language gives participants some degree of flexibility. They stated that it is difficult to put across some of their wishes in a foreign language. They drew examples from traditional praise poetry, which at times is wrongly translated and during the process, some of the original meaning is lost (p. 26).

McLeod (2001) further highlights the importance of language by saying, "[E]very time a story is told, every time one word of Indigenous language is spoken, we are resisting the deconstruction of our collective memory" (p. 31). McLeod's viewpoint speaks to the nexus between language and story in awakening the collective memory of the people. Of course, language is a vehicle in which Indigenous stories are being conveyed.

The level of extinction suffered by Indigenous languages is a source of worry. Foucault (1972) in his *Archaeology of knowledge* pointed out that the change and transformation of language "discourse is snatched from the law of development and established in a discontinuous atemporarily. It is immobilized in fragments: precarious splinters of eternity" (p. 166). The above view is shared by Gudhlanga and Makaudze (2012) who worry about the near extinction of the Indigenous languages of the African continent and Indigenous people the world over considering globalization. As they expressed, "African continent of the 21st century faces a major challenge of failing to use its Indigenous languages and if such a scenario is not seriously looked at would lead to an extinction of some of them" (p. 21).

Onyejieke (2010) has observed that the native Abam language is becoming extinct to the extent that the elderly people in the Abam villages who did not have the opportunity to acquire western education now find it difficult to communicate with the new generations. They need an interpreter to communicate with their grandchildren who come home from cities. Battiste (2008) corroborated Onyejieke's view when she said that knowledge transmission among the Indigenous people is threatened "due to the destruction of their language and culture" (p. 508) by the colonialists. She feared that if nothing were done urgently, the Indigenous people would lose their entire existence.

Furthermore, Mungwini (2012) said, "The violence, threat of extirpation or marginalization of Indigenous African values did not end with the end of colonialism, but it persists and is being championed by Africans as they seek to recognize themselves in the ideals of the Enlightenment" (p. 347). If the Indigenous languages become completely extirpated, how then could Indigenous stories be told? It is worthy of note here that the colonizers might have officially taken down their flags, but they are still in charge using their languages throughout Africa as an instrument of trade, instruction, research, and official government languages (Bamgboes, 1991; Benjamin, 1994; Chilisa, 2012). This may have a negative effect on the practice and the transmission of storytelling traditions among the Indigenous societies.

The Transfer of Knowledge Through Stories

In the course of my master's thesis, I came across several authors and theories of knowledge transmission. A review of a cultural theory of learning by Wenger (1998) concludes that learning or knowledge is a social activity. This implies that knowledge is not an individual affair; rather it takes place within a social milieu. People negotiate and renegotiate meaning they give to learning to suit the context. As Hulan and Eigenbrod (2008) suggest, "Indigenous people shared their knowledge systems with each other, and they simply wowed each other with their fanciful modifications to the original idea" (p. 4). Oral traditions receive the voice of authenticity and authority from family members who have experienced life in each setting or community and have acquired a great deal of knowledge as a result of a long period of social interaction. The main point here is that Indigenous people usually have occupied a certain area of land for an extended number of years. Their epistemology and worldviews are formed as a result of long years of experience and accumulated knowledge in the location (Hulan and Eigenbrod, 2008). It could be deduced here that Indigenous stories are as old as the land and can hold information about the land from generation to generation. However, these stories would only remain with the land if nothing interrupted the process of transmission.

Consequently, Okpewho (1992) corroborated the work of Charles Darwin on evolution in his work, *Oral Tradition* when he said that cultural evolutionists presume that stories found among present-day Indigenous people have survived in their memories through several generations of transmission. Hanson and Fox Griffith (2016) conducted a study on intergenerational learning in Indigenous textiles among Indigenous peoples in Canada (Saskatchewan) and Chile. They discovered that Indigenous knowledge ideas, patterns and stories remained among the people when they are passed on to the succeeding generations. In the same manner, the Igbo people and Abam in particular had a system that was already put in place from succeeding generations about how their younger generations were being enculturated through storytelling. The Indigenous people Abam started early in life to pass these stories to the younger generations.

Challenges of Oral Storytelling Traditions of Abam

From the study, I discovered that globalization is an upshot of colonialism and it attempts towards reconfiguring the world towards Western market orientations (Blaser, 2010; Chilisa, 2012). The Indigenous people of Abam seem to be strangers in the global culture that undermines, 'if not destroys' their epistemologies, their languages; ontology, and ways of living. This finding is in line with Kovach's (2012) view that the colonial outlook of our ancestors' time has shifted, while the relationship continues undiminished. This manifests at the international level as "globalization and consumerism, which feed an economic system that preys on Mother Earth striving to sustain the human species even as we abuse her" (p. 76). Kovach discusses how colonialism was perpetuated through globalization thereby extending the colonial legacies that deny the colonized their autonomy of choice.

Speaking on how globalization has undermined the autonomy of the Indigenous people, Held (cited in Blaser, 2010) laments on how globalization has affected the choices of the Indigenous people. He says that globalization has significantly affected the formulation of aims, beliefs and choice pattern of the Indigenous people on how to seek out ways to participate in socio-economic life in pursuit of their choices. He further states that globalization has negatively affected the ability of the Indigenous people to evaluate their success through "Self-reflection based on empirical evidence and phenomenological experience in working towards these aims" (p. 5). This action undermined the capacity of the Indigenous people to practice their cultural heritage, storytelling inclusive. This seems to "separate individual human beings and societies from the natural worlds of which they are a part" (p. 6). This kind of subordination by which the Indigenous people were stripped of their choice ability and personal responsibilities aided the entrenchment of alienation and power relations between the colonizers and the colonized. It could as well be the origin of the concept of *othering*[66] that tends to divide the world into two- developed and the third world, etc.

Ways of Revitalizing the Indigenous People's Language

From the research, it was discovered that oral storytelling and intergenerational would be impossible without the people's language. Therefore, the study also suggested ways of revitalizing the Indigenous people's languages in the following ways: Encouraging parents to teach their children the indigenous language and incorporating Indigenous languages in formal institutions.

Encouraging Parents to Teach Their Children Their Indigenous Language

The participants stressed that it was difficult to teach Abam stories without understanding Abam local dialect. They suggested the need to encourage parents to teach their children the local dialect of Abam at home since the children would still learn the English language at school. Teaching the children their local dialect of Abam at home will be a double advantage to the child to first know the language of their birth and the second language. During FGD, one of the participants bemoaned the current situation where the upcoming generations of the Abam people could no longer interact with their local dialect. They want to speak English like the Europeans. She said that the situation could be handled if the parents start teaching their children Abam local dialect from childhood. The participants suggested passing on this information in every gathering that involved men and women.

Incorporating Indigenous Languages in Formal Institutions

The research participants suggested that the Indigenous communities should build synergy with formal institutions, especially schools and religious institutions to work out modalities to incorporate the language of the host communities in their operations. The synergy would help the communities to be part of what was happening in the schools within their communities as well as incorporate the Indigenous language in the teaching curriculum of the schools. In a similar way, if a religious teaching is transmitted through the language of the host communities, it will promote learning.

Conclusion

There is no gainsaying that language, oral traditions, and intergenerational learning are the tripartite elements that form the identity of the human race, the Indigenous people in particular. The people will systematically cease to exist once these three elements are missing. It is disheartening that most Indigenous people are living in the past or worst still what Macedo (2000) calls "being for others" (p. 25). This work is an awakening call for the Indigenous people to retrace their steps and reclaim their identities.

References

Achebe, C (1958). *Things fall apart.* New York, NY: Anchors Books.

Baldasaro, M. M., Maldonado, N., & Baltes, B. (2014). Storytelling to teach cultural awareness: The right story at the right time. *Journal of Learning Landscapes* 7(2), pp. 219-231.

Bamgbose, A. (1991). *Language and the nation: The language question in subsaharan Africa.* Edinburgh, Scotland: Edinburgh University Press.

Battiste, M (2008). Research ethics for protecting Indigenous knowledge and heritage: Institutional responsibilities. In Denzin, N., Lincoln., & Smith, L (Eds.), *Handbook of critical and indigenous methodologies* (pp. 497-510). Los Angeles, CA: Sage Publications.

Benjamin, J. (1994). Language and the struggle for racial equality in the development of a non-racial southern African nation. In R. Fardon, and G. Furniss, (Eds.) *African languages, development and the State* (pp. 97-110). Abingdon, London: Routledge.

Blaser, M. (2010). *Storytelling globalization: From the Chaco and beyond.* Durham, NC: Duke University Press.

Bourdieu, P. (1977). The economics of linguistic exchanges. *Social Science Information,* 16(6), pp. 645-668.

Chilisa, B. (2012). *Indigenous research methodologies.* Washington DC: Sage Publications.

Deloria, V., Jr. (2002). *Evolution criticism, and other modern myths: A critical inquiry.* Golden, Co: Fulcrum.

Emeagwali, G and Dei, J. G .[Eds.] (2014). *African Indigenous knowledge and the disciplines.* Boston, MA: Sense Publishers.

Fanon, F (1967). *The wretched of the earth.* London, England: Clays Ltd, St Ives plc.

Field, M and Cuero, M. J. (2012). Kumeyaay oral tradition, cultural identity, and language revitalization. Retrieved from: http://muse.jhu.edu/article/520813.

Foucault, M. (1972). The archaeology of knowledge and discourse on language. New York, NY: Pantheon Books.

Freire, P (1970). Pedagogy of the Oppressed. New York, NY: Continuum

Gudhlanga, E. S and Makaudze, G (2012). Battling against marginalisation: Towards the elevation of Indigenous languages in Zimbabwe. Ife PsychologIA 20(2) pp. 21-30

Hanson, C and Fox Griffith, H (2016). Engaging with Indigenous communities. The Engaged Scholar Journal: Community-Engaged Research, Teaching and Learning 2(1) pp. 225-245.

Hornberger, N. & Mckay, S (2010). Language and identity in *Sociolinguistics and language education*. Toronto, ON: Multilingual Matters.

Hulan, R. & Eigenbrod, R [Eds.] (2008). *Aboriginal oral traditions: Theory, practice, ethics*. Halifax, NS: Fernwood Publishing.

Kovach, M. (2012). *Indigenous methodologies: Characteristics, conversations, and contexts*. Toronto, ON: University of Toronto Press.

Kramsh, C (1998). *Language and culture*. Berkley, CA: Oxford University Press.

Macedo, D (2000) *Pedagogy of the Oppressed Paulo Freire: Thirtieth anniversary edition*. New York, NY: Continuum.

McLeod, N. (2001). Coming home through stories. In G.A. Rufo. (Ed), *(Ad)dressing our words: Aboriginal perspectives on Aboriginal literatures* (pp. 17-36). Penticton, BC: Theytus Books Ltd.

Mungwini, P. (2012). Surveillance and cultural panopticism: Situating Foucault in African modernities. *South African Journal of Philosophy* 31(2) p. 340-353.

National Population Commission (2011). *Abia State population subdivision*. Retrieved from: http://www.citypopulation.de/php/nigeriaadmin.php?admlid=NGA001.

Nielson, C.R. (2013). *New approaches to religion and power: Foucault, Douglass, Fanon, and Scotus in dialogue on social construction and freedom*. New York, NY: Palgrave Macmillan.

Obuba, N. E. (2008). *The history and culture of Ohafia*. Ebem Ohafia, Nigeria: Lintdsons Publications.

Odege, O (2001). Oral tradition and modern storytelling: Revisiting Chinua Achebe's short stories. Retrieved from: https://journals.lib.unb.ca/index.php/ifr/article/view/7692/8749

Okpewho, I. (1992). *African oral literature*. Bloomington: Indiana University Press.

Onyejieke, M. O. (2010). *Socio-political and economic functions of market among the Igbo: Ethnography of Abam in Arochukwu Local Government Area of Abia State, Nigeria*. Unpublished thesis: University of Nigeria, Nsukka.

Tedlock, D (1971). On the translation of style in oral narrative. *Journal of American Folklore* 84(331), pp. 114-133.

Wenger, E. (1998). *Community of practice, meaning, and identity*. Cambridge, UK: Cambridge University Press.

notes

[66] *Othering* is use here to denote the European concepts of themselves and others. It splits the world into binary-European colonizers and others, where European colonizers were quintessence of everything good and others who were the colonized were regarded by the colonizers as evil that needed to be fixed (Nielson, 2013).

Chapter Fourteen

Han—Korean—Ontology
Similarities and Differences from Indigenous Ontologies

JuSung Kim

> The
> cosmic energy
> of our universe, Higgs
> boson that is an extremely infinitesimal
> particle of atomic substance as the primary
> cause or creator, should not be extinct or extinguished,
> but it should continue to exist in space and
> time, in fact, in the cyclic endless and
> eternal process of the creation
> and extinction of all the
> phenomenal objects
> elements/new
> planets.

(Kang, 2015, p. 38-39)

Prologue

We are talking about Han ontology in this chapter with an itinerary as follows: Korean philosophy and Han; Han ontology and its atmas; an atma of oneness; an atma of collective spirit; an atma of brightness and hope; an atma of circular and immortal spirits; and an epilogue ending with a wholistic, ontological riddle as storytelling. Atma is understood as true character, genuine personality/self/I, and vitality, but atma cannot exist without considering our cosmos (Kim, 2018).

Experimenting with structure, I started my writing with a circle-like shape which stands for the heaven/sky/dad; in the middle of this chapter, the paragraphs are all square/rectangular shapes to symbolize the earth/mom. The last paragraph of my writing ends with a triangle shape representing humans/children as a new life created through interrelationships between the heaven/dad and the earth/mom. These circle, square/rectangular, and triangle shapes harmonize and balance each other to reach the final destination of their journey that is another beginning, a new journey. Based on an orientation of Korean and Indigenous philosophies, I have made a deliberate effort to resist the conventional way of writing that is engrained and propelled by a linear Western philosophy. Writing different in styles (e.g., poetics, cartoon, drawing) can move us beyond the scientific objectivity, truth, and authority of traditional writing (Markides, 2018; Meyer, 2008; Wilson, 2008).

Korean Philosophy and Han

Rarely do we pay close attention to Korean philosophy. Yet, Korean philosophy plays a nurturing-mother role in giving rise to Korean ontology, epistemology, axiology, methodology, and vitalogy (e.g., a branch of philosophy studying the virtue of life and living). When Korean philosophies are understood, they should be called *Han* (한; 韓) philosophy. Kovach (2012) writes "Reclaiming is naming, and identifying Indigenous inquiry is a political act" (p. 176). The term Han originates from the number one (- = Hana = 하나), but it transcends the numeric number one. The term Han appears simple at the beginning but profound at the end. Let us dig a little deeper to better comprehend contexts of Korean philosophy. Regarding a spiritual root of Han identity, Han has multiple and complex meanings: one/oneness, all, heaven/sky, prime, full, sacred, ultimate, sun rising nation, respecting the sun, hope, bright, light, big, high, many, great, gigantic, unity, God, king, leader, right, or same (Donga, 1987;

Naver, 2016). These meanings of Han are very important because they express an essence of Han (Korea), Han philosophies, and Han cultural practices.

Han Onthology and its Atma

I am you; you are me; therefore, they are me and you = us.

Ontology is defined as a branch of philosophy to study the nature of realities and existences. That is, ontology delves into the fundamental and global nature and structure of samjae (the heaven/sky, humans, the earth) in the cosmos. Naturally, an origin of Han ontology runs from the *wellspring* of Korean philosophy. In this sense, Han ontology is related to living and breathing per se (Kang, 2015; 2017; Lee, 2016). The reason is when we are born, we grow, we age, die, and return to nature and keep repeating the same cycle of these intricate relationships within samjae. If the essence of Han philosophy is life/living, I can see Han ontology as an organic living entity rather than a simple cognitive concept/idea. Why? Because Han ontology lives in harmony with our body, mind, and spirit as well as with samjae in everyday life (An, 1996; Jo, 2016; Kang, 2015; 2017: Kim, 1997; Lee, 2016).

Based on these assumptions, some crucial atmas characterize Han ontology. Examples of such atmas include oneness and the unity in trinity; collective spirits, brightness and hope spirits; and circular and immortal thoughts (An, 1996; Choi, 2012; Jo, 2016; Kang, 2017; Kim, 1997). All these atmas of Han ontology are deeply related to epistemology, methodology, axiology, and vitalogy. Thinking of a research paradigm as an inseparable circle, Wilson (2008) understands that "The ontology and epistemology are based upon a process of relationships that form a mutual reality. The axiology and methodology are based upon maintaining accountability to these relationships" (p. 71). However, to the best of my knowledge, none of the current literature specifically draws upon vitalogy as part of conceptualizing philosophies of Han or Indigenous paradigms, although many mentioned the importance of diverse spirits and realities.

An Atma of Oneness

Unity/oneness would represent one of the most important qualities of Han ontology. A spirit of oneness indicates the root of all existences and the cosmic phenomena. It is a metaphysical concept that implies an infinite beginning and ending or no start and no finish of samjae. In fact, the prototypical nature of Han philosophy centres on oneness or unity through harmony, balance, and cooperation. That is, Han philosophy can embrace virtues of cosmic unity and peace (An, 1996; Baker, 2007; Kang, 2017; Rhee, 2007). The term oneness implies that heaven, earth, and humanity, which are all essential elements of the one universe, construct a cosmic unity. This implies that we are one and the same irrespective of skin tones or cultural/ethnic groups. "In other words, Hananim (the Supreme one) philosophy sees all human beings as equally valuable and equally worthy of respect" (Baker, 2007, p. 475).

However, Han philosophy is not the only one explaining the virtue of oneness. A transnational African feminism emphasizes the idea of "an age-old concept of a human oneness or human wholeness" (Dillard & Okpalaoka, 2013, p. 321). Oneness means an infinite magnitude that is seemingly impossible to explain in the mathematical, reasoned, and physical ways that can be understood from a Western perspective (Lee, 2008). Thus, oneness is not a numerical notion of one, but oneness has profound spiritual meanings that transcend a simple Arabic number one. That being said, the concept of oneness implies a rudimentary meaning regarding the creation of samjae on which Han philosophy and its ontology is based.

Oneness alludes to the unity of the three elements of samjae via harmony and balance. Simply put, oneness is trinity (the trinity in unity), and trinity is oneness (the unity in trinity) (An, 1996; Choi, 2012; Kang, 2015; Lee, 2008). To better understand this paradox, such a concept can be put into a paradoxical mathematical equation: 1 the heaven + 1 the earth + 1 humans = 3 oneness/unity and 1 the heaven = 1 the earth = 1 humans = 1 oneness. Our ancestors think of the heaven (e.g., the sun, sky, Polaris, etc.), humans (e.g., all races and ethnicities), and the earth (e.g., plants, animal, water, etc.) as interconnected organic entities through harmony, balance, and cooperation. Consequently, samjae cannot be separated into individual elements because samjae itself is *not* an independent object but interrelated living unities. In other words, an original root of oneness is holistically one but includes 'many-ness' within one at the same time (An, 1996; Baker, 2007; Lee, 2008). This paradoxical idea of samjae is the central tenet of Han philosophy and practice. For such a paradox to exist, the spirits of harmony, balance, and cooperation, are required among the three elements of samjae. Likewise, African philosophy has a similar ontology, saying "*I am we; I am because we are; we are because I am, I am in you, you are in me*" (Chilisa, 2012, p. 108). Thus,

CHAPTER FOURTEEN

oneness, embedded with the elemental spirits of samjae, is an important ontological assumption of Han philosophy.

Only when each unity in samjae harmonizes and balances each other in accordance with the law of the heavenly movement of the cosmos, can trinity in samjae exist and prosper (Kang, 2015; 2017). For this reason, it is easy to see how the virtue of Han trinity does not fit with the Western notion of dualism, separating nature-human, subject-object, man-woman, or black-white. This taken-for-granted polemical universe has caused "untold horror and helped create a rigid epistemology we now assume cannot evolve" (Meyer, 2008, p. 225). This dualism acts to encourage human- and self-focused hierarchical ideologies and practices in order to achieve what an individual wants at the expense of groups, others, and nature. Thus, spirits of competition, measurement, struggle, and control rather than harmony, balance, and cooperation tend to be dominant modes of ontological references to the actions of an individual (Baker, 2007; Darder, 2015; Ermine, 1995 as cited in Markides, 2018; Hart, 2010; Meyer, 2008; Smith, 2012). In contrast, Han worldviews highlight interconnected relationships among body, mind, spirit, and nature (e.g., cycle and life) rather than separate and fragmented phenomena seen through Western paradigms (e.g., linear and data-driven).

Borrowing from a geometric notion of triangle, the trinity concept of Han ontology appears to be the most stable vitality embracing harmony, balance, and cooperation/symbiosis rather than the dichotomous idea that symbolizes struggle, power/control, and competition. Similarly, Aluli-Meyer (2008) suggests that the tetrahedron composed of four triangular faces is "the sacred geometry of infinity, energy, and the perfect balance of equilibrium found in post quantum physics" (p. 225). Naturally, the development and prosperity of nature, groups, and others (samjae) matter as much as self-development and personal interest.

An Atma of Collective Spirit

Given the importance of oneness through harmony and balance, an atma of collective spirit is another hallmark of Han ontology. An embodiment of collective spirit would not be possible without taking into account the equation of harmony and balance within samjae. To become "oneness" requires the collective spirits and practices for the common good, in which samjae lives and thrives. The prominent Canadian scholar of Korean studies Don Baker argues that:

> Hana (one) in Hananim (the Supreme One) means that all things in the universe are essentially the same thing, in that everything in the universe is

interrelated and intermingled and forms one and only one universe. This means that Hananim, human beings, and all the animals in the animal kingdom have the same foundation---the universe itself. That is why a philosophy with belief in Hananim at its core must be a philosophy that emphasizes peace and life. (2007, p. 474)

The quest of Han ontology is to construct collective community and society. Collective spirits emphasize the practice of the socially desirable morals and behaviours for human beings in everyday life in order to live for others and community/nation as well as nature (Jeong & Kang, 2013; Lee, 2016). Along with the value of personal human development, the principles of harmony and collectivism are intended to be lived out in the light of giving love, caring/sharing, and showing mercy/homage to our brothers and sisters (Jeong & Kang, 2013; Lee, 2016). Caring for our parents at home and for others in our community can be a starting point to transfer such spirits to our neighbours, our country, the world, and even the cosmos beyond national boundaries. In this manner, the focus on the interrelationships of samaje, rather than a separated self, leads to a communal life and symbiotic society.

Baker goes as far as to say that:

We should treat the simplest forms of life with the same respect we show Hananim and should hold them just as dear. If that's the case, how much more should we human beings respect each other, love each other, and treat each other as valuable in our own right? If we all do that, then there will be peace on earth. (2007, p. 474)

This collectivism culture highlights the virtues of human interdependence, group orientation, positive relationships, and wholism. From the perspective of collectivism culture, the universe is understood as interconnected webs of people, society, and nature (Kang, 2015; 2017; Oyserman, Coon, & Kemmelmeier, 2002). As the old saying goes, "The nail that sticks up shall be hammered down," which succinctly represents the value of group harmony and the social connectedness/relatedness/collectivism of Han ontology.

An Atma of Brightness and Hope

Han ontology has the spirits of brightness, hope, and human completion. What this means is that we, humans, can achieve human completion and self-actualization (e.g., good citizen or saint) through continuous practices in everyday life (An, 1996; Jeong & Kang, 2013; Lee, 2008). As such, we have a strong belief in humans specifically and samjae broadly that we can become God-like figures (not Abrahamic gods/goddesses) or the cosmos, as long as we make ongoing efforts to become them across our life course. Each element of samjae embraces the other two elements of samjae. That is why the heaven, the earth, and human beings have the shared atmas among them that reflect love and sincere care. Thus, human beings can nurture these atmas as if the heaven and the earth provide humans with such atmas. Anyone, regardless of who they are, can become a wise person/saint (Jeong & Kang, 2013; Kang, 2015; Lee, 2008; Park & Jeong, 2014) who attains the ultimate wisdom of the heavenly path. This is a realization of the importance of vitality and respect for all life.

Suffice it to say, God-like figures are everywhere and may exist at any time (e.g., our parents, ancestors, pets, friends, trees, etc.). Hence, we should treat samjae with respect and honour because they have the spirits of the God-like entities/saints and the vitality of life (Baker, 2007; Kang, 2015; 2017). Every aspect of our ancient social systems and community praxis is designed to help us achieve our ethical human completion/self-actualization through improving ourself in community practices in our everyday life. The practices of everyday life are connected to the journey, in the service of achieving self-completion and self-actualization (e.g., good citizenship) that often lead to group and collective prosperity and social justices (Jeong & Kang, 2013; Park & Jeong, 2014).

An Atma of Circular and Immortal Spirits

Circular and immortal virtues of Han ontology cannot be ignored either. The belief that 'forms come and go, but spirits will resurrect' clearly reflects Han ontology. The prominent Korean folklore scholar Kim Tae Gon (1997) shows us that a worldview of an inner world (e.g., after life belief) is based on the premise that our spirit is immortal and continues to live forever. The core of this circular, immortal worldview is an infinity of life so that the essence of such ontology could embrace a dimension of mythic thought about living that extends and develops our life into infinity (Kim, 1997). In doing so, our ancestors liberate us, such that we can cope with our apocalyptic fears and anxieties over our deaths (Kim, 1997). Naturally, a journey of Samjae keeps coming, going, and repeating itself continuously; there is no beginning and no ending (An, 1996; Kang, 2015; Kim, 2004). In Han ontology, truth or reincarnation can be countless because atma, the principle of the cosmos, always exists without beginning and ending (Naver Encyclopedia, 2018).

From what our ancestors have learned by observing the cosmic movements (samjae), they teach us that samjae operates in the infinite and reciprocal ways of the cosmos across a long human history (Cajete, 2000; Kang, 2015; 2017). Thus, circular Han philosophy (An, 1996; Kang, 2017; Kim, 1997; Lee, 2016) contrasts with the idea of linear thought in Western philosophy (Darder, 2015; Ermine, 1995 as cited in Markides, 2018; Hart, 2010; Smith, 2012). Each season in a specific year is seemly gone, but it will keep coming back next year and so on. To support this ontological spirit, there is a Korean proverb saying that "Humans come from the earth and return to it," and this Korean proverb can be proven relevant these days supported by Steven Hawking's Big Bang and Black Hole theories arguing that subatomic substances (e.g., Higgs boson of an infinitesimal particle = $10^{-44} \times 10^{-33}$) have created the cosmos (Kang, 2015; 2017).

Combining both perspectives mentioned above, we can see that our ancestors are living and breathing now and will keep living with us in the future (An, 1996; Kang, 2015; 2017). Thus, Koreans hold memorial rites, the Lunar New Year, and Thanksgiving Day for worshipping our ancestors every year, because we believe that our ancestors co-exist with us and considered them to be living spirits (Kim, 1997; Kang, 2015; 2017; Lee, 2016). In this sense, the notions of time-space, for the past, the present, and the future, can be co-existing beyond the traditional concept of a separate time and space, just as the three elements of samjae are interconnected and circular/immortal because we are one in trinity as inseparable organic entities (An, 1996; Baker, 2007).

Unfortunately, these cultural beliefs and practices, along with Han philosophy, have been continuously eroded since the advent of Christianity in Korea (An, 1996; Baker, 2007; Park & Jeong, 2014). If we have faith in this circular/immortal ontology, then we are less likely to be afraid of death because our life is not limited/linear. Looking through a circular/immortal eye, death is just another rite of passage in life, so there is less religious fanaticism. Given the emphasis of cycles in life, believers are less likely to waste time and energy on self-centred, pleasure seeking. The idea of aging is also viewed differently in our Han ontological eye.

We are concluding the atma of circular and immortal spirit by citing the first and last clauses of the Korean bible, "The Heavenly Manu's Light Sutra" offers: "One began from nothing but one… The end of one is nothing but one" (Rhee, 2006).

CHAPTER FOURTEEN

Epilogue

In Han ontology there are similarities among oneness; the unity in trinity; spirits of collectivism, brightness, and hope; and circular/immortal thoughts. Han ontology is connected to epistemology and vitalology. The traditional Korean shamanism researcher, Jo Seong Je (2016), reminds us that all the livings and the non-livings in the cosmos have life; valuing life, loving, and caring for each other are the ways of a Han spirit that allow all of us (the heaven, the earth, and human beings) to live/co-exist together. Likewise, Kim Jeong Min (2016) emphasizes the importance of a *pan-global worldview,* as our ethnicities and races are directly and indirectly connected in the globalized *One* world. The Han ontology shared in this chapter is but one of the Han-Korean ontologies. I encourage readers to further explore other Han ontologies.

As
a closing remark
of this chapter, let me
share one of the Korean riddles
that we used to hear from our grannies,
as it explains our Han onto-/epistemology. Our
grannies asked their grand kids a riddle like this "Do you know
how many trees are in the world?" The grand kids wander around
seeking the answer to this riddle. All the while, they are thinking about
their immediate surroundings first and then they expand their boundaries.
They try to count the number of trees starting from their yards,
neighbourhoods, communities, provinces, nations, even to the world.
However, they cannot find any clue of how to answer the riddle. After
many days, they cannot help but ask their grannies for the answer.

"Grannies, please
teach us the number
of trees in the world." Grannies
reply to their grand kids' begging
"Shall I give you the answer for the number of
trees in the world? The number of trees in the world
is the same as the riddle for fish in the sea." Do you see
how our ancestors teach us the interrelated relationships/ontologies
among the three elements of samjae (e.g. the heaven, the earth, and
human beings) through this wholistic, onto-/epistemological riddle? If you

did, then it's time to climb down the mountain. Otherwise, keep searching for a lesson from this riddle. Here our story ends...

References

An, C. B. (1996). *The lost Bae-Dal thought and the origin of Eastern thoughts*. Seoul, Korea: The Guk-Hak Archive Council.

Baker, D. (2007). The Korean god is not the Christian god: Taejonggyo's challenge to foreign religions. In R. E. Buswell Jr. (Ed.), *Religions of Korea in practice* (pp. 464-475). Princeton, USA: Princeton University Press.

Cajete, G. (2000). *Native science: Natural laws of interdependence*. Santa Fe, USA: Clear Light Books.

Chilisa, B. (2012). *Indigenous research methodologies*. Los Angeles, USA: SAGE.

Choi, J. M. (2012). *The aesthetic thought of Korean traditional music. Korean traditional music and rhythm study 2*. Seoul, Korea.

Darder, A. (2015). Decolonizing interpretive research: A critical bicultural methodology for social change. *The International Education Journal: Comparative Perspectives, 14*(2), 63-77.

Dillard, C. B., & Okpalaoka, C. (2013). Feminist qualitative research in the millennium's first decade: Developments, challenges, prospects. In N. K. Denzin & Y. S. Lincoln (Eds.), *The landscape of qualitative research: Theories and issues* (4th ed., pp. 305-337). Thousand Oaks, USA: SAGE.

Donga Korean Dictionary. (1993). Seoul, Korea: Donga Publishing.

Hart, M. A. (2010). Indigenous worldviews, knowledge, and research: The development of an Indigenous research paradigm. *Journal of Indigenous Voices in Social Work, 1*(1), 1-16.

Jeong, Y, H., & Kang, J. M. (2013). Hongiginkan humanitarian and the development model of creative economy. *Humanity Policy Journal, 17*, 7-134.

Jo, S. J. (2016). *Musok (Shamanism) stories in ancient Korean history I*. Seoul, Korea: Narute.

Kang, S. W. (2015). *The heavenly manu's light sutra & Dhanuraja authentic politics*. Seoul, Korea: Diyo-Sun Myung-Ryun Royal Academy.

Kang, S. W. (2017). *Critical essay: Exegenesis of errors exposed to light ever since cir. 600 years*. Seoul, Korea: Diyo-Sung Myung-Ryun Academy.

Kim, J. S. (2018). Korean Indigenous epistemologies with notes on the corresponding epistemologies of Indigenous scholarship. In J. Markides, & L. Forsythe (Eds.), *Looking back and living forward: Indigenous research rising up* (pp. 105-113). Leiden, NL: Brill | Sense.

Kim, J. M. (2016). *A nation of Dangun: Kazakhstan*. Seoul, Korea: Global Contents.

Kim, S. D. (2004). *Kim Seong Dong's Thousand words: The principle of the heaven and the tao of the earth*. Kyunggi, Korea: Cheongyeonsa.

Kim, T. G. (1997). *Musok (Shamanism) of Korea*. Seoul, Korea: Daewonsa Publishing.

Kovach, M. (2012). *Indigenous methodologies: Characteristics, conversations, and contexts*. Toronto, Canada: University of Toronto Press.

Lee, B. Y. (2016). The humanistic spirits in the Korean cultural heritage and its globalization. The 8th World Congress of Korean Studies. *Korean Culture, Seeking Insights for the Future*. Philadelphia, the University of Pennsylvania, USA. October 5-7, 2016.

Lee, K. M. (2008). *A study of taekwondo spirit*. Seoul, Korea: Taekwon Maru.

Markides, J. (2018). Reconciling an ethical framework for living well in the world of research. In J. Markides, & L. Forsythe (Eds.), *Looking back and living forward: Indigenous research rising up* (pp. 291-300). Leiden, NL: Brill | Sense.

Meyer, M. (2008). Indigenous and authentic: Hawaiian epistemology and the triangulation of meaning. In N. K. Denzin, Y.S. Lincoln, & L. T. Smith (Eds.), *Handbook of critical and Indigenous methodologies* (pp. 217-232). Los Angeles, USA: Sage.

Naver Encyclopedia. (2018). Knowledge search. Retrieved from https://www.naver.com/

Oyserman, D., Coon, H., & Kemmelmeier, M. (2002). Rethinking individualism and collectivism: Evaluation of theoretical assumptions and meta-analyses. *Psychological Bulletin, 128*, 3-72

Park, S. J., & Jeong, K. H. (2014). A study on the contents and directions of the uniqueness of Korean thought. *Korean Association of National Thought, 8*(4), 37-62.

Rhee, H. B. (2007). *Asian millenarianism: An interdisciplinary study of the Taiping and Tonghak rebellions in a global context.* Youngstown, USA: Cambria Press.

Smith, T. L. (2012). *Decolonizing methodologies: Research and Indigenous peoples.* London, UK: Zed Press.

Wilson, S. (2008). *Research is ceremony: Indigenous research methods.* Winnipeg, Canada: Frenwood Publishing.

Chapter Fifteen

Application of Malthusian Theory in Colonization Schemes in Canada

Kseniya Zaika

Thomas Malthus is one of the paradigmatic thinkers who formulated the basics of political economy for the emerging industrial capitalism in the second half of the 18th through the first half of the 19th centuries. The attitude given by Thomas Malthus to characterize capitalist economic activity communicates the basic imbalances in the human condition which are brought about in the modern era: "If no man could hope to rise or fear to fall in society, if industry did not bring its reward and indolence its punishment, we could not expect to see that animated activity in bettering our condition which now forms the master-spring of public prosperity".[67] Any scholar in Indigenous Studies discerns the diametrical opposition of capitalist parameters of public prosperity to, employing Marshall Sahlins' brilliant phrase, originally affluent and self-sustained non-capitalist economic wellbeing.

However, it should be contextualized that Malthus wrote his first essay during the decade (the 1790s) when population probably grew at twice the rate that had been the case during the decade when the Wealth of Nations by Adam Smith was written". That fact influenced the reception of Malthusian ideas in England and Scotland at that time. The development of industrial capitalism had brought a huge amount of pauperism in urban areas, especially in London. English urban pauperism had been caused, to a considerable extent, by such a factor as intensive industrial development in the last third of the 18th century. This condition had been accompanied by the marginalization of the masses of rural population and was complemented by serious crop failures experienced across Britain in 1794 and 1795. "The rise in food prices was aggravated by the wartime difficulty of purchasing grain from overseas (the war with revolutionary France). Adding to this difficulty was growing unemployment and rising population. The consequent hardship was felt especially by the labouring poor. Real distress combined with war weariness drove them to rioting".[68]

At the end of the 18th – the first half of the 19th centuries emigration to the New World was viewed in Britain as a means of "cleansing" the metropolitan land of the so-called "excessive population" and as a political instrument to reduce the revolutionary capacities of the destitute paupers. We know that industrialization eventually proved the Malthusian theory wrong, though during some decades before industrialization his principles "concerning the social psychology of preindustrial rural migrants provide partial answers to what motivated so many early nineteen century Britons to emigrate."[69] Some scholars argue that the European conquest of the New World instigated the population growth in England and Scotland: "By 1600, even before English settlements were established in the New World, the discovery had already transformed England significantly: London had already multiplied its size by a factor of more than three becoming the fourth largest city of Europe".[70] We can state that it is an intrinsic character of capitalism its exploitative schemes tend to produce "superfluous" population. "England's population did not grow between 1400 and 1500, but it multiplied by a factor of more than 3.5 between 1500 and 1800".[71] The Conquest of North America unlocked an array of employment opportunities for the British. The scope of the newly created jobs embraced all human activities because the politics of colonization required not only traders and servicemen, but also priests, agricultural resettlers, "educators" and so on. We should not ignore the fact that the new products found in North America and exported to Europe, such as potatoes and sugar, boosted the calories rationing and contributed to the gradual increase in the life expectancy of the colonizers.

Hence, emigration and intensive colonization of North America "alleviated" the transition to industrial capitalism in England and Scotland and helped to avoid "Malthusian stagnation." "Malthusian" stagnation is a term that might be used to describe the phenomenon of early industrial development in European countries, especially in England. That phenomenon is characterized by a dramatic increase of urban population during a couple of decades and a fundamental pauperization of the entire population in a country. The common feature of "Malthusian stagnation" is a fear of starvation. Malthusian recipes have proven wrong since the consolidation of the industrial capitalism, whose typical characteristic is "systematic growth in production," that has been achieved by an increasing level of exploitation and displacement of Aboriginal peoples in North America and other indigenous lands.

The Paris peace agreement of 1815, by which European powers agreed upon inter-national relations after the Napoleonic Wars, built the political

CHAPTER FIFTEEN

capacities for Britain to focus on domestic societal problems and consequently stimulated the shift to apply the recipes developed within political economic theories into practical actions. "Between 1820 and 1840 one of the most significant examples of a close relationship between the theoretical and the pragmatic in the social sciences (and social praxis) was Robert John Wilton-Horton. As Undersecretary of State for War and the Colonies from 1822 to 1828, ... Horton was able to apply the principles of political economy to a wide range of national social and economic problems".[72]

Wilmot Horton's mindset and his designs of state-assisted emigration schemes were influenced by the works of Thomas Malthus. Population economy and emigration recipes were part of the political economy in the early 19th century. Malthus considered emigration from Britain as a temporary measure that could not solve all the issues associated with the overpopulation though it could contribute to the transition to industrial capitalism and diminish the level of poverty in urban areas: "it is clear that labour will continue flowing into the market, with almost undiminished rapidity, while the means of employing and paying it have been essentially contracted. It is precisely under these circumstances that emigration is most useful as a temporary relief; and it is in these circumstances that Great Britain finds herself placed at present".[73] Robert Wilton-Horton, facing the burning issue of "redundant" and riotous population in Ireland additionally accommodated emigration on the general imperial scale of "progressive development". Contemplating the economic growth in the colonies and interrelating it directly to the amount of population. R. Wilton-Hortons wrote: "where the want of rapid improvement ... and the retardation of (their) general development ... arose mainly, if not entirely, from want of an adequate population."[74]

Horton's state-aided emigration plan as a national campaign was aimed at colonizing Upper Canada (An Outline of a Plan of Emigration to Upper Canada). Undoubtedly, Canada appeared to be one of the most attractive settlement destinations to accommodate the distressed Irish population and urban paupers from the metropolitan area. In the late 1810s, Thomas Malthus made a trip to Ireland, after which he accentuated in the 1817 edition of his Essay on Population that emigration could be "most useful as a temporary relief."[75]

In his letter to Horton concerning the Wakefield System of colonization of Australia and New Zealand, Malthus fully placed (re)settler colonization in accordance with the colonial political economy: "The true policy of the settler would undoubtedly be to cultivate that land from which he could derive the greatest profit."[76] In Malthusian view, intensive colonization would skyrocket not only the capital inflow and rapid economic development but also the "corresponding" growth of the population in the resettler colonies.

Malthus was a typical product of his time and his being more interested in the questions of overpopulation, he demonstrated racist stances towards the issues of political economy and cultural geography. Malthus regarded "non-Christian" practices in the non-European lands, for example, polygamy, as a means to restrain population growth. Although Malthusian theory was most often related to the studies of the densely inhabited agrarian societies, he "devoted more attention to North American Indians, Australian Aborigines and Polynesians than to the heartland of agrarian Asia – because explorers and voyagers with a scientific bent were more frequently reporting on the former in the second half of the 18th century".[77] In Chapter 3 of his essay on the Principle of Population", Malthus employed a classical colonial racist vocabulary analyzing the state of living of Aboriginal North Americans. His writing is abundant in such words as "savage" versus "civilized mode of production": "in the savage state it rarely happens that above one or two (children) in a family grow up to maturity. These facts prove the superior power of population to the means of subsistence in nations of hunters".[78] Making his assumptions on the ethnographic material that was available to him, Malthus merely contributed to the colonial myth-making and about Aboriginal peoples and colonial policies in North America and Australia, explaining the absence of population density in Aboriginal communities by the fact that it was harmonized to the amount of food accessible. Overall, a Malthusian method of demographic estimations was debunked soon after the industrial capitalist development began to demonstrate a systemic growth in production. Additionally, one of the main Malthusian assumptions, the foundation of population theory, that is the exponential population growth would outrun the subsistence eventually, was widely approved by capitalist proponents who insisted on the acceleration of industrial development and corresponding dispossession of Indigenous people of their lands in the colonies.

The historiographic worth of Malthusian intellectual legacy is compromised due to the fact that he based his assumptions on the ideologically-biased Jesuit accounts, the travelogues and the memoirs of the 18th-century voyagers.[79] While composing Chapter iv of the 1803 edition, Malthus wrote about Native Americans that "small independent tribes in the vast continent of America subsist nearly like the natives of

New Holland on the production of unassisted nature... hunting and fishing".[80] Additionally, one of the predominant intellectual inspiration for Thomas Malthus was Benjamin Franklin and his elaborations on American Manifest Destiny theory and western territorial expansions in North America. One of the pivotal Franklin's essays titled "Observations Concerning the Increase of Mankind, Peopling of Countries" was issued in 1751 just on the eve of the Seven Years Wars, a historical clash between France and Britain over North American colonies. In this essay Franklin elaborated the hypothesis of the exponential growth of population in North America and justified the need to facilitate industrial development of the colonies, thus postulating directly proportionate interrelatedness between the two phenomena. Stating that bush mode of production, which was typical though not prevailing for Native Americans could sustain only a small amount of population: "America is chiefly occupied by Indians, who subsist mostly by Hunting. But as the Hunter, of all Men, requires the greatest Quantity of Land from whence to draw his Subsistence, (the Husbandman subsisting on much less, the Gardner on still less, and the Manufacturer requiring least of all). ... Therefore, Britain should not too much restrain Manufactures in her Colonies. A wise and good Mother will not do it".[81]

Thomas Malthus familiarized himself with Franklin's essay after the completion of the first edition of his own essay, thus he mostly clarified his stance towards Native Americans in the second edition of the essay on the Principles of Population (1803). As mentioned above, the underpinning of Malthusian theory was the assumption that small numbers of Native population in Australia and North America had been predetermined by hunting and gathering mode of economic production: "Under such circumstances, that America should be very thinly peopled in proportion to its extent of territory is merely an exemplification of the obvious truth that population cannot increase without the food to support it".[82] In order to specify Malthusian "methodology" and its political implications for colonization of Canada, I need to refer to the history of colonial human geography of North America in general. In his 1803 edition of the essay, Malthus referred to the United States as a paradigmatic case to "prove" his assumptions, as the population of the states doubled from 1790 (3,929,214) to 1810 (7,239,881).[83] However, the above-mentioned statistics did not include, first, Native Americans; secondly, it is unfeasible to estimate the exact number of Native Americans suffered from genocide, and American Holocaust is estimated at 100 million people.[84] Furthermore, justifying the exponential growth of the U.S population from

1790 to 1810, Malthus indicated the land as a key component accountable for that process. Malthus's understanding of land as a resource was purely utilitarian: the land should be cultivated with the application of the appropriate institutions in order to contribute to the population growth: "plenty of good land" and social/legal systems to ensure its maximized cultivation."[85]

Final Note

Malthusian political economy and demographic estimates were effectively applied in substantiating colonization campaigns on the alleged scientific basis, even though his simplistic assumptions that population growth increases exponentially while food production grows linearly have never been confirmed by any empirical evidence. Malthus's political influence on the emerging (re)settlement schemes for Upper Canada can be explained by the fact that his views "reflected the overall societal situation and mind of the industrializing Victorian England."[86]

Also, we cannot disregard the fact that Malthusian inquiries into "moral restraints" and their influence on societal development has significantly contributed to the growth and elaboration of contemporary population economics and human (cultural) geography, not mentioning the notorious report presented by the Rome Club in 1972 "On the Limits to Growth" based on the computerized modelling of the global population growth and ecological confines of the resource extraction and industrialization. The testing ground for such a systemic approach to human development within the capitalist framework was sampled, in particular, in Upper and Lower Canada during the intensive colonization of the lands in the end of the 18th and the first third of the 19th centuries. I find it relevant to further investigate Malthus's influence on Darwinism and evolutionary anthropology, which throve in the second half of the 19th century and fueled the contemporary field of human geography, though this issue is out of scope in this paper.

References

Malthus T. R., An Essay on the Principle of Population as it Affects the Future Improvement of Society. With Remarks on the Speculations of Mr. Godwin, Mr. Condorcet, and other writes (1798)//in Silber Jacque, Malthus' Preconditions to Moral Restraint and Modern Population Economics, Genus, Vol. 42, #3/4;

Nobuhiko Nakazawa, Malthus's Political Views in 1798: a "Foxite Whig? //History of economic Review, Summer 2012;

CHAPTER FIFTEEN

Victorian Studies, vol. 58, #2, review Empire, Migration and Identity in the British World, edited by Kent Fedorowich and Andrew S. Thompson; Manchester: Manchester University Press, 2013;
Daniel Gorman, Victorian Studies, Winter 2016, pp. 339-341 (Review);
Juan-Carlos Cordoba. Malthus to Romer: On the Colonial Origins of the Industrial Revolution. Munich Personal RePEc Archive// https://mpra.ub.uni-muenchen.de/4466/1/MPRA_paper_4466.pdf;
Clark, G., 2005. The Condition of the Working Class in England, 1209-2004. Journal of Political Economics 113(6);
Edward Brynn, Politics and Economic Theory: Robert Wilmot Horton, 1820 – 1841, The Historian, February 1, 1972; vol. 34; iss. 2;
T. Malthus. Essay on Population, edition of 1817, vol. ii, pp. 304-5// In R. N. Ghosh. Malthus on Emigration and Colonization: Letter to Wilmot-Horton. Economica, New Series, Vol. 30, No. 117 (Feb., 1963)// http://www.jstor.org.uml.idm.oclc.org/stable/pdf/2601711.pdf;
Wilmot Horton, "Statement" (Personal memorandum addressed to William Huskisson), July 6, 1828, British Museum, Huskisson MSS, 38762/173;
John C. Caldwell. P. 680. Malthus and "the Less Developed World". Population and Development Review, Dec. 1998, vol. 24 (4);
Thomas Malthus. An Essay on the Principle of Population. Chapter 3//https://www.marxists.org/reference/subject/economics/malthus/ch03.htm;
Seidl Irmi, Tisdell, Clem A., Carrying Capacity Reconsidered: From Malthus' Population Theory to Cultural Carrying Capacity, Ecological Economics 31 (1999), pp. 395 – 408;
Alison Bashford. Malthus and Colonial History. Journal of Australian Studies, 36:1, pp. 99 – 110;
Observations Concerning the Increase of Mankind, 1751//in Not Your Usual Founding Father, Selected readings from Benjamin Franklin, Yale University Pres, 2007;
Chapter Z. Colonial and pre-Federal Statistics// https://www2.census.gov/prod2/statcomp/documents/CT1970p2-13.pdf;
Stannard, D. E. American Holocaust: Columbus and the Conquest of the New World, 1993; A Brief Account of the Destruction of the Indies by Bartolome de las Casas; Demography: Analysis and Synthesis, Four Volume Set: A Treatise in Population, 1st edition, Vol. 1.

notes

[67] Malthus T. R., An Essay on the Principle of Population as it Affects the Future Improvement of Society. With Remarks on the Speculations of Mr. Godwin, Mr. Condorcet, and other writes (1798)//in Silber Jacque, Malthus' Preconditions to Moral Restraint and Modern Population Economics, Genus, Vol. 42, #3/4, pp. 13-21; p. 13.

[68] Nobuhiko Nakazawa, Malthus's Political Views in 1798: a "Foxite Whig? //History of economic Review, Summer 2012, 56, p. 21.

[69] Victorian Studies, vol. 58, #2, review Empire, Migration and Identity in the British World, edited by Kent Fedorowich and Andrew S. Thompson; pp. xviii + 275. Manchester: Manchester University Press, 2013, review by Daniel Gorman, Victorian Studies, Winter 2016, pp. 339-341 (Review), p. 340.

[70] Juan-Carlos Cordoba. Malthus to Romer: On the Colonial Origins of the Industrial Revolution. Munich Personal RePEc Archive// https://mpra.ub.uni-muenchen.de/4466/1/MPRA_paper_4466.pdf, p. 22.

[71] Clark, G., 2005. The Condition of the Working Class in England, 1209-2004. Journal of Political Economics 113(6): 1307-1340.

[72] Edward Brynn, Politics and Economic Theory: Robert Wilmot Horton, 1820 – 1841, The Historian, February 1, 1972; vol. 34; iss. 2, p. 260.

[72] T. Malthus. Essay on Population, edition of 1817, vol. ii, pp. 304-5// In R. N. Ghosh. Malthus on Emigration and Colonization: Letter to Wilmot-Horton. Economica, New Series, Vol. 30, No. 117

(Feb., 1963), pp. 45-62
http://www.jstor.org.uml.idm.oclc.org/stable/pdf/2601711.pdf, p. 46.

[73] Wilmot Horton, "Statement" (Personal memorandum addressed to William Huskisson), July 6, 1828, British Museum, Huskisson MSS, 38762/173// in Edward Brynn, Politics and Economic Theory: Robert Wilmot Horton, 1820 – 1841, The Historian, February 1, 1972; vol. 34;iss. 2, p. 262.

[74] Edward Brynn, Politics and Economic Theory: Robert Wilmot Horton, 1820 – 1841, The Historian, February 1, 1972; vol. 34;iss. 2, p. 263.

[75] Ibid. P. 57.

[76] John C. Caldwell. P. 680. Malthus and "the Less Developed World". Population and Development Review, Dec. 1998, vol. 24 (4), p. 680.

[77] Thomas Malthus. An Essay on the Principle of Population. Chapter 3//https://www.marxists.org/reference/subject/economics/malthus/ch03.htm

[78] For example, Malthus used such literature as the following: Cook's Voyage towards the South Pole, and round the world (1777); Vancouver's Voyage of Discovery to the North Pacific Ocean, and round the World (1798);

[79] Malthus, Essay (1803), p. 24//in Alison Bashford. Malthus and Colonial History. Journal of Australian Studies, 36:1, pp. 99 – 110, p. 101.

[80] Observations Concerning the Increase of Mankind, 1751//in Not Your Usual Founding Father, Selected readings from Benjamin Franklin, Yale University Pres, 2007, 303 p., pp. 151-152.

[81] Ibid, p. 25// in Alison Bashford. Malthus and Colonial History. Journal of Australian Studies, 36:1, p. 102.

[82] Chapter Z. Colonial and pre-Federal Statistics//
https://www2.census.gov/prod2/statcomp/documents/CT1970p2-13.pdf

[83] Stannard, D. E. American Holocaust: Columbus and the Conquest of the New World, 1993; A Brief Account of the Destruction of the Indies by Bartolome de las Casas; Demography: Analysis and Synthesis, Four Volume Set: A Treatise in Population, 1st edition, Vol. 1, p. 42.

[84] Alison Bashford, Malthus and Colonial History, Journal of Australian Studies, 36-1, pp. 99 – 100, p. 103.

[85] Seidl Irmi, Tisdell, Clem A., Carrying Capacity Reconsidered: From Malthus' Population Theory to Cultural Carrying Capacity, Ecological Economics 31 (1999), pp. 395 – 408, p. 397.

Chapter Sixteen

Anishinaabe *Mino-Bimaadiziwin* in Margaret Atwood's *MaddAddam*

Bryn Skibo-Birney

In the cultural movement surrounding Canada's 150th anniversary (or "Colonialism 150"), scholars and the public alike debate the country's colonialist past, forms of decolonization and allyship in the present, and the possibility and nature of a post-colonial future. The arguments presented by Audra Simpson (Mohawk), Andrea Smith, and their collected authors in *Theorizing Native Studies* (2009) gain special significance during this anniversary. The authors argue that a combined theoretical framework of Indigenous and non-Indigenous critical theories could prevent lateral violence between marginalized groups and "intellectual isolationism" in academia, while simultaneously promoting "intellectual sovereignty" through "intellectual promiscuity, sympathy, and solidarity" (11). Furthering the message of *Theorizing*, scholars like Jodi Byrd (Chickasaw Nation of Oklahoma), Vine Deloria Jr. (Oglala Sioux), Lawrence Gross (White Earth Chippewa), Kwes Kwentin (Musqueam), and Zoe Todd (Red River Métis/Otipemisiwak), among others, have also addressed and argued for the value in using Indigenous epistemologies as critical theories in a largely non-Indigenous academic context, or "to start sharing the law with our neighbors" (Kwentin, n.p).

Following the practice laid out by these scholars, this essay reads Margaret Atwood's post-apocalyptic novel, *MaddAddam* (2013), through the lens of *Mino-Bimaadiziwin*, the Anishinaabe[87] philosophy and "ontological, ethical, epistemological, and aesthetic directives" of "the way of the good life" (Rheault 104). The philosophy's comprehensive instruction on living in harmony with one's relations and environment inspires my argument that *MaddAddam* is entirely composed around the idea and necessity of interconnectivity, using it as a structuring device, a central thematic, and a means of plot resolution. Subsequently, the novel offers a sustained critique of, and an alternative to, ingrained Euro-American ontologies of rigid binaries, linear time, and human exceptionalism. This is demonstrated through an analysis of the novel's use of discontinuous narrative, time, and multi-voiced discourse read through a short scene which encapsulates the primary importance of interconnectivity to the novel's structure and story. Overall, the essay aims to provide a narratological analysis of one of Atwood's most popular novels; in doing so, to offer an alternative theoretical approach to the novel which relies upon Native epistemologies; and, thus, to participate in the necessary and valuable work of ontological and academic decolonization by challenging the commonly accepted "wisdom" of who "owns" theory (Simpson 6). Deloria Jr. argues that "[i]f we change the very way that Western people think, the way they collect data, which data they gather, and how they arrange that information, then we are speaking truly of liberation" (qtd. in Simpson 4). In its prioritization of Anishinaabe epistemologies to advance the critique of mainstream Canadian literature, this essay hopes to provide a small step in the efforts to rebalance the relations between Indigenous and non-Indigenous participants in literary criticism.

Scholars of *MaddAddam,* as a novel and as a part of the larger trilogy (comprised of *Oryx and Crake* [2003] and *The Year of the Flood* [2009]), have used a variety of approaches to address the novel's post-apocalyptic story world, fragmented narrative structure, and genetically hybrid characters, including Revelation, Apocalypse, and ecocriticism; Christianity and "Paganism"; Indigeneity and Indigenous myths; victimization and trauma studies; and posthumanism.[88] While many of these critiques address Atwood's known interest in environmentalism and the dystopic implications of the planet's current trajectory, few scholars have approached the trilogy through the lens of Indigenous ways of seeing and being part of an interconnected world.[89] Thus, there exists a significant gap in the literature. However, some readers may question the relevance of Atwood in the conversation of Indigenous studies due to her role in Indigenous erasure or cultural appropriation, as seen in works like *Survival* (1972), *Surfacing* (1972a), and *The Journals of Susannah Moodie* (1970). More recently, Atwood gained notoriety on social media for her part in discussions regarding the claims to Indigenous identity purported by Joseph Boyden and Stephen Galloway. Her support for these claims – which she has no authority to give – is unusual, since she discusses elsewhere this very problem of "claiming kin," arguing that "many white Canadians claim, as a matter of pride, some 'Indian blood,' perhaps to convince themselves that the land they live in is one they 'ought' to be living in" (2004, 45).[90] Atwood admits that there seems little chance that non-Indigenous Canadians will stop making fake claims regarding their desired Indigenous identities. However, one potential "benefit" that she hopes will result from this trend is "if white Canadians would adopt *a more traditionally Native attitude* towards the natural world, *a less exploitative and more respectful attitude*, they might be able to reverse the galloping environmental carnage of the late twentieth century and salvage for themselves some of that wilderness they keep saying they identify with and need" (emphasis added; 72).

Atwood's conclusion is troubling for its reiteration of the "Native-as-Nature" stereotype and its apparent acceptance of Indigenous identity theft. However, her subtler point – regarding the value of bringing Indigenous philosophies into more mainstream Euro-American ways of seeing and being in the world – coincides with the aforementioned projects of Simpson, Byrd, Deloria Jr., and others. It seems, then, that despite Atwood's troubled/troubling relationship with Indigeneity, reading her novel in terms of Anishinaabe worldviews would have a variety of benefits. For example, the respectful use of *Mino-Bimaadiziwin*, alongside more "conventional" theoretical frameworks, does the important work of decolonizing theory as it rewrites colonial notions of who produces theory and about whom, as aptly demonstrated in *Theorizing*. Part of this work is the very simple, yet vital matter of representation and visibility. In a more localized benefit, *Mino-Bimaadiziwin* clarifies Atwood's vague statement regarding the need to adopt a more "traditionally Native attitude towards the natural world" by referring to actual Indigenous beliefs and worldviews: specifically, those of the Anishinaabeg. *Mino-Bimaadiziwin*, therefore, offers a unique and underrepresented means through which to engage with Atwood's most strident environmental text and to expand upon the critical literature.

This alternative approach is possible because *Mino-Bimaadiziwin* has a thorough and concrete manner of seeing and being in an interconnected world. The philosophy is evident from the Anishinaabe Creation Story, in which Gitchi Manitou has a dream vision of all of Creation and decides it must be made. In making the sun, moon, stars, and Earth; the trees, flowers, grasses, and vegetables; the walking, flying, swimming, and crawling beings, Gitchi Manitou gives a piece of their self into each part of Creation.[91] Subsequently, Creation is, as D'Arcy Rheault (Anishinaabe) describes it, the unity, balance, and harmony of *all the parts*, set to the cyclical temporal rhythm of generation, growth, death, and regeneration (145). Euro-American ontologies – shaped by Christian ideologies – are formed by oppositional relationships of good and evil, right and wrong, which are easily transformed into dichotomies of nature and culture, human and "animal," civilized and savage, set within a teleological timeframe aimed at "progress." Violence and exploitation – of humans, nonhumans, and the land – have been, and continue to be, the result of such a worldview. In contrast, Lawrence Gross explains that the Anishinaabe sacred stories push the Anishinaabeg of all ages and stages of life to see themselves within a "peopled universe," inhabited by Gitchi Manitou and Nokomis, Sky Woman and her Twins, Nanabozho and Muskrat, the Animikiig and Mishipeshu (238). Connecting with the "other-than-human" beings, through fasting visions, dreams, songs, and drumming, allows the Anishinaabeg to learn wisdom, love, respect, courage, honesty, humility, moderation, and truth, and thereby maintain and participate in the harmony and rhythm of Creation (Hallowell 22). A significant portion of knowing one's place within Creation means that one respects the role and purpose that others have to play, whether they are a child, elder, porcupine, drum, story, or song. Thus, in the *Mino-Bimaadiziwin* worldview, you become a part of Creation by living in harmony with your relations, which include your immediate and extended family as well as your clan, your totem "animal," your personal manitous, and the nonhuman "animals" and spirits in the environment around you (including the environment itself). This worldview of relationality clarifies Atwood's statement about being less exploitative towards the natural world, but it also provides an all-encompassing worldview of interconnectivity through which to read Atwood's ecological disaster story.

The three novels of the *MaddAddam* trilogy tell the past- and present-tense stories of the human survivors of a plague that was purposefully spread to eradicate humankind, in the hopes that the Earth would then have a chance to heal from rampant climate change. The protagonists are affected by psychological, sexual, or emotional traumas from before the plague; subsequently, they try to construct boundaries – such as physical separation, emotional distance, and selfishness – to prevent further trauma. However, the discontinuous narrative structure of each novel demonstrates that this kind of self-isolation is untenable and ultimately harmful – to the individual, society, and the planet. The novels all feature an alternating pattern of two protagonists' perspectives, told from oppositional spaces and time-frames; this pattern is often interrupted by first-person stories. For example, in *MaddAddam*, Toby, a former member of an eco-Christian cult, tells the present-tense story of the world after the pandemic, while Zeb, her lover, tells the past-tense story of his difficult life before the pandemic. Toby also tells stories of the past to the Crakers, a group of human/"animal"/plant genetic hybrids. In *Crake* and *Flood*, this alternating pattern is eventually disrupted, leading to a reunification of the split protagonists in time and space. Yet, the first two novels end inconclusively on the question of how to behave in this new world, leaving open the question of whether the protagonists will continue to follow their isolationist mindset or chose one of relationality and community. In contrast, in *MaddAddam,* a potent scene of inter-species vulnerability reveals that the community's isolationist and anthropocentric beliefs are dangerous to their survival. The discontinuous narrative dramatizes this shift in worldview by *adding* a third voice, rather than *unifying* the previous two.

This new narrator, a Craker boy named Blackbeard, reframes the previously binary narrative pattern: from that of Zeb and Toby – past and present, emotionally closed off and anthropocentric – to that of Toby, Zeb, and Blackbeard – a multi-voiced narrative of blended time-frames and representative of a non-anthropocentric community. Mid-way into the novel, Toby receives a vision that requires her to move away from her denial of the past and her avoidance of emotional intimacy. While asking her deceased mentor for advice, she initially receives no *linguistic* response which prompts Toby to think, "there is no magic, there are no angels. It was all child's play" (Atwood 2013, 222). The "it" which Toby thinks is fake refers to the religious teachings of the cult, who believed that the Christian god is omnipresent in the world. However, at the moment when she realizes God is not going to answer, Toby is brought face-to-face with a genetically enhanced pig and her piglets, the same type of pigs who have repeatedly attempted to eat the human survivors. In her vision, Toby sees the sow as "Such enormous power. ... She could run them down like a tank. Life, life, life, life, life. Full to bursting, this minute. Second. Millisecond. Millennium. Eon" (223). In this moment of intense physical and spiritual vulnerability, Toby has a perception of the world as interconnected and cyclical, a realization that directly contradicts her own linear, Euro-American worldviews of oppositional categories: human and "animal," life and death, past and present. Toby's reference to "power" seems to imply the sow's strength, which could kill them. But this reference to possible death is juxtaposed by Toby's uncharacteristic repetition of "life": the five repetitions highlight the sow's *regenerative* power – she is the mother to five piglets – as well as the sow's power to spare or to take away the lives of the five humans – whom she could "run down like a tank." The repetition is powerful precisely because it is unclear to whom the repetition refers: the humans and the pigs are equally likely to be the implied objects of the phrase and are thus drawn together as mutual participants in Creation, or "life."

The connection between the pigs and the humans then expands across time. Whereas Toby previously warned Zeb of delving too much into his past, for fear of reliving the trauma of his childhood, here, she sees "life" – a power shared between the human and the pigs – expanding from this moment of tension to the micro- and macroscopic perspectives of time, from the "millisecond" to the "eon." This moment of shared "life" becomes a synecdoche, a representative part of the overall balance and rhythm of Creation; as Rheault explains, "each individual (human and nonhuman) is as much a representation and manifestation of the whole of Creation as the whole of Creation is a representation of itself" (111). The description of Toby's vision is representative of what elder Edward Benton-Banai describes as humility, or "to know yourself as a sacred part of Creation" (64), one of the seven lessons of *Mino-Bimaadiziwin*. Therefore, it makes sense that Toby only arrives at this simple, yet profound, realization of shared "life" by meeting and returning the pig's gaze. The vision she receives is far from the vision she sought, yet it nevertheless begins to radically reframe Toby's understanding of being in the post-pandemic world.

The encounter between Toby and the sow has a significant effect on the narrative structure and the plot, in which the implications of Toby's awakening to a *Mino-Bimaadiziwin*-esque worldview of interconnectivity become evident. Following the encounter, Toby initially refuses to tell a story to the Crakers, asking instead for Blackbeard's help; when the story is eventually recounted in the narrative, it is revealed to be a story Toby tells herself. These changes offer the first two significant disruptions to the previously predictable narrative pattern and foreshadow Blackbeard's introduction as a new storyteller, which adds a third, and distinctly non-anthropocentric voice (Blackbeard includes the perspective of nonhuman beings in his stories) to the narrative. At the same time that the narrative structure shifts towards a multi-voiced, non-anthropocentric discourse, the vision also causes several important changes to the plot, foreshadowing the novel's peaceful resolution via an inter-species community. For example, the vision prompts Toby to stop eating pig meat, a rare source of protein, because, Toby claims, of "what the sow communicated to her [...] though she couldn't put it into words. It was more like a current. A current of water, a current of electricity" (Atwood 2013, 261-62). An Anishinaabe understanding of Creation is one of "unity in movement," of always being in the process of creation; as Rupert Ross writes about Anishinaabe beliefs, "each person's primary focus is not on a separate thing but on all the movements and relationships between things" (Rheault 104; Ross 103-4). By describing the pig's communication through nature-based similes of movement and flow, Toby demonstrates a significant shift in her worldview, moving away from fixed states of being and towards a perspective of Creation as a state of flux: for example, between a pig, a woman, and the movement of elements. Following this scene of recognized interconnectivity, the previously antagonistic pigs offer a truce between the human survivors in order to join forces against two men who have been killing and eating members of the pig and human communities alike. This truce leads to a successful trial and execution and the continued peace and communality between the humans, the pigs, and the Crakers, thereby resolving various conflicts left open in the previous novels. In short, recognition of vulnerable interconnectivity provides the impetus for a significant shift towards non-human voices in the narration and towards a more egalitarian, and less anthropocentric, community in the story world, thereby leading to a successful plot resolution.

There remains one final suggestion regarding the epiphany between Toby and the sow: it occurs immediately after Toby's recognition that the Christian God she was encouraged to believe in was "child's play" (Atwood 2013, 223). Atwood has stated that, in Canada, Christianity is an "imported" religion and that "the only sort of good, authentic kind of thing to have is something that comes out of the place where you are, [...] the reality of your life" (Gibson 30). In *God is Red*, Deloria Jr. suggests that "the traditions, beliefs, and customs of the American Indian people are the guidelines for mankind's future" *specifically* because they come from revelations stemming from a particular *place*, as opposed to a re-articulated belief based in history. It seems that, despite the problems which arise from Atwood's participation in discourses about Indigeneity, she and Deloria are saying similar things. For Indigenous Studies scholars, Atwood's post-apocalyptic trilogy is valuable for its representation of ontological revelations stemming from experiences with the "other-than-human beings" with whom we share our environment (itself an "other-than-human being"). For readers of Atwood's trilogy, Indigenous worldviews and philosophies need to be recentered as a vital and valuable part of the mainstream critical theory, for their rich and nuanced understanding of living in an interconnected world and its forms of representation in literature and stories.

References

Atwood, Margaret. *Oryx and Crake*. 2003. London: Virago Press, 2012.
———. *The Year of the Flood*. 2009. London: Virago Press, 2011.
———. *MaddAddam*. London: Bloomsbery, 2013.
———. *Strange Things: The Malevolent North in Canadian Literature*. 2004. London: Virago Press: 2012.
———. *Survival: A Thematic Guide to Canadian Literature*. 1972. Toronto: House of Anansi Press, 2012.
———. *Surfacing*. 1972a. London: Virago Press, 2014.

Atwood, Margaret and Charles Pachter. *The Journals of Susannah Moodie*. 1970/1980. London: Paramount Printing Company, Ltd., 1997.
Barnouw, Victor. *Wisconsin Chippewa Myths and Tales and Their Relation to Chippewa Life*. Madison: University of Wisconsin Press, 1977.
Benton-Banai, Edward. *The Mishomis Book: The Voice of the Ojibway*. 1988. Minneapolis: University of Minnesota Press, 2010.
Bergthaller, Hannes. "Housebreaking the Human Animal: Humanism and the Problem of Sustainability in Margaret Atwood's *Oryx and Crake* and *The Year of the Flood*." English Studies. Vol. 91, No. 7 (Nov. 2010): 728-43.
Byrd, Jodi A. *The Transit of Empire: Indigenous Critiques of Colonialism*. Minneapolis: University of Minnesota Press, 2011.
Deloria Jr., Vine. *Custer Died for Your Sins: An Indian Manifesto*. London: Collier-Macmillan Ltd., 1969.
—. *God is Red*. New York: Grosset & Dunlap, 1973.
DiMarco, Dannette. "Going Wendigo: The Iconic Monster in Margaret Atwood's *Oryx and Crake* and Antonia Bird's *Ravenous*." College Literature. Vol. 38, No. 4 (Fall 2011): 134-55.
Frew, Lee. "'A Whole New Take on Indigenous': Margaret Atwood's *Oryx and Crake* as Wild Animal Story." Studies in Canadian Literature / Études en littérature canadienne. Vol. 39, No. 1 (2014): 199-218.
Gibson, Graeme. "Margaret Atwood." *Eleven Canadian Novelists Interviewed by Graeme Gibson*. 1973. Toronto: House of Anansi Press, 2014. 1-30.
Gross, Lawrence. *Anishinaabe Ways of Knowing and Being*. Surrey, UK: Ashgate Publishing, Ltd., 2014.
Hallowell, Irving A. "Ojibway Ontology, Behavior, and World View." *Culture in History: Essays in Honor of Paul Radin*. Stanley Diamond, ed. New York: University of Columbia Press, 1960. 17-49.
Johnston, Basil. *Ojibway Heritage*. 1976. Lincoln: University of Nebraska Press, 1990. Print.
Kwentin, Kwes. NAISA, 22-24 June 2017, University of British Columbia, Vancouver, Canada. Opening Address.
Mosca, Valeria. "Crossing Posthuman Boundaries: Apocalypse and Posthumanism in Margaret Atwood's *Oryx and Crake* and *The Year of the Flood*." Altre Modernità. Vol. 9 (May 2013): 38-52.
Ni, Zhange. "Wonder Tale, Pagan Utopia, and Margaret Atwood's Radical Hope." *The Pagan Writes Back: When World Literature Meets World Religion*. Charlottesville, Virginia: University of Virginia Press, 2015. 97-121.
Northover, Richard Alan. "Ecological Apocalypse in Margaret Atwood's *MaddAddam* Trilogy." Studia Neophilologica. Vol. 88 (2016): 81-95.
Osborne, Carol. "Mythmaking in Margaret Atwood's *Oryx and Crake*." *Once Upon a Time: Myth, Fairy Tales and Legends in Margaret Atwood's Writings*. Sarah A. Appleton, ed. Newcastle upon Tyne: Cambridge Scholars Publishing, 2008. 25-46.
Rheult, D'Arcy. *Anishinaabe Mino-Bimaadiziwin (The Way of a Good Life): An Examination of Anishinaabe Philosophy, Ethics and Traditional Knowledge*. CreateSpace Independent Publishing Platform, 1999.
Simpson, Audra and Andrea Smith, eds. *Theorizing Native Studies*. Durham: Duke University Press, 2014.
Snyder, Katherine V. "'Time to go': The Post-apocalyptic and the Post-traumatic in Margaret Atwood's *Oryx and Crake*." Studies in the Novel. Vol. 43, No. 4 (Winter 2011): 470-89.
Todd, Zoe. "An Indigenous Feminist's Take on the Ontological Turn: 'Ontology' is Just Another Word for Colonialism." zoestodd.com 24 October 2014. Web. Accessed 4 October 2017. https://zoestodd.com/2014/10/24/an-indigenous-feminists-take-on-the-ontological-turn-ontology-is-just-another-word-for-colonialism/

notes

[87] This essay uses the broader term, Anishinaabe(g), to refer to the collection of Algonquin-speaking tribes who share the beliefs of *Mino-Bimaadiziwin*. When referring to individuals, their specific tribal identity (e.g. Anishinaabe, Ojibwa, Chippewa, etc.) will be provided. When referring to Indigenous identity in general, the terms "Indigenous" or "Native" will be used interchangeably.

[88] For Revelation, Apocalypse and ecocriticism, see Northover, whose work traces the shift from *Flood*'s Christian tradition of ecological domination through to the apocalyptic/revelatory possibilities of the genetically hybrid narrator, who reveals a "more just dispensation" of power between humans and nonhumans (94). Similarly, Bergthaller claims that the Christian sermons provided in *Flood* reconcile the human followers to live in harmony, as opposed to destructive antagonism, with their environment. Ni also argues that the sermons taught by Atwood's eco-cult offer a "pagan" form of "radical hope" that allows readers a means to "think otherwise" (117). While Northover, Bergthaller, and Ni find a need to change an anthropocentric, domineering stance towards the environment to a more interdependent position, none of them address Indigenous philosophies which would provide realistic means to arrive at such a relationship with the world. Some scholars do address Indigeneity specifically, such as Frew, who argues, troublingly, that the Crakers are "post-human indigenes [who] ... serve as the noble savages from whom [the protagonist of *Oryx and Crake*] might continuously attempt to 'acquir[e] Indian" (Goldie, qtd. in Frew 212)). That is to say, the Crakers take the position of "the Other," against which the human survivors define themselves. DiMarco discusses Atwood's use of the Wendigo as "a cautionary tale that questions the ethics of humans motivated by greed and profit" (140) but DiMarco erases Indigenous perspectives from her analysis of the myth, thereby missing nuance regarding this mythical figure and its links to more-than-human social relations with adults, children, bears (via the healing tallow), and dogs (see Barnouw). For victimization and trauma, see Snyder, who argues that Atwood's doubled and fragmented temporal structure "emphasizes the futility of attempting to quarantine an individual's subjective interiority from relations," including connections of family, nation, and the non-human (473). Interestingly, Snyder's reading does not take into account the protagonist's deeply held emotional connections *with* non-humans and their relation to his trauma and the global catastrophe. For posthumanism, see Mosca, who argues that *Crake* and *Flood* present "the end of 'the human' as it is traditionally perceived": that is to say, the end of the human subject as perceived within a strictly *Euro-American* ontology (48). Despite their disparate approaches, these studies share their assertion regarding the importance of the trilogy's emphasis on living with more awareness of interdependence, in terms of religion, myths, epistemologies, and ontologies, yet none of them refer to Indigenous philosophies which have asserted these points for centuries and which could offer valuable insight and development of their arguments and analyses of the trilogy.

[89] Osborne argues that the protagonist of *Crake* acts like an Aboriginal Australian "medicine man" to the Crakers, as he creates myths and rituals (43). While I agree with much of Osborne's textual analysis, she does not acknowledge the protagonist's interconnected state with nonhuman "animals" and the Crakers, whom Osborne characterizes as "blank slates" (25). This oversight of the nonhumans' and the Crakers' active role in reshaping the protagonist's worldview negates the very interconnectivity that is at the heart of many Indigenous ontologies. By maintaining a top-down approach (a "medicine man" creating the rituals and "giving" them to the "blank slates"), Osborne reiterates a linear, arborescent epistemology rather than a more rhizomic, interconnected epistem-ontology.

[90] Deloria, Jr. also makes a similar point regarding white Americans in *Custer Died for Your Sins* (3-4).

[91] Paraphrased from the Creation Stories told by Basil Johnston (Ojibwa) in *Ojibway Heritage* and Edward Benton-Banai (Ojibwa) in *The Mishomis Book*.

Chapter Seventeen

Residential School Photography

From Photographic Propaganda to Empowering Pictures

Melanie Braith

I saw a photograph of Cree playwright Tomson Highway in residential school. The picture, taken in the 1960s, shows Highway as a young boy standing in front of Guy Hill Residential School in Manitoba, together with a group of other boys. It is impossible for me, however, to be sure which of the boys Highway is because the description on the back of the photograph merely reads "T. Highway – centre." The picture is archived at Library and Archives Canada in Ottawa where I was given permission to make a personal copy. When asking the archivist whether it would be possible to show this copy at academic conferences, she hesitated, saying that she was not sure about the privacy rights of the other children in the photograph. For me, her answer caused many questions which eventually led to the present research. In *On Photography*, Susan Sontag writes: "[T]he more I thought about what photographs are, the more complex and suggestive they became" (Sontag n.p.). I had the same experience when I started to think more about residential school photographs. In this article, I present some of my thoughts and research but rather than providing exhaustive answers, I intend to open up a conversation about residential school photography, its history, and its functions. Photographs of children in residential school were taken in extremely coercive contexts and emerged from asymmetrical power relations. Often, the pictures were staged with the goal to create propaganda for settler society and children were forced to perform as the objects of successful assimilationist endeavours. In present-day Canada, historical photographs of children in residential schools have become a ubiquitous and powerful tool for teaching the public about the atrocities of Canada's residential school system. However, while the photographs have become crucial testimonies, their creation involved invasive processes that violated children's privacy rights—a fact that complicates their display, even if it is for important purposes such as decolonization and redress. Linda Warley articulated a question that has been haunting me throughout this research: "What if a photograph of you at a residential school is the only photograph of your childhood that you have?" (Warley 208).

In this article, I delineate how the public discourse around residential school photographs developed and argue that its narratives changed from colonial propaganda to testimony and commemoration. I furthermore intend to demonstrate how Indigenous artists choose to engage or not to engage with these photographs in order to create empowering alternative visual discourses which counter the legacy of the schools by celebrating kinship relationships. In order to do so, I will offer an analysis of Cree poet and residential school survivor Sky Dancer Louise Halfe's poetic residential school testimony *Burning in this Midnight Dream*. I argue that by contrasting her haunting poetry about dysfunctional families and residential school trauma with personal family portraits rather than residential school photographs, Halfe engages in the act of what Anishinaabe scholar Leanne Simpson calls "generative refusal" (Simpson 176). Thereby, Halfe creates an empowering visual counter discourse to foster the restoration of relationships.

In section 1, I give a brief overview of different historical contexts in which residential school photographs were created and reflect on the ways in which processes of objectification and intrusion affected Indigenous children as their pictures were taken. In section 2, I demonstrate how the work of Canada's Truth and Reconciliation Commission (TRC) resulted in the repurposing of residential school photographs for commemoration and education and I look at the role which archives such as the National Centre for Truth and Reconciliation (NCTR) play in the reframing of the discourse around the photographs. In section 3, I analyze the use of family photographs in Halfe's poetic residential school testimony *Burning in this Midnight Dream* and demonstrate how the alternative memories captured by the photographs potentially (re)create relationships.

The Coercive Origins of Residential School Photographs

Métis scholar Sherry Farrell Racette identifies three kinds of residential school photographs: "Photographs to illustrate government reports and other official publications, those taken by staff and visitors, and a remarkable group of photographs taken by students" (Farrell Racette "Haunted" 51). This article focuses on the first two categories because they enact what Farrell Racette refers to as "photo colonialism": "the use of photography to collect evidence for and construct a colonial narrative" (Farrell Racette "Returning" 79). For the construction of a propagandistic colonial narrative which present residential schools as places of successful assimilation, school staff and government officials relied on one photographic genre in particular: so-called before-and-after portraits. These pictures were common in the context of Canadian residential schools and US-American boarding schools and "displayed the Other in his or her allegedly degenerate state before Americanization, and again following its conclusion" (Mauro 1). At Carlisle Indian Industrial School in Pennsylvania, these propagandistic pictures were taken to convince supporters to give money to the schools and to convince Indigenous leaders "to send their own children to the schools" (Mauro 56). At the same time, the photographs perpetuated a colonial narrative that suggests that the schools performed an evolution from savagery to civilization within months and the "apparent speed of this process [...] proved the wisdom and power inherent in white reformist agendas" (Mauro 77). The most prominent example of before-and-after-pictures in a Canadian context is the photograph of Thomas Moore at the Regina Indian Industrial School; and the photograph evokes the colonial narrative described by Mauro. Farrell Racette discusses Moore's photograph in detail and points out the staged nature of both parts of the picture by describing the inaccuracies of the boy's clothing (Farrell Racette "Haunted" 53).

Another well-known residential school photograph is included in Métis author Patti LaBoucane-Benson and Kelly Mellings' graphic novel *The Outer Circle*. It depicts nine young boys in a dormitory, kneeling on their bunk beds, apparently praying. In the background stands a woman who oversees the scene, holding a book in her hands, her glasses reflecting the light in a way that creates the ghostly impression of two vacant white holes. Despite the obviously staged nature of the photograph—or maybe because of it—the viewer gets the impression that "the camera is intrusive; it is an unwelcome presence in the room; it violates" (Warley 211). The boys' bodies seem to be arranged for the photograph, and the bedroom, a private space for the privileged settler society, turns into a public space, demonstrating that there is no privacy in residential school. One of the boys is half-naked, merely wearing a white towel around his waist. The way in which the boys were presumably coerced into, and through the photograph forever frozen in, the angelic posture of prayer, speaks to the fact that the children as photographic objects "were not only objectified and repressed, they were created epistemologically for their various audiences" (Mauro 69). Susan Sontag argues that "[t]o photograph is to appropriate the thing photographed" (Sontag *On Photography* 4) and Roland Barthes emphasizes that "[p]hotography transformed subject into object, and even, one might say, into a museum object" (Barthes 13). Residential school photographs appropriated bodies and used them to create colonial narratives. The way in which those photographs enforce identities complicates their status as testimonial objects—an issue the next section will touch upon.

Despite the fact that residential schools created one of the most coercive environments imaginable, students found many ways to enact resistance which "cannot very well be seen in photographs" (Margolis & Rowe 219) and which were emphasized in the TRC's final report (TRC *Summary* 114). Merely discussing the ways in which the children were coerced and turned from subjects into objects without acknowledging their resistance would constitute yet another act of silencing and taking away their agency.

Residential School Photographs Today: Archives, Commemoration, Education

Given the complicated original contexts of these photographs, I am interested in how these propagandistic pictures have become vehicles for commemoration and education. The most encompassing collection of residential school photographs can be found in the archive of the National Centre for Truth and Reconciliation (NCTR) at the University of Manitoba. The NCTR houses all documents the TRC collected from individuals, church and state archives between 2009 and 2015. Throughout its work, the TRC emphasized the importance of residential school photographs for truth-telling, education, and commemoration and thereby contributed to changing the discourse around those photographs away from its propagandistic nature. At its National Events, the TRC redistributed copies of photographs to survivors and stated in its final report that "[f]or many Survivors, especially those who had no visual record of their own childhood or no pictures of siblings who have since passed away, this proved to be one of the most treasured aspects of the National Events experience" (TRC *Summary* 253-4). When thinking about this potentially healing effect of the photographs, it needs to be emphasized, however, that it can be potentially triggering for grown-up survivors to encounter photographs that capture traumatic times of their lives. The NCTR's online collection of the photographs demonstrates an awareness of this potential as it is accompanied by the number of a health support line.

The NCTR continues the TRC's mandate to provide survivors access to these documents and to utilize them to foster education and commemoration. In doing so, however, the archive faces various challenges. Susan Sontag points out that there is a general sense that a photograph captures reality, but she emphasizes that "its meaning—and the viewer's response—depends on how the picture is identified or misidentified; that is, on words" (Sontag *Pain* 26). The identification of children depicted in residential school photographs is a complicated matter the NCTR continues to grapple with. The photographs gathered by the TRC were often poorly described, the lack of names for the students reflecting colonial attitudes and dehumanizing processes occurring in the schools. Like the vague description of the Highway photograph I encountered myself, the archival descriptions of the NCTR are filled with phrases such as "unidentified student," "no title," or "unknown." While the NCTR endeavours to offer adequate descriptions, identifying all students in the thousands of pictures seems nearly impossible given the fact that many of those photographed are no longer alive today.

When trying to identify students, contextualizing the photographs, and bringing them together with survivors' testimonies, the NCTR attempts to make students' voices heard. However, given the traumatic nature of residential school history, it is no surprise that at times, there might be survivors who refuse to have their story become part of the archive. This is where the tension between the importance of testimony and the right to privacy as discussed in the previous section becomes apparent. Next to every photograph in its online archives, the NCTR placed a "Request Take Down"-button for privacy reasons. The NCTR thereby demonstrates an awareness of the potential privacy-violating nature of these pictures. Rodney Carter argues that it is "essential that archivists not undermine the right of groups to remain silent" (Carter 227) because there lies power in the decision "to speak or to be silent, to have control over one's own person and possessions, to co-operate or to resist" (Carter 228). Giving survivors a choice to not share their stories grants them the agency to make their own decision. The tension between survivors' rights to privacy vs. the importance of truth-telling and commemoration was also at the heart of the court processes around the Independent Assessment Process Records which contained the detailed protocols of abuses recounted by residential school survivors. In 2017, the Canadian Supreme

Court rule that these protocols will be destroyed if a survivor does not explicitly ask for them to be preserved.

Susan Sontag states that "[t]he photographer's intentions do not determine the meaning of the photograph, which will have its own career, blown by the whims and loyalties of the diverse communities that have use for it" (Sontag Pain 39). The meaning of residential school photographs is currently actively changed as photographs are returned to survivors and their communities. According to Farrell Racette, several "communities have initiated major projects to reclaim silenced voices and reconstruct a lost history. Photographs have played a critical role in these healing projects" (Farrell Racette "Haunted" 78). In other cases, artists, such as Edward Poitras with his photo installation *Rez Girls*, have engaged with residential school photographs in order to reframe them in new contexts and to dismantle the colonial propaganda they once were intended for (Bell 169). Writers of fictional residential school diaries such as Nlaka'pamux author Shirley Sterling include residential school photographs in their narratives, drawing attention to the staged and performative nature of these photographs. In *My Name Is Seepeetza*, Seepeetza wonders about a photograph of herself as a residential school student: "It was funny because I was smiling in those pictures. I looked happy. How can I look happy when I'm scared all the time?" (Sterling 36-7). A photograph similar to the one Seepeetza describes but showing Sterling herself is printed on the novel's cover, prompting the reader to think about the intersections between photography, narrative, and performance. As the photographs become repurposed and re-appropriated by Indigenous communities and survivors, former students reclaim their agency.

Sky Dancer Louise Halfe's Visual Counter-Discourse

In this section, I take a closer look at one Indigenous artist's engagement with residential school photography—or, more specifically, her refusal to engage with it. Cree poet Sky Dancer Louise Halfe is a survivor of Blue Quills Indian Residential School in Alberta. Residential school experiences and their legacy come up as themes in all of Halfe's poetry collections— most prominently so in her 2016 collection *Burning in this Midnight Dream*. Former TRC Director of Research Paulette Regan contributed the foreword, stating that Halfe's poems "are testimonies of truth, justice and healing" (Halfe xii). In an interview with Shelagh Rogers, Halfe talks about how her poetry was inspired by her own memories, her family's memories, and the stories of others and how sharing these stories is necessary for healing trauma: "They need to be validated and witnessed and be given their own life so that a person can move forward. In order to move forward in a healing way, we have to go into that darkness and rip it out and give it legs to walk away from us once it's been told (Halfe "Interview"). In the collection, the boundaries between Halfe's own experiences and her poetic retelling of other people's stories become blurry as Halfe weaves all memories—those of experiences and those of stories—together to create a poetic testimony of residential school experiences and their legacy. The collection of photographs is similarly comprised of pictures that show Halfe herself but also of pictures that show her parents, grandparents and other family members whose stories are part of her testimony. Photographs of Blue Quills Residential School, including pictures of the building as well as group pictures of children, can be found in the NCTR archive and the United Church of Canada Archives. Halfe chose not to include any of these photographs, and I argue that she thereby refuses to draw on the connotations of residential school photography discourse in favour of an alternative visual discourse: that of kinship and relationships evoked by family portraits. In doing so, Halfe engages in what Anishinaabe scholar Leanne Simpson refers to as "affirmative" or "generative refusal" (Simpson 176): Halfe refuses to draw on residential school photography discourse which calls on non-Indigenous Canadians to acknowledge and be educated about this part of colonialism. Instead, Halfe employs photographs that focus inward on her own family, evoke relationships, and thereby reclaim positive memories.

    The first photograph is placed directly under the dedication which reads: "This book is dedicated to my children Usne Josiah Butt and Omeasoo Wahpasiw as well as my grandsons Josiah Kesic Butt and Alistair Aski Butt" (Halfe v). The photograph depicts two little boys, Halfe's grandsons, holding a copy of her collection *Blue Marrow*. In combination with the dedication, the photograph suggests that Halfe writes for her family and for the next generation of Indigenous readers. As the reader turns the page, they encounter the second photograph which depicts a group of about 30 people standing in front of a building. The caption reads: "Mom and Dad's wedding, November 4, 1939" (Halfe vi). After depicting the future symbolized by Halfe's grandsons, the book now turns to the past and the many faces in the picture connect to a line from the book's second poem "aniskostew-connecting" in which Halfe reflects on her parents' lives and time in residential school, stating: "That little story is bigger than I can tell" (Halfe 2). The story is bigger because it affects all of Halfe's family, all of the faces visible in the wedding photograph and Halfe emphasizes how the residential school legacy affects generations. Through the first two photographs, Halfe connects future and past. However, rather than letting this future and past be determined by residential schools, Halfe chooses photographs that emphasize family relations.

Reflecting on family photography, Susan Sontag argues that "[t]hrough photographs, each family constructs a portrait-chronicle of itself—a portable kit of images that bears witness to its connectedness" (Sontag 8). The photographs in Louise Halfe's collection are such a kit of connectedness. Notably, all of the photographs include captions with the names of the people who are depicted—the anonymity of residential school photography does not exist in Halfe's work. The captions also indicate how a person is connected to Halfe. In the captions of pictures of her grandparents, Halfe refers to them as "nimosôm" (grandfather) and "nôhkum" (grandmother). As a student in an Introduction to Cree class, I was taught that the Cree word for grandmother does not exist without a possessive pronoun prefix indicating a connection to another person ("ni-" for "my," in this case, "n-" because it is followed by a vowel). Halfe's use of this Cree noun which comes with in-built relationships strongly affirms her relationships to her kin. The photographs have also an effect on the reader : Anishinaabe scholar Celeste Pedri-Spade argues that as a viewer, one establishes relationships to portraits of people and that "[i]ndividuals find, for example, their grandmother or grandfather in images that are not of them" (Pedri-Spade 109). This, according to Pedri-Spade, helps the viewer "to reclaim and develop relationships with significant characters in their life" (Pedri-Spade 109).

As the reader engages with Halfe's collection, they will notice a discrepancy between the poems and the photographs. While the poems engage with experiences in residential school, with violence in families, residential school trauma and its effects, dysfunctional and disrupted relationships, the photographs depict family members who gather together, united, sometimes the arms around each other. Halfe's photographs testify to the importance of relationships and thereby counter the content of the poems which speak of their disruption. Pictures of Halfe herself as a child are included: a picture of Halfe standing next to her father (Halfe 29), a picture of Halfe being hold by her grandmother (67) and a picture of Halfe being hold by her father (Halfe 79). The picture in which Halfe is held by her father is the last photograph in the collection and it is also the one on its cover. This photograph stands in stark contrast with the poems which tell of a father (whether Halfe's own or someone else's remains unclear) who violently attacks his own kin: "My niece was two when my father / took her by her feet / and threw her across the room" (Halfe 8). The way in which the photographs emphasize relationships while the poems discuss their disruption creates a multidimensional picture of the complicated nature of the residential school legacy. Thinking about the complicated nature of relationships in dysfunctional families, Halfe states: "We love those people that hurt us and who also in their own way try to love us" (Halfe "Interview). The way in which the photographs in *Burning in this Midnight Dream* testify to relationships while the poems testify to their dysfunction captures this complicated love.

While it is impossible to offer an exhaustive study of residential school photography in the concise format of this book chapter, I endeavoured to discuss some of the main questions and complexities around these photographs. Residential school photographs were created in coercive contexts, objectify former students and often violate their privacy rights, and capture trauma. At the same time, however, these photographs can play important roles for survivors' reclamation of agency, truth-telling, and commemoration. How photographs are interpreted depends to a certain extent on how they are presented to an audience. In order to fulfill the empowering functions described above, residential school photographs rely on being framed or re-framed in the "right way" by Indigenous archives such as the NCTR, Indigenous communities, and Indigenous artists. As I hope to have shown in my analysis of Louise Halfe's *Burning in this Midnight Dream*, it can also be important to refuse to participate in the discourse around residential school photographs in order to create alternative visual discourses for healing. After having reflected on the complexities of residential school photographs, I am still confronted with the question of whether to display the copy of the Highway photograph when presenting on my work. Not only will I have to consult with Library and Archives Canada's copyright experts, I will also have to decide how to ethically engage as a witness in the discourse around residential school photographs and whether my purposes of commemoration and education are substantial enough to outweigh the potential violation of privacy rights.

References

Barthes, Roland. Camera Lucida: Reflections on Photography. New York: The Noonday Press, 1981.
Bell, Lynn. "Unsettling Acts: Photography as Decolonizing Testimony in Centennial Memory." Carol Payne and Andrea Kunard Eds, The Cultural Work of Photography in Canada.   Montreal& Kingston: McGill-Queen's University, 2011: 165-181.
Carter, Rodney G.S. "O Things Said and Unsaid: Power, Archival Silences, and Power in Silence." Archivaria Vol. 61 (Spring 2006): 215-233.

Farrell Racette, Sherry. "Returning Fire, Pointing the Canon: Aboriginal Photography as Resistance." Carol Payne and Andrea Kunard Eds, The Cultural Work of Photography in Canada. Montreal& Kingston: McGill-Queen's University, 2011: 3-22.

----. "Haunted: First Nations Children in Residential School Photography." In Loren Lerner (ed.) Depicting Canada's Children. Waterloo: Wilfried Laurier University, 2009: 49-84

Halfe, Louise Bernice. Burning in This Midnight Dream. Regina: Coteau Books, 2016.

----. Interview by Shelagh Rogers. CBC Books: The Next Chapter, 14 Nov. 2017, http://www.cbc.ca/books/burning-in-this-midnight-dream-1.3988108. Accessed 16 May 2018.

Margolis, Eric. "Looking at discipline, looking at labour: photographic representations of Indian boarding schools." Visual Studies 19:1 (2004): 71-96.

Margolis, Eric/Jeremy Rowe. "Images of Assimilation: Photographs of Indian Schools in Arizona." History of Education. Vol 33.2 (2004): 199-230.

Mauro, Hayes Peter. The Art of Americanization at the Carlisle Indian School. Albuquerque: University of New Mexico, 2011.

McCracken, Krista. "Archival photographs in perspective: Indian residential school images of health/Photos d'archives en perspective: images de santé des pensionnats Indiens." British Journal of Canadian Studies, Volume 30, Number 2, 2017, pp. 163-182.

Miller, J. R. "Reading Photographs, Reading Voices: Documenting the History of Native Residential Schools"

Pedri-Spade, Celeste. "But they were never only the master's tools": the use of photography in de-colonial praxis." AlterNative: An international Journal of Indigenous Peoples. (2017) Vol. 13.2: 106-113.

Simpson, Leanne. As We Have Always Done: Indigenous Freedom Through Radical Resistance. Minneapolis: University of Minnesota, 2017.

Sontag, Susan. On Photography. New York: Farrar, Straus and Giroux, 1978.

----. Regarding the Pain of Others. New York: Farrar, Straus and Giroux, 2003.

Sterling, Shirley. My Name is Seepeetza. Toronto: Douglas & McIntyre, 1992.

Strathman, Nicole. "Student Snapshots: An Alternative approach to the Visual History of American Indian Boarding Schools." Humanities Vol. 4 (2015): 726–747.

Truth and Reconciliation Commission of Canada (TRC). Honouring the Truth, Reconciling for the Future: Summary of the Final Report. TRC, 2015.

Warley, Linda. "Captured Childhoods: Photographs in Indian Residential School Memoir." In Marlene Kadar, Jeanne Perreault, and Linda Warley (eds) Photographs, Histories, and Meanings. New York: Palgrave Macmillan, 2009. 201-221.

Chapter Eighteen

Indigitalgames.com and Representations of Indigenous Peoples in Video Games

Naithan Lagace

Digital identity has become an influential aspect of Indigenous representations in the 21st century. With the rise in popularity of social media, blogging sites and other social platforms, identity can become skewed or assimilated in digital media. The Indigitalgames.com project wants to show the complexities and various factors that contribute to representations seen in video games throughout the decades. Initially, the plan was simple, examine images similar to those seen in other media forms like Hollywood Western movies, or Western comics. As I began to investigate more diverse genres of games, there were multiple types of representations involving Indigenous people that didn't follow the Noble Savage characteristics. Not all representations wore headdresses and threw tomahawks. This discovery allowed me to examine other images seen in video games and compare the tropes and stereotypes. As technology continues to develop and expand concepts of space, people use said space to inform, to connect with others over long distances and to explore ideas and values that otherwise would not be accessible in the physical area. By using technology like blogs, social media outlets, and cellular devices, local space becomes intertwined with technology, often, used as a starting point for discussions and relationships. This paper will discuss the complexities that digital media has on Indigenous identity and by using Indigitalgames.com to show video games like Until Dawn and Assassins Creed 3's complex tropes of Indigenous cultures can be used to counteract negative representations of Indigenous people through digital content aimed at educating multiple generations of peoples on video game stereotypes.

Digital media can reshape the way people perceive cultures, and communities as generations of younger people continue exploring this media through technology. Digital technology is an interest for many Indigenous communities who wish to pursue etiquette ways of including their cultures into newer forms of technology. Perceptions surrounding space and the importance of physical space come into question as more Indigenous peoples rely on digital space for connecting with their communities. As younger generations of Indigenous peoples continue to move away from their traditional homelands, the higher the reliance on digital media to stay connected with family back home becomes. Messaging, however, can consistently change within digital spaces as there becomes more input from people sharing similar backgrounds, experiences, and relationships. For many communities, this becomes a concern when representations within digital media become intertwined traditional roles and other information associations. As Joshua describes in his book; *No Sense of Place: The Impact of Electronic Media on Social Behavior;* "the change in the information characteristics of traditional groups lead to two complementary phenomena: the decreasing importance of traditional group ties and the increasing importance of other types of association" (Meyrowitz, 131). Connectivity through digital media for Indigenous communities raises concerns as many feel digital space assimilates communities and traditions. It is up to re-establishing the importance of roles and responsibilities within communities through digital media to rebalance what potential disconnections may arise while incorporating digital space into physical spaces.

Roles and responsibilities can continue to resemble parts in natural communities if input and relationships continue to be reflected similarly within digital spaces. Reconnecting physically disconnected people to communities through digital space is essential, as technology can quickly bring individuals back into their respective communities. It is important to note, that because physical presence declines within Indigenous communities with every generation, roles of elders and youth can still preserve the importance of relationships through contributions in digital space. Knowledge can again be passed down, and relations can always be upheld using technology. As Joshua explains; "electronic media affect social roles because they bypass the communication networks that once made particular places unique. More and more, people are living in a national (or international) information system rather than a local town or city" (Meyowrityz, 146). Reconstructing relationships within Indigenous communities by using digital media allows families to reconnect that are separated by physical space. However, concerns arise as aspects of identity become harder to simulate within digital media outlets that involve larger, multi-ethnic groups, which incorporate more substantial inputs from people that undermined or underestimate essential aspects of a particular culture.

Relationships within the digital realm have considerably more identity issues when relating to physical ones. Part of the problem, as Joshua describes is that; "The integration of social spheres does not simply give people new places to play their old roles; it changes the roles that are played. As place and information access become disconnected, place-behaviors and activities begin to fade" (Meyrowitz, 148). Within physical connections, roles of elders or community leaders become tied to community presence. These social spheres reinforce the importance of continuing roles and responsibilities, tying people back into their culture. Digital media plays a significant role in rebuilding mentioned relationships, as more and more Indigenous youth travel away from their home communities pursuing a career or personal interests. Using social media sites, blogs or even digital phone channels like Skype or Discord, youth can now reconnect and often teach older generations to harness these technology gifts as tools for reinforcing positive relationships. What digital sites achieve is significant, as on the one hand they can strengthen roles and responsibilities of older people in the community, but can change how to address challenges from being physically distant from their community. As technology continues to develop and expand concepts of space, people use this space as an opportunity to inform and to connect with others over vast distances.

Additionally, to explore ideas and values that otherwise would not be accessible in the physical area. As Eric explains;

> local space is defined by a users ability to locate information flows... local information acquisition, once regulated to the sidewalk conversation, church meetings, town halls, is now potentially extended to the internet or mobile phone... In each case, they are privy to local information without setting foot in the physical space to which information is accessed, in a networked society... (26)

Video games differentiate from other popular forms of media like comic books and television shows or movies, that loosely identify Indigenous characters only through visual and auditorial ques, whereas video games combine these formats to enhance representations.

Video games present information to a multitude of different generations that play them. For comparison, books have confidently separate age groups according to the complexities of the material, whereas digital media like video games allow the more adult-oriented content to be accessed more readily for younger generations. Eric describes this as; "a child's age was once a prime determinant of what he or she knew. Very different types of children were exposed to similar information because they were in the same age group. Now, children of every age are presented with "all-age" social information through electronic media" (Meyerowitz, 151). An "all-ages" information system dissolves the restrictive order placed on written information, as the specific or adult-focused content is more available or accessible on the platform. Information in digital media consistently shifts and changes depending on who or what factors contribute within them. Multiple aspects of Indigenous imagery portray the complexities facing identity, culture and traditional values when describing what makes an Indigenous person Indigenous. Using examples like Until Dawn, Assassins Creed 3 as well as others, provides examples of non-Indigenous video game companies reconstructing Indigenous cultures in their games. Indigitalgames examines some of the portrayals that famous video game developers use to devalue Indigenous people. Some examples that are used by non-Indigenous video game developers are mystical, or Wendigo depictions that are used to reconstruct essential traditions surrounding spiritual lessons. As well as hyper-violent warrior imagery, that deconstructs vital roles warrior teachings have on Indigenous men. Both examples show that adverse impacts are displaying beyond what the game visually presents to the player.

Mystical and Wendigos in Until Dawn

A dominant contributing trope continuing to restrict representations of Indigenous cultures, communities, and traditions is through mystical and Wendigo tropes. These tropes share similar relationships with the "savage" or "noble savage" tropes as their representations other and limit mystical or traditional ties of Indigenous communities to their past. In video game media, mystical or Wendigos are used as historical lore within the game as a justification for the demonic nature that the game takes place within. Mystical representations include tropes like spiritual creatures such as the Wendigo in Until Dawn are the antagonists that the player must conquer to fight their way out of a remote cottage in the northern Alberta winter. Shape-shifters are a part of many First Nations cultures and have become popular plot devices in recent popular literature- especially the subgenre of horror/science fiction. In *Shape-shifting: Images of Native Americans in Recent Popular Fiction,* Macdonald, Macdonald and Sheridan (2000) describe shape-shifting as;

> a human being changing into another living creature- for example. The shamanistic idea of the Lakota Sioux warriors shape-shifting into buffalo or

CHAPTER EIGHTEEN

wolves to enhance hunting skills and to honor the animal hunted... In general, it carries the idea of metamorphosis, of transformation from one form to another, or to some degree, becoming the other, sharing point of view and lifeway (Adare, xvii; MacDonald et al., xiv-xv).

One example that uses the Wendigo or mystical tropes as the backbone to their storylines is Until Dawn. This game reinforces a character that "others" or disassociates essential teachings involving traditions, vital lessons or cultures that many Indigenous cultures would use to reiterate fundamental cultural ties that are passed down through younger generations.

Until Dawn is a 3rd person horror adventure game set in an isolated cabin in the northern mountains of Alberta, Canada. In the game, you take control of 9 friends who return to the family cabin one year after a tragic event. Throughout the game, the player controls multiple characters between chapters, often exploring both new and familiar surroundings previously examined. The main story revolves around the teenagers, as shortly after reaching the cabin, something or someone begins to hunt them down. Every interaction, dialogue choice and button press or button miss press impacts the character's path through their portion of the story. The "butterfly effect" as the game describes it early on, is the primary mechanism that revolves around the player's choices and weaves them into pieces of the story. Every decision the player makes shifts the story into another direction. For example, if the player decides one character should be killed or accidentally fails a chase scene, where button combination completions are required to see a character safely cross a dangerous section of the level, the player will lose a piece of the story that only that player can acquire. Ultimately, player choice having such a substantial impact on the story is an essential mechanic that keeps the player emotionally invested in ensuring every character contributes to their portion of the game.

The story involving the playable characters is not the only story told, however, as the player explores the mountain environment, they will find side story tidbits revolving around the previous residents living up on the mountain. The game describes the mountain as having a checkered history. The game details that in 1893, "the Cree" were the original inhabitants amongst the mountain. Upon colonial expansion, Tin and Radium were discovered in the region causing a massive mining boom. After a lack of maintenance, a devastating structural collapse in the mine caused 30 miners to be trapped in the intricate tunnels of the pit. After numerous days of surviving on only a small stream of water, 12 miners resorting to cannibalism. The miners were found and rescued and placed into the recently built Blackwood Asylum, where the miners would slowly turn into cannibalistic creatures. In the early 1990's, property near the Asylum was purchased by the American movie mogul Bob Washington and a vacation home was soon constructed. This vacation home is the location surrounding the player's main story.

Until Dawn uses multiple examples of Cree people in both the primary and side missions in the game. The Wendigo depicted in the game are based on legends that describe a creature or monster who transforms from a human into a cannibalistic monster. The story states that anyone who ate human flesh would run the risk of being possessed by the Wendigo around the Blackwood Mountain. During a playthrough, if the player finds the "Strangers Journal," it describes that the Cree believed that the Blackwood Mountain was sacred land. It also details that prophecies were foretold of butterflies guiding ones to wither good or bad fortune. As mining began to disrupt the holy grounds, the Wendigo was released. The attachment that once solidly connected the Cree nation to the Blackwood Mountain region would dissipate by the destructive measures of mining in the area.

Over consuming resources are also described as another symptom of transforming a person into a Wendigo. Basil Johnson argues in; *The Manitous: The Spiritual World of the Ojibway,* that overconsumption of an individual rather than supporting his/her family can also contribute to the Wendigo becoming stronger.

> There is nothing more harmful in humankind's inclination to rest, play, celebrate, feast, and pursue hobbies. The trouble is that some people don't know when to stop and appear not to care, because nature, or Kitchi-Manitou, has endowed them with slightly more than is good for them: appetites, passions, and desires that dilute their talents, common sense, and judgment. It doesn't take much. A fraction too much or too little of anger, envy, or lust is enough to create an imbalance in a person's character to impair his or her judgment and weaken his or her resolution (Johnston 223-224).

Johnston describes the rapid western colonial expansion, similarly to the development mentioned in the game, as a crucial contributor to the survival of the Wendigo entity. As Johnson indicates that the ends of business deal with power, wealth, and profit. Anything that diminishes the return, ensuring not to violate the rights of others or; "to ensure the land remains fertile and productive for future generations…"(Johnston, 237). When exploring the miner's side story clues, the player would find out the history of the miners themselves and 1952 mine collapse. The game also makes mention in a Journal clue found as a secondary source of information about the slow transition into Wendigo's as some would resort to cannibalism. It is important to note that the game designers did not use resource extracting as another symptom that would lead the miners to turn into Wendigo's, only the idea of resorting to cannibalism set the transformation into play.

Until Dawn plays with an iconic 1980's horror movie trope setting to tell a story of isolation, desperation, and revenge. The mystery surrounding the Wendigo is solely upon the fear surrounding nonhuman actions like cannibalism rather than a multitude of factors that could change a character into a Wendigo like greed, or cannibalism as Johnston describes earlier. The depiction of wendigoes as a "mythical" or nonhuman like entity that completely dissociates the creature from a human. The game uses Wendigoes as creatures that only transform through nonhuman actions (cannibalism) and not that of massive resource extraction. Another example that takes on a different form of negative stereotyping is through the Warrior representation used in Assassins Creed 3.

Warrior and "Hyper Violence"

The player portrays the warrior representation in the game Assassin's Creed 3. In Assassin's Creed 3, the player controls the character named Desmond Miles, who uses a futuristic device called the Animus to travel back in time to fight an organization trying to run the world called Templars. During this setting, Desmond will use the Animus to live out one of his Native America relatives during the American Revolutionary War period. Connor, Ratonhnhaké:ton who is a half-English, half-Mohawk man whose father is a part of the Templars. The player may play an active role in warriorhood in Assassin's Creed 3, but some factors continue to reinforce unhealthily aspects involving Indigenous men and violence within Assasins Creed 3. In Assassin's Creed 3, Ratonhnhaké:ton must build up an army in which helps him continue his search throughout the Americas for his father, Haythem Kenway. Kenway, early on within the game finds, kills and burns down Ratonhnhaké:ton community. The player experiences the harsh realities of interactions between early colonial settlers and Indigenous communities. Showing Ratonhnhaké:ton as a small child losing his community gives the player the understanding of his struggles throughout the game, forcing the player to explore and interact with the environment and continue to grow with Ratonhnaké:ton. The destruction of the community by his father paints Ratonhnaké:ton as an underdog being forced to overcome such obstacles to survive. This event occurs while, Ratonhnhaké:ton is still a young child, attempting to get the player to sympathize with Ratonhnhaké:ton as after seeing his community destroyed, he must kill everyone involved. What Assassins Creed 3 illustrates is a very violent event of "warrior" mentality where Ratonhnhaké:ton must then partake in violently assassinating everyone held responsible for his communities extinction.

Hyper "warrior" mentality is a destructive accomplice in many Indigenous communities surrounding the men. However, one example of warriorhood that is described by Thomas Ka'auwai Kaulukui Jr in the book; *Indigenous Men and Masculinities* as warriorhood coming from the deity Ku, which represents the god of war. In the interview, Ty.P. Kawika Tengen writes: "In actuality, Ku is a deity of male generative force and productivity, and including statecraft, governance, farming, fishing, and healing; even more broadly, Ku is seen as the masculine component of society that compliments Hina, the Feminine" (Tengan, 229). Kaulukukui explains that Ku mainly represents responsibility. The responsibility of one's self regarding ethics, morality, having good values, being in substantial physical strength. All factors contribute to responsibilities surrounding "protection, building, and carrying the heavy physical loads and all of those things which are necessary for a male role in society" (Kaulukui, 230- 231). Roles and responsibility then sprout out from self to family, then to the community and finally to nations. Throughout the interview, there are conversations about Kaulukui's time serving in the military and the experiences he sees in other Indigenous men dealing with their Kus. In the interview Kaulukukuis discusses that one of the most important things in which Indigenous warriors need to do when dealing with this built up Ku is to rather than fighting with that aspect of life, there needs to be recognition that Ku is a part of who Indigenous men are. Secondly, Kaulukukui mentions that recognition of the community needs is vital for what is acceptable conduct within a civilized society, separating that from the violent actions appropriate in war. Lastly, Kaulukukuis mentions that then the men would need to:

> deal with the experience itself and try to translate the experience of battle into something that is positive, has made you stronger so that you can move forward to carry your community responsibilities in the peacetime effort... take those things in which can be seen as a negative experience and look at the positive aspects of it that make you stronger and better to live a better life to carry your kuleana here (Kaulukukui, 232).

Ultimately suggesting, that the warriorhood mentality is something that is inside every Indigenous male and that for that kuleana to remain positive, violent actions that only hurt oneself or the people around them must be dealt with accordingly.

Throughout Assassins Creed 3, the family values that Kaulukukui mention in his interview with Kawika Tengen are absent in Ratonhnhaké:ton as he ventures through his story. The character deals with his "warriorhood" by lashing out, assaulting and killing the people responsible, continuing to address the pain of loss through violence. The character never looks at his actions as destructive within the community he makes. Often, Ratonhnhaké:ton divides his new community and the "real" world, even more, apart from as the player progresses through the game. The community that Ratonhnhaké:ton creates is that in which all have similar desires. That desire is to kill every Templar (who are British colonizers) and to obtain an abundant amount of wealth. This community is not family or that of even nationhood; it forms the image of the colonizers.

Concluding Thoughts

With video games like Until Dawn and Assasins Creed 3 incorporating harmful tropes and stereotypes of Indigenous peoples as the games main narratives, the importance of Indigenous identity dissolves. The lack of identity leaves younger Indigenous peoples lacking traditional teachings, or the desire to seek out that knowledge as they feel mainstream media has portrayed their cultures as harmful or destructive. However, by providing analyzed information surrounding multiple types of tropes and stereotypes, numerous generations of Indigenous peoples can seek out educational opportunities that constructively display harmful tropes. Having blog type entries like Until Dawn and Assassins Creed 3 shown as examples, the project can enhance the significance of essential roles involving spirituality, the importance of warriorhood, as well as other factors that greatly hinder positive aspects of Indigenous cultures, communities, and traditions for generations of Indigenous peoples. The continuation of blog entries that present both positive and negative tropes continue to expand concepts of Indigenous identity, as well as address concerns about cultures expanding into digital media. Roles, responsibilities, and communities can draw upon video games that detail specific examples that either incorporate examples of positive cases or as shown with the examples given in this essay, dissolve essential aspects of

Indigenous culture. As each game adds another example of the complex nature surrounding Indigenous representations in video games, Indigitalgames.com wants to present these issues in a suitable way that can be consumed by multiple generations of Indigenous and non-Indigenous peoples that further the conversations surrounding positive digital media relationships of cultures, traditions, and communities.

References

Adare, S. (2005). "Indian" Stereotypes in TV Science Fiction. University of Texas.
Anderson, K., & Innes, R. A. (2015). Indigenous Men and Masculinities; Legacies, Identities, Regeneration. Winnipeg: University of Manitoba Press.
Bergland, R. (2000). The National Uncanny: Indian Ghosts and American Subjects. Press of New England.
Gordon, E. (2009). Redefining the Local: The Distinction between Located Information and Local Knowledge in Location-Based Games. Peter Lang Publishing.
Macdonald, A., Macdonald, G., & Sheridan, M. (2000). Shape-Shifting: Images in Native Americans in Recent Popular Fiction. Westport, CT: Greenwood Press.
Mayerfeld Bell, M. (1997). The Ghosts of Place Theory and Society 26. Kluwer Academic Publishers.
McKegney, S. (2014). Masclindians; Conversations About Indigenous Manhood. University of Manitoba Press.
Meyrowitz, J. (1985). No Sense of Place: The Impact of Electronic Media on Social Behaviour. Oxford University Press.
Tengan, T. K., Kaulukukui Jr, T. K., & Richards Jr., W. K. (2015). "The Face of Ku:" A Dialogue on Hawaiian Warriorhood. In K. Anderson & R. A. Innes (Eds.), Indigenous Men and Masculinities (pp. 229–242). University of Manitoba Press.

Chapter Nineteen

Expanding Métis Curriculum[92]

Chantal Fiola

Too often Indigenous content is included in curriculum in a tokenistic way. The focus is usually on First Nations rather than Métis; this is true from early years through to post-secondary education including within Indigenous Studies departments. To emerging (and established) scholars and educators, I encourage finding ways to increase Métis-specific content in curriculum.

In this chapter, I explain how historic and contemporary Métis exclusion is predicated upon the denial of Métis indigeneity as part of the larger colonial agenda of assimilation. Educators can eliminate pernicious stereotypes about Métis people and more accurately teach about Métis identity and nationhood. New Indigenous Course Requirements (ICRs) being implemented by some universities may be useful (in combination with other strategies) in addressing Métis erasure in education. I also spend time debunking stereotypes regarding Métis spirituality and discuss the latest research in this area. I appeal to educators to create greater space in their classrooms and institutions for Métis-focused curriculum and, in so doing, promote Métis self-determination and sovereignty.

SIDELINING MÉTIS: FROM THE PAST TO THE PRESENT

Historical examples of Métis exclusion by settler governments abound. Before Canada existed, British treaty negotiators were given instructions to only deal with "Indians;" according to racist logic "Halfbreeds" and Métis were half-civilized due to their partial white ancestry and, therefore, less in need of civilizing or Indigenous rights. During the Robinson Treaties negotiations in 1850, in the Great Lakes region of present-day Ontario, Chief Shingwauk insisted that his Métis kin be included in the treaties but white treaty commissioner, William Robinson, "would do nothing for the half breeds, because his instructions ordered him to treat with Indians, not whites" (Surtees, 1986). The Canadian government preferred to exclude Métis from the numbered treaties and continue this exclusion in comprehensive land claims (modern treaties). When the government did negotiate agreements with the Métis, they refused to acknowledge them as *treaties*. Métis scholars Dr. Adam Gaudry and Professor Larry Chartrand launched the Métis Treaties Research Project (2017) to "challenge this common understanding and to show that Métis-settler relations in Canada, from the 19th century to the current times, have been marked by the conclusion of treaties." For instance, the Manitoba Act (1870), which brought Manitoba into confederation thanks to the Métis provisional government headed by Louis Riel, was referred to by Riel as the "Manitoba Treaty" and the "Métis Treaty" (Gaudry, 2016; Shore, 1999, p.76).

Two more examples of the Canadian government's fickle treatment of Métis people that continue to have ramifications are residential/day schools and the Sixties Scoop. Biological determinism enabled the racist logic that Métis children were less Indigenous than First Nations children because of their partial Eurocanadian ancestry; therefore, the Canadian government preferred separating Métis children into day schools and First Nations children into residential schools (Fiola, 2015). Some Métis children did go to residential schools; moreover, the day schools were run by the same clergy as the residential schools, the same abuses existed, and the same intergenerational impacts are experienced. Yet, the Residential Schools Settlement (IRSS) agreement (2007) excluded day schools, and thereby, excluded most Métis survivors from compensation (Fiola, 2015; Indigenous and Northern Affairs Canada, n.d.).

Conversely, Métis children were taken into the child welfare system earlier than First Nations children — provincial child welfare was only extended to children on reserves in 1951. During the "Sixties Scoop," thousands of Métis and First Nations children were taken from their homes and placed in (white) homes due to the racist government belief that white people were better parents (York, 1990). Neglect, abuse, and forced Christianization continued to occur as they did in residential/day schools, and similar intergenerational effects plague survivors. The Canadian government reached an agreement regarding the Sixties Scoop including $750 million to compensate First Nations and Inuit survivors taken between 1951-1991 (Tasker, 2017). Like the IRSS agreement, the Sixties Scoop agreement excludes Métis survivors; the Métis National Council (MNC) was not consulted or alerted about the negotiations (Kirkup, 2017).

In 1982, with the patriation of the Canadian Constitution, the Government of Canada officially recognized Métis people as *Aboriginal* alongside First Nations and Inuit. Frustratingly, the provincial and federal governments continued to argue over which level of government held jurisdiction over the Métis. In 2016, the Supreme Court of Canada (SCC) declared that the federal government has jurisdiction over Métis peoples (Daniels v. Canada, 2016). This makes the exclusion of Métis survivors from these settlements unjustifiable. Despite government and judicial systems, there are other avenues which can counter the erasure of Métis people.

INDIGENOUS COURSE REQUIREMENT

A shift is occurring in post-secondary institutions as illustrated by the implementation of Indigenous Course Requirements (ICRs) at the University of Winnipeg (UW) and Lakehead University. Beginning in September 2016, all students who enroll must complete a minimum of one three credit-hour course to graduate. For UW, this was a student-lead initiative approved by Senate as promoting the university's mandate of indigenization. According to Lakehead University (2017), ICR-approved courses contain "at least 50% (equivalent to 18 hours) of Indigenous knowledge and/or Aboriginal content." Similarly, at UW (n.d.) ICR-approved "course content is derived from or based on an analysis of the cultures, languages, history, ways of knowing or contemporary reality of the Indigenous peoples of North America."

ICR implementation is presenting early challenges including: backlash from (especially white) scholars who are against indigenizing the academy and denounce Indigenous scholarship (Widdowsen, 2016); (white) students who resent being "forced" to take classes which privilege worldviews other than their own; Indigenous students and faculty experiencing backlash; increased pressure on existing Indigenous faculty asked by non-Indigenous faculty for "assistance" in indigenizing their syllabi or to guest lecture; a lack of Indigenous representation among faculty; increased demands for supports/resources; the realization that Indigenous content isn't enough, and a subsequent call for Indigenous ways of teaching as well as questions regarding non-Indigenous professors and the potential for cultural appropriation.

Despite these challenges, ICRs can lessen ignorance among Canadians regarding Indigenous realities and (neo)colonization (Fiola & MacKinnon, forthcoming). There are many ways we can participate in these efforts;

one suggestion for educators is to correct stereotypes and misinformation about Métis people and make space for Métis-specific content in curriculum.

MÉTIS IDENTITY AND NATIONHOOD

Educators can do better regarding the topics of Métis identity and nationhood. When Métis issues are discussed at all, too often the starting point is a reduction of Métis ethnogenesis (origins) and identity to racial mixing. British then Canadian governments encouraged a definition of Métis identity based on biological determinism and implied that such mixing amounts to a lack of authenticity. Denying Métis indigeneity inhibits Métis nationhood and rights thereby bolstering a colonial agenda of privileging foreign (Canadian) government and settler rights over Indigenous nationhood and rights. Educators can help correct this harmful definition of Métis identity and re-center it around nationhood.

Métis scholar Chris Andersen (2014) documents the evolution of Métis as an administrative concept used to deny Métis rights and nationhood. He explains that "Métis are understood as mixed, diluted missives of a deeper and more legitimate indigeneity, namely, that of our First Nation ancestors" (p.36) and that the supposed "'purity' of 'Indians' and 'whites' is naturalized at the expense of Métis peoplehood" (p.32). Countering the stereotype of *Métis-as-mixed*, Andersen and others (Gaudry & Leroux, 2017; Fiola; 2015) maintain a definition of Métis that "refer[s] to the history, events, leaders, territories, language, and culture associated with the growth of the buffalo hunting and trading Métis of the northern Plains, in particular during the period between the beginning of the Métis buffalo brigades in the early nineteenth century and the 1885 North West Uprising" (Andersen, 2014, p.24). One is Métis if one is descended from the historic Red River Métis and our kinship networks which extend from Red River east to the Upper Great Lakes, west into eastern British Columbia, south into the northern United States, and north to the Northwest Territories (Andersen, 2014, p.18).

Racial definitions of Métis that minimize our indigeneity are linked to government refusal to engage with Métis as Indigenous people (Fiola, 2015). One example is Métis exclusion from the Indian Act (1876) which is used to prevent us from treaty-making. The Indian Act explicitly prohibited "half-breeds" in Manitoba from coming under the the Act (Lawrence, 2004; Lawrence, 1999), and later excluded "half-breeds" beyond Manitoba (Dickason, 1992). Section 3 stated, "no half-breed head of family (except the widow of an Indian, or a half-breed who has already been admitted into a treaty) shall be accounted an Indian, or entitled to be admitted into any Indian treaty" (Green, 1997, p.79). The Act created "non-status Indians" who did not meet the government's requirements for obtaining registered Indian status.

The administrative categories of *Métis* and *non-status Indian* became conflated. In the prairies, this conflation was understandable given that Métis culture, language, and spirituality are closely tied to our parent cultures, especially Anishinaabe (Saulteaux, Ojibwe) and Nêhiyaw (Cree); our kinship ties run deeply and intermarriage is common (Innes, 2013). However, conflating Métis and non-status Indians east of the Great Lakes is illogical because there are no recognized historic Métis communities there (Gaudry & Leroux, 2017). Conflation increased in 1982 with section 35 which recognized Métis people as Aboriginal and acknowledged Aboriginal and treaty rights. Legally, this meant that the federal government could no longer deny Métis indigeneity and rights. Indeed, in R. v. Powley (2003), the SCC recognized Sault Ste. Marie, Ontario as a historic Métis community with section 35 hunting rights affirmed for Métis descendants. However, the SCC's definition of "Métis" only required that a "claimant's historical community be composed of Indigenous members who, living apart from Indian or Inuit communities, had not been classified by contemporaneous official taxonomies (whether British or Canadian) as members of either one" (Andersen, 2014, p.168), as opposed to requiring proof of historical attachment to the Red River Métis. This racial definition of Métis could include *any mixture* of Indigenous and EuroCanadian ancestry. After 1982 and since 2003, there has been an increase in non-status Indians self-identifying as Métis attempting to gain federal recognition and rights. One example was the "Labrador Métis Nation"; however, they now call themselves NunatuKavut in recognition of their *Inuit* and EuroCanadian ancestry (Andersen, 2014).

Settler self-indigenization further complicates Métis identity and inhibits Métis nationhood – the phenomenon of white settlers finding one Indigenous ancestor in their genealogy from 200 years ago, then self-identifying as "Métis" and demanding Aboriginal rights. Since 1982 and 2003, the potential for federally recognized Métis rights has been growing; as a result, that period has seen an explosion of self-identification as "Métis" by people without connection to the historic Métis Nation (Gaudry & Leroux, 2017).

Settler self-indigenization, and a preference for calling themselves Métis (as opposed to First Nations), is linked to the Métis-as-mixed racial definition of Métis and to the difficulty of gaining registered Indian status -

government attempts to decrease the number of people with registered Indian status continues (Gehl, 2017). This phenomenon is being fuelled by two recent SCC cases. In MMF v Canada (2013), the SCC declared that the Crown (i.e. federal government) failed in its constitutional duty to distribute 1.4 million acres of land promised to the Métis (Manitoba Act, 1870). In Daniels v Canada (2016), the SCC declared that in section 91(24) of the Constitution Act (1867), the term "Indian" includes Métis and non-status Indians; this section outlines federal jurisdiction over "Indians and lands reserved for Indians." These cases open the door to Métis land claims and rights and many settlers want access to them. Self-identifying as Indigenous distances white settlers from guilt over benefitting from settler privilege – what Tuck and Yang (2012) call "settler moves to innocence" (p.9). Some of these "Métis" people and their organizations claim they are more legitimately Métis than Red River Métis and dispute First Nations rights (Gaudry & Leroux, 2017). Settler self-indigenization and the Métis-as-mixed stereotype inhibit Métis self-determination including our right to define our identity, membership, and rights.

Educators can illuminate the conflation of Métis and non-status Indians, and white settler self-indigenization, and expose how these phenomena are based on racist definitions of Métis. Rather than a definition based on biological determinism, educators can emphasize that Métis people are a post-contact Indigenous *nation* (Andersen, 2014, p.207). Teaching accurate understandings of Métis could help curb the incidence of white settlers co-opting Métis identity, and protect the space required for legitimate members of our nation displaced via residential/day schools and the Sixties Scoop to find their way home.

MÉTIS SPIRITUALITY

Spirituality is another misunderstood aspect of Métis identity and nationhood; here, too, educators can assist in debunking stereotypes. Much has been written about Métis relationships with Christianity, especially Roman Catholicism (Widder, 1999; McCarthy, 1990; Huel, 1996); almost nothing has been published regarding our relationships with traditional Indigenous spirituality. Educators can create space to further this dialogue. Below, I outline a longstanding stereotype regarding Métis spirituality, briefly trace Métis relationships with Indigenous spirituality and Christianity, and examine ways that colonization has impacted these.

It is not by chance that many (including Indigenous) people believe the stereotype that Métis people only go to church and First Nations people only go to ceremonies (Fiola, 2015). Colonial legislation (e.g. Indian Act outlawing Indigenous ceremonies) and colonial systems (e.g. residential/day schools, child welfare eradicating Indigenous cultures) have disconnected many Métis and First Nations people from Indigenous spirituality (Fiola, 2015). Debunking the stereotype above, syncretism (blending Christianity and Indigenous spirituality) is common in many Métis and First Nation families.

Préfontaine, Paquin, and Young (2003) argue that Métis spirituality exists on a continuum from Christianity to traditional Indigenous spirituality with syncretism in between. This is true of Métis spirituality historically and today. Historically, distinct Métis culture and spirituality were influenced by our parent cultures including their spiritualities – especially Anishinaabe, Nêhiyaw, and French. Early factors impacting the continuum of Métis spirituality included proximity to First Nations communities and relatives, and to white settler communities and relatives, and the presence or absence of a Christian church in the community (Fiola, 2015).

In the early 1800s, writing about the Saulteaux, Métis, and Cree population of Duck Bay, MB, Father Simonet was disappointed that despite converting to Catholicism, "nearly half of them had abandoned their Catholic religion and renewed their Native beliefs and practices" (McCarthy, 1990, p.113). By 1858, Henry Youle Hind noted "forty to fifty 'halfbreed indians' living there.... Métis who lived a life very similar to that of the Sauteux [sic]" (p.112). Ten years later, Père Camper documented a large gathering there for "la Grande Medicine" (Midewiwin); despite his conversion efforts, he "realized that their faith was somewhat uncertain. They sometimes attended his services and sometimes those at the medicine lodge" (p.114). Father Belcourt, a predecessor to Camper, witnessed such a gathering at Manitoba House (en route to Duck Bay): "This large number had gathered for the Midewiwin ceremony, the type of native religious practice which was abhorred by the missionaries because it posed such an obstacle to the inculcation of Christianity" (p.103-4). Priests' journals confirm that Red River Métis people participated in ceremonies in the early nineteenth century.

Métis spiritual syncretism meant that Métis would adopt Christian beliefs in a way that was consistent with Indigenous cosmology. Huel (1996) notes that Indigenous people who had converted to Christianity in the Red River region and attended the Pilgrimage at Lac Ste. Anne in Alberta participated on "terms consonant with native modes of thought and relevant to perceived needs" (p.270-1). Payment (2009) explains that ongoing adherence to Indigenous spirituality frustrated clergy including belief in the immortality of the soul, the "happy hunting ground," and customs like "serial monogamy, polygamy, conjuring rituals, and casting of spells practiced" which priests condemned as 'pagan' and 'savage' (p.95). Consequently, Christian missionaries redoubled their efforts to disconnect Métis from traditional spirituality.

By 1818, Joseph Provencher, Sévère Dumoulin, and Guillaume Edge, the first missionaries to arrive permanently in the Red River settlement (Siggins, 1995), drastically increased Christian influence upon Red River Métis people. Priests accompanied us on our bi-annual bison hunts (Huel, 1996) and often wintered with us (Payment, 2009). Priests sometimes learned Indigenous languages to promote conversion – around Red River, Métis people preferred attending mass in Saulteaux (McCarthy, 1990, p.18). By 1845, Red River had six priests, four Grey Nuns, and several Oblates; ten years later, there were 30 priests, and by the end of the nineteenth century, the Diocese of St. Boniface (in present-day Winnipeg) had 60 priests, 350 nuns, and 140 Oblates – it had become the "gateway to the Catholic Northwest" (Duval, 2009, p.67-8). In addition to Christian missionaries, colonial legislation and systems also significantly impacted Métis spirituality.

Not only did colonial legislation and systems impact Métis identity and nationhood, they also influenced Métis spirituality. The Indian Act and treaty-making impacted Métis identity by excluding Métis people and creating divisions between us and our First Nations relatives (Fiola, 2015). Forced divisions were also created by the differential treatment of Métis and First Nations children in residential/day schools and the child welfare system which further removed Métis children from traditional Indigenous spirituality (Fiola, 2015). Conversely, Métis and First Nations have shared intergenerational trauma stemming from these colonial systems including disconnection from Indigenous spirituality.

Such divisions are heightened in our current rights-based climate with Section 35 rights and recent court case wins – to claim these rights, Métis people must prove we are wholly distinct from our First Nations relatives. Having to prove complete distinction/separation from First Nations encourages Métis people to distance ourselves from all things First Nations including ceremonies (due partly to the stereotype discussed above) despite our historic and contemporary participation in them (Fiola, 2015).

My doctoral research found that Catholicism is lessening its hold on some Red River Métis as we increasingly find our way back to traditional

Indigenous spirituality including Sundance and Midewiwin (Fiola, 2015). My current research explores Métis reconnection to ceremony at the community level in selected Manitoba Métis communities. I argue that contemporary Métis spirituality continues to exist on a continuum from Christianity to traditional Indigenous spirituality (with syncretism in between), and that Métis people are increasingly reconnecting with ceremonies. Historically, *Métis spirituality* included participation in ceremonies such as sweat lodge, Sundance, and Midewiwin, and these relationships are being revived within Métis spirituality today. In other words, *Métis spirituality* includes ceremonies in its own right.

Increasingly, educators want to *indigenize* their curriculum and courses, I encourage debunking the false stereotype that Métis people only go to church, and First Nations people only go to ceremonies. Métis spirituality is one aspect of Métis nationhood that has been ignored and is deserving of respectful attention.

A WAY FORWARD

With this chapter, I expose ongoing Métis erasure and encourage rectifying this in educational settings including in classrooms and curriculum. The growing interest among Canadian universities to decolonize and indigenize academia, as evidenced by ICRs, brings hope of addressing such erasure. In these efforts, we must take care not to fall into the traps of tokenism, lip service, romanticization, and oversimplification.

Much of the work to develop Métis-specific research and curriculum should be done by Métis scholars, researchers, and educators; however, non-Métis allies can help. Stereotypes such as "Métis-as-mixed," and "Métis people only go to church (and First Nations only go to ceremonies)" continue to misinform Indigenous and non-Indigenous people. Educators have a responsibility to help clear away such misunderstandings and teach updated and more respectful information.

I have highlighted selected areas where emerging (and established) educators can assist in such work; namely, Métis identity, nationhood, and spirituality. I invite educators to think of ways to help make space in our educational institutions for further development in these areas. In so doing, we will promote Métis self-determination and nationhood. Educators can use their platform to expand content and curriculum to include more and relevant information on Métis people and issues. Educators can use their influence to teach healthy respect for Métis nationhood and self-determination; we can all do more to be better neighbours on these Indigenous lands we now call *Canada*.

Miigwetch

References

Andersen, C. (2014). "Métis": Race, recognition, and the struggle for Indigenous peoplehood. Toronto: UBC Press.
Daniels v. Canada (Indian Affairs and Northern Development). (2016, April 14). Supreme Court Judgement. Government of Canada. Retrieved from https://scc-csc.lexum.com/scc-csc/scc-csc/en/item/15858/index.do
Dickason, O. (1992). *Canada's First Nations: A history of founding peoples from earliest times*. Toronto: Oxford University Press.
Duval, J. (2001-2003). The Catholic Church and the formation of Métis identity. *Pat Imperfect*, 9: 65-87.
Fiola, C. (2015). *Rekindling the sacred fire: Métis ancestry and Anishinaabe spirituality*. Winnipeg: University of Manitoba Press.
Fiola, C., & MacKinnon, S. (forthcoming). Urban and inner-city studies: Decolonizing ourselves and the University of Winnipeg. In S. Cote-Meeke & T. Moeke-Pickering (Eds.), Decolonizing the academy. WILL FLESH THIS OUT AS DETAILS EMERGE.
Gaudry, A. (2016). Are the Métis treaty people? *Weweni Indigenous Scholars Speaker Series*. University of Winnipeg. Retrieved from https://www.youtube.com/watch?v=oU8b5QFB53g
Gaudry, A., & Leroux, D. (2017). White settler revisionism and making Métis everywhere: The evocation of métissage in Quebec and Nov Scotia. *Critical Ethnic Studies* 3(1), 116-142.
Gehl, L. (2017). Understanding "6(1)a all the way!" Blog retrieved from https://www.lynngehl.com/black-face-blogging/understanding-61a-all-the-way
Green, J. (1997). Exploring identity and citizenship: Aboriginal women, Bill C-31 and the 'Sawridge Case' (Unpublished doctoral dissertation). Edmonton: University of Alberta.
Huel, R. (1996). *Proclaiming the Gospel to the Indians and Métis*. Edmonton: University of Alberta Press.
Indigenous and Northern Affairs Canada. (n.d.). Indian residential schools. Retrieved from http://www.aadnc-aandc.gc.ca/eng/1100100015576/1100100015577#sect1
Innes, R. (2013). *Elder brother and the law of the people: Contemporary kinship and Cowessess First Nation*. Winnipeg: University of Manitoba Press.
Kirkup, K. (2017, October 10). Métis feel left out of '60s Scoop settlement. *The Star*. Retrieved from https://www.thestar.com/news/canada/2017/10/10/mtis-feel-left-out-of-60s-scoop-settlement.html
Lakehead University. (2017). FAQ's about the Indigenous content requirement (ICR). Retrieved from https://www.lakeheadu.ca/faculty-and-staff/departments/services/ai/icr
Lawrence, B. (2004). *'Real' Indians and others: Mixed-blood urban Native peoples and Indigenous nationhood*. Vancouver: University of British Columbia Press.
—. (1999). 'Real' Indians and others: Mixed race urban Native people, the Indian Act, and the rebuilding of Indigenous nations (Unpublished doctoral dissertation). Ontario Institute for Studies in Education, University of Toronto.
Manitoba Act. (1870). Government of Canada. Retrieved from http://www.solon.org/Constitutions/Canada/English/ma_1870.html
Manitoba Metis Federation Inc. (MMF) v. Canada (Attorney General). (2013, March 8). Supreme Court Judgment. Government of Canada. Retrieved from https://scc-csc.lexum.com/scc-csc/scc-csc/en/item/12888/index.do
McCarthy, M. (1990). *To evangelize the nations: Roman Catholic missions in Manitoba 1818-1870*. Winnipeg: Manitoba Culture Heritage and Recreation Historic Resources.
Métis Treaties Research Project. (2017). Homepage. Retrieved from

http://www.metistreatiesproject.ca/
Payment, D. (2009). *The free people – Li gens libres: A history of the Métis community of Batoche, Saskatchewan*. Calgary: University of Calgary Press.
Préfontaine, D., Paquin, T., & Young, P. (2003). Métis spiritualism. *The Virtual Museum of Métis History and Culture*. Gabriel Dumont Institute. Retrieved from http://www.metismuseum.ca/media/db/00727
R. v. Powley. (2003, September 19). Supreme Court Judgement. Government of Canada. Retrieved from https://scc-csc.lexum.com/scc-csc/scc-csc/en/item/2076/index.do
Shore, F. (1999). The emergence of the Métis nation in Manitoba. In L. Barkwell, L. Dorion & D. Prefontaine (Eds.), *Métis legacy: A Métis historiography and annotated bibliography* (pp.71-78). Winnipeg: Pemmican Publications.
Siggins, M. (1995). *Riel: A life of revolution*. Toronto: Harper Perennial.
Surtees, R. J. (1986). "The Robinson Treaties (1850)." Treaties and Historical Research Centre, Indian and Northern Affairs Canada. Aboriginal Affairs and Northern Development. Retrieved from http://www.aadnc-aandc.gc.ca/eng/1100100028974/1100100028976
Tasker, J. P. (2017, October 5). Ottawa announces $800M settlement with Indigenous survivors of Sixties Scoop. *CBC News*. Retrieved from http://www.cbc.ca/news/politics/ottawa-settle-60s-scoop-survivors-1.4342462
Tuck, E., & Yang, K. W. (2012). Decolonization is not a metaphor. *Decolonization: Indigeneity, Education & Society*, *1*(1): 1-40.
Widder, K. (1999). *Battle for the soul: Métis children encounter Evangelical Protestants at Mackinaw mission, 1823-1837*. East Lansing: Michigan State University Press.
Widdowson, F. (2016, Nov. 4). Academic freedom and indigenization: Should the dissemination of pseudoscientific "ways of knowing" be protected? Paper Presented at the Pseudo-Science and Academic Freedom Colloquium, Saint Mary's University.
University of Winnipeg. (n.d.). Indigenous course requirement criteria. Retrieved from https://www.uwinnipeg.ca/indigenous/indigenous-course-requirement/ICR-criteria.pdf
York, G. (1990). *The dispossessed: Life and death in Native Canada*. London: Vintage UK.

notes

[92] This is a modified version of the keynote address I delivered at the Rising Up Graduate Students Conference on Indigenous Knowledge and Research at the University of Manitoba in the spring of 2018.

**Honouring Identity and Strengthening Community
Through Resistance and Personal Narratives**

Chapter Twenty

Honouring our Relations

Exploring a Wider Acumen of Métis Spaces

Victoria Bouvier, Angie Tucker, Jason Surkan, and Chuck Bourgeois

Looking at the diversity within Métis consciousness, both historically and contemporarily, the discussions that envelop Métis self and collective understandings are complex and multidimensional. These complexities are understood on micro-individual scales and within larger communal spaces that are informed by ancestral knowing, practices and everyday lived experiences. Because of the historical racialized discourse of Métis identity (Andersen, 2014; Gaudry, 2014; Vowel, 2016) there is continuing contention in how people are claiming Métis identities and spaces across the Canadian landscape. Therefore, the (re)telling of stories of how we historically practiced our Métis self and collective understandings in both place and space is imperative. Moreover, even more crucial is storying the ways in which we **are and still continue to** use our ancestral historicity to inform our everyday lived experiences in the present. This chapter will explore how four Métis individuals are honouring their ancestral knowing and connectedness through affirming, defending, and creating Métis spaces.

Shoohkishtikwanew avik shakihi[93]

Victoria Bouvier

Taanishi, Victoria Bouvier, *dishinikawshon niya Michif*. I am writing from within the traditional territories of the *Niitsitapi* (Blackfoot), from *Moh'kins'tsis* (Calgary). I was born in Calgary, but live away from my ancestral homeland of the St. Francois Xavier community of the Red River and Boggy Creek, Manitoba. I was born into the traditions and experiences of my ancestors, but through dwelling in the city, I have been and continue to be shaped and formed by this urban setting. Being re-created by my environment is a continual process; I am always within and enacting relationships every day. I am repeatedly being called by my experiences to make meaning and participate with/in the world in meaningful ways – there is something at stake if I do not. This is a story of how an unsettling experience, within an urban space, provoked an act of resistance - a tribute to my Michif ancestors.

Stories are dynamic, animate, multidimensional, and powerful. They are steeped in and reinforce worldviews, beliefs, values, protocols, and practices. However, those whose stories are marginalized, oppressed, and silenced are assaulted when the telling of a story, that prescribes how history is conveyed, relayed, is told from one perspective. The implications of the assertion of a single story is the erasure of others. Marie Battiste (2013) coins the erasure of stories and histories as **cognitive imperialism**, "When Indigenous knowledge is omitted or ignored in the schools, and a Eurocentric foundation is advanced to the exclusion of other knowledges and languages, these are the conditions that define an experience of cognitive imperialism" (p. 26). Although Battiste (2013) is referring specially to cognitive imperialism in educational environments, I extend this notion into urban spaces. Tuck and Yang (2012) echo these sentiments as they describe the implications of settlers' move to innocence, "In order for the settlers to make a place their home, they must destroy and disappear the Indigenous peoples that live there" (p. 6). There are continued attacks through the erasure of Indigenous minds, bodies, spirits, stories, and histories.

I was attending an event, focussed on creating meaningful discussions on the topic of Reconciliation with agencies and organizations in Calgary. Conversations were generating from the Truth and Reconciliation Commission (2015), but lunch approached, and I had to return to my vehicle so I left the gathering. As I crossed the street toward my car, I scanned my surroundings and noticed a large construction site adjacent to the centre hosting the event. Blocking off the site from the public, were impermanent walls that were placarded with posters. As I read the advertisements along the wall, my eyes fell upon one particular poster that stood out from all the others. There, from the middle of the street, I was confronted by a large six by four-foot Roots Canada advertisement. The poster stopped me dead in my tracks.

CHAPTER TWENTY

Photograph 1. Celebrating 150 years of being nice. #benice

Instantly, I was struck by the propaganda on this poster – Celebrating 150 year of being nice. I stood there, frozen in the middle of the street, feeling assaulted – feeling like I had just been hit in the stomach and robbed of both my history and my presence. I remember thinking *'the last 150 years has been anything but nice for Métis people'*. Mentally and emotionally, I flipped through the atrocities that have been endured by my ancestors; the execution of Louis Riel, the exodus from the Red River, the legacy of the road allowances, perpetuated acts of racism and discrimination, the genocidal attacks on our languages and culture, and sadly, the list goes on. This ad was trying to invalidate and erase our historicity while creating a benevolent narrative of Canadian history.

After returning to the reconciliation event, I was haunted by my encounter with the poster while still trying to weed through the trauma I felt so I could continue to participate in the dialogue. In our afternoon discussions about truth and reconciliation, I shared my experience while affirming—until we learn the TRUTHS of the impacts of on-going settler-colonialism, we will not be able to form meaningful relationships.

Over the last 150 years, Métis individuals and communities have countless stories that exemplify resistances toward genocidal strategies and settler-colonial tactics. Resistances of my ancestors are reflected in the fleeing from the Red River after the Riel resistance of 1885 into North Dakota and subsequently returning to Canada in 1903 with their Michif language still intact. Only in the late 1950's were the effects of imposed colonial education felt as the English language began to take hold on our way of life. My aunt, who is 92 years young, can still speak the Michif language today, a testament to our subtle acts of resistance.

The benevolent message Roots Canada is trying to promote for Canada's sesquicentennial celebrations is a settler move to innocence (Tuck and Yang, 2012) by trying to promote a nostalgic and romanticized Canadian history however, for me, the narrative of settler-colonialism is wrought with inflictions, wounds, and scars that are easily traceable. Dwayne Donald (2012) affirms, "We need more complex understandings of human relationality that traverse deeply learned divides of the past and present by demonstrating that...perspectives on history, memory, and experience are connected and interreferential" (p. 534). Donald (2012) further articulates the challenge of traversing learned divides is held within finding "a way to hold these understandings in tension without the need to resolve, assimilate, or incorporate" (p. 534). The challenge then, is understanding that we must "pull on the threads that feed the story (diaspora, sexism, racism, patriarchy, homophobia, etc.) and that constructed the cultural fabric" to uncover the tensions that exist (Maracle, 2015, p. 246) which will allow us to imagine and create better stories (Donald, 2016).

Leaving the hall that afternoon and returning home *Celebrating 150 years of being nice* stalked me. I was disturbed, yet not surprised, that colonialism is still trying to erase me from the Land. I repeatedly asked myself: *How are we to build meaningful relationships while settler-colonialism is ongoing?* I knew I had to do something – the nagging in my gut, the voices of my father and my ancestors would not let me sit idle.

One June evening, I decided to create a poster that reached into my own tensions to tell a story of the last 150 years, a story that acknowledged our history -- *I could not allow another colonial narrative to swallow me up whole*. The poster I created, privileges the story of Métis resistances to settler-colonialism. I drew inspiration from Louis Riel and the Metis provisional council and the courage and defiance they embodied when petitioning the government for land and cultural rights. While compiling the poster, I channelled the love for my father and my grandmother, drawing strength from the lives they led as Michif people. This was a small act of loving resistance -- a tribute to all who have gone before me who resisted the eradication of language, land, culture, and beliefs so that I could be a proud Michif today.

CHAPTER TWENTY

Photograph 2. Celebrating 150 years of RESISTANCE. #resistance150

My friend and I returned to the space where I felt assaulted, to fulfill my small act of loving resistance, and make peace. Together, we put up *Celebrating 150 years of RESISTANCE*. I could have chosen to 'cover-up' the propaganda but I knew that these two perspectives on Canada's 150 celebrations, had to sit in relation in order to speak to one another. As we put the poster up, people passed by, curiously glancing at what we were doing, nobody stopped to inquire. I wanted to share my poster, I wanted to talk about Louis Riel and his provisional government, but instead I was left contemplating – *are people **ready** to listen to OUR stories?* Donald (2012) insists that, "the task of decolonizing in the Canadian context can only occur when Aboriginal peoples and Canadians face each other across historic divides, deconstruct their past, and engage critically with the realization that their present and future are similarly tied together" (p. 535).

Framing settler-colonialism as benevolent (re)traumatizes individuals and communities by continuing to erase Indigenous presence. As we tell stories of history and experience, especially at a time where the success of this country is predicated on (re)newing Indigenous-non-Indigenous relationships, we must ensure that our stories do not induce harm, but rather ignite a space that shapes a new relationship rooted in mutually beneficial abiding principles and enactments. *This is not an easy task.* Uncomfortable discussions will have to be endured, truths will not only have to be told, but understood and taken to heart. Each day as we enact our relationships we are bound together by our histories, our experiences, and the Land. Because we are bound together we are responsible and accountable, when called upon by our own experiences and the experiences of others, to not only make meaning, but to participate with/in the world in loving meaningful ways that allow all of us to flourish.

awinawa? Who is this one?: Reclaiming Power in Identity

Angie Tucker

The most recent Daniels Decision (*Daniels vs. Canada*, 2016) has become controversial in cases involving Métis identity claims. The Supreme Court did not outline any specific defining criteria for the inclusion of Métis or non-Status Indians and therefore, has opened the doorway for false claimants of Métis identity. The Supreme Court chose to side-step the identity issue all-together, demonstrating their lack of knowledge of the Métis people.

The uncovering of a distant Indigenous relative does not give the right to claim a contemporary Métis identity (Anderson, 2016; Gaudry, 2014; Leroux & Gaudry, 2017). Furthermore, receiving results from DNA tests that indicate the presence of Indigenous ancestry does not offer membership to the Métis Nation. In a collective work by members of both Ojibwe and Métis communities, the unknown author of the article, "On Métis Identity and Sovereignty" states, "those people who use the term "Métis" rather than "person of mixed ancestry" to incorrectly identify themselves are not decolonizing. They are choosing to use the colonialist definition for the term Métis to mean mixed-blood, rather than the Indigenous definition which connotes the distinct and sovereign Métis Nation" (Dibaajimowin, 2018). Therefore, having a distant Indigenous relative does not give access to claiming Métis as part of your identity - which is confusing, because what non-Indigenous society has learned, is that this *mixedness* is exactly what determines 'being' Métis.

I can understand this confusion of identity because I too have lived and embodied these complexities. Despite having multiple family members who signed scrip within the boundaries of the historic Métis territory, and ancestors who were deeply connected to the Métis resistance in Manitoba, my grandmothers silenced this history. I have struggled to reconcile this fact, but I am aware of how Indigenous people have been marginalized politically, legally, and socially. I believe that my family

CHAPTER TWENTY

(particularly the women), chose to exercise their resistance through silence. I understand that this history provides a difficult framework to enter this argument. However, in Arjun Appadurai's (1988) work, *Putting Hierarchy in its Place*, he looks at the construction of the 'Native' from anthropological perspectives, and how some knowledges are privileged over others. In his work he states, "proper Natives are somehow assumed to represent themselves and their history, without distortion or residue" (p. 37). Appadurai (1988) is suggesting that although Indigenous people are expected to have clear understandings of who they are, it is not always possible. The restrictions that have been continually imposed on Métis by the Canadian Government have affected how we know ourselves today. Yes, it is messy. Yes, it is confusing. But there is a difference between 'being' and 'becoming.'

The State has been responsible for altering definitions that have acted, at times, to be more exclusive than inclusive, or more inclusive than exclusive - silencing not only the contemporary effects of colonial diaspora and forced assimilation but the processes in which Métis, as 'other' has found ourselves bound. These restrictive definitions are then recreated and perpetuated in society in their understanding of Métis people. In non-Indigenous circles, it has sometimes been difficult for me to talk about our family's connections to our Métis genealogy. I am charged to describe how I am biologically Métis; I am asked which of my parents are 'full-blooded,' and am asked to quantify my percentage of Indigenous blood. Furthermore, my physical features do not resemble what society expects to see when visualizing an Indigenous person. I never know exactly how to respond to these questions, but know that if I had just said that I was Ukrainian (because my mother is), nobody would have been arguing with me to begin with. But, can we claim identities based on a continued and uninterrupted cultural history? I argue that we cannot - particularly within a landscape that has continued to privilege the historical records, fieldwork and ethnographies of biased non-Indigenous researchers who have created racialized and romanticized notions of our Metisness. Inclusion based on preconceived categories of traditional practice is more often ignorant of territory, kinship connections, roles, and gender. Some Metis have become lost within our own territories, estranged from the very families, mobility, and ways of knowing that once informed them due to the effects of being oppressed and rejected within their own landscapes. Furthermore, specific traditional activities are assumptive and rooted in historical colonial contexts. Theses categorizations reject contemporary Métis experiences and continue to position us in an historical context. Métis are very much present today, but just maybe not as we have been expected to be. But more troublesome, these colonial theories have become responsible for how Métis people themselves, continue to determine membership within their own communities, using the social and legal definitions that continue to be defined and redefined by the Canadian State.

Using the Cree/Michif teaching of *wahkohtowin*, or natural law, Brenda Macdougall (2014) argues in her text, *One of the Family*, "cultures are not born but are developed as people live, work, play, and make families together. It is the process of how people behave and react to each other and outsiders that shapes their values and, in turn, defines their worldview" (p. 49). Macdougall (2014) is stating that relationships within communities and within families shapes whom one becomes. Therefore, with families over time, it is evident that there is a possibility for an incredible amount of variation based on independent experiences. If culture is developed through living, working, playing and making families together, and colonial aims were to destroy all aspects of these categories, then maintaining a singular culture among Métis groups is nearly impossible, and a difficult argument for those of us who have lost our communities and connections.

Federal and provincial decisions therefore, cannot, nor should not, provide a unified definition of Métis identity. These definitions collectively define Indigenous groups using non-Indigenous categories of inclusion. We have repeatedly learned that the Canadian State continues to create and define Metis identities for its own specific use, and we are guilty of attempting to fit ourselves and others into these narrow qualifying definitions. Métis identities must be disentangled and decolonized from static legal and social definitions by recognizing the colonial role of the Canadian State in contemporary Métis understanding and how this in turn, has created fluidity in both the recognition of and recognition within ourselves. 'Being' Métis can no longer rely on historical definitions that have been fabricated within imperialistic empires. Therefore, I choose to approach my doctoral work by shifting the power back to Métis people and critiquing how the true 'other', that is, the colonizer, the State, the government bodies, and non-Indigenous people have continued to objectify us through the continued colonial gaze, the verbal rhetoric of policy, and the devouring and regurgitation of ethnic identifying categories.

CHAPTER TWENTY

Kîhokêwin Kumik

Jason Surkan

> My people will sleep for one hundred years, but when they awake, it will be the artists who give them their spirit back.
>
> - Louis Riel, 1885.

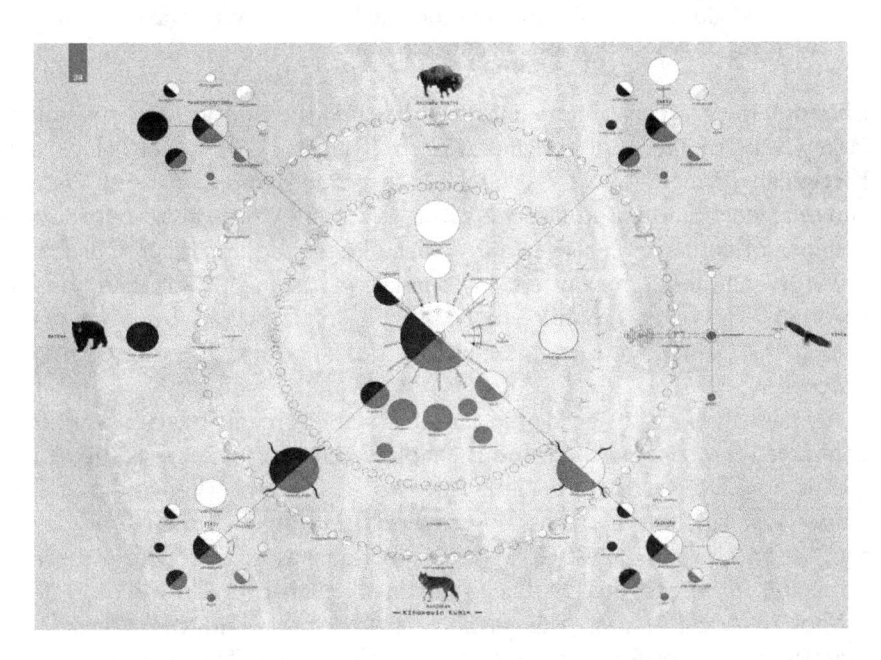

Figure 1. This diagram illustrates a cyclical design process, program diagram, and cosmological elements showing a way of working that honours natural law teachings and lays out the relationship of the four artists residents' cabins to the central cultural centre.

The following research was carried out on the homeland of the Métis Nation, near the Forks in Winnipeg, Manitoba. This is the ancestral lands of my maternal family and a place all Métis people hold close to their hearts. It holds significant cultural and political meaning to our communities as it is the historical birthplace of our Métis Nation. I come from a complex history, carrying my maternal families Métis blood and my paternal families homesteading blood. These two cultures were often in competition for land and resources, and space on the prairies, often resulting in Métis families being pushed to road allowance communities to make room for homesteaders, I acknowledge both sides of this history. In the foreword for *Contours of a People: Métis Family, Mobility and History*, Maria Campbell (2012) writes the following regarding this history:

> After the resistances were put down, the leaders hanged, imprisoned, or exiled, and their homelands settled by new immigrants, our people were forced out by fear of violence and imprisonment. Many fled to the United States or to isolated areas of the Northwest and were forgotten by authorities. They settled on crown lands, or road allowances and were, according to the government, squatters; their inherent right to their land not recognized. They became known as Road Allowance People, and they were left alone, out of sight, out of mind, until it was again time for settlement or resource development. (p.iv)

I honour my maternal Métis lineage, a lineage of resilience and resistance in my way of life and design research (Figure 1). My upbringing near Kistapinân (Prince Albert, Saskatchewan) grounds me in a rural lifestyle and enabled a land based lifestyle My sisters and I were raised outside the confines of an urban centre in a log house immersed in nature. Our family grew up spending time out picking berries, gardening, fishing, and hunting together. This close connection to a land, its flora and fauna form my cosmology, which in turn informs my design work and space making processes.

My path through my academic career is semi-nomadic by nature and has connected me to other Indigenous scholars and relatives across the globe. This is how life was for our Metis Ancestors as they worked and travelled across vast landscapes connecting two cultures through their work; long ago, is once again. In 2016, I began working as a Graduate Research Assistant, for Professor Dr. David Fortin through Laurentian Universities School of Architecture. This project is an inquiry into the origins and practice of a specifically prairie Métis architecture. This research work helped foster personal connections across Métis country and form the foundation of a personal Métis architectural design process, including the following thesis project. I was honoured to be connected with Métis Elder, author, scholar, playwright, artist, visionary, and relative, Maria Campbell on a warm summer day at the site of the thesis, Gabriel Dumont's Crossing, Saskatchewan. The vision for this thesis work came through a dream that was gifted to Maria a long time ago, while she was visiting the site (Figure 2).

CHAPTER TWENTY

Figure 2. This is the first of a series of four images that draw out the dream vision for Kîhokêwin Kumik. It shows a canoe travelling back and forth across the South Saskatchewan River bringing people back to their culture. This thesis work metaphorically represents that canoe, as it functions as a vessel for cultural resurgency.

The thesis work explores a collaboration with Maria Campbell on a design proposal for a space that facilitates cultural resurgence through a process of Kîhokêwin (visiting) which included storytelling, dreaming, art, music, language, craft, ceremony, and cultural activities at the historic site of Gabriel Dumont's Crossing along the Apihtâkîsikanohk Kisiskâciwani-Sîpiy (South Saskatchewan River) near the historic site of Batoche, Saskatchewan. This main cultural lodge (Figure 3) is supported by a total of four satellite artist residency studios (tipinawahikan, sipîy, wacistwanihkân, and wâkâyôsi-wâti) that respond to four distinct landscapes present at the crossing: Prairie, River, Hill, and Coulee respectively (Figure 5). The design of each studio is tectonically, spatially and experientially unique and aims to foster creativity in the artist residents through the design of Métis spaces. The construction of the structures is a community led process, that utilizes local materials and sustainable design.

Figure 3. Wacistwanihkân // A Nest Like Structure. These two renderings illustrate one of four artist residency studios.

One of the primary spatial conditions that has historically distinguished the Métis from other groups in the Canadian prairie provinces emerged from their overriding emphasis on egalitarian principles of social organization and consensus that evolved out of their Buffalo hunting culture during the 19th century (Fortin & Surkan, 2016). The Métis have built and continue to build spaces across the prairie provinces that respond to each local environment in ingenious, sustainable, egalitarian, and resourceful ways. This Métis vernacular architecture is the physical manifestation that developed when the lived consequences were too severe to make error. These responses have been learned through inherited experiences that were and continue to be distilled by countless generations of lived experience in harsh environmental and even harsher social conditions.

CHAPTER TWENTY

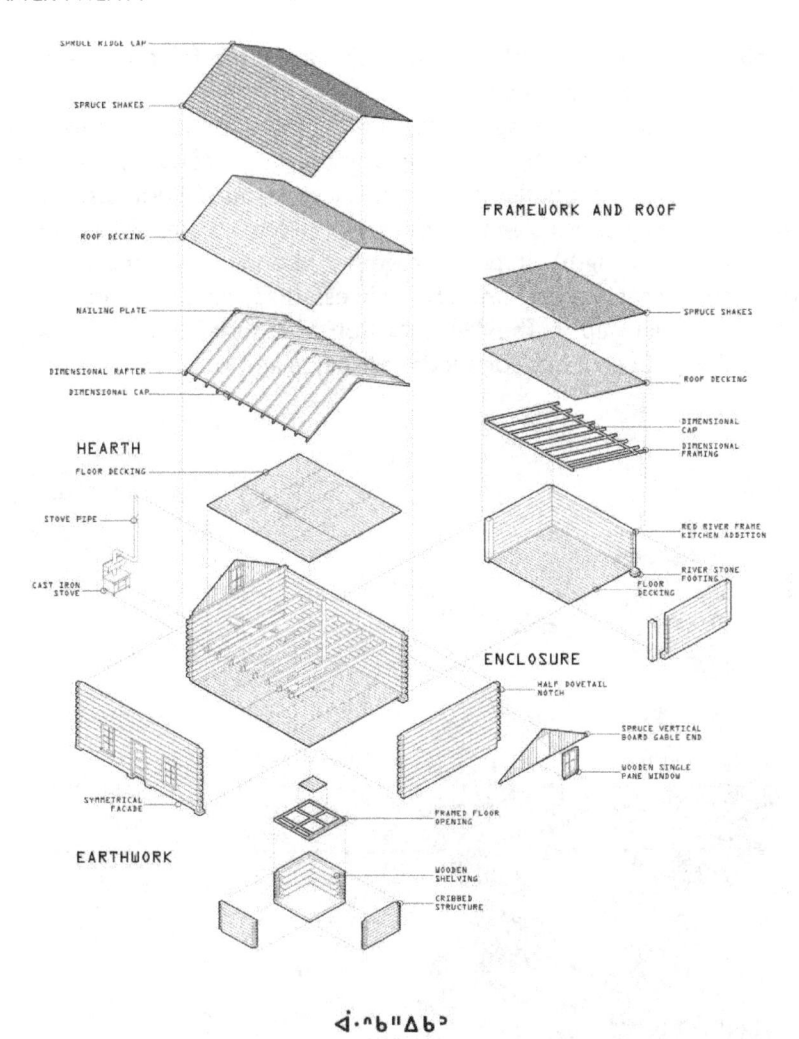

Figure 4. This diagram illustrates the tectonics of the Folk Home, a Métis vernacular building typology constructed in the 19th century along river lots in this region. It was a dovetail aspen log home standing one and a half stories night. The design of the home honoured both their maternal and paternal lineages. The exterior of the home was Georgian in appearance and served as a colonial mask for the strongly Indigenous interior of the home. The interior was like that of a Plains Tepee with a central hearth and no interior partitions.

Historical and contemporary examples of Métis architecture to better understand 'what is Métis architecture?' Other Indigenous cultures in Canada have recognizable vernacular typologies such as the igloo, tipi, longhouse, and wigwam. What then is Métis architecture beyond log cabin nostalgia and pasted visual lexicons? Is there a place for a contemporary Métis architecture in the prairies?

Kîhokêwin Kumik (Visiting Lodge) is an exploration of not only a Métis Vernacular (Figure 4), but an exploration in a contemporary Métis architecture that is grounded in the teachings of our Elders, kisêwâtisiwin (kindness), kwayaskwatisiwin (honesty), nikwatisowin (sharing), and maskawisiwin (strength). It braids together the past, present, and future through an Indigenous architectural process that creates a catalyst space to strengthen kinship in the Métis Nation at Gabriel's Crossing, a place that has always been a hub for Métis resistance and culture.

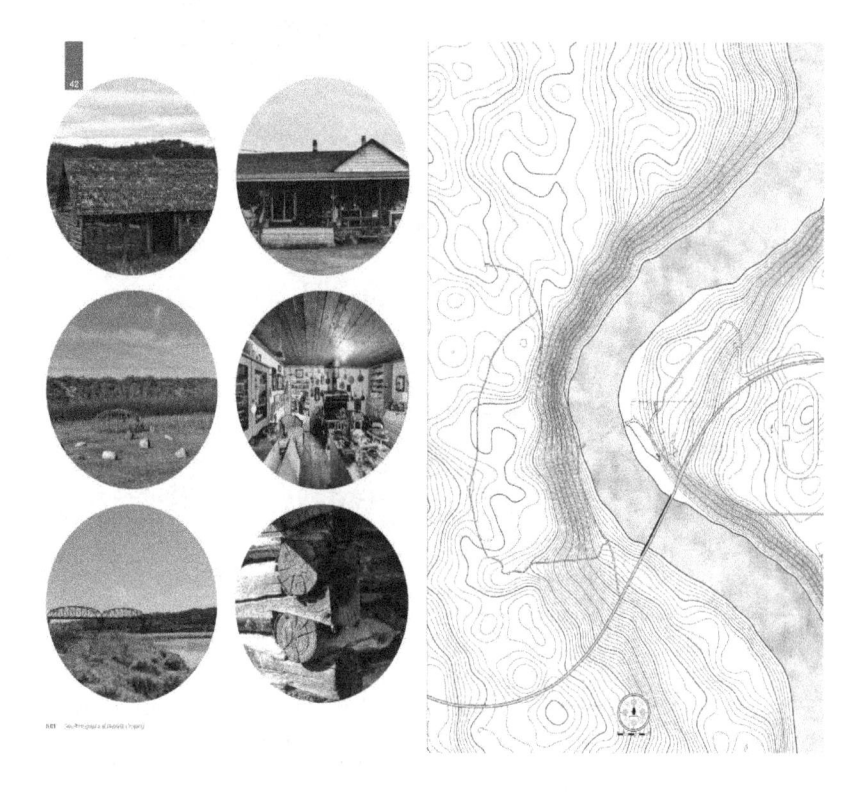

Figure 5. This site plan illustrates the central hub of the project that includes Maria's house and the main cultural centre. The sipîy studio sits near the river at the historical site of Gabriel Dumont's Crossing. Across the river are the tipinawahikan, wacistwanihkân, and wâkâyôsi-wâti studios.

CHAPTER TWENTY

Oshki Izhiwebiziwin: Towards New Ways of *Being* Métis[94]

Chuck Bourgeois

Boozhoo indinawemaaganag, I am a proud Métis person from the community of St. Pierre Jolys, which sits along *Wazhushk Ziibins*, or Muskrat Creek. My great-great-great grandparents, Mélanie Nault and Louis Larivière lived there on a river lot long before a clergyman arrived and named their little paradise after a Christian saint. Being a Métis person in Manitoba today is much different than it was for my ancestors in the nineteenth century. For them, being Métis did not entail a process of rediscovery, or sifting through stacks of dusty archives; nor did they require federal recognition to be who they were. They were brought up in the world *as* Métis people. The languages they spoke, the places they called home, and their beautiful way of life were all a part of what made them Métis. Again, for myself and my relations today, things are much different.

Today, many of us carry official photo identification cards. Some Métis people explore their identities through academic study, drawing from the fields of law, history and even archeology. Others believe that we are Métis because Canada's constitution recognizes us as such (Shore, 2017, p. 131). This begs the question, is there such a thing as 'Métis' beyond a legal category in Canadian law, or as Chris Andersen (2010) muses, are "colonial nation-states [...] so elementally powerful that nothing Indigenous exists 'outside' them?" (p. 23). I often wonder what stories will be told about the Métis of the 21st century – that we were politicians, lawyers, and historians? That we accepted our lot, and made good with the very state that subdued our families with Gatling Guns just over a century ago? Would our Cree relatives still recognize us as *otipêyimisowak*, or 'those own themselves', if they saw us today?

I know many stories about Mélanie Nault and Louis Larivière. They were both supporters of Louis Riel, who was Mélanie's first cousin. The Riel House National Historic Site in Winnipeg was purchased from Mélanie and Louis, back in the day. In October of 1869, when William MacDougall was making his way northward to assume authority over our territory, Louis and Mélanie stood at *La Barriere* with their comrades. This was a time when activism was meted out at gunpoint, rather than from the comfort of social media platforms. According to one account, during the siege of Fort Garry, Louis Larivière "was one of the guards placed on the Governor's House, [and] was specifically detailed to watch over Donald A. Smith, Commissioner from Canada." (Barkwell, 2014, n.p.). Another story tells us that the day before Elzéar Goulet was lynched by Orangemen, he had declined an invitation to Mélanie and Louis' wedding – had he accepted, he may not have met his brutal fate in the Red River (Vermette & Ferland, 2006, p. 199). These stories tell me a lot about who my ancestors were, and who I am; but how do I embody that same resolve and conviction in my own life?

Where our ancestors were recognized by their relations as apihtawikosisanak, or *otipêyimisowak*, today, these monikers are largely considered historical, and our identities are increasingly framed in political or legal terms. Where we once defended the land shoulder to shoulder with our Saulteaux and Cree relatives, today, we squabble with them over meagre state handouts. Consequently, "[t]he unfortunate reality is that Métis identity is confusing for everyone" (Teillet, 2013, p. 1-4). In my own thinking, I try to look beyond mere essentialisms in my exploration of contemporary Métis identity. Essentialist ideas tend to dominate this discourse however; many still consider sashes, Louis Riel, and fiddle music to be hallmarks of Métis identity. Métis Elder Carole Leclair (2003) once wrote that "Métis in the 21st century are looking forward to finding new ways to speak of, and for ourselves" (p. 1). And indeed, speaking *of* and *for* ourselves is a privilege Métis people have only recently begun to enjoy. To this, I would humbly add that we are also looking for new ways of *being* Métis. Our task, I believe, is not to replicate the culture, beliefs or practises of our ancestors. Nor should we seek to cobble together an essentialized, utopian prototype of Métis identity out of our history – one completely irrelevant to our current circumstances, and ultimately unattainable. I interpret Rita Bouvier's (2004) poem, *Riel is dead, and I am alive* as a call to action – "this time", she warns "the gatling gun is academic discourse" (p. 28). Are we doomed to regurgitate the same old discourses, or is it time to start putting up roadblocks of our own?

I am Métis of French and Saulteaux descent; Saulteaux being the French name for the Anishinaabe People. Louis Larivière's grandmother was an Anishinaabe woman who appears in the records only as *Marie Sauteuse*. This would make sense, as St. Pierre is located only a short distance from a large Anishinaabe community. I am proud of this heritage. For some years now, I have been slowly reclaiming the beautiful language spoken in our homeland. Speaking Anishinaabemowin feels good; every time I greet a relative in our language or learn a new word, I feel more complete. This is the honor song I sing to my ancestors, this is one of the ways that I practice *being* Métis each day. I have discussed my thoughts on Métis identity with my Elders, and they have encouraged me to continue searching. They call what I am looking for, *oshki izhiwebiziwin*, or a 'new way of being'. That is the story I hope will be told about the Métis of our time – that we carried our ancestors' gifts forward, and envisioned new ways of *being* Métis.

> I went back and dug in the prairie soil. There among the buffalo bones and memories, an ancient language sprang from the earth and wet my parched tongue. In that part of the country we were always katipâmsôchik – and our displaced history is as solid as every railroad tie pounded into place, linking each stolen province

-Gregory Scofield, Policy of the Dispossessed, 1996

Conclusion

The lifeways and practices of our ancestors were deeply connected to the Land and places that they both inhabited and interacted with. We have always been and continue to be formed by the processes of our geographical places and the influences of our ancestral wisdoms and traditions. Each of us, as depicted through our scholarly work and reflections, illustrate how Métis people are claiming traditional wisdom to reshape to redefine the spaces and relationships to which we find ourselves. By affirming our voices within colonial landscapes, and rejecting colonial narratives of erasure, we are shifting the lens to centre our own languages, stories, and teachings not only within our research, but within our daily lives. With the guidance of Métis Elders, past and present, we remain connected to our ancestors, our homelands, and all of our relations. Through our continued resilience and resistance, we are and will remain present.

References

Bouvier, Victoria
Andersen, C. (2014). *"Metis": Race, recognition, and the struggle for Indigenous peoplehood.* Vancouver, BC: UBC Press.
Battiste, M. (2013). *Decolonizing education: Nourishing the learning spirit.* Saskatoon, SK: Purich Publishing Limited.
Donald, D. (2012). Indigenous metissage: A decolonizing research sensibility. International Journal of Qualitative Studies in Education, 533-555. Retrieved from http://dx.doi.org/10.1080/09518398.2011.554449
Donald, D. (2016). From what does ethical relationality flow: An Indian act in three artifacts. In J. Seidel, & D. Jardine (Eds.), *The ecological heart of teaching: Radical tales of refuge and renewal for classrooms and communities* (pp. 10-16). New York, NY: Peter Lang.
Maracle, L. (2015). *Memory serves.* Edmonton, AB: NeWest Press.
Truth and Reconciliation Commission of Canada. (2015). *What we have learned: Principles of truth and reconciliation.* Retrieved from: http://nctr.ca/assets/reports/Final%20Reports/Principles_English_Web.pdf
Vowel, C. (2016). *Indigenous writes: A guide to First Nations, Métis, & Inuit issues in Canada.* Winnipeg, MB: High Water Press.

Tucker, Angie

Andersen, C. (2014). *Métis: Race, recognition and the struggle for Indigenous peoplehood.* Vancouver, BC: UBC Press.

Appadurai, A. (1988). "Putting Hierarchy in its Place." *Cultural Anthropology* 3 (1), 36-49.

Daniels v. Canada, Supreme Court of Canada. (2016)

Gaudry, A. (2014). *Kaa-tipeyimishoyaahk* – 'We are those who own ourselves': A political history of Métis self-determination in the North-West, 1830-1870. (Unpublished doctoral dissertation). University of Victoria, Victoria, BC. Retrieved from https://dspace.library.uvic.ca:8443/handle/1828/12/browse?value=Gaudry%2C+Adam+James+Patrick&type=author.

Leroux, D.R.J., & Gaudry, A. (2017, October, 26). How 'race-shifting' explains the surge in the number of Métis in Eastern Canada. *Macleans.* Retrieved from https://www.macleans.ca/news/canada/the-rise-of-eastern-metis-canada.

Macdougall, B. (2010). *One of the family: Métis culture in nineteenth-century Northwestern Saskatchewan.* Vancouver: UBC Press.

Dibaajimowin. (2018, March 20) On Métis Identity and Sovereignty. Retrieved from https://www.dibaajimowin.com/metis/on-metis-identity-and-sovereignty.

Surkan, Jason

Fortin, D., and Surkan, J. (2016). Towards an Architecture of Métis Resistance. *SITE Magazine.* Retrieved from https://www.sitemagazine.com/

St-Onge, Nicole., Podruchny, Carolyn., & Macdougall, Brenda. (2012). *Contours of a people: Metis family, mobility, and history.* Norman, OK: University of Oklahoma Press.

Bourgeois, Chuck

Andersen, C. (2010). Mixed Ancestry or Métis? In B. Hokowhitu, N. Kermoal, C. Andersen, M.Reilly, A. Peterson, I. Altamirano-Jiménez, & P. Rewi (Eds.), *Indigenous Identity and Resistance: Researching the Diversity of Knowledge* (pp. 23-37). Dunedin, New Zealand: Otago University Press.

Barkwell, L. (2014). *Personalities of the 1869-70 Resistance, Laderoute's Dicté.* Winnipeg, MB: Louis Riel Institute.

Bouvier, R. (2004). *Papîyâhtak.* Saskatoon, SK: Thistledown Press Ltd.

Leclair, C. (2003). *Métis environmental knowledge: La tayr pi tout li moond* (Unpublished doctoral dissertation). York University, Toronto, ON.

Scofield, G. (1996). *Native Canadiana: Songs From the Urban Rez.* Vancouver, BC: Polestar.

Shore, F. (2017). *Threads in the Sash: The Story of Métis People.* Winnipeg, MB: Pemmican Publications, Inc.

Teillet, J. (2013). *Métis law in Canada.* Vancouver, BC: Pape Salter Teillet.

Vermette, A., & Ferland, M. (2006). *Au temps de la Prairie.* Saint Boniface, MB: Éditions du Blé.

notes

[93] Resistance with love

[94] We would like to acknowledge the contribution of the late Chuck Bourgeois, Métis scholar and friend. We were fortunate to present on a panel with him in March 2018 to which this chapter was based upon. To honour his work, his contribution stands in his own original expression. Maarsii Chuck, for your wisdom and insight. Kaawaapamatin.

Chapter Twenty-One

I am told I was fierce

A Personal Narrative on Decolonization through Written and Spoken Word

Liberty Emkeit

Words. Carry. Power. Do they not? They have the power to heal, to harm, exclude and include. They have the capacity to enlighten minds or murder thousands. Language can create spiritual self-awareness alongside violent narcissistic justifications, depending on who is doing the speaking and who is listening. We can follow blindly, never questioning the truth behind the vernacular we read and hear. We can also utilize words, written and spoken, to decolonize our minds and world. Language can, has and will, continue to be a powerful tool for resistance.

Words have been used to enslave Indigenous peoples for centuries (Acoose, 1995). Stereotypes and unjust, one-sided storytelling have abounded and perpetuated long standing beliefs about the supposed inferiority of Indigenous people (Acoose, 1995). In addition, well-chosen words have also been used to cloak privilege and denial behind Eurocentric language that elevated colonialists to be heroes and hid their centuries of genocide and unchecked greed. LaRocque (2010) astutely noted that "colonizers require a system of thought and representation to mask their oppressive behavior" (p. 37). As a result, after generations of dismissal and dehumanization, many Indigenous ancestors were lost and those left behind were silenced.

My Story: From Suppression to Celebration.

Coming from a long line of storytellers, I witnessed how severing of the voice through oppression can often lead to dysfunction. Without a voice, there is no passing on of knowledge to the next generation, speaking our truths are erased before they even leave our lips, and with no voice there is no way to purge trauma. Silenced, the person fades away, often falling into abuse, and addiction, buried under generations of pain.

I know this story all too well. For myself and my family. As a small child, I am told I was fierce. My father shared that the first time he met me, bundled and tiny in the hospital, he said he peered into my eyes and saw and felt my power. He also told me that when I was a toddler, I would stand, with my hands on my hips, and give him heck, if I felt he was stepping out of line. Apparently, at just three years old, I would stare down any adult I had just met. My father believed wholeheartedly that I was peering into their soul and could read the intent of their spirit. He said I was always right. It would appear I was a force to be reckoned with (and slightly cheeky too).

Clearly from these stories, my father believed that I was special. That I was powerful. He saw that I was unafraid, not only of myself but of speaking my truth. My father loved sharing these stories with me. As a young woman, I loved listening to them. It made me feel proud and wistful at the same time. I longed to hear of her because the little child he spoke of was a heroine in my story that I did not recall. The fierce little girl my dad knew was not the woman that I would become.

Today, I do not know that little girl. I am not sure the exact moment she vanished from my spirit. But at some point, my fierceness was replaced with fear. Life would strip away my strength, voice and power. I became timid, damaged, and broken.

In an oppressive and unequal colonialist society, I wonder, how many women, especially Indigenous women does this happen to? Fierce little girls transformed into muted shadows? Abuse and trauma happening all too often, removing innocence and autonomy before we even develop a sense of who we are or what we have to say?

I understood by the time I was in middle school, as a teenager, a young woman and then as a wife and mother, that my story, words, truth, and autonomy were not valued nor recognized. My body and physical appearance was my only worth. My voice became a dream I could not quite remember.

I am still searching for that little girl. I often ponder, how could she, strong and assured, rest within the same soul as the diminished adult version of me? I do not have the answer for that. All I know, is that I miss that little girl.

Many years would pass before I saw a glimpse of her again. Whispers of her began at age twenty-eight, where as a newly separated single mother, I returned to university. Initially, I went to gain the piece of paper so that I would have more choices in providing for my children, but it quickly evolved into something much deeper. I cannot express enough how impactful my education has been in all aspects of my spiritual, emotional, mental, and activist development. This is the place where my voice began to grow roots.

My journey of higher education was and is, soul altering. It blew apart my understanding of the world and my place within it in the best possible way. It was there I discovered that I am far smarter and far more capable than I ever realized. University is the place that re-connected me to myself, to my writing. As a little girl, I had dreamed of being a writer. Ironically before I even actually knew how to read.

The campus buildings have become a sacred site for me, a pilgrimage that I travel to each week. It is the place where my ancestors sit, waiting for me. I searched for them in the history books and found them not only there within those pages but everywhere within the walls, halls and grounds of the campus. And when I am still and silent amongst my words and the books I read, I feel my ancestors in every thought, every moment, and every word. They are the reason I am there. To realize dreams that they were not allowed to have. They guided me to school. Learning and writing is as much of a need for my spirit as breathing is. It is what feeds my soul.

Higher education and writing was a strong act of empowerment for me. Suddenly, my critical analysis on an issue mattered. Even if the only person who ever read it was the professor, that never made a difference to me. Being silenced and dismissed for so many years, the incredible moment where my written words carried their own power for the first time is indescribable and the importance of this is without an equivalent within my soul's journey in this life.

University also reunited me with my Métis roots. As I am disconnected from my family and culture, I have sought out, all my life, to understand who I am and where I belong. I have had to fight to be recognized as an Indigenous woman, a Métis woman. It seems I am too light for some and one drop of blood too many for others. It has not been an easy path.

Within my studies, I took in class lectures from others who had followed the same search for their roots as I did. I read of Indigenous people who reclaimed their identity in their own way, outside of mainstream state definitions of who is an Indian and who is not. I cried and cheered alongside Indigenous academics who wrote at length about that process of reclamation and remembrance to their ancestors and traditions.

Being given that gift of knowledge, previously unknown to me, about residential schools, the Indian Act, the 60s scoop, racism, sexism, oppression and violence, privilege and greed, helped me to understand the context of my life as a disconnected Métis woman. I found myself amongst the pages of their words. As such, being taught about the centuries of colonialism and the resistance to it, to deny all of who I am, would be to deny my ancestors struggles for survival. I would never disrespect them in such a way. I am here today because of them. Now, I fully identify as an Indigenous woman and a settler woman. I honor all the peoples that I come from. I am done asking permission to be who I am and to claim my own people. I know where I come from. University gave me that foundation.

The next evolution of my finding my voice, my place in the world of resistive and reclamation of words, was completely unforeseen. There are only a small amount of moments where I have felt the hand of spirit directly on my heart. It may sound dramatic to say it, but my first poetry slam event was one of those times. It was like coming home. Spoken word/slam poetry combined all my lived experiences, my education, my thoughts and hopes for the world and my sorrow and pain, all into one wonderful medium. Suddenly, I was no longer writing from solely an academic lens but my own narrative as well. And there was audience participation, validating what I had written.

Combining my truth with paper and performance, gave me such a feeling of freedom. I could say what I thought, and people listened to me. My words, my voice mattered.

I am still a quiet mouse. I am still afraid. I still do not feel assured of myself or my truth. But, when I write, when I perform, I am fierce. That is where she and I, reunite.

While my story is my own, I know that am not the only person who has found my narrative and my strength stripped away through life experiences and systemic problems of inequality and marginalization. I also understand that I am not alone in the journey of reclaiming one's identity, and personal truths through written and spoken word.

Words carry power, but how much?

Indigenous peoples have been speaking their truths in all manner of methods, for many a century. They were not mere victims, passively taking the colonialist domination (Stote, 2015). "Native writing shows that Natives have been resisting colonizing practices as long as they have been writing" (LaRocque, 2010, p. 25). However, writing, speaking, shouting, and crying does not seem to change an entrenched systemic labyrinth that only benefits some settlers and harms the original peoples of this land.

CHAPTER TWENTY-ONE

We may use the colonizers language as a tool of resistance, but does it change the lived realities of our narratives? Are we not still oppressed? Smith stated that... (as cited in Hargreaves, 2017, p. 17) "We assume that when the 'truth comes out' it will prove that what happened was wrong or illegal and that therefore the system, will set things right...(However), a thousand accounts of the 'truth' will not alter the 'fact' that Indigenous peoples are still marginal and do not possess the power to transform history into justice". I wonder, when examining the power of language, how much of providing words and research regarding 'the other' translates into change? Do the words themselves create transformative power on its own or is it within the listener, who hears it, that is the catalyst?

And what if the listener is not interested in hearing an Indigenous truth? If the words fall upon the deaf ears of privilege, should we still resist, reclaim, and remember when we are constantly fighting an uphill battle? Do we still fight anyways and write our narratives? And do our stories even matter? If suppression of Indigenous peoples still exists, why would I, tiny little mouse, try to leave behind my insignificant story? Why would any of us?

For that, I look toward Spirit for the answer. Several years ago, in December of 2008, I attended a Prairie Lily Feminist Society conference in Saskatoon, Saskatchewan. Their key note speaker was Morning Star Mercredi. Her story and message were compelling.

It was many years ago, so I am paraphrasing what she said. I hope I do right by her. Mercredi (2008) began her talk by discussing the idea of prayer. And how often, when we pray, we are praying for something in the present and for a resolution within our lifetime. Morning Star then went on to state that perhaps those prayers, when given, go out into the ether, and take on a life of their own. She said that perhaps those words of prayer are not meant for our lifetime. Mercredi then began to speak of generations past and what they may have prayed, dreamed and fought for. Then, she paused, looked at us intently and said to us, "So, maybe YOU are the answers to your Grandmother's prayers" (Mercredi, 2008).

Just like our prayers, our words of resistance and truth narratives may not be for our lifetime. I am here because my ancestors survived. They perhaps did not see the change they prayed for. But we should, like them, still resist and challenge. We must. If nothing else, to pay tribute to our ancestors who fought so that we could have a chance at freedom. We do not know how the actions of today will affect generations of tomorrow. Perhaps my grandchildren will see the realization of my hopes, dreams, prayers and words. That is why I write.

The Power of One

How do we create change knowing the odds we are up against? What method is the most apt for success? Mass production or one person at a time? From a capitalistic ideology, the only true measure would be in the realization of the end goal. Anything but that would be considered a failure. And, if our words do not become books and or lectures, seen and heard by thousands, then we should not even bother.

I disagree. Each of us has something to say. No matter the outcome. Each of us has value within our own narratives.

Is the unknown woman who writes in her journal so that she has an outlet for her voice any less powerful at shifting the world than a famous author or orator? Writing in her journal gives her a reprieve, allows her to bleed her soul through the pages, instead of on her wrists, so that she may have the strength to get up the next day fighting to survive in a racist and sexist society. She tucks the journal away under her bed, where no one sees it, in the same way she tucks away herself because she learned long ago, no one is interested in who she is and what she thinks.

But her story matters. Is her silenced voice not the most powerful? She is the one we should be listening to.

For every person out in front of the podium or microphone, there are countless sisters and brothers (and every gender in-between), standing beside and behind them engaging in the same acts of strength and resistance. We do not know their names. But does that matter? Their contribution exists and is important.

And if nothing else, if our words only go as far as our own lips, written by our hands, seen by our eyes alone, should not that be enough to begin the process of decolonization? If my words, whether spoken, written, whispered or dreamed enables my voice to find a place to call home, to find the source within my soul, is that not enough to begin healing and reclaiming myself?

I believe it is possible to transcend past the current status quo and continue to decolonize. It may seem naïve and idealistic. But said in a different way, idealism and naivety have other meanings. Hope. Endurance. Resistance. A reimagining of what is possible. One person, one narrative, joined together is a mighty opponent against injustice. The power of one become some, becomes many, becomes all. The power of one is enough. You. I. We. Matter.

Conclusion

I can feel that little girl coming back. I thought she had left me, but she was always there. She simply hibernated until I began to find my way back to her. No longer patiently waiting, she is pounding drums inside my chest screaming her truth. She knows her power. She wants me to remember. My father named me Liberty so that I could be free. My words have been my deliverance.

Marilyn Dumont stated (as cited in Hargreaves, 2017, p. 84), "Writing has saved my emotional, spiritual, and intellectual life in a country where I wasn't supposed to exist, let alone survive". We research, write and speak what we do so that our stories are not lost, to ensure our stories are told, and so we can remember those who came before us. Words cannot be permanently taken. They can be silenced. Forgotten. But they eventually always find their way back to the speaker and to the listener. The truth always finds a way to survive.

Write.

Speak.

Share.

Yours.

References

Acoose, J. (1995). Reclaiming Myself. In Iskwewak – Kah' Ki Yaw ni Wahkomakanak Neither Indian Princess Nor Easy Squaws (17-39). Toronto: Women's Press.

Acoose, J. (1995). Literature, Image and Societal Values. In Iskwewak – Kah' Ki Yaw ni Wahkomakanak Neither Indian Princess Nor Easy Squaws (39-55). Toronto: Women's Press.

Hargreaves, A. (2017). Introduction. In Violence Against Indigenous Women: Representation and Resistance (1-29). Waterloo: Wilfred Laurier University Press.

Hargreaves, A. (2017). Narrative Appeals: The Stolen Sisters Report and Storytelling in Activist Discourse and Poetry (65-101). In Violence Against Indigenous Women: Representation and Resistance (1-29). Waterloo: Wilfred Laurier University Press.

LaRocque, E. (2010). Insider Notes: Reframing the Narratives. In When the Other is Me: Native Resistance Discourse 1850-1990 (17-37). Winnipeg: University of Manitoba Press.

LaRocque, E. (2010). Dehumanization in Text. In When the Other is Me: Native Resistance Discourse 1850-1990 (37-59). Winnipeg: University of Manitoba Press.

Mercredi, M. (2008, December). Key Note Speaker on Women's Empowerment. Presented at the Prairie Lily Feminist Society symposium, Saskatoon, SK.

Stote, K. (2015). Indian Policy and Aboriginal Women. In An Act of Genocide: Colonialism and The Sterilization of Aboriginal Women (28-46). Winnipeg: Fernwood Publishing.

Chapter Twenty-Two

Decolonization? What is it? Does anyone know what it is? Let's find out!

Patricia Siniikwe Pajunen

Many academic institutions and disciplines are decrying their intent to decolonize. Unfortunately, the people making the declarations are using 'decolonize' in a way that connotes something completely different than what actual decolonization would be. Due to the overuse of 'decolonization', the word has become empty word, tossed about like a leaf caught in the breeze. I will argue in this paper that many who use this word keep using it without knowing what it means to decolonize.

There are many great Indigenous initiatives happening in academia all over North Turtle Island. In January of 2017, the University of Guelph hired six Indigenous professors. Indigenous philosophers are rare, so I remain the only 'publicly out' Indigenous philosopher in my department. It hasn't been an easy path to walk: there have been assaults on my body, my intelligence, and my methods. All of this, at the same time some folks are talking about 'decolonizing the department'. These are the same people who reject the Anishinaabe storytelling method of engaging philosophy and attempt to assimilate me into the Western way of questioning the world and how we interact with it.

Hiring sprees, adding Indigenous scholars to syllabi, and allowing space for Indigenous voices in classrooms are all great ways to open the academy to the First Peoples of this land. Are they acts of decolonization? Not exactly. As long as the acts above are done to serve 'diversity points', they are not acts of decolonization. Margaret Kovach (2009) points out that, "[in] post-secondary education, Indigenous students experience the burn of colonial research on a consistent basis most evident in the suppression of Indigenous knowledges" (76). Consequently, "decolonization becomes personally embodied within the lives of Indigenous researchers" (Kovach 76). I will let this sit with you for a moment.

While Indigenous scholars are rising up the academic ranks, Indigenous knowledges seem to be left behind. I barely remember my nookomis.[95] What I do remember, when my immediate family visited her in Red Rock, is her sitting on her rocking chair in her pyjamas, leaning over a coffee table rolling cigarettes while watching her soaps on a small black and white TV. She would often send my cousin, my sister, and me to the store to buy her a package of cough candies. I think she did this because we were being too loud, and she couldn't hear her stories. There was a picture of Jesus hanging on the wall above the door way into the kitchen from the living room. Nothing in her house lead me to believe she was Anishinaabe. We were 'normal'. When the law changed in 1985[96] and thousands of Indigenous women across North Turtle Island were able to reinstate their community membership, my family was faced with an identity change: my nana and my mum suddenly became Anishinaabe.

My mum applied for and received an Indian Status card. Our lives didn't change too drastically. We still lived off reserve and we still weren't really stigmatized in the same way the people who lived on reserve were. We were still 'normal people' according to my folks' friends. A drastic change was that my folks, who were hesitant on buying large priced items, no longer had qualms about buying the things we needed for the house, the yard, and hunting since being a 'legal Indian' and having status decreased the amount of sales tax paid by 8%. But that never meant my mum never paid taxes. Yes, my mum paid taxes. My mum had several different jobs over her years and she paid taxes. I pay taxes. Indigenous people in the 'Ontario' portion of North Turtle Island do not get free handouts. The agreement 'Ontario' made with the communities is that we didn't need to pay provincial sales tax on certain items. Save your take-out receipts because take-out meals are tax exempt.[97]

Everything else in my family was status quo. My mum still (barely) followed the Roman Catholic teachings that she grew up in because of her parents. Our house was not a religious house. My mum had some crucifixes and crosses, but we never went to church or prayed or said grace. My nookomis never made us go to church or pray or say grace either. It didn't dawn on me then, even, that my nookomis and my mum were Anishinaabe. After they got their membership back, we still rarely went to visit family living in the community. I like to imagine that nookomis was protecting us from the very real dangers involved with being Anishinaabe just like I'm sure her Ojibwe parents did for her.

So, what does this have to do with embodied decolonization? Decolonization starts with rejecting internalized hatred and reconnecting with who we are as Anishinaabeg. All the colonial lies told about

Anishinaabeg need to be purged from our own beliefs about ourselves. When my peers imply that I am in grad school because I fill a quota or got a free-ride, I start to believe it. Decolonization, then, starts with purging the internalized beliefs that lead to the conclusion that Anishinaabeg are inferior. For all the settlers in the privileged section, please stay seated; a list of your responsibilities is being handed out next.

While decolonization starts with Indigenous people defiantly rejecting the colonial state's narrative about Indigenous people, decolonization does not end there. Unfortunately, here is where things get tricky. I can continue to mention all the things Indigenous people can do to decolonize themselves: learn the language, participate in the culture, and help create community sovereignty and sustainability. Assuming Indigenous people are solely responsible for decolonization is 'bootstrappy' and leaves out what settlers must do to decolonize. Since there is no reason for me to 'preach' to Indigenous people, I refuse to talk any further about what Indigenous people can do. We know what we need to do. And we are doing it now all over North Turtle Island. So, let's talk about settlers since 'decolonization' seems to be the Settler Buzzword of the Day.

Prime Minister Justin Trudeau created a bold definition of 'decolonize' in Ottawa on December 12, 2016 as reported by the National Observer:

> "It basically means looking at the impacts of the wide swath of federal laws and legal frameworks to remove and to eliminate the elements that, instead of providing justice and opportunity, and opportunities for reconciliation, have been impediments for opportunities for growth and success of indigenous communities across the country," Trudeau said. He said the key would be to find tangible ways to improve Canada's relationship with its First Nations by providing better health care, for example, and closing economic gaps between indigenous and non-indigenous Canadians.[98]

Concerning the split of INAC into two departments,[99] the new Minister of Crown-Indigenous Relations, Carolyn Bennett, was quoted as saying the change

> "is a story that is about decolonizing," Bennett said Monday. "It is about getting rid of the paternalism and being able to understand that we have to move to a new way of working together. It is ... about us stopping delivering government programs and begin to build Indigenous-led institutions and Indigenous-led governments."[100]

And let's not forget that 'decolonization' involves taking a look at the Indian Act. Bennett describes the act of decolonization as "more and more communities trying to get out from under the Indian Act with our help."[101] Whether intentional or not, the implications of the previous quote are that the government is filled with heroes saving Indigenous people from the evil Indian Act and that abolishing the Indian Act is not going to happen.

There are plenty of fancy words and, possibly, good intentions in the above quotes. Not a single one mentions what settlers can do to decolonize themselves. Do you remember that bit above about how decolonization starts with eliminating the colonial internalized beliefs about Indigenous people? It is not only Indigenous people who need to eliminate those beliefs; settlers also need to work toward rooting out and eliminating those beliefs. At this point, you might want to declare that you hold no harmful beliefs about Indigenous people. Unfortunately, due to colonial rule, biased education systems, and social norms (to mention a few), it is highly likely that you have at least one harmful belief about Indigenous people. It might be the case that you think Indigenous people cannot help themselves and, thus, need you to save them. Perhaps you think we are lazy for not being able to find steady employment. Maybe you think we are bad parents because many of our children have been apprehended. And it is likely that you have a lingering belief that Indigenous people are stubborn. At least two philosophers have implied that I am stubborn. As a philosopher, it is my job to argue points. Somehow me being a philosopher translates into stubbornness to those who know I am Anishinaabe.

There are many examples I could give on various harmful beliefs one could have, but that would detract from the purpose of pointing this out: in order for Trudeau and his cabinet to take any action toward reconciliation or decolonization, they need to decolonize themselves. No, it is not easy. It is, perhaps, less easy for settlers since most believe wholeheartedly that they are good allies and do not hold harmful beliefs. In the face of an Indigenous person telling a settler they are being hurtful and harmful, it is typical for the settler to get defensive. It is especially worse when the Indigenous person is angry. I will say more to the problem of anger below. The point I want to make here is that settlers, people whose ancestry is not from Turtle Island, need to realize their place on North Turtle Island. It does not matter if you were born here; you are a settler. Hell, even I am part settler. The important part is that, even though I am a mix of Finnish, French, and Ojibwe, Turtle Island still claims me. I still have a fundamental spiritual, emotional, mental, and physical connection to Anishinaabe territory. Settlers need to come to terms with the fact that a different land claims them even if they cannot go, have no way to go, or have a severed connection to that land. That brings me to the second unmentionable in the above quotes: land stewardship/ownership.

Before I get to a discussion on land, however, a lesson in anger is necessary. A lovely kwe[102] from a community in Northern Ontario once referred to a common trope as 'Stoic Indian Face'. This vulgar term is meant to make fun of the colonial idea that all Indigenous people are calm, cool, and collected at all times. Any sort of emotional outburst is regarded as irrational and as, perhaps, a precursor to physical violence. It is the case that being calm and cool is the ultimate way of being (when a person is mentally, physically, emotionally, and spiritually well, the person will be calm and cool). However, it is not the case that Indigenous people are the 'unemotional Stoic Sage' or ought to be. Also, there are far too many injustices o be angry about. So, the colonial narrative of the 'Stoic Indian' is what is expected of Indigenous people. When someone does something significantly wrong to an Indigenous person, the expectation is the Indigenous person will remain calm. Some Indigenous people may remain calm. Others will not. If you self-identify as an ally to Indigenous people and you find Indigenous people getting angry with you for things you say or do, be a better ally by figuring out what you are doing wrong and stop doing those things.

There is also a narrative which makes it so that being calm and cool in an extremely tough situation lessens the impact of the situation such that bystanders or the one causing the situation can believe that whatever aggression just happened was not an aggression or was an aggression with a significantly small impact. If you are not mad, it could not have been that bad, right? For example, if someone referred to my people and their problems as appetizers for consumption, and I did not feel safe raising an objection to what was said, I will probably try to keep a stoic expression so that further violence is not directed at me. The stoic expression can be interpreted to mean that the comment was not a problem or did not cause harm. If Patricia is not angry about it, it must be okay! Often, out of self-preservation, Indigenous people will grin and bear aggressions from settlers. If any sort of complaint were to happen after the fact, then the aggressor could claim that the recipient of the harm is inflating aggression because, while it was happening, the Indigenous person was calm and cool, shrugging off the aggression. What I have come to realize at a young age is that displays of anger are necessary as a means of addressing the severity of the aggression. Displaying anger is a risk because non-Indigenous people can see the 'angry indian' as a threat needing to be killed rather than a person who is legitimately angry over an injustice.

The crux of the problem is that I must show anger to address the severity of the impact and, yet, I must not show anger because the colonial narrative dictates that angry Indigenous people are physically aggressive. This 'damned if I do; damned if I don't' situation makes standing up to oppression much more difficult. I cannot get angry when being oppressed because it could be taken as me preparing to physically attack, but I have to get angry to make it known that the impact was significantly harmful. So, depending on the situation, I show anger in an equal level to the impact. If I do not feel safe or supported to show anger, I suppress and miss the chance to stand up to oppression.

Perhaps it is understandable now why Indigenous people across Turtle Island are angry when government officials say nothing about land when speaking about decolonization. First, I am not referring to the land claims.[103] Second, I am not referring to the land acknowledgements.[104] I am referring to the 99.65% of the land that Canada claims it owns.[105] It is rather baffling that any Canadian government leadership can speak of decolonization in a meaningful way without giving thought to diverting stewardship of crown land back to the First Peoples. Food security, safe drinking water, and economic stability/growth are a few of the benefits First Nations, Inuit, and Metis people will reclaim when decolonization involves reinstating Indigenous stewardship of the land.

Indigenous stewardship is not a novel idea and it is not my purpose here to figure out how Indigenous stewardship is supposed to work. Being Ojibwe does not give me the right to dictate what stewardship is for communities. I know my place here; I have a toddler's worth of knowledge about land stewardship. My focus is still decolonization and what it is supposed to refer to. Like I said above, decolonization starts with the individual. This is a necessary step. Unfortunately, this individualistic step does nothing to decolonize the system we are living in. It is also a strange hybrid of the bootstrap argument and victim blaming. Canada needs to maintain the focus on individuals decolonizing themselves because Canada cannot (and will not) decolonize the land; Canada needs the land to maintain itself as a country and governing body. As Peter Kulchyski (2013) points out, "our old friend capital, private interest, needs certainty in order to 'invest,' in order to continue to tear up the land at its unsustainable pace" (108). Without Canadian control over almost all the land, Canada starts losing its ability to make deals with corporations (foreign or local) or enact change that benefits the country; hence, land control equals certainty.

In the first half of 2018, the Prime Minister of Canada, Justin Trudeau, had set aside Canadian tax dollars to purchase the Kinder Morgan

Pipeline.[106] We can see, in real time, the government of Canada burning treaties by relying on supreme court rulings (needing to gain consent is tricky and often fails to protect Indigenous sovereignty over lands, including unceded lands)[107] to push through a pipeline Kinder Morgan does not have consent for. The takeaway is Canada cannot back down over land ownership because, if it does, Canada cannot sustain itself or entice business since Canada cannot make decisions on land it does not own.

One short and clear section of the United Nations Declaration on the Rights of Indigenous Peoples (UNDRIP) states that the General Assembly is

> *Concerned* that indigenous peoples have suffered from historic injustices as a result of, inter alia, their colonization and dispossession of their lands, territories and resources, thus preventing them from exercising, in particular, their right to development in accordance with their own needs and interests, *Recognizing* the urgent need to respect and promote the inherent rights of indigenous peoples which derive from their political, economic and social structures and from their cultures, spiritual traditions, histories and philosophies, especially their rights to their lands, territories and resources… [and] *Convinced* that control by indigenous peoples over developments affecting them and their lands, territories and resources will enable them to maintain and strengthen their institutions, cultures and traditions, and to promote their development in accordance with their aspirations and needs.[108] (2, their emphasis)

Article 26, point 1, of UNDRIP states that "Indigenous peoples have the right to the lands, territories and resources which they have traditionally owned, occupied or otherwise used or acquired" (see footnote 12, 10). Points 2 and 3 of Article 26 state that Indigenous peoples have the right to own the lands and the state needs to legally acknowledge and protect that ownership (see footnote 12, 10).

While UNDRIP is not the penultimate document of decolonization, it references what the Canadian government cannot: Indigenous stewardship of land. Even though the scholarship of some Anishinaabe and other Indigenous groups does not explicitly include land in their definitions of decolonization, land stewardship is a key component in self-determination, self-governance, and healing from the violent acts of colonization. As Sheila Cote-Meek (2014) points out,

> decolonizing is very much about healing. This means that it takes time to become decolonized, and we do not become decolonized without engaging in a lengthy process of freeing ourselves from colonial and imperial domination and control at multiple levels, including the mind, body, and

spirit, and within many contexts, such as family, community and larger society. (35)

Cote-Meek does not explicitly mention land stewardship and she does not have to; her point about 'colonial and imperial domination' involves the stealing of land and the implementation of the reserves system. It might be the case where people (academics or not) may not know this because colonized classrooms have narratives that exclude such information. It is not Cote-Meek's job to recount 500 years of colonization. The details of colonization are out there, and one needs only to search for those details. Also, explicitly talking about land stewardship opens a 'rabbit hole' of nightmarish strawman arguments. If I had a nickel for every time someone asked, "If we give the land back, where are we supposed to go," I would have a nice chunk of change to drop on my existing student loans. This and other strawman arguments over land signify gross ignorance of Indigenous ways and implicitly agree that the treatment of Indigenous people over the last 500 years is not something they want done to them.

So, where does that leave us? Decolonization is used in this weird, one-off sort of way by government officials, implying that they are decolonizing. For example, repealing the Indian Act (I know this is complicated), implementing Jordan's Principle, honouring consent, and increasing funding for First Nations, Inuit, and Metis education are just a few things that can be done, but they do not classify as 'decolonizing'. At the root of decolonization is land. Reclamation of ceremony, language, and practices are minimized when land is not decolonized. Why? Because our lives as Indigenous people are directly tied to the land. Ceremony is based on the land. So is language. The land gave us our lives, practices, and languages. Without the land, we are disconnected.

Pair the reclamation of land with every other aspect of decolonization mentioned above and we start to get a taste of what decolonization is to First Nations, Inuit, and Metis. There are many aspects not mentioned that are significant and specific to communities. What matters to all communities is the land. And that is where decolonization needs to start. When people say 'decolonize', it is vital to make sure the person using the word gives their understanding and definition so that this crucial word is not left empty. And, if the speakers of the word do not talk about land stewardship in their definitions of 'decolonization', we must ask them why they left it out.

On February 9, 2018, Indigenous people all over Turtle Island expressed their disappointment because Gerald Stanley was acquitted from both second-degree murder and manslaughter in the killing of a Red Pheasant First Nation youth.[109] The acquittal solidified the Canadian belief

CHAPTER TWENTY-TWO

that Turtle Island is Canadian land and Canadians can protect their land by any means necessary. A quick google search will find all the comments from settlers who cheered because now they can shoot Indigenous people on sight. I have argued that decolonization is often an empty term or a term with many meanings based on the context it appears in. After the Stanley verdict, it is unclear to me that we can work toward decolonization in a meaningful way now that Canada has a champion in Stanley to argue that this land is settler land only. Unfortunately, it does not seem likely that decolonization as many Indigenous people mean it to be is possible: Canada giving much of the stolen land back to Indigenous peoples. What we can do is come together to create the semantics or referents of the settler language. This way we maintain our narrative. Decolonization needs to be something that everyone does as defined by Indigenous groups. No longer should we allow Canada to use empty words.

References

Cote-Meek, Sheila. 2014. Colonized Classrooms: Racism, Trauma and Resistance in Post-Secondary Education. Halifax: Fernwood Publishing.
Kovach, Margaret. 2009. Indigenous Methodologies: Characteristics, Conversations, and Contexts. Toronto: University of Toronto Press.
Kulchyski, Peter. 2013. Aboriginal Rights are not Human Rights. Winnipeg: Arbeiter Ring Publishing.

notes

[95] Anishinaabemowin (Anishinaabe language) for 'grandmother'.
[96] https://www.ictinc.ca/indian-act-and-womens-status-discrimination-via-bill-c-31-bill-c-3. Bill C-3 was the start of equalizing the Indian Act so that Indigenous women no longer lost status, regained status after losing it due to marriage, and gaining the ability to pass status on to children.
[97] https://www.fin.gov.on.ca/en/guides/hst/80.html. There is a long list of what items are tax exempt and not tax exempt. Oddly enough, take-out meals qualify.
[98] https://www.nationalobserver.com/2016/12/12/news/trudeau-proceed-wide-federal-review-decolonize-canada. A new article where Prime Minister Justin Trudeau expresses a part of the decolonization plan.
[99] Indigenous and Northern Affairs Canada (INAC) has been split into two ministries: Indigenous Services and Crown-Indigenous Relations.
[100] http://thechronicleherald.ca/canada/1498236-bennett-philpott-tag-team-indigenous-file-as-feds-look-to-dissolve-department. An article that explains the split of INAC into two different ministries.
[101] http://www.cbc.ca/radio/thecurrent/the-current-for-january-26-2017-1.3951896/indigenous-leaders-give-trudeau-government-failing-grade-on-delivering-promises-1.3951900. Indigenous people weigh in on Prime Minister Justin Trudeau's performance so far.
[102] Anishinaabemowin for 'woman'.
[103] https://www.aadnc-aandc.gc.ca/eng/1100100030285/1100100030289. The Canadian government's details on land claims.

[104] https://studentlife.uoguelph.ca/aboriginal/territorial-acknowledgement. The University of Guelph's suggested land acknowledgement statement.

[105] Taking the number from INAC (3,554,836) and dividing that by the number from the geography of Canada Wikipedia page (9,984,670 converted to hectares: 998,467,000) gives us 0.35%. Sources: https://www.aadnc-aandc.gc.ca/eng/1359993855530/1359993914323 and https://en.wikipedia.org/wiki/Geography_of_Canada.

[106] https://globalnews.ca/news/4371887/trudeau-defends-government-buying-trans-mountain/. Prime Minister Justin Trudeau's justification for buying a pipeline that Indigenous groups never gave consent to build.

[107] http://www.chamber.ca/media/blog/171106-supreme-court-decision-provides-more-clarity-regarding-Aboriginal-consent-for-projects/. Indigenous consent is now a requirement for any projects built on Indigenous lands, including reserves and unceded lands.

[108] http://www.un.org/esa/socdev/unpfii/documents/DRIPS_en.pdf

[109] https://www.cbc.ca/news/indigenous/colten-boushie-gerald-stanley-indigenous-justice-history-1.4532564. A news article about the acquittal of Gerald Stanley.

Chapter Twenty-Three

Indigenous Student Experience in an Indigenizing Institution

Preliminary Results from a Canadian University

Iloradanon Efimoff

Situating the Author

Háw'aa, Iloradanon hínuu díi kya'áang (Hello, my name is Iloradanon). I am Haida and European settler. I was born in Northern British Columbia, but spent most of my formative years in the lower mainland of British Columbia. I have been in post-secondary institutions for almost 10 years as a student and will likely continue this journey for some time. This paper, in particular, comes from my experience, and the experience of several other students, with Indigenization at the University of Saskatchewan, where I completed my Master of Arts degree in Psychology. Full findings from this study will be published elsewhere at a later date.

Introduction

Indigenization seems to be on every institution's collective mind in recent years. In Canada in particular, there is a focus on Indigenizing institutions. Ranging from a reconciliation totem pole being raised on the UBC campus (CBC, 2017), which intrudes upon unceded Coast Salish territory, to the first mandatory Indigenous studies course credit being required for graduation at Lakehead University in Thunder Bay, Ontario, and the University of Winnipeg (Macdonald, 2015), the efforts to Indigenize post-secondary institutions are sweeping the nation. The University of

Saskatchewan has made much progress towards Indigenization – from a Ph.D. program in Indigenous studies to the largest population of Indigenous students at a U15 institution; there is much to be said about the happenings at this institution. Both accolades and critiques abound.

Indigenization is slippery, elusive, transcending – what the hell does it mean? As an Indigenous and White woman, growing up with both of my cultures (although decidedly more of a general White Canadian culture), it perplexes me. It is no wonder, then, that the institution itself does not have a public definition for the strategic priority they are currently undertaking. So, what is Indigenization? While exploring the multitude of meanings that exist within the concept is not the explicit purview of this paper, it is, of course, imperative that readers have a working understanding of the concept in order to follow along. I only hope that I can provide a mildly lucid explanation to help readers in that regard. Indigenization manifests itself in many ways – on the very surface level, this includes paintings on walls, artifacts in glass boxes displayed for the White onlooker, and on a more in-depth level, changes in policies and curriculum to equally value Indigenous ways of knowing with those of the White world. This is a simple conception, but hopefully gives you a vague understanding of a continuum on which acts of Indigenization can exist. Perhaps on the deep end of this continuum, work blends into decolonization, a dismantling of colonial systems that have attempted to chain us for centuries and continue such attempts.

With a vague idea of Indigenization in your mind, let us get down to business. As an Indigenous student coming from a small undergraduate institution in the lower mainland of British Columbia, I was pleasantly surprised when I began my degree at the University of Saskatchewan. Indigenous art was everywhere, I could take a Cree language course if I wanted (although it would not count for credit towards my degree, and the Haida language is nothing like the Cree language), I could study in the Gordon Oakes Red Bear Student Centre (an entire building dedicated to Indigenous students), I could attend powwows, smudges, sweats, pipe ceremonies… This was a hard deviation from the initiatives at my undergraduate institution, which fell squarely on the shoulders of one individual in one small room in an isolated corner of campus (which was my second home for the final year of my undergraduate studies). Having always had an inclination for organization, leadership, event planning and the like, I had racked up a fairly large laundry list of these types of experiences at my undergraduate institution, although few formalized opportunities with the Indigenous community on campus explicitly. With so much more happening at the University of Saskatchewan, I naturally gravitated towards my community and ended up in several leadership positions, representing hundreds of Indigenous graduate students (and sometimes undergraduate students as well, due to structural inconsistencies within internal governing bodies).

In these positions, at first, I was amazed at the amount of work the institution was doing to Indigenize. I was impressed by my (White) supervisor's understanding of Indigenous issues and my (White) lab-mates empathy and genuine knowledge of the history of Canada. I was impressed by the abundance of Indigenous faculty, staff, and students, the plethora of free Indigenous focused events to attend, and the overwhelmingly welcoming community. Sitting on these committees, I provided what input I could, acutely and explicitly aware of my position as an outsider to prairie culture. After some time in these positions, I began to notice some potential unintended consequences of the Indigenization work happening at the university.

First of all, I was exhausted. I was drinking more coffee than I wanted to, sleeping less than I wanted to, and pestering my friends more than I wanted to, to get engaged. I was one person sitting on these committees, representing hundreds of students (many of whom I barely knew), in a culture I was terribly unfamiliar with. The vast majority of my Indigenous colleagues had an equally large burden to bare – providing input on committees, coordinating student action, organizing and hosting events – all related explicitly to Indigenization. We were dealing with a massive capacity issue. The university wanted many of us to provide input to Indigenize – and a few of us took on formalized roles and were often relied on heavily. We were all doing it in some way or another, even by merely existing in spaces barred to us a few generations ago. But the work was exhausting, which left me exhausted. My friends were exhausted.

Secondly, things started to look a bit odd. It was as if I was blinded by the beauty of the buildings, the art, the songs, the stories, the proudly displayed culture. If there is any beauty to be blinded by, that is it. But substantial long-term changes, changing systems that continue to oppress Indigenous individuals within the ivory tower, were slower moving, and often top-down. This concerned me greatly as a student. I had gained a large amount of knowledge about current Indigenization processes, but upon my graduation, some of this knowledge is inevitably lost, despite attempts to transition incoming leaders. These long-term changes that students push for can fall off the radar as students graduate, and without student advocacy, sometimes they find a quiet corner to sit and wait. This is not always the case at the University of Saskatchewan, but the push and pull between systemic and surface-level changes, long-term and quick fixes, was front and center in my mind.

Who did the university talk to about Indigenization? Lots of people, but I am not sure how many students (Indigenous and non-Indigenous). Whom did they listen to? Whose advice did they take? I wanted other people's ideas. How did Indigenization impact them? What were their experiences with it? Did they like it? Hate it? What could be done better?

Method

I set out upon a treacherous journey, filled with ethics applications, conversations with my supervisor, hours of transcription, even more hours of analysis, and finally, the writing of this paper. At the time of this submission, I have interviewed 8 Indigenous student leaders at the University of Saskatchewan in Saskatoon, Canada, with all identifying as First Nations or of Mixed Ancestry. I read through the consent form and acquired voluntary consent from all 8 participants. I transcribed the interviews and then sent each transcript to each respective participant for their review, so that they had the opportunity to edit them to better reflect what they were trying to express. After this process, seven of the eight participants signed a transcript release form (one could not be contacted), indicating that they were comfortable with me using their transcript for analysis. As an added layer to ensure appropriate representation of participants, all participants included in this analysis were sent excerpts from this paper before submission – none requested changes, and all were satisfied with my representation of them.

Participants ranged in age from 21 to 61 years and were enrolled in a variety of undergraduate and graduate programs: from education, to business, to environmental sciences, to medicine. Half of the 8 participants identified as men, and half as women. Given that detailed analysis of interviews will be presented elsewhere upon completion of the project, only a brief analysis including quotes from 4 participants is presented here.

Results

All participants acknowledged the good work being done by the University of Saskatchewan and were grateful for all of the work being put into Indigenization. Students discussed many opportunities provided by Indigenization: learning while sitting on committees related to Indigenization, connecting with other Indigenous individuals on campus through events hosted with the intent to Indigenize, public speaking

CHAPTER TWENTY-THREE

opportunities, feelings of safety and comfort on campus, and even the chance to meet political figures. When asked about the benefits of Indigenization, one student stated:

> ...The opportunities that I've been actually given since I started to get more involved with the Indigenous aspect of the University of Saskatchewan has actually changed my opportunities as an individual. I would have never had the opportunity to be in that group to privately meet with Justin Trudeau, if I never joined the [Indigenous peer mentor program], so. So that was, y'know, and then on top of that I still have more opportunities coming that are actually, y'know, still in the works, it's really interesting how my life is actually changing because I'm getting more involved.

In this case, the student has had some excellent opportunities due to his engagement with Indigenization efforts on campus. The Indigenous peer mentorship program the student refers to is one that was created in efforts to Indigenize the campus, and a snowballing set of opportunities have developed from the student's engagement in one Indigenous initiative on campus. He even goes as far to say that his life is changing because of his increased involvement. These changes were undoubtedly positive, as indicated by the participant's hopeful tone of voice when discussing incoming opportunities. There are potentially large-scale benefits due to engagement, with this student having the opportunity to meet the Prime Minister of Canada and change his life through engagement with Indigenization. These are obviously positive impacts of Indigenization on this particular student.

However, of course, with opportunity comes responsibility. Several students discussed the pressures that Indigenization puts on students – pressures to engage, to do free work, and to often be the Indigenous "expert" in the room. It is particularly ironic that a process partly intended to assist Indigenous students in succeeding at post-secondary institutions is also negatively impacting them. One student says:

> I've had to make some real big sacrifices in terms of grades... I'd go to class, but my mind wasn't actually there. And then when I was there, I would maybe go for about an hour and then I'd get antsy... so I'd have to get moving... for a lot of these committees that we have and a lot of the meetings that I've been grateful to attend, but it's been a lot of time taken up...

In this case, the student had trouble focusing in class because they are involved in many initiatives and committees related to Indigenization, and this trouble focusing is negatively impacting their grades. While they are grateful to be attending such meetings, they are also acutely aware of the time they are dedicating to these initiatives. Beyond this, they are feeling "antsy" and wanting to get moving – perhaps feeling anxious about the amount of work they were undertaking, and the subsequent impact on grades. Missing class negatively impacts student success; even when missing classes is done to create initiatives to help other Indigenous students succeed. However, it would appear the student is conscious of these sacrifices, partly speaking of them as a choice; perhaps engagement for the betterment of the community is perceived as more important than grades. This highlights the desire to contribute to the community that was common in many interviews.

Other students had negative experiences with Indigenization in the classroom. Some students shared stories of professors attempting to Indigenize. For example, Jacqueline Nokusis, a first-year medical student, recounts the story of a well-intended professor and Indigenization gone wrong.

> ...[The professor] brings up HIV prevalence in Indigenous women... he didn't even get to his point. He just threw up these statistics... Class ended, no time to elaborate... he thought if he makes people aware that it's a problem, maybe we can educate some students...I said but you need to realize that you gave this knowledge to impressionable people, first, second year university students, they're going to take that knowledge, and they're going to do whatever they want with that knowledge... some people are just gunna [think] "ok, Aboriginal women have HIV."

While this particular professor was trying to Indigenize class content, they ended up potentially providing students with dangerous information and no context. These students may remember this piece of information and potentially apply it to many Indigenous women – as an Indigenous woman, it did cross Jacqueline's mind that perhaps other students would then assume she had HIV because of this decontextualized information. This is obviously an incredibly uncomfortable situation for the student. This quote, however, also alludes to the need to build capacity. This professor wants to Indigenize but is clearly having a hard time doing so in a good way. Thus, capacity is needed; resources and information for professors who wish to Indigenize. The student, in this case, goes on to ask if this professor should have been Indigenizing at all. She asserts that there is a time and place for this material, but discussing HIV in Indigenous women is not appropriate in a second-year genetics class. This further illustrates the need for Indigenization capacity – in particular, help with integrating Indigenous content appropriately into classes. Perhaps something more relevant to a second-year genetics class, would be a discussion of genetic components of Multiple Sclerosis, which impacts more people living in

Saskatchewan than anywhere else in Canada (Cameco MS Neuroscience Research Center, n.d.), and has a much lower incidence in Indigenous peoples than White people hailing from Northern Europe (The Mayo Clinic, n.d.).

Similarly, other students discuss poor attempts at Indigenization, however with potentially positive outcomes. One student explains an in-class situation:

> [The professor said] I bet you more Indigenous students here know someone who committed suicide rather than those people who are non-Indigenous." ... I called her out on it in front of class where she actually took a poll... that very quick poll changed her mind... she was by all means really receptive, she said "you know what, you're right, I'm really sorry about that." She did admit that she was wrong. And it was very immediately after class that she apologized...

While the professor was attempting to Indigenize by explicitly discussing content related to Indigenous peoples, the delivery and assumptions were quite problematic. More importantly, despite being challenged on this assumption in front of the class to which they were supposed to be the expert, the professor was able to take a step back and check her assumptions, and acknowledge that she was wrong about something. Further, she very quickly apologized and was receptive; potentially changing how she thought about that particular topic in the future. This is illustrative of the inevitable community learnings that are emerging from this Indigenization process, as multiple different communities with different worldviews and lived experiences come together to create something beneficial for all, but in particular, for (or perhaps with) Indigenous students. Professors being able to take the perspective of Indigenous students appears to be an important part of this process. With these two examples, we can see that there is likely much more learning to be had, but that this learning is likely possible.

However, Indigenous students also learn from non-Indigenous students throughout this Indigenization process. A White-presenting Indigenous student (an Indigenous student who physically appears White) tells a story of a study group at her friend's house:

> I had a study group at a [White] friend's house... and all of the sudden the conversation was about me, they had so many questions, legitimate questions... they all agreed with Indigenization, and what that showed me... maybe I have to be less judgmental also... I did not think that those women would be as interested or as knowledgeable as they were.

In this case, the student is taken aback by her White peers understanding of and attitude towards Indigenization – she is pleasantly surprised. This experience results in her checking her own assumptions and attempting to understand her own biases towards White people on campus. This may be a contentious quote for some readers, but ultimately this is one student's story, and my job as a researcher is to tell that story. These three quotes in combination indicate that members of Indigenous and non-Indigenous communities on campus are learning from each other. There is likely more learning to occur in one direction than the other, but the entire on-campus community may be learning from each other nonetheless.

These examples illustrate the inevitable existence of community and communities on campus that exist throughout this Indigenization process. While in the above examples Indigenization may be perceived as including separate communities (e.g., Indigenous and White people or students and professors), many students discussed the importance of community for them throughout Indigenization. Students talked about community between Indigenous and non-Indigenous students, they discussed community as a way of survival on campus, and even discussed simple examples of the importance of community within the context of an Indigenizing institution. Terrance Pelletier, a senior Ph.D. student, shares the importance of community on campus:

> Terrance: That one time I went into the cafeteria and there was this Indian [Indigenous] guy in there, he was serving something, he was a cook... and he told me this really funny Indian [Indigenous] joke, just in the way of one sentence, and it made me laugh [laughter]. So we like to see that...
>
> Iloradanon: So that helps, to build that sense of community?
>
> Terrance: It does, it does. It builds that up when you see other people.

In this example, Terrance indicates that it helps build a sense of community when students see other people like him, that is, other Indigenous people on campus. It doesn't matter what role they are in, just their presence and a brief expression of culture (in this case, humour), is valued. This sense of community came through a joke, and indeed, humour was very common throughout these interviews.

Discussion

Ultimately, while students acknowledge good work occurring on campus and are appreciative of ongoing Indigenization efforts, they also see many areas for improvement. There is a desperate need to build capacity, on behalf of students (such that they can contribute without putting their success at stake) and on behalf of faculty who are attempting to Indigenize their own classrooms. It is important for the institution to continue to allow the Indigenous community to grow to ensure continued Indigenization. However, perhaps one of the most important things that I learned from this project was the desire for students to voice their ideas, concerns, and critiques on Indigenization. This is said best in the words of one of the participants:

> ...more student input. There's a lot of assumptions being made about what students want, but nothing directly asking students what they want... I think that there should be more involvement to allow our voices to be heard, cause if there's such a focus on Indigenization at the university, well maybe you should ask the students that are here about how that should look.

While it can be easy to criticize and fixate on the negative, it is important to remember that all students appreciated the work the university is doing. Indigenization is undoubtedly a long-term project that walks a winding journey, and adaptability and flexibility are critically important. Furthermore, initiatives for Indigenization should ensure that Indigenous community voice, and in particular student voice, is front and center. As the student above alludes to, the university should listen to student voices to successfully Indigenize. Hopefully, this project has helped to do just that.

Háw'aa (thank you) for the read, I hope you enjoyed it. I enjoyed the write.

Endnote

This research could not have been completed without participants (listed alphabetically by last name): Gabrielle Lee, Jacqueline Nokusis, Terrance Pelletier, Regan Ratt-Misponas, and four other students who wished to remain anonymous.

References

Cameco MS Neuroscience Research Center. (n.d.). *Information about MS*. Retrieved from http://www.usask.ca/healthsci/cmsnrc/msinfo.html

CBC. (2017, April 1). *Reconciliation totem pole goes up at UBC*. Retrieved from http://www.cbc.ca/news/canada/british-columbia/reconciliation-totem-pole-goes-up-at-ubc-1.4050078

Macdonald, N. (2015, November 19). *Required reading: Making Indigenous classes mandatory.* Retrieved from http://www.macleans.ca/education/making-history-2/

The Mayo Clinic. (n.d.). *Multiple Sclerosis.* Retrieved from https://www.mayoclinic.org/diseases-conditions/multiple-sclerosis/symptoms-causes/syc-20350269

Chapter Twenty-Four

Beyond Indigenization

Indigenous Collaboration and Imagining our own Academy[110]

Adam Gaudry[111]

The Canadian academy has undergone significant changes since the release of the Truth and Reconciliation Commission's (TRC) *Calls to Action* in December 2015.[112] While certainly some of this change has been substantial, such as the noticeable increase in the number of postings for Indigenous faculty positions at most Canadian universities, more structural change seems elusive. It is probably obvious to most people in the academy that the pre-TRC university was inadequate in its relations with Indigenous peoples, but it is not quite clear yet what a post-TRC university will look like. We are in a moment of change—what is yet to be determined is if this change will have meaningful impact on Indigenous lives, or if it will just be a shift in how universities market themselves. One significant change stemming from the TRC is that "indigenization" entered the popular lexicon of the university, a marked departure from the previous ignorance of Indigenous policy-making on most university campuses. In our current moment, like many moments of transition before it, almost any outcome is possible. Predicting the eventual outcome is probably a loser's game, yet there is substantial value in knowing the long-term aspirations of Indigenous faculty, staff, students, and our communities in order to address the changing policy directions of Canadian universities as they attempt to adequately respond to the challenges of post-TRC Canada.

I began my academic career two years before the TRC released its *Calls to Action*, and so witnessed the seemingly overnight shift of the Indigenous place in the academy from one of marginal importance with insufficient resources, to one of seemingly central importance, which resulted in a small increase in resources, but with a much greater demand on Indigenous time for committee work, policy formation and the like. I've also taught Indigenous studies at three Western Canadian universities and have been involved in various indigenization and reconciliation initiatives at two of them. Building off this direct experience with the inner mechanics of university policy-making, my more recent scholarly work—done collaboratively with education scholar Danielle Lorenz—surveys Indigenous scholars, instructors and allies working in post-secondary education to gather their thoughts on both the practical directions and the ideals of indigenization policy.

This research, which I will draw on throughout this piece, has culminated in a book chapter, "Decolonization for the Masses? Grappling with Indigenous Content Requirements in the Changing Post-Secondary Environment"[113] and an article, "Indigenization and inclusion, reconciliation, and decolonization: Navigating the different vision for indigenizing the Canadian academy."[114] In these works, Lorenz and I found that many post-secondary educators expressed hesitancy about the growing move to require Indigenous content and courses at Canadian universities. Yet there was a general optimism that if done correctly, and if taught by the right people, that these courses could transform the status quo.[115] We also found that indigenization as an overarching policy goal was generally supported by Indigenous people and allies working in universities, but that these people remained concerned that indigenization could be pursued in superficial ways. The risk was that these new initiatives would fail to substantiate change, to make universities safer for Indigenous faculty, staff, and students, or to effectively transform the consciousness of Canadians.[116] Nonetheless, in both instances we found that most of the people on the front lines of indigenization and reconciliation struggles in the academy expressed cautious optimism for a positive, transformative outcome.

If I could define the current moment in the Canadian academy I would describe it as a time of fundamental tension over the long-term relationship between Indigenous peoples and Canadian post-secondary institutions. While Indigenous faculty, staff, and students, (and our allies) are largely focused on achieving long-term and transformative goals, university administrations are much more focused on quick fixes which produce immediate results, leading in many cases to divergent strategies in addressing the key issues—or even disagreement over what the key issues are. There are, in my view, three concerns about "indigenizing the academy" that will determine its efficacy:

1. A lack of clarity in how indigenization is defined resulting in divergent academic policy directions;
2. A longstanding struggle for the autonomy for Indigenous intellectual communities both inside and outside of the Canadian academy;
3. A need for clear support for Indigenous intellectual futures where indigenization strengthens intellectual independence of Indigenous communities, rather than merely integrates us into the Euro-North American academic norms.

In this chapter, I address each of these concerns, proposing ways that Indigenous students, faculty, and staff can enliven Indigenous intellectual futures that the support self-determination and decolonization of our peoples.

INDIGENIZATION AND ITS PITFALLS: MOVING BEYOND INDIGENIZATION

The term "indigenization" likely originates from language developed in in the edited collection compiled by Devon Abbot Mihesuah and Angela Cavender Wilson, notably called *Indigenizing the Academy: Transforming Scholarship and Empowering Communities* (2004). The volume called for the creation of spaces of consequence for Indigenous peoples in post-secondary education, including the substantial hiring for Indigenous scholars, a cultural shift in research and teaching that held Indigenous knowledges and Indigenous histories in equal esteem, and transforming scholarship in ways that serves Indigenous community needs. This language, in circulation among Indigenous scholars for years, went mainstream with the release of the *Calls to Action,* and while campus indigenization was greeted with optimism by Indigenous people, this has mood has changed, seemingly with the realization that what "indigenization" signifies today is not necessarily in keeping with how it has long been used in Indigenous scholarship. While many people are now arguing for "indigenization," the form that that indigenization takes is the real issue. This was of course a criticism nearly from the beginning,[117] but is only increasing in intensity.

Most notably, on February 28, 2018, the Indigenous Students Council (ISC) at the University of Saskatchewan released a blistering statement which questioned the very nature of indigenization happening on their campus, where calls for reconciliation and indigenization, has yield[ed] little practical results. We take offense to the toe the line speeches and the uplifting of a colonial institution. We are told to maintain hope and toe the line of Reconciliation and Indigenization. However, we have not seen any real systemic change occur on campus.[118]

The ISC, seemingly tired of stalled progress, while still being asked to support university efforts, proposed a radical and empowering solution:

> We are calling for all indigenous students to come together as a community to rescind current ratifications and sever ties from Settler Student Unions and create an Indigenous Students Union. We call on the Gordon Oakes Red Bear Student Centre to be recognized as the Gordon Oakes Red Bear Indigenous Student Union Building. We call for our student fees to be rerouted to our student bodies in the form of this Indigenous Student Union, we have the answers, we have the solutions, but we do not have the financial means and space to meet the needs of our student population.[119]

In taking control of the transformation of their campus, Indigenous students at the U of S are suggesting a very different path for reconciliation and indigenization, a path which fundamentally alters the structure of the contemporary university. This approach empowers Indigenous people to make policy decisions on our own, rather than by appealing to existing university processes. Indeed, the vision articulated in the ISC's is not the indigenization envisioned by most university administrators, it is proposing a different direction entirely.

More importantly, perhaps, is the growing impatience with administrations to implement the policies they've been proposing for years. Where at one time public discussion of indigenization was so novel as to elicit optimism, now the same language is increasingly viewed with skepticism where action does not accompany a rhetorical shift. It is also no mistake that students have taken the lead on this, as they have a shorter time horizon for change than faculty and staff. Most students cycle through university programs in roughly four years and expect to see change within that length of time. The pressure they apply and the urgency that they feel is important for the rest of us to remember, with our careers lasting as long as 35 years, when we do not feel the same time pressures. Indeed, students are an important instigator for effective change at universities for precisely this reason. Students tire of learning about injustice at universities while not seeing their own institutions address injustices in their midst. In many ways, the ISC's statement marks a turning point in discussions of indigenization, a red line in which universities must recognize when they come to it. It is the point where rhetoric is not enough. The ISC statement represents our new context, and so perhaps it's useful to begin thinking "beyond indigenization" and think about how we can martial our goals to pursue truly transformative change in the academy.

THREE DEFINITIONS OF "INDIGENIZATION"

Aside from inaction, there is a rhetorical problem. Indigenization as a concept is not taken up in a systematic way. In our survey of Indigenous academics and allies working in this field, Lorenz and I found that the term gets used in three distinct ways:

1. Indigenous inclusion

We define Indigenous inclusion policy as a strategy "to increase the number of Indigenous students, faculty, and staff in the Canadian academy ... largely by supporting the adaption of Indigenous people to the current (often alienating) culture of Canadian academy."[120] In other words it helps Indigenous people acclimate to current academic and administrative structures of the university, and does so without attempting to change those structures. This means that the burden of change falls on Indigenous faculty, staff, and students, not the institution itself. Indigenous inclusion policy has certainly been beneficial in increasing the number of Indigenous people able to enter post-secondary education, but an inclusion policy's ambition ends there, with little effort directed towards system-wide change. In practice this is largely the dominant approach to indigenization operating in Canadian universities. Even though Indigenous inclusion has ensured access to post-secondary education for more Indigenous people, it has done little to address the exclusionary structures which created the need for such a policy in the first place. While ensuring the inclusion of more Indigenous people is surely important, it is not in itself sufficient to indigenize the academy.[121]

2. Reconciliation indigenization

Going beyond Indigenous inclusion is a more systematic approach we labelled reconciliation indigenization, which "locates indigenization on common ground between Indigenous and Canadian ideals, creating a new, broader consensus on debates such as: what counts as knowledge? how should Indigenous knowledges and European-derived knowledges engage one another? and what types of relationships should academic institutions have with Indigenous communities?"[122] In practice, the adoption of reconciliation language has been more of a rhetorical shift than an actual policy change, with universities still struggling to understand what actual reconciliation looks like. Given that reconciliation requires more fundamental change than policies of inclusion, its implementation is much slower (if it is being implemented at all). The celebratory and transformative rhetoric of reconciliation has certainly resulted in the expansion of inclusion policies, but little else. So, while this is the dominant mode of *rhetoric*, it is not the dominant *approach* of policymakers.[123] This disjuncture between rhetoric and practice has led to frustration, disillusionment, and activism, exemplified by the ISC's statement calling for a fundamental shift in direction and a shift to Indigenous leadership in indigenization decision-making.

3. Decolonial indigenization

The long-term vision of most Indigenous scholars involved in our study was what we termed decolonial indigenization, which "envisions the wholesale overhaul of the academy to fundamentally reorient knowledge production based on balanced power relations between Indigenous peoples and Canadians, transforming the academy into something dynamic and new."[124] One anonymous respondent proposed that we should constitute a "parallel academy," creating two co-existing intellectual spaces, one Indigenous and one Canadian, that inhabit the same institutions, operating simultaneously as interdependent and autonomous entities. This proposal was likely drawn from visions of interdependent yet autonomous political relations from Indigenous treaty-making traditions that envision multiple peoples inhabiting the same space, but not governing one another. This ideal of parallel academies seems also to resonate with the ISC's proposal for a parallel student government in a parallel student union, co-habiting the same campus, but governing themselves independently of the existing student union.

This notion of a parallel academy and the more ambitious approach to indigenization provided by decolonial thought can provide us with some important insights in how we envision our future relationships in the academy. Indeed, an academy specifically for Indigenous intellectual communities that we build ourselves, on our own terms, and for our own purposes would generate a new outlet for intellectual expression, activist scholarship, and increased political autonomy for our peoples. This notion of parallel academies can help jumpstart our thinking, moving us beyond indigenization, changing the dynamics of our campuses, and propelling us towards a world much different than the one we currently live in.

CHAPTER TWENTY-FOUR

A PARALLEL ACADEMY

In advocating for a parallel Indigenous academy, I am not proposing that our intellectual institutions should be modeled after contemporary universities. Rather, I am suggesting that we embrace a broad view of the term "academy," which is according to the *Oxford English Dictionary* is "a society or institution of distinguished scholars and artists or scientists that aims to promote and maintain standards in its particular field."[125] To understand this more broadly, an academy is an intellectual community of learned people, who work together to promote the advancement of a particular knowledge or understanding, and is a place for the deliberation and debate of ideas. Where colonialism has long sought to bring Indigenous knowledges *inside* of Canadian institutions, Indigenous peoples have long resisted by defending, re-establishing, and creating our own institutions. In essence, Indigenous people are already doing a lot of this work both inside and outside of universities. Collectively we are holding parallel conversations about Indigenous issues, we are debating these issues and working to create consensus on many of them, and we are doing this in numerous forums, everything from annual general assemblies to Indigenous Twitter. These forums are populated by diverse Indigenous intellectuals from diverse traditions, who are already working towards this development.

So how can we support the development of an "Indigenous academy" that can work both within and against current Canadian university structures? In particular there is a need for great administrative and intellectual autonomy for Indigenous programs, for Indigenous students, and for Indigenous community-engaged research. And with this focus, the likely end goal is not inclusion in the existing Canadian academy, but the formation of separate intellectual communities that are connected to current university structures but are also autonomous and distinct. In short, we can create our own academy—or for those who dislike that term, our own intellectual community that is governed by our own internal processes and structured by our own internal debates.

We can think of this as a treaty model of universities, which structured political and jurisdictional relationships between Indigenous peoples and the British Crown as co-equal entities, intended to each cohabitate the same space without governing the other, and more importantly without declaring sovereignty over the other. There were always acknowledgements that interaction between the treaty partners would occur, and that was even desirable because learning from each other was one of the ways everyone would benefit from this new relationship. There are obvious parallels in contemporary intellectual relations as well, as Indigenous or Euro-Canadian knowledges can certainly be utilized for the benefit of the other, but problems arise when Indigenous knowledges are either devalued or used inappropriately to the diminishment of their originary community.

At the core of this movement is a different way forward that does not aspire to the Canadian academic refrain of "advancing human knowledge" in ways that bring all knowledges inside a universal (European-derived) intellectual tradition—as if inclusion in this canon is in itself a just result, a kind of intellectual reconciliation. Rather, by embracing the particularities of localized Indigenous ways of knowing, an Indigenous academy supports Indigenous knowledge holders of all kinds in the protection and revitalization of their intellectual inheritance, while keeping the authority to interpret such knowledge where it belongs, with its people. Indeed, this movement away from the mere inclusion of Indigenous knowledges within the Canadian intellectual tradition, and towards a community-rooted, collaborative, Indigenous "academy" is an important shift underpinned by decolonial attitudes of Indigenous independence and intellectual self-determination. A parallel academy likewise calls on Canadians to engage in different academic relationships, to work collaboratively with communities as partners, but while also respecting the intellectual independence of Indigenous communities. In this emerging vision, how intellectuals mobilize their energy and resources is the vital concern, and careful consideration must be given to how Indigenous-focused, community-driven collaborations fit within treaty relationships or in communities where no such relationship exists, the principle of international relations that respects the political independence of other nations. In practice these are ultimately the same.

BREAKING DOWN THE UNIVERSITY-COMMUNITY DICHOTOMY

A parallel academic structure is only one way of conceiving of a new direction for intellectual relations between Indigenous peoples and Canadians. Indeed, there are also many distinct Indigenous post-secondary institutions and educational movements that exist independent outside of the Canadian university structure, such as Indigenous universities and colleges. There are, of course, much older intellectual institutions in Indigenous communities as well, where traditional knowledges are held, passed on, and revitalized quite independent of any university or college apparatus. One of way of moving beyond an indigenization paradigm is to rethink a strict dichotomy that distinguishes between university-based and community-based Indigenous intellectual pursuits, as if they serve totally different ends. We tend to conceptual intellectual labour as if work done in community and work done at the university by Indigenous intellectuals are inherently separate, or that they knowledges that are engaged with constitute two self-contained systems that are somehow incompatible. In much of our work there is surprising overlap, indeed, much of the work undertaken by Indigenous intellectuals transcends these sorts of boundaries. The best work engages both of these spheres, collapses them, and reworks intellectual relationships to break down these distinctions.

It is not surprising then that we are seeing very different research coming out of Indigenous-centred university programs, where community-engagement, partnership, and leadership are the norm. If we're willing to pursue a very different kind of academy—our own academy—it would necessarily involve these kinds of relationships. Indigenous studies scholarship must be in constant conversation with non-university intellectual traditions and if done properly a combination of different approaches to teaching, learning, and research can make for very different kinds of intellectual relationships. If the indigenization approach is bringing knowledge holders into the classroom, the decolonial approach is moving the classroom into the bush. If we're thinking about our own academy, it doesn't need to be cloistered off in a university—the origin of which is a medieval Catholic monastery—the very setting of our learning and pedagogy of our teaching can be immersive, it need not follow university models.

In recognition of different kinds of knowledge, experience, and credentials, an Indigenous academy must also include knowledge holders outside of the university structure, supporting ideals that knowledge comes from many places, and that university campuses are not the best places to learn many of the things we need to know. This is where it's important to move classrooms into communities, particularly on the land—in places where a lot of academics aren't going to be the ones with answers. How can we share intellectual roles with all sorts of Indigenous intellectuals and how can we reflect that in our teaching and research? Thinking about institutional change—structural change, innovative pedagogy, and methodology—is all needed here. It's not just about bringing more Native people into the existing system, it's about us re-establishing our own intellectual spaces. Many of those are out on the land, but these spaces need not be totally separated from university learning either, indeed the growing number of university-connected land-based learning programs attest to these integrated approaches to immersive Indigenous intellectual revitalization.

PRACTICAL STRATEGIES FOR SAFEGUARDING INDIGENOUS INTELLECTUAL FUTURES

If we're looking beyond indigenization, what exactly are we working towards? I have a few suggestions that I think will help us gain more autonomy within the existing academy and allow us to develop a lot more capacity to protect our bright intellectual futures. We can do this in three ways. First, within universities we can strive to building Indigenous studies institutional capacity and intellectual autonomy. Second, we can work to ensure that as our intellectual community grows it remains horizontally organized. Third, that we "future proof" our recent successes by ensuring a culture of support and mentorship throughout this Indigenous academy.

1. Building Indigenous studies institutional capacity and intellectual autonomy

For better or for worse universities are major sites of Indigenous intellectual community-building. There are certainly good arguments for why this shouldn't be the case, but much of the reality is that many universities have intense Indigenous intellectual engagement, even if that engagements occupies a rather marginal part of the university structure. Since this is the case, we must be ready to support the students who come to us to learn and communities that wish to partner with us. One way to ensure that we can best serve our students is to strategically support the development of Indigenous programming that is both well-resourced and autonomous. While almost every Indigenous program in a Canadian university has fewer resources that it should, indigenization commitments by senior administrators are often public commitments to change this reality. Long term sustainable resources, particularly permanent staff and faculty positions are signs that these commitments are genuine, Indigenous people and allies can appeal to this to augment our numbers and allow us to work towards more ambitious goals.

I am fortunate to work in a Faculty of Native Studies, one of a the few. As a faculty we have our own dean, multiple associate dean positions, a large support staff, our own course calendar, and control over the majority of our day-to-day operations. We oversee our own curriculum and we oversee our own tenure and promotion processes. We are not a department or a program that answers to a Faculty of Arts, we mostly report to ourselves. As a Faculty, we have the budget for a greater number of scholars and staff, we now have 25 people that work in the Faculty of Native Studies, plus a growing grad program and the ability to connect with hundreds of undergraduate students. This may seem like a minor distinction for those who are not familiar with the nuances of academic governance, but I've been in an Indigenous studies *program* and an Indigenous studies *department*, but neither has the freedom of a full-fledged Faculty.

I'm not saying this to gloat over our sister units, but rather to suggest that Faculties of Indigenous Studies should be the norm, not the exception. If we are committed to developing parallel academies and to Indigenous intellectual independence more generally, this kind of administrative structure for our Indigenous studies units can provide the space to do this. University administrations need to consider this as part of a program of reconciliation. Not every university has the groundwork for such a move—and even at the University of Alberta, we have our struggles in meeting our ambitious goals—but it is a level of autonomy available in few publicly-funded institutions of higher learning.

Program-building is therefore a vital part of developing this Indigenous academy. In many places, there is a well-defined need for Indigenous-specific programing, to support students and communities in reaching their goals. These programs need to be established, policies built, and ultimately run by Indigenous people who are committed to Indigenous intellectual institution-building. In some cases, these programs already exist and the growth and interest in them has reached a point where they need an increase in resources. In many ways Indigenous students, faculty and staff would be best served by becoming departments, with full-time faculty positions, major and minor degree options, and a graduate program to train future intellectual leaders. There are also many long-established departments who are slotted under faculties alongside several other disciplinary departments. These are places where, if universities are seriously committed to robust Indigenization, the transition into faculties or schools would allow an additional degree of administrative autonomy that many programs struggle to attain in their existing status. More space can be created—or taken—by building administrative capacity geared towards intellectual independence.

A lot of the labour Indigenous faculty, staff, and students are currently asked to do involves building up the capacity of others: we are asked to educate non-Indigenous people, we are asked to provide Indigenous perspectives on committees, we are asked to navigate community-university relations, all of which is in addition to the work we do for our own people. While all of these activities are certainly important—and in many cases necessary—taking the time to critically examine whose capacity-building our energy supports is a key element of moving "beyond indigenization." One of the best pieces of advice I've received was in my first year as an academic. My faculty mentor Winona Wheeler said to me "publishing in a non-Indigenous studies journal will help build up the expertise of that discipline, but publishing with one of our journals ensures that you are helping to build the capacity of Indigenous studies." It has become clear to me in the years since that this is true in a larger sense too, we have a responsibility to support our own institutional and disciplinary development, we need to invest our energies in supporting our people and building our own institutional capacities should come before we build up the capacities of others. In many cases there is no clear line, and sometimes helping universities learn to work collaboratively with Indigenous communities or teaching a class full of non-Indigenous students about colonialism meets those needs. But underneath all of this, and over the long term, the majority of our energies are probably best spent on ourselves—in building our programs into self-sufficient and autonomous spaces and in revitalizing Indigenous intellectual traditions in ways that allow our communities to best respond to the challenges and opportunities they face.

2. Building a horizontal intellectual community

Capacity and institution-building is best done collectively and to do this we need to make sure that we are supporting one another, building communities of like-minded people as we go. In this era of indigenization and reconciliation and being among the people who aspire to more than this, we will face a lot of structural resistance to the changes that are coming. Simply said, it is easier when we push back together. We are strongest in community, in the academy that often means creating our own and supporting each other in ways that advance common interests, but also protect the positions of other Indigenous students, staff, and faculty.

The academy is a place of hierarchy, we need to flatten this vertical structure and make our own relationships horizontal. As we advance in our academic careers, we are often confronted with more opportunities than we have time for. For community-building it is important that we support you friends and colleagues. This can be as easy as recommending someone more junior than ourselves when declining an invitation—when I decline an invite, most of the time the organizers will invite one of the people I suggest in my place. By being strategic and sharing opportunities with one another we can make sure the next wave of Indigenous intellectuals coming up are invited to give high profile talks, are phoned for media interviews, and are offered opportunities to co-author peer-reviewed articles with established scholars. Since university education often means moving around, key introductions to elders and knowledge holders for newly arrived colleagues can also ensure that relationships exist to support communities and build accountable relationships with local people. If we do this well, we will be to ensure that Indigenous scholars complete their education and get jobs with greater ease and more support than we were, allowing all of us to build on our successes. It also requires us to sometimes say to ourselves "I've said a lot lately and got a lot of attention, maybe I should step back for a bit and make sure others have the space to speak as well." It is important that opportunities are spread around, that grad students and junior faculty have the opportunity to learn from new opportunities and that the best gigs don't always flow to the top of the academic hierarchy.

A horizontal intellectual community also thrives on a mentorship model—something our ancestors knew quite well. Part of being in a nurturing academic community is looking out for one another and sharing the skills we've learned with others. It also means having an expansive vision for this community and that we make sure that community-based intellectuals can access the same opportunities as university-based ones.

We're all better off surrounded by a big Indigenous intellectual community. We're less isolated and can call on greater support from larger networks if we help each other get established and succeed. It is important that we always remember that we are all in this together and that we're stronger when we've all built the skill-set, the confidence, and the clout to speak and act for the benefit of our peoples.

3. *Future-proofing our intellectual community*

As a scholar of Indigenous governance, I know the emphasis our ancestors placed on youth involvement in traditional governance. During the big Métis buffalo hunts, for instance, those selected as scouts would also select a young man to apprentice, and the scouts would work in pairs—one senior and one junior—that way the junior scout could learn the contours of the expansive prairie from their senior. In the contemporary academy, much like Indigenous communities, teaching the next generation is a vital part of how knowledge is passed on. Historically speaking, the European academy developed as a kind of guild system—an association of people who shared a common pursuit, people responsible from training new scholars. As much as the neoliberal assault on post-secondary education has worked against these kinds of relationships, principles of mentorship and supervision remain core values of graduate education. Yet, with the many stresses faced by Indigenous scholars working in contemporary post-secondary institutions, the priority of mentorship and support for Indigenous students cannot be sidelined.

For an institution that prizes learning and mentorship, the training students get in navigating university structures, processes, and expectations are not always specifically taught. In many cases students are left to navigate academic processes on their own. Building up our own intellectual communities, our own academy, is about mentoring people not just in intellectual contour pursuits, but in navigating the larger post-secondary landscape as well. For those of us who teach, we can certainly do more to build in explicit training and mentorship programs for students, which could include everything from supporting them through scholarship applications to encouraging them to explore professional or graduate programs.

Throughout a lot of my education, it felt like I was trying to find my way without a senior scout, without someone to help me find my way. I hear this a lot. Sometimes I think once we've learned the way we assume that others either know it already or that they are better off finding it on their own as many of us did. We also simultaneously express frustration at how so many people, feeling unsupported, lose their way. If we want to think about our own academy and doing things differently based on Indigenous values, it's vital we take on the extra work to support each other. For Indigenous grad students this is especially important, we can help each other prepare for the next steps—whether that is support in applying a post-graduation job (academic or otherwise) or applying for a SSHRC grant this fall.

I think so often we only see our own busyness and with all the other stuff we're expected to do, we forget to look at who's coming along behind us. I've always thought that mentorship is a kind of upfront investment of labour, because some day there'll be more of us, more of us to share the workload, more of us to take on faculty positions, to fight the fights over all the things that need to change. With more of us, things get easier.

I think a lot of people avoid mentoring others because they feel like they're not "an expert," or is they aren't knowledgeable enough, but someone is always newer than you and there is always someone to whom your support will make all the difference, in other words there is *never* a point where you are too junior to mentor new students. You can do this right now, you can help undergraduates navigate the challenges of their degree, you can encourage them to apply for grad school or give them advice on the application. If you received a SSHRC award, you can mentor your grad student peers on the application process, you can share your successful application as a model. You can edit their work or hold a workshop so that everyone can edit their SSHRC applications together.

Like many of you, I had opportunities my mentors never had, just as many of you will have opportunities I never did. This is what success looks like. For all that needs to change, we can at least look at the big strides that those before us have already made. But despite these successes, we need to look out for each other, because if we're being honest, who else is going to do that? Future-proofing means that when this Indigenization push ends, as everything always ends, we're in a position where we're so organized that we're already organizing for the next stage of Indigenous intellectual activism. Maybe that is a parallel academy or Indigenous community-led research, or something we don't know yet. Whatever is next, it's our responsibility that we are preparing the next generation to learn the contours of the land and to have the skills to navigate the often-challenging terrain ahead.

CONCLUSION

I think keeping focused on an ethic of obligation—whether through institution-building, community engagement, or mentorship—is the thing that will propel us into a profoundly different academic world than the one we live in. And if we're going to be here for our careers, like many of us are, and if we are working to connect our communities with the universities that we work in, why not start implementing some profound change right now. Look around at your future colleagues the people that you'll be working with to overhaul the academy. This is the community with whom we'll be strategizing about how we move beyond indigenization and how we can support one another in building that better future. It is the kind of place where we can get together. Where we can organize and make plans. Here we can get more people involved. And then we can go out and change the world.

notes

[110] This chapter is the author's keynote address to the Rising Up Graduate Student Conference at the University of Manitoba on March 9, 2018

[111] Associate Professor and Associate Dean (Research & Graduate Studies), Faculty of Native Studies, University of Alberta.

[112] Truth and Reconciliation Comission of Canada, "Calls to Action," 2015. http://www.trc.ca/websites/trcinstitution/File/2015/Findings/Calls_to_Action_English2.pdf

[113] Adam Gaudry and Danielle Lorenz, "Decolonization for the Masses? Grappling with Indigenous Content Requirements in the Changing Post-Secondary Environment," pp. 159-174 in Indigenous and Decolonizing Studies in Education: Mapping the Long View, Linda Tuhiwai Smith, Eve Tuck, and K. Wayne Yang, eds., Routledge. 2018a

[114] Adam Gaudry and Danielle Lorenz, "Indigenization as inclusion, reconciliation, and decolonization: navigating the different visions for indigenizing the Canadian academy," AlterNative: An International Journal of Indigenous Peoples 14(3): 218-227. 2018b

[115] Gaudry and Lorenz 2018a.

[116] Gaudry and Lorenz 2018b.

[117] Rauna Kuokkanen, Reshaping the University: Responsibility, Indigenous Epistemes, and the Logic of the Gift, Vancouver: University of British Columbia Press, 2018. D'Arcy Vermette, "Inclusion is Killing Us," Teaching Perspectives Magazine, St. Thomas University, Issue 17, Fall 2012. 18-19. Adam Gaudry, "Paved with Good intentions: Simply requiring indigenous content is not enough," Active History http://activehistory.ca/2016/01/paved-with-good-intentions-simply-requiring-indigenous-content-is-not-enough/201601/ Daniel Heath Justice, "Seeing (and reading) red: Indian out-laws in the Ivory Tower." Pp. 100-125 in Indigenizing the Academy, D. Mihesuah and A. Wilson eds. Lincoln: University of Nebraska Press.

[118] Indigenous Students Council, Official Statement, February 28, 2018. http://thesheaf.com/2018/03/02/indigenous-students-council-calls-for-autonomous-governing-body-student-council-reacts/

[119] Ibid.

[120] Gaudry and Lorenz, 2018b: 218.

[121] Gaudry and Lorenz, 2018b: 219-221.

[122] Gaudry and Lorenz, 2018b: 219.

[123] Gaudry and Lorenz, 2018b: 221-223.

[124] Gaudry and Lorenz, 2018 b: 219.

[125] Oxford English Dictionary, "Academy," https://en.oxforddictionaries.com/definition/academy

Indigenizing Protocols and Decolonizing Practices in Research and Teaching

Chapter Twenty-Five

The Honourable Harvest

An Indigenous Research Protocol

Silvina Antunes, Kara Passey, Jordan Tabobondung, and Erika Vas

Purpose of "The Honourable Harvest" Indigenous Research Protocol

In September 2017, Neechi Commons Ltd., partnered with Tabitha Robin (PhD student in Interdisciplinary Studies at the University of Manitoba) to collaborate on a project to be designed by students in the Master's in Development Practice: Indigenous Development program at the University of Winnipeg. The purpose of this project was to provide students with an opportunity to utilize their skills as researchers to design a framework for ethical and responsible research practices to the Neechi Commons community.[126]

The "The *Honourable Harvest*" Indigenous Research Protocol utilizes the teachings of Dr. Robin Wall Kimmerer, a mother, plant ecologist, writer, and Distinguished Teaching Professor of Environmental Biology at the SUNY College of Environmental Science and Forestry in Syracuse, New York.[127] "Dr. Kimmerer is the founding director of the Center for Native Peoples and the Environment, whose mission is to create programs that draw on the wisdom of both indigenous and scientific knowledge for our shared concerns for Mother Earth".[128] Her interests include not only restoration of ecological communities, but restoration of our relationships to land. We have applied Kimmerer's TedXSitka Talk, "Reclaiming the Honourable Harvest" to a research context, using her "Honourable Harvest" protocol steps to inform our Indigenous Research Protocol.[129]

It is our belief that the interactions we engage in as researchers are more than just research; they are pivotal in the development and maintenance of relationships. These relationships will be built on the *Four R's* of research: respect, relevance reciprocity, and responsibility.[130] Through this lens, individuals will begin to view their work as contributing to community development and less of a research focus, topic, or subject. Furthermore, in entering this research relationship, there is an expectation that you will also be a contributing member of this community and must abide by their ethics and values.

Neechi Commons & "The Honourable Harvest"

Neechi Commons Ltd. is an Indigenous owned and operated worker co-operative that is a staple of Winnipeg's North End. It is a community business complex, which includes a neighbourhood supermarket, restaurant and catering service, an arts store, and various meeting space.[131] Neechi Commons is a leader of Indigenous business and its commitment to making positive contributions to people and the planet is recognized by its Green Globe certification.[132] It has implemented award-winning diabetes prevention campaigns, and its worker co-op structure is a unique feature of its social enterprise.[133]

The aforementioned initiatives are just some of the many aspects of Neechi Commons which make it a sought-after location for research purposes. While the interest of the academic community is appreciated and supported by Neechi Commons, unfortunately, very few partnerships have been conducted in a respectful manner. During consultations with Neechi Commons, it was expressed that a research protocol outlining the community's values, goals, and expectations would be beneficial. Thus, a methodology outlining best practices for both the community and the researcher was designed to ensure that all individuals involved will pursue their projects in a good way. The result was the creation of *"The Honourable Harvest" Indigenous Research Protocol* which ensures Neechi Commons can continue to nurture the community, exercise its self-determination, and protect its knowledge. This protocol is based on Indigenous epistemology that aligns with Neechi Commons' values but can also be widely applied to conducting research in any community.

The Neechi Commons community is built on and around food. From their local fruits and vegetables, neighbourhood supermarket, bannock bakery, ethnic foods, fish market, cafeteria and restaurant, to their 40-square foot community garden, they have a deep connection to the land and its gifts.[134] One may envision Neechi Commons as a rich meadow of gifts – from the food, to its community members, to its various departments, or its role as a community hub, these gifts are all inherent to Neechi Commons and are responsible for its fruitful, long-standing connection to the land and peoples and the success of its work.

However, Neechi Commons is a meadow where one cannot carelessly extract what they may need without regard for the land or the gifts – these are not commodities ripe for the taking. Rather, one must engage in *"The Honourable Harvest"*, learning from tradition on how to respectfully approach our community meadow, develop a relationship with the community, and how to "Be Grateful and Give Thanks."[135]

As defined by Kimmerer, *"The Honourable Harvest* is a practice both ancient and urgent, applies to every exchange between people and the Earth," or in this case, researcher and community[136]. "It is a set of protocols that governs our taking, so that the world remains as rich for the seventh generation to come as it is for us today.[137] "Currently, we live in a world made of gifts but find ourselves harnessed to institutions and an economy that relentlessly ask, "What more can we take from the Earth?"[138]

> "If we understand the Earth as just a collection of objects, then apples and the land that offers them fall outside our circle of moral consideration. We tell ourselves that we can use them however we please, because their lives don't matter. But in a worldview that understands them as persons, their lives matter very much. Recognition of personhood does not mean that we don't consume, but that we are accountable for the lives that we take. When we speak of the living world as kin, we also are called to act in new ways, so that when we take those lives, we must do it in such a way that brings honor to the life that is taken and honor to the ones receiving it."[139]

Kimmerer's perspectives on harvesting the earth can easily be adapted to the harvesting of knowledge from Neechi Commons or any community; the people and knowledge are not just subjects, or data, and they are not simply assets, resources, or commodities. They are unique community members with personhood, and the knowledge and wisdom of the community provides life-giving well-being and independence. When building a relationship with the community and conducting research, we request that you don't ask what can be learned or taken away from the community, but rather, what can you contribute to the community and how you can conduct your research in a manner that is respectful and reciprocal.

"The Honourable Harvest" Indigenous Research Protocol

The following steps have been adapted from Kimmerer's TedXSitka presentation, "Reclaiming the Honourable Harvest", to create the framework for a research protocol to be used by community organizations.[140]

Step 1: What Are You Bringing to Our Table?

Research with individuals and communities should be reciprocal, and the researcher should avoid extracting knowledge from communities and individuals for their own benefit, without considering how individuals can also become empowered through the work, or how communities might want their knowledge protected and honoured. The research relationship should be formed much like any other - how do our interests align? Are our intentions honourable? How willing are we to protect and nurture this relationship?

When approaching a community or individual for the purposes of research, the researcher should have already done the necessary work to establish their positionality and consider how power dynamics may play into their work. For some, this may look like stating who your family is and where you are from, for others this may be the application of a feminist or anti-oppressive lens wherein the researcher outlines their identity. Ask yourself, which aspects of your experience have contributed to your role as a researcher? Are there any labels or communities that you are a part of, where identifying as such could help the community determine if developing a relationship around research is appropriate? Who are you affiliated with, on a personal, political, or academic level? Do you hold any moral or internal biases that could contribute to, or inhibit your ability to complete this research in a respectful manner?

Recommended reading for this process is the book *Kaandossiwin: How We Come to Know* by Kathleen E. Absolon. This text will take the researcher through their own journey to determine their position within the world and how they came to exist and work within it. It may also be necessary to accompany research inquiries with references relevant to your research project (this could mean a professor or teacher, research organization, government, or past/current community partnerships). If you have established respectful and reciprocal relationships in your past work and life, these efforts will not go unnoticed (and alternatively, if your past work has resulted in negative outcomes and/or disrespectful use of knowledge, these instances will also not go unnoticed).

Step 2: Setting the Table

In extension to setting your own personal positionality, determining the goal and purpose of your research prior to connecting with communities or individuals can help focus the intent, and allow the community in question to decide whether or not it is in their best interest to participate. Furthermore, the self-determination of the community is key in establishing a healthy, respectful relationship, so the researcher should allow for space to have their research question critiqued and their methods altered based on the needs and interests of the community/individuals.

Research proposals should include methodologies which consider the *Four R's* of Indigenous research: *respect, relevance reciprocity, and responsibility*. Research proposals should include consideration for the time and labour contributed by communities/individual(s). How will engaging in your project be a mutually beneficial for you and the community/individual(s)? How will you pay for the cost of labour (whether visible or invisible) contributed by the community/individual(s)? How will you ensure that the knowledge shared with you will be utilized in a respectful manner, which does not capitalize from the contributions of the community/individua(s)?

What is the timeline for your project? Have you reserved an appropriate amount of time to build a respectful relationship with the community/individual(s) that you wish to engage? What will come of the knowledge that is shared with you, once the project is complete? How can your subjects and partners be assured that the knowledge that is shared with the researcher will be shared and implemented in a respectful manner?

Step 3: "Never Take the First"

Many research inquiries are posed to individuals and communities without consideration of the time and labour it takes away from their roles, responsibilities, and obligations. It is crucial to determine if the community in question is the right fit for your research project before inquiring. Have you considered all options for research partnerships before coming to your conclusion? Have you investigated past research that has been published about the community or your research topic before voicing your inquiry? Has the question you are posing already been answered? If so, how will your work reaffirm, refute, or otherwise remain relevant to the community?

Step 4: "Listen for the Answer"

As a researcher, it is crucial to listen carefully throughout the research process. One should be cognizant that there are ways to listen beyond simply hearing the explicit words from a participant.[141] When interacting with any member of a community, pay attention to body language and other social cues to ensure that individuals feel comfortable in the research situation.

Patience is key: take your time when conducting interviews or using any other research methods to ensure that the community/individual(s) has full understanding of the purpose of your questions. Always be respectful; do not push when an individual feels uncomfortable answering a question or has not given you the answer you desire.[142]

Margaret Kovach's *Conversation Method in Indigenous Research*, published in *The First Peoples Child and Family Review* (2010) is recommended reading for the technique of conversational interviews. Conversational interviews are based on the conversational method which stems from Indigenous methods of gathering knowledge, namely oral storytelling.[143] Conversational interviews are often more informal, less structured and focus more on sharing through anecdotes and stories as a method of gathering information.[144]

Step 5: "Take Only What You Need" or What is Given

This step displays a stark difference between Western and Indigenous ideals: Western ideals often dictate that it is beneficial to take everything you possibly can regardless of consent or necessity.[145] These actions are based in capitalist pursuits of power, i.e. to collect resources (including knowledge) in the pursuit of profit - these ideals go against Indigenous ways of being which encourage an individual to only take what is needed or what is given.

As a researcher, you are aware that the research process can be taxing at times, but it is important to remember that this not only affects you, but has the ability to affect the community/individual(s) as well. As with *Step 4* above, do not seek further responses if you did not receive a desired answer. Take what you have been given and use it to the best of your ability.[146] Do not take advantage of the kindness of the members of the community who are participating in your research. Allow individuals to provide you with the information in such a way that makes them comfortable. If there are certain subjects that individuals do not wish to discuss, kindly move on to something else. It is important to always be aware of the needs and desires of those involved.[147]

Step 6: "Minimize Harm"

In order to minimize harm, the researcher must ensure there is ongoing communication and understanding between all partners. It is important that control of the research responses remains solely in the hands of the community prior to public dissemination.[148] Before any knowledge shared by the community in question is published or shared with a third party, the researcher must request approval with the possibility of revision or redaction.

Before writing or printing anything, consider the impact it will have on the community. The end result of your research should benefit you as a researcher as well as the community who has participated in your research.[149] Consider the implications of your work and ensure that you are not bringing any undue harm to the community in the way you are using the information you have obtained.

In short, remember this quote from Robin Kimmerer (2012); "Do not use a shovel where a digging stick will do."

Step 7: "Ask Permission"

Article 19 of The United Nations Declaration on the Rights of Indigenous Peoples (UNDRIP) states the following: "States shall consult and cooperate in good faith with the Indigenous Peoples concerned through their own representative institutions in order to obtain their free, prior and informed consent before adopting and implementing legislative or administrative measures that may affect them."[150]

As a researcher, it is crucial to obtain individual or collective free, prior and informed consent from potential participants in your research. It is the responsibility of the researcher to ensure that they follow ethical guidelines and protocols throughout their research and make themselves aware of the role western research methodology and procedures have infringed on individual and collective Indigenous rights. This means that you are obligated to understand the complexities of navigating Western research methodological paradigms while undergoing research with

Indigenous people and their communities or knowledge systems. Consideration of specific individuals and collective protocols to establish respectful and reciprocal relationships must be done in a way that establishes a recognition of the visions, intent, expectations and informed consent between the researcher and community.

Ensure that those taking part in your research understand the purpose, direction and utilization of the knowledge you are harvesting from the community. When asking for permission it is important to consider your approaches when seeking consent from participants. Are your consent forms full of academic or legal jargon? Did you ask participants in a way that respects their right to refuse? Do you have an awareness and understanding of how to employ Nation specific research ethics such as the First Nations Ownership, Control, Access and Possession (OCAP) Principles? Ensure that you are doing your personal research to understand how to approach your project in a way that is respectful to the spirit by clarifying and being upfront of your intentions and regard for the knowledge and the people you want to include.

Step 8: "Be Grateful and Give Thanks"

How often are reports written only to never be heard of ever again, perhaps placed on the desk of a policy maker only to gather dust. Within both research and community development, it is common for completed projects to only be shared within academic or professional circles – often the communities involved never see the final result, or the outcomes of the researcher's findings. Historically, researchers have conducted research with little to no benefit, accountability, or transparency in their relationships with Indigenous communities, which is evident from Maori scholar, Linda Tuhiwai Smith's statement that:

> It galls us that Western researchers and intellectuals can assume to know all that it is possible to know of us, on the basis of their brief encounters with some of us. It appals us that the West can desire, extract and claim ownership of our ways of knowing, our imagery the things we create and produce and then simultaneously reject the people who created and developed those ideas and seek to deny them further opportunities to be creators of their own culture and own nations (page 1).[15]

"The Honourable Harvest" asks the researcher to work within a state of gratitude of reciprocity, considering the benefits they've received from the communities who choose to share with them – and even further, considering how they can return the favor. Do not design an inconsiderate/harmful process of extracting knowledge from communities to benefit your own career or success - what are you doing to provide your set of knowledge and skills towards positive influences of individuals or communities? Consider these questions: How will you give back to the community for the time, efforts and knowledge you have gained for your research? How will you ensure that individuals in your research are honoured for the time, knowledge, experience and support they are providing to you by participating in your research? How will your presence and/or research benefit the community?

Step 9: "Share What You've Taken"

It is vital for the researcher to work form a place of respect, as outlined in the *Four R's* of Indigenous research - how will you ensure that the community fully understands how and where you will be sharing the information and data that you are harvesting from the community? It is important for researchers to ensure there are direct lines of communication open throughout the many stages of developing, interpreting, revising, finalizing, and presenting your research.

Responsibility for the interpretation of the data falls largely upon the researcher. It is also the responsibility of the researcher to protect the integrity of the community and people included in your research. At times the true intent and meaning of what participants shared in your research may be obscured through the researcher's interpretations. This can be avoided by providing participants with drafts of how you have evaluated and interpreted the data gathered, in order to ensure that the community has an opportunity to correct, clarify, or edit, if they feel it is needed.

After preparing of the knowledge you have harvested from the community, remember to provide a final product of the research. It is also imperative to seek free, prior and informed consent of the community before beginning any future publications or presentations where you would be sharing data that is owned by the community. Allow participants the opportunity to be aware of the information that is being disseminated and presented to the world about them, their families or communities.

Conclusion

This protocol was developed in order to guide the formation of research partnerships based on respect, relevance reciprocity, and responsibility between institutions and the community. The intention of the protocol is to guide all those involved in the research relationship so that positive outcomes may be achieved. "The Honourable Harvest"" model was chosen in order to create a framework that is grounded in Indigenous research methodologies while also explaining protocol processes in plain language so that all researchers may learn and understand how to pursue their work in a good way. The resulting protocol is a marriage of traditional ways of seeking knowledge and acknowledgement of contemporary academic processes. It is crucial to recognize that not everyone has access to traditional knowledge and that it may be difficult to properly implement traditional protocols within an academic context. We hope that *"The Honourable Harvest" Indigenous Research Protocol* will provide guidance to researchers and the communities they are working with as they pursue their learning journeys together.

References

Absolon, Kathleen E. (2011) Kaandossiwin: How We Come to Know. Fernwood Publishing, Manitoba. p65

Assembly of First Nations [AFN]. (2009). Ethics in First Nations Research. Retrieved from: http://www.afn.ca/uploads/files/rp-research_ethics_final.pdf

Carlson, E. (2017) Anti-colonial methodologies and practices for settler colonial studies. *Settler Colonial Studies*. 7:4, 496-517.

Centre for Humans & Nature. (2017). Robin Wall Kimmerer. Distinguished Teaching Professor of Environmental Biology - SUNY. Retrieved from: https://www.humansandnature.org/robin-wall-kimmerer

College of Environmental Science and Forestry. (2018). Robin W. Kimmerer Distinguished Teaching Professor and Director, Center for Native Peoples and the Environment. Retrievedd from: http://www.esf.edu/faculty/kimmerer/

First Nations Information Governance Centre. (2017) The First Nations Principles of OCAP.

Kimmerer, R. (2012). Reclaiming the Honorable Harvest. TEDxSitka. Retrieved from: https://www.youtube.com/watch?v=Lz1vgfZ3etE

Kimmerer, R. (2015). The "Honorable Harvest": Lessons From an Indigenous Tradition of Giving Thanks. Yes! Magazine. Retrieved from: http://www.yesmagazine.org/issues/good-health/the-honorable-harvest-lessons-from-an-indigenous-tradition-of-giving-thanks-20151126

Kirkness, V.J. & Barnhardt, R. (1991). First Nations and Higher Education: The Four R's – Respect, Relevance, Reciprocity, Responsibility. Journal of American Indian Education, 30(3): 1-15.

Kovach, M. (2010). Conversation Method in Indigenous Research. *The First Peoples Child and Family Review*. 5:1.

Kovach, M. (2010). Indigenous methodologies: Characteristics, conversations, and contexts. University of Toronto Press.

Neechi Commons. (2017). About Neechi Commons. Retrieved from: https://neechi.ca/about/

Neechi Commons. (2012). Neechi Foods Co-Op Ltd. Retrieved from: https://neechifoods.files.wordpress.com/2010/12/brochure-feb-2012.pdf

Robin, T. Indigenous Research Methods Syllabus. (2017). University of Winnipeg.

Tuhiwai Smith, Linda. (2012). Decolonizing Methodologies: Research and Indigenous Peoples, second edition. Zed Books Ltd.

The Canadian Community Economic Development (CED) Network. (n.d.) Neechi Foods Co-op Ltd. (Operates Neechi Foods Community Store). Retrieved from: https://ccednet-rcdec.ca/sites/ccednet-rcdec.ca/files/ccednet/Profile_-_Neechi_Foods_Cox.pdf

United Nations (2007). United Nations Declaration on the Rights of Indigenous Peoples. Retrieved from: http://www.un.org/esa/socdev/unpfii/documents/DRIPS_en.pdf

notes

[126] Robin, T. Indigenous Research Methods Syllabus. (2017). University of Winnipeg.

[127] College of Environmental Science and Forestry. (2018). Robin W. Kimmerer Distinguished Teaching Professor and Director, Center for Native Peoples and the Environment. Retrieved from: http://www.esf.edu/faculty/kimmerer/

[128] Center for Humans & Nature. (n.d.). Robin Wall Kimmerer Distinguished Teaching Professor of Environmental Biology – SUNY. Retrieved from: https://www.humansandnature.org/robin-wall-kimmerer

[129] Kimmerer, R. (2012). Reclaiming the Honorable Harvest. TEDxSitka. Retrieved from: https://www.youtube.com/watch?v=Lz1vgfZ3etE

[130] Kirkness, V.J. & Barnhardt, R. (1991). First Nations and Higher Education: The Four R's – Respect, Relevance, Reciprocity, Responsibility. Journal of American Indian Education, 30(3): 1-15.

[131] Neechi Commons. (2017). About Neechi Commons. Retrieved from: https://neechi.ca/about/

[132] Neechi Commons. (2012). Neechi Foods Co-Op Ltd. Retrieved from: https://neechifoods.files.wordpress.com/2010/12/brochure-feb-2012.pdf

[133] The Canadian Community Economic Development (CED) Network. (n.d.) Neechi Foods Co-op Ltd. (Operates Neechi Foods Community Store). Retrieved from: https://ccednet-rcdec.ca/sites/ccednet-rcdec.ca/files/ccednet/Profile_-_Neechi_Foods_Cox.pdf

[134] Neechi Commons. (2017). About Neechi Commons.

[135] Kimmerer Wall, R. (2012). "Reclaiming the Honourable Harvest".

[136] Kimmerer, R. (2015). The Honorable Harvest: Lessons From an Indigenous Tradition of Giving Thanks. Yes! Magazine. Referenced from: http://www.yesmagazine.org/issues/good-health/the-honorable-harvest-lessons-from-an-indigenous-tradition-of-giving-thanks-20151126

[137] Kimmerer, R. (2015). The Honorable Harvest: Lessons From an Indigenous Tradition of Giving Thanks.

[138] Ibid.

[139] Ibid.

[140] Kimmerer Wall, R. (2012). Reclaiming the Honourable Harvest.

[141] Kimmerer, R. (2012). Reclaiming the Honorable Harvest. TEDxSitka. Retrieved from: https://www.youtube.com/watch?v=Lz1vgfZ3etE

[142] Kovach, M. (2010). Conversation Method in Indigenous Research. *The First Peoples Child and Family Review.* 5:1.

[143] Kovach, M (2010). Conversation Method in Indigenous Research.

[144] Ibid.

[145] Kimmerer, R. (2012). Reclaiming the Honorable Harvest.

[146] Assembly of First Nations [AFN]. (2009). Ethics in First Nations Research. Retrieved from: http://www.afn.ca/uploads/files/rp-research_ethics_final.pdf

[147] Assembly of First Nations [AFN]. (2009). Ethics in First Nations Research.

[148] First Nations Information Governance Centre. (2017) The First Nations Principles of OCAP.

[149] Carlson, E. (2017) Anti-colonial methodologies and practices for settler colonial studies. *Settler Colonial Studies.* 7:4, 496-517.

[150] United Nations (2007). United Nations Declaration on the Rights of Indigenous Peoples. Retrieved from: http://www.un.org/esa/socdev/unpfii/documents/DRIPS_en.pdf

[151] Tuhiwai Smith, Linda. (2012). Decolonizing Methodologies: Research and Indigenous Peoples, second edition. Page 1. Zed Books Ltd.

Chapter Twenty-Six

Striving for Authenticity

Embracing a Decolonizing Approach to Research with Indigenous Athletes[152]

Shara R. Johnson[a*,153], Jennifer Poudrier[b], Heather Foulds[a], and Leah J. Ferguson[a]

Introduction

To pursue their sports aspirations and seek more favourable opportunities, some athletes move across both country and cultural borders. For reasons such as lack of facilities, seeking better coaching expertise, accessing more competitive environments and broader opportunities, some Indigenous athletes relocate from their home communities to pursue sports in urban centers (Blodgett & Schinke, 2015). Athletes' relocation often involves moving from multi-dimensional cultural backgrounds to broader dominant cultural contexts often classified as 'mainstream[154].' Mainstream sports, for example, hockey, football, and soccer, and the rules governing mainstream sports continue to be dominated by and give preference to a Eurocentric[155] way of knowing (Blodgett et al., 2014). As a result, Indigenous athletes who choose to pursue these sports at elite levels, must adjust to mainstream culture to achieve their goals. Adjusting to mainstream contexts may involve navigating several challenges such as racism and discrimination, isolation from family, friends, and community, and a dismissed cultural identity (Blodgett et al., 2014). Adjustment challenges may prevent Indigenous athletes from successfully transitioning to mainstream culture and can result in negative effects such as social and cultural isolation, mental fatigue, hindered growth and development, and premature discontinuation of sports (Blodgett & Schinke, 2015). The challenges faced by Indigenous athletes navigating mainstream cultural environments suggest that Indigenous peoples may be at a disadvantage in attaining satisfaction in life and achieving psychological well-being as outcomes of sport.

Psychological well-being, also referred to as psychological flourishing, embodies the scope of human wellness that includes a positive assessment of one's life, lifelong growth and development, a purposeful outlook of life, healthy interpersonal relationships, autonomy, and control over one's environment (Ryff & Keyes, 1995). Understanding psychological well-being within the sport context has become increasingly important as it has the potential to address barriers to athletes performing to their highest potential (Lundqvist, 2011). There is emerging research exploring what flourishing in sport means from Indigenous athletes' perspectives. Ferguson et al. (2018) explored the stories of 16 female Indigenous athletes to understand their meanings and experiences of flourishing in sport. The factors identified as essential to flourishing in sport include having multidimensional community support, achieving personal goals, persistent growth, and realizing wholistic[156] athletic excellence. Following up on Ferguson et al. (2018), the purpose of our research is to explore how the psychological well-being of Indigenous athletes pursuing sport in mainstream context is impacted by their relocation and multicultural adjustment experiences.

Study Design

We were deliberate in engaging in a research study that honours Indigenous ways of knowing and making the research an authentic reflection of Indigenous athletes' experiences. As such, we selected a qualitative case study grounded in an Indigenous research framework. A case study explores the uniqueness and complexity of a single case, achieving an understanding of its activity within significant situations (Stake, 1995). A case study is ideally suited for providing an in-depth exploration of issues or individuals within specific settings or contexts (Creswell, 2007). Since this research focuses specifically on the psychological well-being and adjustment experiences of Indigenous athletes in the mainstream context, a qualitative case study is an appropriate strategy of inquiry.

Indigenous Research Framework

As researchers partnering with Indigenous peoples, it was imperative that the methodological framework we chose would respectfully and ethically illustrate the Indigenous participants' experiences in culturally responsive ways. An Indigenous research framework is centered around an Indigenous epistemology, which is a knowledge system guiding research that is based on Indigenous beliefs, values, languages, and other Indigenous ways of knowing (Kovach, 2009). The other components of the Indigenous research framework include having a decolonizing and ethical aim, preparing researchers about cultural protocols, having a research plan with standard research design, gathering and interpreting knowledges, and giving back to the Indigenous community (Kovach, 2009; see Figure 1). We will discuss three components implemented in our research: decolonizing and ethical aim, researcher preparation, and research preparation.

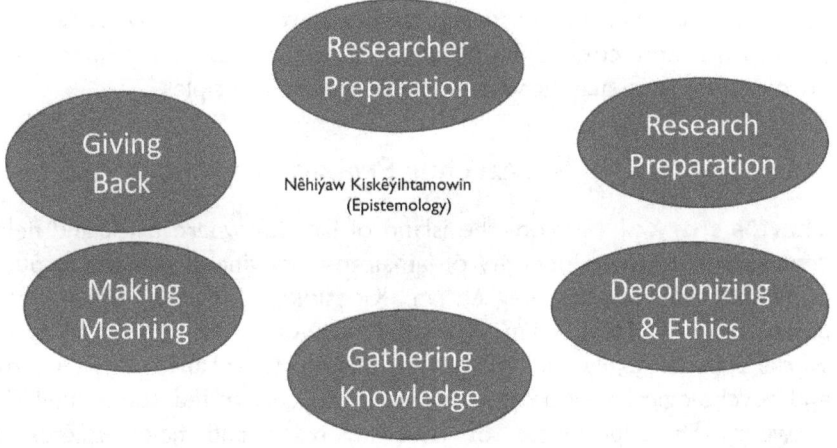

Figure 1. Indigenous research framework. Adapted from Indigenous Methodologies: Characteristics, Conversations, and Contexts (p. 45), by M. Kovach, 2009, Toronto: University of Toronto Press. Copyright 2009 by University of Toronto Press.

Having a Decolonizing and Ethical Aim

Research has traditionally been dominated by Western worldviews such as post-positivist and constructivist, which are deeply influenced by colonialism (Kovach, 2009). Applying a decolonizing lens to research serves to deconstruct the Western knowledges that dominate research and discount Indigenous peoples' ways of knowing (Tuhiwai Smith, 2016). A decolonizing approach to research assumes that the research and researcher are critically reflexive with the aim of achieving social justice for Indigenous peoples (Kovach, 2009). Moreover, a decolonizing approach to research involves ensuring that the research participants are involved in all stages of the research including the planning, knowledge generation, interpretation, and dissemination. Essentially, a decolonizing approach lays the foundation for ethical and authentic research by continuously integrating the following key principles: (a) understanding the power dimensions in research and ensuring that participants and their community are fully engaged in the generation of knowledge; (b) ensuring the research benefits and does not harm any Indigenous participants or communities; and, (c) ensuring the research accurately reflects the participants and community values. We have strived to maintain a decolonizing approach by applying these guiding principles.

Researcher Preparation

Shara's story. I am from the island of Jamaica where track and field is central to the cultural identity of Jamaicans. Moving to Canada to pursue a Master of Science degree in Kinesiology at the University of Saskatchewan (UofS), I am privileged to work with a supervisor who works collaboratively with Indigenous peoples to enhance physical activity and psychological well-being. I immediately recognized some similarities between the experiences of Jamaican track and field athletes and Indigenous athletes who relocate from their home communities to play sports in a mainstream urban context. This piqued my interest in wanting to understand how the psychological well-being of Indigenous athletes is affected when they have to relocate from their home community to pursue sports in an urban mainstream context. I embarked on this research project to authentically explore the relocation and adjustment experiences of Indigenous athletes. As a non-Indigenous student researcher doing Indigenous research, I wanted to ensure this research was conducted in ways that honoured Indigenous cultural traditions, beliefs, and knowledge systems. Therefore, preparation was key in my aim to be authentic.

Firstly, my previous research experience was mainly from a post-positivist perspective, so an Indigenous research framework was novel to me. Training and development became focal points in preparing to undertake this research. I took a graduate-level course in Indigenous methodologies offered by Dr. Margaret Kovach who identifies as a First Nations person and authored the book "Indigenous methodologies: Characteristics, conversations, and contexts." I was also able to further develop my research knowledge, skills, and experiences by working on research projects involving the Indigenous community in Saskatoon. For instance, I embraced research assistantships on provincially- (Saskatchewan Health Research Foundation) and nationally-funded (Canadian Institutes of Health Research) research projects where I assisted with data generation, data transcribing, and community engagement. These training and development activities helped me to self-situate in my own research, understand cultural protocols for Indigenous research, and prepared me to embrace a decolonizing approach with an aim to be authentic and culturally relevant.

Secondly, I adhered to Kovach's (2009) recommendation that relationship building is an essential component when striving to make Indigenous research authentic. I was mindful of the importance of building mutually beneficial relationships with Indigenous communities and being respectful of Indigenous ways of knowing. I set out to build meaningful relationships with the Indigenous peoples in Treaty 6 Territory and the Homeland of the Métis, and to extend my understanding of Indigenous ways of knowing. Relationship building activities included volunteering with community-based initiatives such as an Indigenous sporting event, being a student mentor in the Verna J. Kirkness Science and Indigenous Engineering program, and assisting with an Indigenous Youth Mentorship Program. These ongoing activities help to build my awareness of cultural protocols, generate trust with the Indigenous community, and assist with reciprocity.

Finally, to prepare for our research the research team relied heavily on consultations and collaborations with community advisors, participants, and the expertise of other researchers. As the research design and plan were conceptualized, it was important to receive input and feedback from members within the Indigenous sporting community. Collaborating with and getting advice from sports personnel within the Indigenous sporting community helped us with establishing community connections, gaining research insight, and understanding cultural protocols. Our research team also includes three Indigenous researchers who have collectively done extensive work within Indigenous communities. This has been very helpful in providing guidance to myself as a student researcher, managing my expectations about emerging directions the research may take, and learning best practices for engaging in Indigenous research. The steps I have taken to prepare for this research have been invaluable in laying the groundwork to achieve authenticity.

Jennifer's story. I was born in Winnipeg, Manitoba to a Métis activist father and a nurse mother. Having moved 17 times before I was 12 years old, our family settled in Meadow Lake Saskatchewan, where I completed high school. I then re-located many times as a young adult, completing a Master's degree in Sociology at the UofS and a Ph.D. at Queen's University in Kingston, Ontario in the area of Sociology of Science and Knowledge. At the time, my academic focus concerned the socio-cultural implications of new genetic science and technology. I was then able to secure a tenure-stream position in the Department of Sociology at the UofS in 2003.

My passion for social justice emerged before I could remember, as it was part of my life growing up. My activist father wanted to 'solve the world's problems in a lifetime' by participating in a number of Saskatchewan and Manitoba based initiatives to ensure that Indigenous children had access to education. While he was unable to complete some of the tasks that he hoped, he did teach me many lessons about Indigenous tradition and social justice. My mother, a practicing nurse, continues to work in the Waterhen Lake First Nation community in northern Saskatchewan and it's there that we call 'home.'

The academic work that has most fascinated me is the concept of knowledge systems or knowledge spaces, ranging in seemingly diverse locations such as Indigenous communities and scientific laboratories. I have had some wonderful opportunities to work with Indigenous communities in Saskatchewan and Manitoba, using visual methods to better understand health and the healthy body (body image and sport). While the knowledge and guidance I have gained is humbling, the relationships I have been able to hold are by far the most important to me – and ought to be when doing community-based research.

I am currently very privileged to work with this team and learn more as I go. I have always had a passion for sport and for coaching sport (despite the many years of injuries from basketball and touch football). I've also had a very keen interest to further explore the experiences of Indigenous female athletes and in this case, flourishing.

CHAPTER TWENTY-SIX

Heather's story. Growing up in Lheidli T'enneh traditional territory, away from my extended Métis family, I have always felt drawn to my Métis culture and history. During my graduate school in Musqueam traditional territory, I had the opportunity to participate and learn more about Indigenous cultures and connect with my own culture and history to a greater extent. Since being hired as a tenure-track Assistant Professor in the College of Kinesiology at the UofS, located on Treaty 6 Territory and the Homeland of the Métis, I have greatly enhanced my connection and engagement with my own Indigenous culture and community. Returning to the region of my Métis roots has provided many wonderful opportunities to reconnect with extended family and expand my experience and engagement of Indigenous protocols, knowledge, and histories.

My academic experience in collaboration with Indigenous communities began with my Master's degree. During this degree, I had the opportunity to be part of a collaboration with Indigenous communities across the province. This partnership allowed me to engage and contribute to the Indigenous community through a community-based physical activity program evaluating health benefits of this culturally-appropriate, community-led program. My commitment, interest, and dedication to health research continue as I pursue my career. As I continue to develop, maintain, and expand my relationships with my own Métis community and the broader Indigenous community in Saskatoon, I increasingly recognize the value and importance of community, culture, and connectedness. As an Indigenous female officiating in the mainstream, largely male, Eurocentric lacrosse leagues, I recognize and have experienced the challenges of facing interactions and expectations shaped by mainstream bias and psychological approaches. Merging my line of inquiry in health research with my experiences of the importance of community and culture, I am currently engaged in collaborations to examine the importance of culture and social support for health.

Leah's story. As a Métis woman from Treaty 6 Territory and the Homeland of the Métis, I am compelled to do more for the community and with the community. I was hired as a tenure-track Assistant Professor in the College of Kinesiology at the UofS in 2014. Starting this new adventure was both exciting and terrifying; in fact, I began my position 6 days before I defended my Doctoral dissertation. I jumped right into things in my position at the UofS, which is one of Canada's 15 research-intensive universities. I was trained in sport psychology during my graduate education, and I have a deep-rooted interest in, fascination with, and passion for my discipline. I am intensely curious about exploring ways for athletes to overcome setbacks and adversity to flourish in sport. When I began in my position, I knew I had the opportunity and responsibility to do more in my research. With a personal and professional commitment to truth and reconciliation, I began a somewhat parallel line of inquiry to work with Indigenous peoples to explore ways to promote flourishing collaboratively.

Prior to my point of hire, I had (very) little research engagement with Indigenous peoples. Relationships became – and continue to be – central to everything that I do. I strive to develop, maintain, and enrich relationships with community members, and I have been fortunate to cultivate relationships that have resulted in genuine research collaborations with community advisors (e.g., Ferguson et al., 2018). I aspire to create reciprocal relationships by volunteering my time, energy, knowledge, and resources for community events, as well as working with Indigenous youth, athletes, and the sport community. As part of my relationship-building, I embrace opportunities to learn from Indigenous peoples. The stories I have been told, ceremonies I have had the privilege to experience, and lessons learned have guided me as I move forward in my journey working with Indigenous peoples. I am honoured to collaboratively work with Indigenous athletes, youth, coaches, parents, and community members on various programs, projects, initiatives, and studies. I am committed to maintaining and enriching those relationships in authentic ways, as reflected in this research.

Research Preparation

Research preparation was a fluid process that occurred alongside some of the first author's activities to ready herself to engage in Indigenous research. An example of one activity to prepare for this research was forming a thesis advisory committee (i.e., research team) experienced in working with Indigenous peoples. Creating a reflexive research plan was another deliberate step. Reflexivity is being used increasingly more as a methodological tool to achieve trustworthiness in qualitative research (Finlay & Gough, 2003). Reflexivity is the process of examining and reflecting on how research is co-constructed and transformed through ongoing interactions between the researcher, the researched, and the social contexts involved (Finlay & Gough, 2003). Reflexive collaboration has been a critical feature embraced in our research as we strive for authenticity. To honour the collaborative and decolonizing spirit of an

Indigenous research framework we have made several changes to our research plan, and we share some of those changes below.

Our participant recruitment plan was originally to invite five Indigenous athletes who have relocated to pursue sport in mainstream context to share their in-depth knowledge to inform our research purpose. The recruitment strategy was guided by Creswell's (2007) recommendation that participants be selected for the background knowledge they hold. Coming out of conversations with community advisors as well as interacting with the parents of the first two athletes we recruited, it was suggested that to comprehensively explore this research topic we might also consider the stories of support persons for the athletes. As a result, our participant group changed to include the athletes' parents and billet family. Expanding the participant group has added to the complexity, and layered richness of the knowledges gathered.

To ensure our research involving Indigenous peoples reflects local and cultural relevance, our planned knowledge generating methods needed to be culturally appropriate and aligned with cultural traditions allowing for sharing and storytelling (Kovach, 2009). Storytelling and stories are essential features of Indigenous culture, as stories are means by which Indigenous peoples share their experiences, help with the co-construction of knowledges, and inform research that can benefit the community (Kovach, 2009). Our original research plan included both visual and oral storytelling methods that would facilitate meaningful information exchange to inform our research purpose. Specifically, we had planned to include sharing circles and photovoice reflections.

Sharing circles are sometimes implemented as Indigenous research methods to exchange and gather stories. Sharing circles resemble the Western method of focus groups, but differ based on the sacred meaning, growth, and healing aspect that is sharing circles have within Indigenous cultures (Lavallée, 2009). Sharing circles make the knowledge generation process somewhat ceremonial and align with Indigenous traditions, as they create a safe space, provide an opportunity for respectful listening, and cultivate an environment that engenders sharing feelings, experiences, and emotions (Kovach, 2009).

Photovoice is a qualitative research method whereby photographs are used by people to depict, reflect, and improve their community (Wang & Burris, 1997). Photovoice is useful for giving insight into the lives of people whose viewpoint differs from those who traditionally control the means of reflecting the world (Wang & Burris, 1997). Photographs are also seen as a form of visual diaries and an unobtrusive method of gathering data from participants' perspectives (Brooks, Poudrier & Thomas-Mclean, 2008). In their study exploring the health and body image of First Nation girls, Shea, Poudrier, Thomas, Jeffrey, and Kiskotagan (2013) found that using a visual storytelling method was integral in engaging the girls in the research, fostering creative expressions, and facilitating the co-creation of knowledge. Photovoice was considered a relevant method to generate knowledge in our research.

As a result of interacting with community advisors, changes were made to our knowledge generation methods. One community advisor noted that the sanctity of sharing circles allows for openness with the intent that what is discussed in the circle remains in the circle. The community advisor suggested not using sharing circles as a knowledge generation method to honour the sacredness of the circle. Instead, he taught us that the use of sharing circles in research might be a means of building relationships. Taking his advice, we substituted the sharing circles with conversational group interviews, which are considered to be the most open-ended knowledge generation method and allow for authentic uncovering of unique perspectives (Blodgett et al., 2010). Furthermore, conversational interviews are culturally appropriate, as conversations are Indigenous knowledge gathering methods that combine storytelling, reflection, and dialogue (Kovach, 2009).

As the research progresses, we anticipate there may be more changes in later stages of the research plan, particularly when we approach meaning making and knowledge translation. We continue to embrace reflexivity and collaboration as we strive to make our research authentic.

Conclusion

To understand and reflect how the well-being of Indigenous athletes who have relocated from their home communities have been shaped by their multicultural adjustment experiences, striving for authenticity is critical. As a research team, we are very deliberate in our intent to ensure that our research accurately captures and reflects the stories of the participants. Using an Indigenous research framework facilitates striving for authenticity. Being ethically sound, taking a collaborative and decolonizing approach to research, building reciprocal relationships, and using culturally relevant research methods are key underpinnings in our quest for authenticity. The Indigenous research framework utilized throughout the research process keeps us grounded in our aim to be authentic. This research framework, and our subsequent decolonizing approach has been critical in helping us accurately and ethically capture stories of the participants as we seek to understand and represent their experiences.

References

Blodgett, A., & Schinke, R. (2015). "When you're coming from the reserve you're not supposed to make it": Stories of Aboriginal athletes pursuing sport and academic careers in "mainstream" cultural contexts. *Psychology of Sport and Exercise*, 21, 115–124. http://dx.doi.org/10.1016/j.psychsport.2015.03.001

Blodgett, A., Schinke, R., McGannon, K., Coholic, D., Enosse, L., Peltier, D., & Pheasant, C. (2014). Navigating the insider-outsider hyphen: A qualitative exploration of the acculturation challenges of Aboriginal athletes pursuing sports in Euro-Canadian contexts. *Psychology of Sport and Exercise*, 15, 345-355. https://doi.org/10.1016/j.psychsport.2014.02.009

Blodgett, A., Schinke, R., Peltier, D., Wabano, M., Fisher, L., Eys, M., Ritchie, S., Recollet-Saikkonen, D., Pheasant, C. & Pickard, P. (2010). "Naadmaadmi": Reflections of Aboriginal community members engaged in sport psychology co-researching activities in mainstream academics. *Qualitative Research in sport and Exercise*, 2 (1), 56-76.

doi: 10.1080/19398440903510160

Brooks, C., Poudrier, J., & Thomas-MacLean, R. (2008). *Creating collaborative visions with Aboriginal women: A photovoice project.* In: Liamputtong P. (eds). Doing cross-cultural research. Social Indicators Research Series, 34. Springer, Dordrecht. https://doi.org/10.1007/978-1-4020-8567-3_13

Creswell, J. (2007). *Qualitative inquiry and research design: Choosing among five approaches* (2nd ed.). Thousand Oaks: Sage

Ferguson, L., Epp, G., Wuttunee, K., Dunn, M., McHugh, T., Humbert, L. (2018). 'It's more than just performing well in your sport. It's also about being healthy physically, mentally, emotionally and spiritually': Indigenous women athlete's meanings and experiences of flourishing in sport. *Qualitative Research in Sport Exercise and Health*, 1-19. https://doi.org/10.1080/2159676X.2018.1458332

Finlay, L., & Gough, B. (2003). *Reflexivity: A practical guide for researchers in health and social sciences.* Malden, Ma: Blackwell Science.

Kovach, M. (2009). *Indigenous methodologies: Characteristics, conversations, and contexts.* Toronto: University of Toronto Press.

Lavallée, L. (2009). Practical application of an Indigenous research framework and two qualitative Indigenous research methods: Sharing circles and Anishnaabe symbol-based reflection. *International Journal of Qualitative Methods*, 8 (1), 21-40. https://doi.org/10.1177/160940690900800103

Lavallée, L., & Lévesque, L. (2012). Two-eyed seeing: Physical activity, sport, and recreation promotion in Indigenous communities. In Forsyth, J. & Giles, A. (Eds.), *Aboriginal peoples and sport in Canada: Historical foundations and contemporary issues* (pp.206-228). Vancouver: UBC Press.

Lundqvist, C. (2011). Well-being in competitive sports – the feel-good factor? A review of conceptual considerations of well-being. *International Review of Sport and Exercise Psychology*, 4 (2), 109- 127. http://dx.doi.org.cyber.usask.ca/10.1080/1750984X.2011.584067

Mainstream. (2018). In *Oxford Dictionary.* Retrieved May 14, 2018 from https://en.oxforddictionaries.com/definition/mainstream

Ryff, C. D., & Keyes, C. L. (1995). The structure of psychological well-being revisited. Journal of Personality and Social Psychology, 69, 719-727. https://doi.org/10.1006/pmed.2001.0963

Shea, J. M., Poudrier, J., Thomas, R., Jeffrey, B., & Kiskotagan, L. (2013). Reflections from a creative community-based participatory research project exploring health and body image with First Nations girls. International Journal of Qualitative Methods, 12(1), 272-293.

Stake, R. E. (1995). The art of case study research. California: Sage Publications, Inc.
Tuhiwai Smith, L. (2016). *Decolonizing methodologies: Research and Indigenous people*. Zed Books. Retrieved April 29, 2018 from
https://ebookcentral.proquest.com/lib/usask/detail.action?docID=1426837.
Wang, C., & Burris, M. (1997). Photovoice: Concept, methodology, and use for participatory needs assessment. *Health Education & Behaviour*, 24 (3), 369-387. doi:10.1177/109019819702400309

notes

[152] This work was supported by a Saskatchewan Health Research Foundation Establishment Grant awarded to L. J. Ferguson.

[153] aCollege of Kinesiology, University of Saskatchewan, Saskatoon, Saskatchewan, Canada; bDepartment of Sociology, University of Saskatchewan, Saskatoon, Saskatchewan, Canada;
*Corresponding author. Shara Johnson, College of Kinesiology, University of Saskatchewan, 87 Campus Drive, Saskatoon, SK, Canada, S7N 5B2, Canada. Email: shara.johnson@usask.ca

[154] Mainstream refers to the "ideas, attitudes, or activities that are shared by most people and regarded as normal or conventional" (Oxford Dictionary, 2018).

[63] Eurocentric is defined as favouring White, European cultural values and belief systems (Blodgett et al., 2010).

[156] "Wholistic is spelt with a 'w' to signify the concept of wholeness when the four areas of health-physical, mental, emotional, and spiritual-are in balance" (Lavallée, & Lévesque, 2012, p.208).

Chapter Twenty-Seven

Miýo-Pimātisiwin

Decolonizing Self Through Culturally Responsive Pedagogy (CRP)

Obianuju Juliet Bushi

Introduction

Ndewo, Aham bu Obianuju, a bu m <u>onye</u> si n'ala <u>ndi igbo</u>. A <u>lu'rum onye</u> Kalanga o bu <u>ihe</u> mere m <u>ji</u> wu <u>ndi beh</u> ha. I begin this paper by respectfully introducing myself in <u>Igbo</u> language because it sets my aim and framework of how my interpretation of achieving a decolonized mindset (self), relates directly to the process and aim of decolonization. In the colonizer's language this translates to: "Hello, my name is Obianuju (meaning – I came in the midst of abundance or wealth), I am from the land of the Igbos, I am married to a Kalanga man (Botswana), which also makes me a member of their community. This particular African tradition makes an individual who is married into another community, a full participating member of their spouse's community. One does not need an identification card, or a certificate to prove one's membership.

The purpose of this research paper is to identify ways in which culturally responsive pedagogies (CRP) of relations can be applied in my work as an educator and a graduate student. This paper will also discuss the effects of colonization and its implications in the Canadian education curriculum. Applying critical pedagogy and CRP of relations as a lens to frame my work, I argue that in order to achieve miyo pimatisiwin (the good life) and ubuntu (humanity towards others), a decolonized mindset (Ladson-Billings, 1994; Pirbhai-Illich, Pete, Martin, 2017), must be achieved and practiced. I recognize that this cannot be accomplished in one day; it is a work-in-progress because the practice of CRP is complex and challenging coupled with educational disparities which have impacted the health and wellbeing of Indigenous people significantly, stemming from colonization and the resulting intergenerational traumas (Siope, 2013; Sasakamoose, Bellegarde, Sutherland, Pete, & McKay-McNabb, 2017). A decolonized mindset is aware of these disparities, aims to address these challenges, and works to achieve justice and equity. I do not claim to represent any Indigenous peoples of Canada, nor do I speak for all Indigenous people; rather, I represent myself, my thoughts, my journey, and my interpretations on the topics discussed in this paper.

Value in Decolonized Education

Gay (2013), defines culturally responsive pedagogies (CRP), as "using the cultural knowledge, prior experiences, frames of reference, and performance styles of ethnically diverse students to make learning encounters more relevant to and effective for them" (p. 49). CRP recognizes rich and diverse cultures, social wealth, epistemologies, and competencies of learners from various cultures by trying to change the very fabric of society for underserved groups (Siope, 2013). This approach seeks to develop a philosophical view of teaching that is dedicated to nurturing students' academic, social, emotional, cultural, psychological, and physiological well being (Battiste, 1998; Gay, 2013; Ladson Billings, 1994;). CRP makes it essential to provide multiple perspectives when discussing historical information to counteract the negative discriminations and distortions perpetuated in conventional conceptions of knowledge and truth, in schooling generally and in society at large (Gay, 2013). Gay argues that:

> Education must be specifically designed to perpetuate and enrich the culture of a people and equip them with the tools to become functional participants in society, if they so choose. This education cannot progress smoothly unless it is based upon and proceeds from the cultural perspectives of the group of people for whom it is designed. Since all Americans do not have the same set of beliefs, attitudes, customs, values, and norms, a single system of education seems impossible to serve everyone . . . [Educators] must accept the existence of cultural pluralism in this country and respect differences without equating them with inferiorities or tolerating hem with an air of condescension". (2013, p. 35)

For more than a decade, educators from minoritized and marginalized backgrounds including Gloria Ladson-Billings, Geneva Gay, Fatima Pirbhai-Illich, Marie Battiste, & Shauneen Pete, have advocated for the education system to move from western hegemony pedagogies that favours only people from dominant societies (mostly White, privileged students), to culturally responsive pedagogies (CRP), that also encourages critical intercultural communications about culture and identity, so that white students and educators can examine their privileges and whiteness in the educational space and society and their contributions to social reproduction of hegemonic discourses and conflicts. CRP has been noted to benefit students from various cultural backgrounds because it opens up the opportunity to think and do in ways that are culturally responsive and allows every learner to feel that their identity and culture is welcomed and safe (Pirbhai-Illich, Pete, Martin, 2017). Nakata, Nakata, Keech, and Bolt (2010), suggest

> "An alternate pedagogical approach for equipping students with understandings and analytical tools that can make explicit the conditions of the knowledge complexity Indigenous peoples confront as they move forward in their efforts to 'decolonize' knowledge, assert Indigenous analysis, reassert Indigenous 'ways of being, knowing and doing', or generate new knowledge to transform Indigenous social conditions" (p. 120).

The effects of colonization have had a profound negative effect on generations of Indigenous people. Unequal and inequitable access to social institutions and services have impacted Indigenous peoples and children especially. Specifically, educational disparity takes on diverse forms depending on context. In Canada, as it is in New Zealand, academic disparities exist between the Indigenous people and non-Indigenous people whose culture dominates the education system (Penetito, 2010; Siope, 2013; Shields, Bishop, & Mazawi, 2005). It is also safe to say that Canada's education system may be strengthening the idea of social reproduction where children from rich families are more likely to end up being rich, and children from poorer families are more likely to remain poor due to low engagement in the absence of culturally responsive practices (Castagno & Brayboy, 2008; Cothran & Ennis, 2000).

Silencing Indigenous History in Curriculum Content

Canada continues to produce policies and education reforms that fail to address social, political and economic issues faced by Indigenous people. Education reforms have to date not been able to meet the educational needs of diverse Indigenous people. Issues such as systemic racism, negative stereotypes endured by Indigenous people embedded in legislature such as the Indian Act continues to dictate the lives of

Indigenous people. According to St. Denis (2011), Indigenous teachers continue to face resentment, and rejection when trying to incorporate Indigenous content into their curriculum. Indigenous teachers recognize the need for meaningful Indigenous content and perspectives that address the ways in which racism and colonialism shape the lives of Indigenous people in Canada. Canadian data from 2010 census indicates that only 50% of Indigenous students graduated from high school in contrast to an 88% graduation rate among non- Indigenous students (Battiste, 2013; Pirbhai-Illich, 2010). Many scholars such as Fatima Pirbhai-Illich, and Marie Battiste, suggest that this is a direct link to the racist aftermath of colonization. Research findings indicate that dominant colonial educational epistemologies fail to address or support Indigenous ways of living and learning (Malin, 1990; Pirbhai-Illich, 2010). In addition, the failure to consider linguistic and cultural diversity and the lack of culturally responsive pedagogies creates an attitude and practice that perpetuates a dogma of cultural inferiority that is mutual among oppressed people. Significantly, Indigenous people often come to believe that they are incapable of learning and that the degrading images and beliefs perpetuated by the colonizers are true (Hart, 2002; Pirbhai- Illich, 2010, p. 257). This is evident in the low percentage of high school graduates among Indigenous students (Pirbhai-Illich, 2010). It is not that these studens are not smart or are incapable of grasping classroom content, rather it is because they are forced out of school due to racism and discrimination, and the obvious fact that the conventional/ colonial Canadian curriculum reinforces cultural inferiority and ultimately creates binary opposites (Good vs. Bad, Us vs. Them). In addition, the conventional educational system continues to uphold a colonial worldview (Battiste, 1998), which marginalizes Indigenous students on the basis of their race, class, gender, religion, and language (Pirbhai-Illich, 2010). These oppressive factors create more problems for Indigenous learners and manifests itself in behavioural problems, abuse of alcohol and drugs, physical and mental health problems, and low levels of literacy (Hains, 2001).

St Denis (2014), in her article titled "Silencing Aboriginal Curricular Content and Perspectives Through Multiculturalism: "There are Other Children Here"" describes her encounter at a ministry of education meeting where discussions around merging Native studies, history and social studies as one course brought about disconnection and disagreements by a non- Indigenous person present at the meeting who stated that "Aboriginal people are not the only ones here " (St Denis, 2014). This statement refers to the idea that when the course is created, Indigenous history will be put on the spotlight, ignoring the white-dominant sugar-coated Canadian history. Over the years, we have seen school boards approving courses that limit Indigenous history and culturally responsive teaching at the both elementary and the high school levels. This does not only affect Indigenous students, but Indigenous teachers are silenced, oppressed as they continue to face resistance, racism and are not given the opportunity to incorporate Indigenous content in their curriculum (St. Denis, 2014).

Language, Connections and Relationships

At the beginning of my paper, I used my first language to make meaning of words, sentences and phrases that are difficult to translate effectively with the use of English, a colonial language. I also used my language because it reminds me of who I am, and where I come from, my responsibilities and purposes as a non-white educator and how I need to pass on this language and knowledge to my children. Ultimately, decolonization cannot occur without Indigenization, justice and equity; Language is what defines a people (Makokis, 2008). Language is crucial because it is through this medium that history and culture are passed on from one generation to the other - it is no wonder why Indigenous children who attended Residential Schools were refused and forbidden to speak their language. The colonizers understood the power of language and thus forbidding Indigenous children from speaking their language was a way of breaking down their identity and memories of their history and cultural guidance. Although we can see that language is very important in the learning process, Indigenous students and teachers continue to experience discrimination and are made to feel ashamed of their language and identity. It is my belief that CRP can provide innovative pedagogies by incorporating the language of the learners into the learning process. This leaves me to believe that our education system does not value the culture of people from lower classes as much as it does for the culture of the people who have more resources, who come from the higher or privileged classes (Apple, 1982).

Beyond Abyssal Thinking

The idea that the education system somehow values ideas and theories of European scholars and empirical findings makes educational institutions a supporter of neo-colonialism and the center for Abyssal thinking. Western ways of thinking is abyssal thinking because it functions through radical lines that divide social reality. De Santos describes these two realms as "this side of the line" and the realm of "the other side of the line" (De Sousa Santos, 2007). This separation acts in a way "that the other side" eventually becomes erased, or seen as non-existent Thus, Abyssal thinking creates invisible and visible layers and structures that ignore social, systemic, economic and political inequalities, and puts so much blame on cultural diversity, and identity (Pirbhai-Illich, Pete, Martin, 2017). This example also illustrates the relations of dominance and subordination and the conflict to change these processes. The fact that Western thinking operates in abyssal lines, tensions between this side and the other side is created, and violence is stemming from these ways of thinking can affect marginalized and racialized groups who are place on the other side, the less-human side. Across the globe, Indigenous peoples in common with other colonized populations, also assert a "definitive rejection of 'being told'…what we are, what our ranking is in relation to the ideal of *humanitas* and what we have to do to be recognized as such" (Mignolo, 2009, p. 161). Our ways of knowing, learning and teaching are ultimately ignored because we do not fit into this side of the abyssal line and because abyssal lines continues to structure modern knowledge and law, Indigenous pedagogies are buried as though they never existed and when they are consulted, they are measured critically with the lens of Western thinking.

Conclusion

In conclusion, I strongly believe that schools and teachers can be contributing to educational inequity if they choose to ignore that disparities exist or do nothing to address them. Addressing these disparities through reforms leading to fundamental changes in schools and classrooms are necessary but also very crucial is the process of consultation with Indigenous communities, students, educators and elders, because addressing inequalities promotes equity and justice for all.

Decolonized education is a process that has to start with self. As educators and students, we have to build that mindset free of prejudice and colonized ideology by embracing decolonized pedagogies and epistemologies. Institutions such as the government, schools, Indigenous government and provincial and federal governments need to support Indigenous teachers and allies to build a better environment that enriches culturally responsive pedagogies and academic freedom.

I argue that the education of racially, ethnically, and culturally diverse students should connect in-school learning to the out-of-school living; promote educational equity and excellence; create community among individuals from different cultural, social, and ethnic backgrounds; and develop students' agency, efficacy, and empowerment (Gay, 2010).

The importance of language also needs to be emphasized and supported in research and in the classroom. Consultations with Elders and community members' needs to occur to implement programs that not only benefit and puts students' priorities first but also that of the communities in which they reside.

References

Apple, W. M. (1982). Cultural and economic reproduction in education: Essays on class, ideology, and the state. Boston: Routledge & Kegan Paul.

Battiste, M. (1998). Enabling the autumn seed: Toward a decolonized approach to aboriginal knowledge, language, and education. *Canadian Journal of Native Education, 22*(1), 16–27.

Castagno, A., & Brayboy, B. M. (2008). Culturally responsive schooling for Indigenous youth: A review of the literature. *Review of Educational Research, 78*(4), 941-993.

Chartrand, R. (2012). Anishinaabe pedagogy. *Canadian Journal of Native Education, 35*(1), 144-162,221. Retrieved from https://login.libproxy.uregina.ca:8443/login?URL=https://search-proquest-com.libproxy.uregina.ca:8443/docview/1370197105?accountid=13480

Christie, M.J. (1985). Aboriginal perspectives on experience and learning: The role of language in aboriginal education. Geelong, VIC, Australia: Deakin University Press.

De Sousa Santos, B. (2007). Beyond abyssal thinking: From global lines to ecologies of knowledges. *Review (Fernand Braudel Center), 30*(1), 45-89. Retrieved from http://www.jstor.org/stable/40241677

Geneva Gay (2013) Teaching to and through cultural diversity. *Curriculum Inquiry, 43*(1), 48-70, DOI: 10.1111/curi.12002

Goulet, L.& Goulet, K. (2014). Teaching each other. Nehinuw concepts & Indigenous pedagogies. Vancouver, BC: UBC Press.

Hains, S. (2001). Establishing success with native students. *Principal Leadership, 1*(8), 44–47.

Hart, M.A. (2002). Seeking mino-pimatisiwin: An Aboriginal approach to helping. Halifax, NS: Fernwood.

Imbo, S. (1998). An introduction to African philosophy. Lanham, Maryland: Rowman and Littlefield Publishers.

Kanu, Y. (2002). In their own voices: First Nations students identify some cultural mediators of their learning in the formal school system. *Alberta Journal of Educational Research, 48*(2), 98-121.

Ladson-Billings, G. (1994). The dream keepers: Successful teachers of African American children. San Fransisco, CA: Jossey-Bass.

Lewthwaite, B., & McMillan, B. (2010). "She can bother me, and that's because she cares": What Inuit students say about teaching and their learning. *Canadian Journal of Education, 33*(1), 140-176. Retrieved from https://login.libproxy.uregina.ca:8443/login?url=https://search-proquest com.libproxy.uregina.ca:8443/docview/366291336?accountid=13480

Malin, M. (1990). The visibility and invisibility of Aboriginal students in an urban classroom. *Australian Journal of Education, 34*(3), 312–329.

Makokis, J. A. (2008). Nehiyaw iskwew kiskinowâtasinahikewina - paminisowin namôya tipeyimisowin: Learning self determination through the sacred. *Canadian Woman Studies, 26*(3), 39-51. Retrieved from https://login.libproxy.uregina.ca: 8443/login?url=https://search-proquest-com.libproxy.uregina.ca:8443/docview/217445726?accountid=13480

Mignolo, W. (2009). Epistemic disobedience, independent thought and decolonial freedom. *Theory, Culture & Society, 26*(7/8), 159–181.

Nakata, M., Nakata, V., Keech, S., & Bolt, R. (2012). Decolonial goals and pedagogies for Indigenous studies. *Decolonization: Indigeneity, Education & Society* 1(1), 120-140

Pirbhai-Illich, F. (2011). Aboriginal students engaging and struggling with critical multiliteracies. *Journal of Adolescent & Adult Literacy, 54*(4), 257-266. Retrieved from https://login.libproxy.uregina.ca:8443/login?url=https://search-proquest-com.libproxy.uregina.ca:8443/docview/817784495?accountid=13480

Pirbhai-Illich, F, Pete, & S. Martin, F. (2017). Eds. *Culturally responsive pedagogy. Working towards decolonization, indigeneity and interculturalism.* Switzerland: Palgrave Macmillan.

Sasakamoose, J., Bellegarde, T., Sutherland, W., Pete, S., & McKay-McNabb, K. (2017). Miýo-pimātisiwin developing Indigenous cultural responsiveness theory (ICRT): Improving Indigenous health and well-being. *The International Indigenous Policy Journal, 8*(4). Retrieved from: http://ir.lib.uwo.ca/iipj/vol8/iss4/1 DOI: 10.18584/iipj.2017.8.4.1

Siope, A. (2013). A Culturally Responsive Pedagogy of Relations': Coming to Understand. Waikato Journal of Education: Te Hautaka Matauranga o Waikato, 18(2). Retrieved from: file:///Users/israelbushi/Downloads/160-561-1-PB.pdf DOI: 10.15663/wje.v18i2.160

Wilkins, D. F. (2017). Why public schools fail first nation students. *Antistasis, 7*(1), 89-103. Retrieved from
https://login.libproxy.uregina.ca:8443/login?url=https://search-proquestcom.libproxy.uregina.ca:8443/docview/1903429172?accountid=13480

Chapter Twenty-Eight

Decolonizing/Indigenizing

(Re)Imagining Educational Systems, even those Mathematical

Shana Graham

Introduction

According to Castagno and Brayboy (2008), Indigenous nations have called for improved schooling "since at least the early part of the 20th century" (p. 944). This call stems from inadequate facilities (Angus, 2015) as well as statistical disparities between Indigenous and non-Indigenous counterparts, including teenage high school dropout and adult unemployment rates (Bell & Brant, 2014). When considering disparities in relation to mathematics education in particular, "Aboriginal students tend to be over-represented in special education classes and low-track mathematics courses and under-represented in higher level mathematics courses" (Nicol, Archibald & Baker, 2013, p. 73). Mathematics classes and schooling systems have also generated devastating doubt among Indigenous students (Battiste, 2013; Nicol, Archibald & Baker, 2013). Thus, decolonizing/Indigenizing[157] practices are more recently being sought, especially in response to the educational Calls to Action within the *Final Report of the Truth and Reconciliation Commission of Canada* (2015).

Mathematics education literature tends to rely upon notions of incorporation, inclusion, and integration when suggesting Indigenous onto-epistemologies become part of curricula (Aikenhead, 2017; Gavarrete, 2015; Kaino & Kasanda, 2015). The purpose of this paper, therefore, is to express concern that the majority of related practices continue to reflect understandings of *making space within* rather than (re)imagining and *making changes to* present education systems, including those mathematical. I challenge the reader to reflect upon the writing that follows so as to think about how to similarly resist and change present educational limitations, wherever possible. Through such means, perhaps future educational systems might better reflect decolonization/Indigenization and, eventually, reconciliation.

Situating Myself

I was not born in the province of Saskatchewan but I have considered the capital city of Regina and part of the nearby Qu'Appelle valley to be my homelands since I was less than a year old. Although I lived elsewhere, when I was an undergraduate student and beginning teacher, the Saskatchewan prairie region remained home. My grandparents and parents were born and raised within the region and my husband and I chose to reside in Regina to have our family. The Treaty 4 territory in which we live is the traditional territory of the Nêhiyaw, Saulteaux, Nakota, Lakota and Dakota peoples, aas well as the homeland of many Métis people. The University of Regina, where I am presently a doctoral candidate, is also predominantly situated in Treaty 4 territory but it does have a presence in Treaty 6 territory as well.

While my doctoral research journey brought me to my present research interest in exploring interfaces of Indigenous worldviews and mathematics education, my capacity for (re)imagining mathematics education was actually initiated through Master of Education experiences. Prior to these experiences, I assumed that there was only one way to learn and teach mathematics. Through experiences as a student of mathematics, no matter the teacher, sample questions with procedural solutions were demonstrated and then I was expected to practice what had been modelled. This way of teaching and learning is referred to as transmissive, traditional, or didactically teacher-centered (Boaler & Greeno, 2000). The problem with only learning mathematics in this way was that I was also learning how I thought mathematics should be taught. As a result, and without question, I practiced the same transmissive/traditional or received ways of learning/teaching mathematics for the first decade of my professional career. From 2005-2010, however, through Master of Education study of complexity theory and introduction to the notion of a collective learning community, I became aware that received ways of learning/teaching were not the only ways of knowing mathematics. I developed a consciousness that it was possible to practice learning/teaching differently. More specifically, through complexity theory, I came to understand that when conditions[158] are suitable, interactions and relations between learners can enable collective ways of learning that can supersede the possibilities of individual learning. I enjoyed my Master of Education research because I felt it afforded me an onto-epistemological leap, from positivistic to complex ways of knowing and being.

Through doctoral experiences, I have again been drawn to different ways of thinking about mathematics and mathematics education. This time though, Indigenous knowledges[159] have led to an onto-epistemological leap from complex to relational ways of knowing and being. Perhaps by now the reader might be wondering, "Isn't math just math? How can you think about it differently? And, why would you want to?" For me, thinking about mathematics in a variety of ways opens up the possibility of (re)imagining mathematics education, beyond the teaching of mathematics as a language or as a defined process with universal rules. This opening allows me to realize that our minds are, or at least mine was/is, colonized/controlled (Fasheh, 2015; Mukhopadhyay & Roth, 2012a; Skovsmose, 2014; Waziyatason & Yellow Bird, 2012). What I mean is that mathematics education tends to project that mathematics is universal (Barton, 1999), neutral (Ernest, 2009; Klein, 1997; Weist, 2006), objective (Ernest, 2009; Weist, 2006), culture free (Barton, 1999; Foote & Bartell, 2011), "supposedly apolitical, ahistorical, immutable" (Klein, 1997, p. 68), and non-negotiable (Nolan & Weston, 2015). But mathematics actually holds none of these characteristics.

A Demonstration

As a result of the understanding that mathematics is negotiable, whenever I have an opportunity (as an instructor or graduate teaching assistant for undergraduate pre-service teachers and graduate student teachers) I often introduce the idea that our minds have been colonized and that mathematics is neither universal nor objective by using the following demonstration:

– I begin with any sort of solid objects to show a seemingly universal and basic mathematical concept that is taught in schools, namely 1 + 1 = 2

Figure 1. A demonstration that 1 object + 1 object = 2 objects

– Next, I change the medium of the objects (presently I find playdough works well but, in the past, I have used water) to demonstrate that 1 + 1 ≠ 2.

Figure 2. A demonstration that 1 object + 1 object = 1 object

In this part of the demonstration, I acknowledge it could be argued that the amount of material represented by the total sum is doubled but, in reality, there is only one object displayed.

– For my final act, I talk about piles to demonstrate an understanding that 1 + 1 could be reflective of many objects, in other words, perhaps 1 + 1 = many

CHAPTER TWENTY-EIGHT

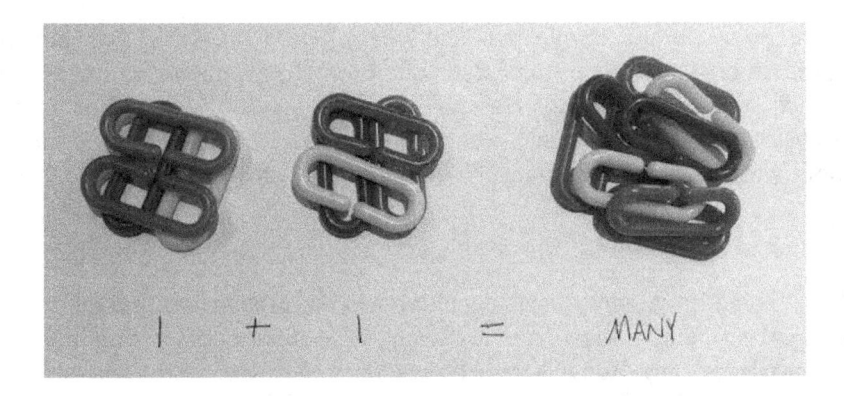

Figure 3. A demonstration that 1 pile + 1 pile = many objects

I add the final demonstration because it similarly reflects what happens with the addition of playdough whereby 1 + 1 = 1 when only speaking of piles but clearly another dimension is present in that many objects are displayed as components of the summation.

I use these demonstrations in hopes that at least some of the educators who stand witness might begin to ponder why the mathematics that is taught in schools tends to reduce complex realities. In other words, why is it that children only learn 1 + 1 = 2 with simple solid objects when there are other possibilities to discuss? Authors within mathematics education literature, who notice school mathematics is so restricted and unchanging, are concerned about whether mathematics is actually dead (Fasheh, 1997; Greer, Mukhopadhyay & Roth, 2012a) or merely serves a purpose in societal obedience training (Skovsmose, 2014) and cultural hegemony (Greer, Mukhopadhyay & Roth, 2012b). Bishop (1990) asserts that through the use of simplifications, abstractions, and decontextualizations "western mathematics [is]...one of the most powerful weapons in the imposition of western culture" (p. 51). Other authors agree with Bishop because "the mathematical activity of those without power is always characterized as non-mathematical" and, I would add, therefore omitted from mathematics education (Greer, Mukhopadhyay & Roth, 2012a, p. 5).

Curricular omissions of complex mathematics-like Indigenous worldviews and related practices appear to serve at least a few purposes. First, omissions perpetuate an "epistemological ignorance" (Calderon, 2014, p. 314). Second, such ignorance sustains the normalization of Eurocentric "discourses and discursive practices" (Battiste, 2013, p. 106). And, third, normalization protects Eurocentric futurities by maintaining grand narratives that "hide the social and economic structures of

Eurocentrism, white dominance, and racism" (p. 106). Thus, I do believe that it is necessary to consider decolonization/Indigenization efforts within mathematics education, not only *for Indigenous* students but rather *for the well-being of everyone* so that we might all learn to think more critically about what it is that our educational systems actually do.

Decolonization/Indigenization Efforts

With respect to my own decolonization/Indigenization efforts as a doctoral student, I share the following two experiences which may be beneficial for any administrators, teachers/educators and students to consider, even beyond the context of mathematics education.

Story 1 – graduate student seeking policy change

This first story discusses how graduate student policies can actually limit research capacities. It stems from my experiences with limitations that were placed on me because of my identification as a doctoral student. In most universities, I assume it typical that graduate students are not allowed to take undergraduate courses, however, after having finished my graduate course requirements I requested to take an additional undergraduate course reflective of Indigenous culture and history. In looking back, I took a rather harsh stance in my request when suggesting that it was time for the Faculty of Graduate Studies and Research (FGSR) to develop policy and actions rather than lip service to the idea Indigenization. The premise of my argument, however, was that without access to Indigenous worldviews, cultures and languages, the notion of Indigenization would likely never become anything more than token.

I explained that my request stemmed from multiple understandings, including:

- it would probably be my last chance to learn from the course instructor, a valued Indigenous scholar who had announced retirement;
- 'Indigenization' was identified as an "overarching area of emphasis" within the 2015-2020 Strategic Plan but few people on campus were sure about what that involved (University of Regina, 2015, p. 9);
- "decolonization of education is not just about changing a system for Indigenous peoples, but for everyone" (Battiste, 2013, p. 22); and,
- reconciliation involves "following through with concrete actions that demonstrate real societal change" (Truth and Reconciliation Commission of Canada, 2015, p. 11), especially revitalizations of

Indigenous "spirituality, cultures, languages, laws, and governance systems" (p. 12).

I further argued that in order to participate in decolonizing/Indigenizing and reconciliatory actions and revitalizations, "in order to find new ways of living together on this land [Canada], Settler people need to take up the responsibility of learning about Indigenous ontologies" (Battell Loman and Barker, 2015, p. 20). In accepting such responsibility, I stated that I wanted to continue to "work at changing myself" (Mason, 2002, p. iv) by developing a worldview beyond Euro-Western onto-epistemologies through Pinar's (2012) method of currere. Through currere, Pinar (2012) advocates for teachers to forever remain as students, "always studying across the disciplines, as well as reading in depth and over time in at least one [discipline]" (p. 231). He goes so far as to say that "teachers should be enrolled in universities each term, and not only in education departments or in the academic subject they teach" (p. 231).

I rationalized that my area of study was mathematics education and my research interests lay in disrupting Euro-Western onto-epistemologies and (re)imagining possibilities for mathematics education through/with Indigenous knowledges and complex conversations. I argued that taking an Indigenous culture and history course could occasion opportunities for disruptions and (re)imaginings. Thus, I challenged FGSR to begin to change patriarchal policies so that graduate students could push past current program policy limitations. I asked to exceed the doctoral course requirements so that I might research what it meant to decolonize/Indigenize with "radical hope ... 'directed toward a future goodness that transcends the current ability to understand what it is'" (Lear quoted by Wiseman, Onuczko and Glanfield, 2015, p. 237).

The final point I made was that my research journey began before I realized my path. I explained that my research was emergent, requiring development of opportunities for learning in unexpected ways, perhaps in ways not yet accepted as normal or common sense, such as through exposure to extra coursework reflective of Indigenous worldviews. Indigenous onto-epistemologies teach that "no one [can] dictate the path that must be followed" (Ermine, 1995, p. 108) and so I ended my request with a few questions – Why does the FGSR have policies in place that limit graduate student research paths? How can the FGSR know what path is best for me when it does not know/understand my research? And, if the FGSR wants to emphasize Indigenization, then when/how can it be made possible for graduate students to be able to take any/all courses reflective of Indigenous worldview and language?

In the end, my request was granted.

Story 2 – mathematics sessional lecturer seeking policy change

At most universities I would wager that a project instead of an exam is not an unusual method of final evaluation within education departments. A project as a method of final evaluation, however, is unusual within departments of mathematics, especially with respect to introductory mathematics courses. My request that I be allowed to set a project instead of exam when instructing a mathematics course for first-year Métis and First Nations pre-service teachers stemmed from multiple experiences, including the following:

- While attending an Indigenous mathematics education conference, I was reminded of Lisa Lunney-Borden's work, Show Me Your Math, which provides students with an opportunity to explore connections between mathematics and local/cultural community knowledges (https://www.youtube.com/watch?v=sqFb4VZ_D44).
- While teaching a university-level course to pre-service teachers I was asked, "What would a math project look like? I have never done a math project before." Thus, knowing that most teachers are inclined to teach as they were taught (Boaler & Greeno, 2000; Nadelson, et al., 2013), I believed that it was important to provide my students with opportunities to explore other forms of assessment/evaluation besides those with which they were already familiar; namely, mathematical quizzes, tests, and exams.
- The university identified Indigenization as an "overarching area of emphasis" within the 2015-2020 Strategic Plan (University of Regina, 2015, p. 9) and the mathematics project would allow pre-service teachers to explore this emphasis in the context of mathematics education.
- The project, as designed, could also allow pre-service teachers to explore mathematics in languages besides English and to present alternative vocabularies and understandings that relate to mathematical topics/concepts.

I was fairly certain, however, that it would remain most important that the mathematics content/curricula be thoroughly evaluated. Thus, I proposed to decrease the usual weighting of the final evaluation so as to be able to also provide a full assessment of all of the mathematical concepts presented throughout the semester via a number of quizzes. In this way, I suggested that a final exam would be unnecessary for its sole purpose would only be to re-evaluate the concepts that had already been assessed. Thus, in place of the final exam I offered to use the exam time slot to hold a public exhibition or math fair so that the pre-service teachers could present their projects.

The math fair project outline was as follows:

1. Students were asked to find mathematics within their communities and to share their understandings of what they found through the creation of a poster for public exhibition (and possibly a presentation of an artifact, if applicable).
2. Students were asked to relate local/community knowledges/artifacts to at least one of the six universal mathematical activities identified by Bishop (1988): counting, locating, measuring, designing, playing and explaining.
3. Students were assessed for their ability to apply a mathematical lens along with the correct use of mathematical concepts, terminology and calculations to explain the mathematics they perceive related to the local/community knowledges/artifacts.
4. Because the project was being developed for elementary pre-service teachers, they were expected to link the mathematical understandings identified to specific Saskatchewan Elementary Mathematics Curricula Outcomes and/or Indicators, especially within K-8 curricula.
5. In an effort to explore the notions of decolonization/Indigenization, students were also asked to discuss whether application of a mathematical lens to the local/community knowledges/artifacts actually enhanced such knowledges/artifacts, in their particular case.

The fifth requirement stemmed from my own dissertation work which asks: Just because we can apply a mathematical lens, should we? The requirement also came from once listening as a participant of a conference round table discussion in which it was emphasized that Indigenous peoples should be able to choose for themselves the mathematical language and mathematical applications that they want to draw into their communities, such as those that do not undermine present languages and knowledges.

In the end, my request was again granted.

Thus, I challenge the reader to begin to think about how to take action to decolonize/Indigenize within their own contexts for we are "not everything we could be" (Battell Lowman & Barker, 2015, p. 123). "[W]e *are* allowed to think about alternatives [because] the world *can* be other than what is the case" (original emphasis, Greer, Mukhopadhyay & Roth,

2012a, p. 7). Like Skovsmose (2014), "I am...not convinced of the irrelevance of small-scale educational changes" (p. 296).

References

Aikenhead, G., & Michell, H. (2011). Bridging cultures: Indigenous and scientific ways of knowing nature. Don Mills, ON: Pearson.

Aikenhead, G. S. (2017). Enhancing school mathematics culturally: A path of reconciliation. Canadian Journal of Science, Mathematics and Technology Education, 17(2), 73-140. doi: 10.1080/14926156.2017.1308043

Angus, C. (2015). Children of the broken Treaty: Canada's lost promise and one girl's dream. Regina, SK: University of Regina Press.

Barton, B. (1999). Ethnomathematics and philosophy. Zentralblatt für Didaktik der Mathemati (ZDM), 31(2), 54-58.

Barton, B. (2008). The language of mathematics: Telling mathematical tales. New York, NY: Springer.

Battell Lowman, E., & Barker, A. J. (2015). Settler identity and colonialism in 21st century Canada. Halifax, NS: Fernwood Publishing.

Battiste, M. (2013). Decolonizing education: Nourishing the learning spirit. Saskatoon, SK: Purich Publishing Limited.

Bell, N., & Brant, T. (2015). Culturally relevant Aboriginal education. Toronto, ON: Pearson.

Bishop, A. J. (1988). Mathematical enculturation: A cultural perspective on mathematics education. Dordrecht, NL: Kluwer.

Bishop, A. J. (1990). Western mathematics: The secret weapon of cultural imperialism. Race & Class, 32(2), 51-65. doi: 10.1177/030639689003200204

Boaler, J. & Greeno, J. G. (2000). Identity, agency, and knowing in mathematics worlds. In J. Boaler (Ed.), Multiple perspectives on mathematics teaching and learning, (pp. 171-200). Westport, CT: Ablex Publishing.

Calderon, D. (2014). Uncovering settler grammars in curriculum. Educational Studies, 50, 313-338. doi: 10.1080/00131946.2014.926904

Castagno, A., & Brayboy, B. (2008). Culturally responsive schooling for Indigenous youth: A review of the literature. Review of Educational Research, 78(4), 941-993. doi: 10.3102/0034654308323036

Davis, B., & Simmt, E. (2003). Understanding learning systems: Mathematics education and complexity science. Journal for Research in Mathematics Education, 34(2), 137-167. doi: 10.2307/30034903

Ermine, W. (1995). Aboriginal Epistemology. In M. Battiste & J. Bearman (Eds.), First Nations education in Canada: The circle unfolds (pp. 101-112). Vancouver, BC: UBC Press.

Ernest, P. (2009). New philosophy of mathematics: Implications for mathematics education. In B. Greer, S. Mukhopadhyay, A. B. Powell & S. Nelson-Barber (Eds.), Culturally responsive mathematics education (pp. 43-64). New York, NY: Routledge.

Fasheh, M. (1997). Is mathematics in the classroom neutral – or dead? For the Learning of Mathematics, 17(2), 24-27.

Fasheh, M. (2015). Over 68 years with mathematics: My story of healing from modern superstitions and reclaiming my sense of being and well-being. In S. Mukhopadhyay & B. Greer (Eds.), Proceedings of the Eighth International Mathematics Education and Society Conference, June 21-26, 2015 (Vol. 1) (pp.33-60). Portland State University, OR: Ooligan Press.

Greer, B., Mukhopadhyay, S., & Roth, M. (2012a). Celebrating diversity, realizing alternatives. In S. Mukhopadhyay & W.-M. Roth (Eds.), Alternative forms of knowing (in) mathematics: Celebration of diversity of mathematical practices (pp. 1-8). Rotterdam, NL: Sense Publishers.

Greer, B., Mukhopadhyay, S., & Roth, M. (2012b). Part 1: Mathematics and politics of knowledge: Introduction. In S. Mukhopadhyay & W.-M. Roth (Eds.), Alternative forms of knowing (in) mathematics: Celebration of diversity of mathematical practices (pp. 9- 15). Rotterdam, NL: Sense Publishers.

Foote, M. Q., & Bartell, T. G. (2011). Pathways to equity in mathematics education: How life experiences impact researcher positionality. Educational Studies in Mathematics, 78(1), 45-68. doi: 10.1007/s10649-011-9309-2

Gavarrete, M. E. (2015). The challenges of mathematics education for Indigenous teacher training. Intercultural Education, 26(4), 326-337. doi: 10.1080/14675986.2015.1073878

Goulet, L. M., & Goulet, K. N. (2014). Teaching each other: Nehinuw concepts and Indigenous pedagogies. Vancouver, BC: UBC Press.

Kaino, L. M., & Kasanda, C. (2015). Some Indigenous strategies in mathematics teaching: Taking the artefacts into the classroom. Journal of Communication, 6(1), 67-74. doi: 10.1080/0976691X.2015.11884849

Klein, M. (1997). Looking again at the 'supportive' environment of constructivist pedagogy: An example from preservice teacher education in mathematics. Journal of Education for Teaching, 23(3), 277-292. doi: 10.1080/02607479720015

Lunney Borden, L. (2011). The 'verbification' of mathematics: Using the grammatical structures of Mi'kmaq to support student learning. For the Learning of Mathematics, 31(3), 8-13. doi: 10.2307/41319601

Mason, J. (2002). Researching your own practice: The discipline of noticing. New York: Routledge.

Nadelson, L., Callahan, J., Pyke, P., Hay, A., Dance, M., & Pfiester, J. (2013). Teacher STEM perception and preparation: Inquiry-based STEM professional development for elementary teachers. The Journal of Educational Research, 106(2), 157-168. doi: 10.1080/00220671.2012.667014

Nicol, C., Archibald, J., & Baker, J. (2013). Designing a model of culturally responsive mathematics education: Place, relationships and storywork. Mathematics Education Research Journal, 25, 73-89. doi: 10.1007/s13394-012-0062-3

Nolan, K., & Weston, J. H. (2015). Aboriginal perspectives and/in mathematics: A case study of three grade 6 teachers. in education, 21(1), 12-22. Retrieved from http://ineducation.ca/ineducation/article/view/195/702

Pinar, W. F. (2012). What is Curriculum Theory. New York, NY: Routledge.

Skovsmose, O. (2014). Critique, generativity, and imagination. In O. Skovsmose (Ed.), Critique as uncertainty (pp. 289-299). Charlotte, NC: Information Age Publishing. (Reprinted from For the Learning of Mathematics, 31(3), 2011, 19-23.

Truth and Reconciliation Commission of Canada. (2015). Final report of the Truth and Reconciliation Commission of Canada, Volume one: Summary: honouring the truth, reconciling for the future. Toronto, ON: James Lorimer & Company.

University of Regina. (2015). University of Regina Strategic Plan 2015-2020: peyak aski kikawinaw – together we are stronger [online pdf document]. Retrieved November 23, 2015 from, http://www.uregina.ca/strategic-plan/assets/docs/pdf/sp-2015-20-together-we-are-stronger.pdf

Waziyatawin, & Yellow Bird, M. (2012). Introduction: Decolonizing our minds and actions. In Waziyatawin & M. Ywllow Bird (Eds.), For Indigenous minds only: A decolonization handbook (pp.1-14). Santa Fe, MN: School for Advanced Research.

Weist, L. (2006). Teaching mathematics from a multicultural perspective. Equity & Excellence in Education, 34(1), 16-25. doi: 10.1080/1066568010340103

Wiseman, D., Onuczko, T., & Glanfield, F. (2015). Resilience and hope in the garden: Intercropping Aboriginal and Western ways of knowing to inquire into science teacher education. In H. Smits & R. Naqvi (Eds.), Framing peace: Thinking about & enacting curriculum as "radical hope" (pp. 237-252). New York, NY: Peter Lang Publishing.

notes

[157] Indigenization is defined by The Aboriginal Advisory Circle to the President of the university as:
The transformation of the existing academy by including Indigenous knowledges, voices, critiques, scholars, students and materials as well as the establishment of physical and epistemic spaces that facilitate the ethical stewardship of a plurality of Indigenous knowledges and practices so

thoroughly as to constitute an essential element of the university. It is not limited to Indigenous people, but encompasses all students and faculty, for the benefit of our academic integrity and our social viability. (University of Regina, 2015, p. 9)

[158] Davis and Simmt (2003) identify five conditions of collective learning systems but these conditions are not necessarily sufficient in order for learning to occur in a collective way. The conditions are: internal diversity (the diversity represented by individual agents within the system); redundancy (a sameness with respect to the focus of learning for the system); decentralized control (diffuse authority within a collective/system); organized randomness (the possibility of flexibility and variation within constraint and boundary); and neighbor interactions (the intersection of ideas and representations but not necessarily of people).

[159] When initially reading about Indigenous epistemology, I came across the idea that "coming to know is a journey toward wisdom-in-action, not a destination of discovery" (Aikenhead & Michell, 2011, p. 69-70). The authors introduce the term 'knowledges' and the phrase 'ways of knowing' to express an understanding of learning as dynamic and lifelong. In this way, definitions and interpretations of knowledge are no longer noun-based. In other words, knowledge is disconnected from being about facts to be discovered or obtained. Knowledges and ways of knowing instead offer a form of agency, releasing me from a necessity to seek indisputable certitude or truth. Rather, enrichments of understandings and interpretations remain open to change through language that pushes positivistic vocabulary from the foreground. I also use the term knowledges, however, in place of the notion of worldview within my own writing to express that I only know very little about that which might be deemed Indigenous. Languages, which I lack, are critical to worldviews because translations to English are not always possible (Barton, 2008; Goulet & Goulet, 2014; Lunney Borden, 2011).

Chapter Twenty-Nine

Research, Technology, and Neocolonialism

Orest Kinasevych

This chapter will examine how modern information technologies are not neutral, that they have been co-opted by corporations and the nation-state and, especially where Indigenous peoples are concerned, these technologies have become vectors of neocolonization. An examination is essential because information technologies such as mobile devices can be of great benefit in bridging geographic and temporal gaps between members of any community. There appear to be opportunities to enhance Indigenous language learning through the appropriate use of technology. However, these potential benefits are not without significant risks that may not be immediately apparent.

Author Positionality

The author's acknowledgement of positionality is intended to be congruent with an Indigenous world-view (Absolon & Willett, 2005):

> The circumstances of colonial history have positioned me as a settler on Turtle Island. I was born and raised on Treaty I territory, in the North End of Winnipeg where I reside today. My parents were Ukrainian refugees of the Second World War who fled the imperialist and genocidal ambitions of Nazi Germany and Stalinism (Brubaker, 1996; Connelly, Roseman, Portnov, David-Fox, & Snyder, 2011). My refugee parents and grand-parents sought safety in Canada but at a dear price. They left behind the lives they had built for themselves, their relations and extended families, friends, their belongings, and the places, traditions, and the communities to which they belonged. As refugees, my parents dearly hoped to one day return "home." As a settler, I recognize that I have been positioned this way as a tool of colonization of the Canadian nation-state. However, I assert my agency as a sovereign individual and disavow my instrumentalization by any nation-state.

Rather, I offer my words and actions to bring justice and peace to my relations, near and far.

The Bias of Technology

Hlynka & Yeaman (1992) and Woolgar (1991) have characterized technology as the writing and then reading of a text, equating any technology to a cultural record that is set down and then retrieved. Selwyn relates the following characterization:

> ...Grint and Woolgar (1997) proposed the notion of 'technology as text'. ... 'written' (configured) ... 'read' (interpreted) ... technologies can have preferred readings built into them by dominant interests.... The metaphor of treating 'technology as text' elegantly draws attention to the often unseen work by designers, financiers, marketers and others in both crafting the materiality and interpretations of devices. It also provides acknowledgment of the opportunities that exist for alternative appropriations and uses of technology (2011, p. 86)

This characterization of technology as text recognizes that on one side there are the creators of technologies and on the other side there are the users of those technologies. Each party plays a role in the interpretation of how a given technology will be applied and in embedding and revealing the values implied through those applications. Consider a circular, analog clock face. This instrument provides indicators that spin from the centre of the face and point to static markers which may be visible or implied by the relative position of the indicators. The original designers of the clock face, using cultural contexts, decided on the division of increments, the number of indicators, the velocity of movement of the indicators, and so on, to create the archetype of the clock face. These indicators and markers likely take their design from that of sundials. Sundials communicate their meaning through how the sun casts a shadow across its face. In the sundial's case, there is a connection between the natural traversal of the sun across the sky and how far along the sun has moved based on the shadow it has cast. A clock face has no direct connection to the natural world. Because of this disconnect from natural, diurnal cycles, the reading of a clock face must be taught and users of the clock face must learn to read, or tell, the time from the relation its indicators and markers.

The clock face, as a technology, offers certain innovations compared to the sundial. It may continue operating in the absence of the sun's light, such as during cloud cover and or at night. It may be placed indoors. It may be positioned in any manner, without reference to the sun's position or the user's position in terms of geographic latitude. At the same time, it introduces an array of potential challenges. The precision of mechanical (or, today, electronic) clock movement allows for greater granularity in how a day can be partitioned. One may well ask whose interests, ultimately, are served? An answer to this question points to the biases written into this simple, yet culturally complex, technology.

One's values are surfaced by how closely one aligns their life to the clock's movements. To what degree does anxiety arise when one's plans do not align with the clock's movements? To what degree do these anxieties dissipate in the absence of clocks? What is the source of values such that they are emotionally linked to a technology? As much as any technology has aided human beings, it has also demanded of them certain adaptations. Humans beings, thereby, have become a part of the technology, adjuncts to its full function.

Figure 6. A machine-readable code representing a short, English-language phrase.

Figure I depicts a graphic that can be read and decoded into plain text by specialized software that understands the particular encoding of the graphic. Meaning is absent in this technology to the human observer: if anything, it asserts its rootedness in technology. The graphical code was generated by software and, so, a device with the appropriate software must be directed at it in order for it to be decoded. The intermediary would be a human operator who would direct one technology at the other in order for these algorithmically-generated codes to be of any human meaning. In this example, humans are instrumental to the technology. They must intercede and they must be aware of how these technologies are to be used. There is no innate indication to a meaning which has not been fully fabricated. Feenberg has remarked that

> The computer simplifies a full-blown person into a 'user' in order to incorporate him or her into the network. Users are decontextualized in the sense that they are stripped of body and community in front of the terminal

and positioned as detached technical subjects. At the same time, a highly simplified world is disclosed to the user... (2010, p. 9)

The "poverty" that results in this "simplified world" is that of an absence of human affective, social, or experiential traits (Feenberg, 2010, p. 9). Marcuse observed that "only in the medium of technology, man and nature become fungible objects of organization" (1991, p. 172). That is, because of technology's demands for intercession, human beings become another resource to be exploited in technology's application.

McLuhan (1966) and Hall (1959) have remarked on how technology and media are extensions of the human person. Clothes are an extension of the skin, claimed McLuhan, and electricity is an extension of the human nervous system. The character of any technology is to be a human extension in order to manipulate the natural world (McLuhan, 1966). However, these extensions insert layers of distance and barriers between people. They also become tools for othering. Storr made the following observation regarding the nature of human aggression:

> It is obviously true that most bomber pilots are no better and no worse than other men. The majority of them given a can of petrol and told to pour it over a child of three and ignite it, would probably disobey the order. Yet, put a decent man in an aeroplane a few hundred feet above a village, and he will kill, without compunction, drop high explosives and napalm and inflict appalling pain and injury on men, women and children. The distance between him and the people he is bombing makes them into an impersonal target, no longer human beings like himself with whom he can identify. (1968, p. 112)

At industrial scales of manufacture and consumerism, and with the concentrations of power in state, military, corporate, and academic institutions, certain technologies become favoured. Furthermore, contemporary media and consumer culture creates an environment amenable to this power. The works of Dusek (2006), Ellul (1964), and Said (1994), provide support to the idea that contemporary information technology is inherently colonialist and imperialist in its design and creates a path for colonization in the realms of language, culture, and world-views. In terms of world-views, Marcuse observed that technology's:

> supreme promise is an ever-more-comfortable life for an ever-growing number of people who, in a strict sense, cannot imagine a qualitatively different universe of discourse and action, for the capacity to contain and manipulate subversive imagination and effort is an integral part of the given society (1991, p. 26)

Indigenous scholars have echoed these concerns about technology. Smith laments that "the unrelenting imperative of corporations and governments to promote technology as a solution to our lives is the same imperative which suppresses and destroys indigenous alternatives" (Smith, 2012, p. 115). At worst, the purpose of any given technology may be deliberately and even maliciously obscured by its creators (Bösch, Erb, Kargl, Kopp, & Pfattheicher, 2016).

Neocolonialism

Neocolonialism is defined by globalization (Kanu, 2006) and through the exploitation of human labour through its "multinational division" (Bhabha, 1994) resulting in "a much more complete capitalist infrastructure" (Spoonley, as cited in Whiteford & Barns, 2002). It is insidious and happens without boats or invading armies but through transnational bureaucracies and processes. This new form of colonialism is an incursion that, like a second wave, washes over societies while they still endure an earlier colonization which had never receded.

Colonial-academic research is a locus of the exploitative use of technology and rational technique. Party to neocolonialism have been not only the military and corporations but also universities (Giroux, 2015). Universities have claimed the creation and legitimization of knowledge as their exclusive purview. This positioning of academia as the font of all knowledge has been problematic due to neocolonialism. Expanding on the work of Smith, Anderson elaborates:

> The promotion of the internationalization of higher education has not been without critique, particularly regarding the role it plays in the spread of (neo)colonial and neoliberal discourses from the west 'outwards,' and the standardization of English-mediated and Anglocentric epistemologies and ontologies, including a bias towards western-based knowledge creation, research methods, methodologies, and academic discourses. What constitutes 'legitimate' research and knowledge has long been determined by colonial powers, who act as gatekeepers to academic communities, both within the west and outside it (2015, p. 176)

This, Anderson claims, is what can be understood as "academic neocolonization" (2015, p. 176). "Research methods, methodologies, and academic discourses" have been the means through which this power was applied. Technology, as a collection of material objects, has been an instrument of the application of this exercise of power. In addition however, also, the instrumentalization of human researchers, as the adjuncts and intermediaries in the use of technology, and the processes they have made routine, must be understood as part of the technological process. Ellul elaborates at length on technology as technique and process in his work (1964). Taken together, research, the circumscription and commodification of knowledge, and the methods and processes of research constrained by technocratic thinking can be seen to contribute to neocolonialism.

Research Methodologies

The imposition of neocolonialism through academic research has been met with resistance from several quarters, among them Indigenous scholars and scholars of emancipatory research methodologies. In particular, Indigenous scholars have asserted critiques of positivist and neocolonial research methods, tools, and techniques (Brown & Strega, 2005; Kovach, 2010). There are several ideas that these critiques espouse that centre on Indigenous world-views. In addition, these critiques align with research discourses that embrace post-positivism, critical theory, and emancipatory research approaches. This alignment could be seen as a progressive effort on the part of Indigenous and non-Indigenous researchers to bring together the most just and inclusive ways toward a shared knowledge of the world.

In this discussion, it must be recognized that colonization brought forth a challenge to the world-views of Indigenous peoples and the colonizers. The dominant powers of colonialism held certain world-views as superior to all others. Since world-views can be seen to inform research, a single world-view constrains research to a single, accepted epistemology. However, according to Wilson, the "awareness of colonization, and the firm belief that Indigenous peoples have their own worldviews,... [has] led to the present stage in the articulation of our own research paradigm" (2008, p. 53). Furthermore,

> 'Humans—feeling, living, breathing, thinking humans—do research. When we try to cut ourselves off at the neck and pretend an objectivity that does not exist in the human world, we become dangerous, to ourselves first, and then to the people around us.' (Hampton, as cited in Wilson, 2008, p. 56).

Positivism as a research approach can be seen as supporting the assertion of a single, objective world-view. Post-positivism re-examines this stance and acknowledges that researchers are themselves fallible and prone to errors in commission or omission (Wilson, 2008). This cannot be otherwise since human beings are creatures of the cultures that they create and the social worlds that they construct. These inform human values which then differ from one society to the next, and even from one era to the next. O'Reilly expands on the observation that post-positivist research approaches

> attempt to reconcile the tension between positivism and various forms of relativism. They acknowledge the real existence but infinite complexity of the social world, that can only be known through the focussed collection of evidence. They also recognise that all knowledge is always limited, open to being proved false, and requires constant reflexive elaboration (2012, p. 58).

Further still from positivism is critical theory "in that it holds that reality is more fluid or plastic than one fixed truth. Critical theorists contend that reality has been shaped into its present form by our cultural, gender, social and other values" (Wilson, 2008, p. 36). Therefore, not only are research questions value-laden and prone to bias, so, too, is the understanding of what might constitute knowledge and truth. Evans agrees, adding that "since science is an inherently social process, in which egos and ideologies frequently overcome rational thought, it must be riddled with nontheoretical interests" (2011, p. 801). Challenging the notion of monolithic, colonialist knowledge, Nichols and Allen-Brown contend that knowledge is mutable "depending on the culture, the history, and the power in which it is embedded" (1996, p. 226). Critical theory provides a social justice perspective, in that it confronts "what is taken for granted in culture" and offers opportunities for equity (McCarthy, as cited in Nichols & Allen-Brown, 1996, p. 226). Nichols and Allen-Brown add that "because critical theories run contrary to that which oppresses people, the theories usually are positive and hopeful" (1996, p. 226). Critical theory challenges "rationality, science, and the technical" and in doing so brings "balance with other aspects of life, such as moral perspectives" (Nichols & Allen-Brown, 1996, p. 228). In its analysis of social constructs of knowledge, critical theory is also important in understanding the role of technology and media in human societies (Feenberg, 2010).

Equipped with approaches such as post-positivism and critical theory, researchers can begin to take an anti-oppressive stance in the research they undertake. Such a stance respects the humanity of participants and the value of their world-view, their communities, and the non-human aspects that comprise their world. More meaningfully, it shifts the power inherent in research activities over to participants. Potts and Brown underscore this aspect of the anti-oppressive stance, stating that

Being an anti-oppressive researcher means that there is political purpose and action to your research work.... It means making a commitment to the people you are working with personally and professionally in order to mutually foster conditions for social justice and research. It is about paying attention to, and shifting, how power relations work in and through the processes of doing research (2005, p. 255).

These approaches may serve Indigenous communities well. The source of what counts as knowledge is shifted from the colonial centres of power. Research becomes, in these ways, more respectful of the humanity of Indigenous participants and of their needs. These approaches may also reflect, to some degree, how "'Indigenous researchers ground their research knowingly in the lives of real persons as individuals and social beings, not on the world of ideas'" (Weber-Pillwax, as cited in Wilson, 2008, p. 60).

Conclusion

Can, then, technology play an emancipatory role in research? A tentative 'yes' would be possible if technology is truly a value-neutral tool. However, as has been argued in this chapter, just as there are varying epistemologies that inform research methods, so, too, are there values that inform technologies and the purposes to which they can be applied. A relationship that is mediated through technology is one where the human values of both researcher and participant may be smothered in the name of science. Where the research purpose is to improve the condition of human societies, research that acknowledges relationships through social interaction at a human scale is more likely to yield the kind of answers that researchers may truly be seeking.

References

Absolon, K., & Willett, C. (2005). Putting Ourselves Forward: Location in Aboriginal Research. In L. Brown & S. Strega (Eds.), *Research as Resistance: Critical, Indigenous and Anti-oppressive Approaches* (pp. 97–126). Canadian Scholars' Press.

Anderson, T. (2015). Seeking Internationalization: The State of Canadian Higher Education. *The Canadian Journal of Higher Education, 45*(4), 166–187.

Bhabha, H. K. (1994). *The location of culture*. London and New York: Routledge. Retrieved from https://ia601303.us.archive.org/24/items/TheLocationOfCultureBHABHA/the%20location%20of%20culture%20BHABHA.pdf

Bösch, C., Erb, B., Kargl, F., Kopp, H., & Pfattheicher, S. (2016). Tales from the Dark Side: Privacy Dark Strategies and Privacy Dark Patterns. *Proceedings on Privacy Enhancing Technologies, 2016*(4), 237–254. https://doi.org/10.1515/popets-2016-0038

Brown, L., & Strega, S. (Eds.). (2005). *Research as Resistance: Critical, Indigenous and Anti-oppressive Approaches*. Canadian Scholars' Press.

Brubaker, R. (1996). *Nationalism Reframed: Nationhood and the National Question in the New Europe*. Cambridge, UK: Cambridge University Press.

Connelly, J., Roseman, M., Portnov, A., David-Fox, M., & Snyder, T. (2011). Timothy Snyder, Bloodlands: Europe between Hitler and Stalin. *Journal of Genocide Research*, 13(3), 313–352. https://doi.org/10.1080/14623528.2011.606703

Dusek, V. (2006). *Philosophy of Technology: An Introduction*. Wiley.

Ellul, J. (1964). *The Technological Society*. (J. Wilkinson, Trans.). New York: Alfred A. Knopf, Inc.

Evans, M. A. (2011). A critical-realist response to the postmodern agenda in instructional design and technology: a way forward. *Educational Technology Research and Development*, 59(6), 799–815. https://doi.org/10.1007/s11423-011-9194-5

Feenberg, A. (2010). *Critical Theory of Technology*. Manuscript. Retrieved from http://www.sfu.ca/~andrewf/books/Critical_Theory_Technology.pdf

Giroux, H. A. (2015). *University in Chains: Confronting the Military-Industrial-Academic Complex* (EPUB). New York: Routledge.

Hall, E. T. (1959). *The silent language*. New York: Doubleday.

Hlynka, D., & Yeaman, A. R. J. (1992). Postmodern Educational Technology. ERIC Digest. Retrieved from http://eric.ed.gov/?id=ED348042

Kanu, Y. (Ed.). (2006). *Curriculum as Cultural Practice: Postcolonial Imaginations*. University of Toronto Press.

Kovach, M. (2010). *Indigenous Methodologies: Characteristics, Conversations, and Contexts*. University of Toronto Press.

Marcuse, H. (1991). *One-Dimensional Man: Studies in the Ideology of Advanced Industrial Society* (Second edition). Oxon, UK and New York: Routledge.

McLuhan, H. M. (1966). *Understanding media: The extensions of man* (2nd edition). New York: Signet Books.

Nichols, R. G., & Allen-Brown, V. (1996). Critical theory and educational technology. In D. H. Jonassen (Ed.), *Handbook of research for educational communications and technology* (1st edition, pp. 226–252). Retrieved from http://www.aect.org/edtech/ed1/

O'Reilly, K. (2012). *Ethnographic Methods*. Oxon, UK: Routledge.

Potts, K., & Brown, L. (2005). Becoming an Anti-Oppressive Researcher. In L. Brown & S. Strega (Eds.), *Research as Resistance: Critical, Indigenous and Anti-oppressive Approaches* (pp. 255–286). Canadian Scholars' Press.

Said, E. W. (1994). *Culture and Imperialism*. New York: Vintage Books.

Selwyn, N. (2011). Making sense of young people, education and digital technology: the role of sociological theory. *Oxford Review of Education*, 38(1), 81–96. https://doi.org/10.1080/03054985.2011.577949

Smith, L. T. (2012). *Decolonizing Methodologies: Research and Indigenous Peoples* (Second edition). Dunedin: Otago University Press.

Storr, A. (1968). *Human Aggression*. London: Allen Lane, Penguin Press.

Whiteford, G., & Barns, M. (2002). Te Ao Hurihuri. In W. E. Pentland, A. S. Harvey, M. P. Lawton, & M. A. McColl (Eds.), *Time Use Research in the Social Sciences* (pp. 211–230). Springer US. Retrieved from http://link.springer.com/chapter/10.1007/0-306-47155-8_10

Wilson, S. (2008). *Research is ceremony: Indigenous research methods*. Black Point, NS: Fernwood Publishing.

Woolgar, S. (1991). The Turn to Technology in Social Studies of Science. *Science, Technology & Human Values*, 16(1), 20–50. https://doi.org/10.1177/016224399101600102

Decolonizing Through Counter-Narratives

Working to Disrupt Colonizing Systems and Structures

Chapter Thirty

"In this war of words"

Canada 150 and the (re) Telling of History

Wanda Hounslow

Introduction

In this war of words, Whites explore, Indians wander; Whites have battles or victories, Indians massacre and murder; Whites scout, Indians lurk; Whites go westward, Indians go bloodthirsty; Whites defend themselves, Indians "seek revenge"; Whites appear as officials who simply assume authority, Indians are "haughty," "insolent," "saucy," or "impudent" (when they assume equality); Whites have faiths, and so they pray; Indians have superstitions, and so they conjure: whites may be peasant, Indians are primitive; Whites may be "brutes," but Indians remain savage and barbaric in the "heathen" lands (LaRocque, 2011, p. 60).

This chapter examines the ways in which contemporary discourses reflect and reinforce unequal power-relations and structures of oppression. The aim of the project is to uncover implicit assumptions embedded in contemporary re-settler and colonial discourses that justify and maintain the power structures that underlie them. A critical analysis of this nature seeks to problematize narratives that have historically been utilized to validate settler-colonial domination through nation-building and forced assimilation projects and continue to inform institutions, policies and programs today.

The analysis is situated in post-colonial and decolonizing paradigms which understand colonial domination as structural in form, yet processual in nature; as an adaptive and ongoing force (Regan, 2010; Smith, 1999; LaRocque, 2011; Brown and Strega, 2005; McLeod, 2013; Memmi, 2013;

Coburn and LaRocque, 2015; Alfred and Corntassel, 2005; Blaut, 1993). From this perspective, language and the production of knowledge are enmeshed with social and political context that sustain narratives, and ultimately the structures of, dominance and oppression. Critical discourse analysis will explore the ways in which the Government of Canada's 'Canada 150' web-based promotional material functions to maintain the meta-narrative of colonial superiority in its (re)telling of history.

I conclude that decolonization requires actively "unsettling" (Regan, 2010) colonial and Eurocentric regimes of power; to move beyond symbolic forms of reconciliation and recognition towards transformative action (Tuck and Yang, 2012; Coburn and LaRocque, 2015; Brown and Strega, 2005). One way to do this is to interrogate ontological and epistemological assumptions underpinning national and historical discourses (Anderson and Robertson, 2011; Berkhofer, 1979; Dickason, 1984; Francis, 1993; Harding, 2006; Mangan, 1993; Duchemin, 1990).

Methodology, Terminology, and Reflexivity

Decolonizing methodologies interrogate the ways in which Eurocentric and colonial ideologies are embedded in scholarship and thus, problematizes these taken-for-granted 'truths' (Smith, 1999; Brown and Strega, 2005; Regan, 2010; Coburn and LaRocque, 2015; Alfred and Corntassel, 2005; Blaut, 1993). This approach acknowledges the role that power plays in the production of knowledge and compels us to examine implicit assumptions and narratives that reinforce colonial domination and violence; it acknowledges the colonial present which discourses of reconciliation overlook (Coulthard, 2014). In keeping with this approach, this project uses critical discourse analysis to interrogate how discourses of nationalism are used to maintain and reproduce settler-colonial power and justify its ongoing violence.

Critical discourse analysis (CDA) provides needed insight into the ways in which language is used to produce, reproduce and maintain unequal and destructive power relations; it conveys not only what is said and who has the power to define its truth, but also who is to be silenced. (Foucault, 1990; Fairclough, 2013; van Dijk, 2015; Jørgensen and Phillips, 2002; Henry and Tator, 2002). Likewise, contemporary historical narratives are a subjective interpretation of events; in a colonial context, these discursive representations can undermine Indigenous people's claims to self-determination while advancing colonial superiority and domination (Green, 1995). In this way, discourses are able to naturalize structural and institutional oppression that, in this instance, reproduce settler-colonial power.

In keeping with decolonizing methodologies, I acknowledge the problematic nature of the term 'Indigenous' as one that "appears to collectivize many distinct populations whose experiences under imperialism have been vastly different" (Smith, 1999, p. 6). When appropriate, I use the term 'Indigenous peoples' in an understanding of the "right of peoples to self-determination" (Smith, 1999, p. 7).

Additionally, I employ LaRocque's (2011) concept of re-settler which challenges the notion that Europeans "own the notion of 'settler' and 'settlement'" (p. 8). As LaRocque and others argue, colonial expansion relied on the myth of emptiness; uninhabited, unsettled and savage lands and peoples to which civilization and progress was gifted by the Europeans (Blaut, 1993, Memmi, 2013; Jennings, 1975). To label all non-Indigenous people as 'settler' assumes that Indigenous peoples were not settled inhabitants of this land and perpetuated Eurocentric ideologies which facilitated the initial colonial project (LaRocque, 2011).

Lastly, I acknowledge that the term 'decolonization' might act as yet another discursive trope to further entrench racist ideology (Tuck and Yang, 2012). As Tuck and Yang (2012) state,

> Decolonization as a metaphor allows people to equivocate these contradictory decolonial desires because it turns decolonization into an empty signifier to be filled by any track towards liberation. In reality, the tracks walk all over land/people in settler contexts. Though the details are not fixed or agreed upon, in our view, decolonizaton in the settler colonial context must involve the repatriation of land simultaneous to the recognition of how land and relations to land have always already been differently understood and enacted; that is, *all* of the land, and not just symbolically (p. 7).

As such, I recognize the role that deconstruction, dismantling and repatriation must take in decolonization. As a non-Indigenous scholar, I situate myself, and this study, in   allyship to this transformative effort by confronting and exposing "colonial mentality, moral indifference, and historical ignorance as part of a massive truth-telling about Canada's past and present relationship with the original inhabitants of this land" (Alfred, 2010, p. x).

Knowledge, Discourse and the Colonial Project

Language and knowledge production have historically been utilized to validate the colonial project and, by extension, Western superiority and dominance (Smith, 1999; Blaut, 1993; LaRocque, 2011; Walker, 1971; Duchemin, 1990; Walker, 1971; Berkhofer, 1979; Dickason, 1984). For example, the theory of diffusionism assumes that there is a central point of innovation through which all other communities are changed; Eurocentric diffusionism places Europe at this central point (Blaut, 1993). As Blaut (1993) argues, the production of knowledge became an essential component to the rapid expansion of colonialism in the eighteenth and nineteenth centuries, and diffusionism, a "super theory" (p. 11) upon which all other theories were developed. These theories were able to justify the colonial project as a natural, progressive, and inevitable process, indeed as benevolent, by developing race-related stereotypes of colonized lands and peoples as uninhabited, unsettled and savage (Woolford, 2015).

Discursive representations of European civilization (superiority) and Indigenous savagery (inferiority) served as justification for numerous policies of dispossession and genocide throughout the eighteenth and nineteenth centuries, such as forced relocation to reserve lands and forced assimilation in the Indian Residential Schools (IRS) system (Regan, 2010; TRCC, 2012; Milloy, 1999; TRCC, 2015). The *Indian Act* federally mandated and legally enforced the attendance of Indigenous children in the IRS and, through forced assimilation, was intended to "bring Indian status to an end" (TRCC, 2012, p. 11) and to "continue until there is not a single Indian in Canada that has not been absorbed into the body politic (Duncan Campbell Scott, cited in TRCC, 2012, p. 12). Despite economic strains and rampant criticisms of inadequate care, poor living conditions, illnesses, deaths and abuse, a total of 130 residential schools existed during the system's operation (TRCC, 2012; Milloy, 1999; TRCC, 2015).

During the 1950s and 1960s, the Canadian government made amendments to the *Indian Act* that began the transfer of Indigenous health, schooling and welfare services to the provinces, and emphasizing the integration of Indigenous children into the public education system (Bennett, Blackstock and De La Ronde, 2005). While some cite this era as a time when colonial assimilationist policies came to an end, a critical interrogation reveals that, while the push towards assimilation had eased, new sites of control were being developed (Woolford, 2015; Bennett, Blackstock and De La Ronde, 2005). The analysis to follow seeks to examine this shifting form and its persistent structural underpinnings.

'Canada 150' and the (re)Telling of History

Green (1995) suggests that historical representations are a subjective interpretation of events that, in a colonial context, are meant to undermine Indigenous people's claims to self-determination while advancing colonial superiority and domination. Following this line of thinking, I analyze the Government of Canada's 'Canada 150' web-based promotional material (http://canada.pch.gc.ca/eng/1468854891549) and consider how it functions to maintain the meta-narrative of re-settler superiority, thereby reinforcing the structural undergirding of colonialism's shifting form. Guided by post-colonial and decolonizing methodologies, I pay particular attention to three main tropes of colonial myth-making:

1. The Myth of European Progress
2. The Myth of the Colonizer
3. The Rhetoric of Reconciliation

The Myth of European Progress

Colonial narratives that define progress as a linear movement through time, in which the central point of innovation hails from Europe, naturalizes the colonial model; it presumes that civilization occurs from the diffusion of progressive European ideas and assumes Western superiority (Blaut, 1993). Early colonial models utilized discourses of uninhabited and savage lands and peoples in order to justify intrusion, resource extraction, accumulation, and expansion (Memmi, 1993; Berkhofer, 1979; Jennings, 1975; Milloy, 1999; Harding, 2006; Walker, 1971). However, discourses of progress shift over time in order to adapt to emerging technologies of control, yet its structural undergirding remains intact; the maintenance of power through the establishment of superiority. Thus, contemporary forms of colonial power utilize discourses of modernization and development, rather than civilization and savagery. However, they establish a similar result: a justification for colonial oppression (Alfred and Corntassel, 2005; Bennett Blackstock and De La Ronde, 2005; Woolford, 2015).

A critical reading of the 'Canada 150' promotional material exposes a similar narrative. A page titled, "Aboriginal arts, culture and heritage" invites the reader to:

> Learn about Aboriginal arts, culture and heritage that are woven into the fabric of our country. Indigenous and Northern Affairs Canada (INAC) works with Aboriginal partners to help celebrate, raise awareness of, and preserve Aboriginal arts, culture and heritage. As well, INAC supports Aboriginal people (First Nations, Inuit and Metis) and Northerners in their efforts to: improve social well-being and economic prosperity; develop healthier, more sustainable communities and participate more fully in

Canada's political, social and economic development – to the benefit of all Canadians(http://www.aadncaandc.gc.ca/eng/1100100012788/1100100 012792).

Several discursive markers throughout this text convey elements of colonial paternalism such as "support," "improve," "develop" and "benefit." The passage, in its entirety, denotes a level of superiority to colonial governing bodies, in their assistance to, what Berkhofer (1979) cites as "domestic dependent nations" (p. 164). In particular, the passage that suggests that INAC supports Indigenous communities to "improve social well-being and economic prosperity, develop healthier, more sustainable communities and participate more fully in Canada's political, social and economic development – to the benefit of all Canadians" provides a stark example of a persistent colonial narrative in which colonial "civilization stands for what is illuminated, progressive, and decent" (LaRocque, 2011, p. 41).

The Myth of the Colonizer

Glorification, as the "creation of language celebrating colonial identities" (Green, cited in LaRocque, 2011, p. 37), justifies unequal power relations and applies a sense of nobility to the colonizer (LaRocque, 2011). This false representation of the colonizer rewrites historical events through explicit omission of the violence enacted on Indigenous peoples in order to achieve said accomplishments (Memmi, 2013). As Memmi (2013) suggests, "self-justification thus leads to a veritable ideal reconstruction" (p. 55). By ascribing positive traits to colonial pursuits, actions of the colonizer are presented as justified, and the history is rewritten accordingly.

Such a tactic is exemplified in the 'Canada 150' promotional material that offers additional links to "Events, celebrations and commemorations" (http://canada.pch.gc.ca/eng/1444411481693/1444411709508). This page invites us to celebrate the life of Sir John A. Macdonald, the first prime minister of Canada. It states:

> Sir John A. Macdonald is remembered for his role in the expansion of Canada's boundaries from sea to sea, the completion of the Canadian Pacific Railway, the creation of the North-West Mounted Police, and the development of a National Policy that levied high tariffs on imported goods to shield Canadian manufacturers from American competition. (https://www.google.com/culturalinstitute/beta/exhibit/QRFWD7Z-).

The site also quotes Sir Wilfrid Laurier, the seventh Prime Minister of Canada, as stating: "As to his statesmanship, it is written in the history of Canada. It may be said without any exaggeration whatever, that the life of Sir John A. Macdonald...is the history of Canada."

However, James Daschuk (2013), author of *Clearing the Plains*, details a very different history of Sir John. A Macdonald's conservative leadership and the treaty-making process following 1867; one that was driven by "a policy of submission shaped by a policy of starvation" (p. 114). This was during a time of increasing Indigenous resistance to colonial intrusion that encumbered Macdonald's pursuit of expansion from "sea to sea." This was also a time of national famine and under MacDonald's leadership, rations, or a lack thereof, were used as a means of coercing starving Indigenous peoples into submitting to treaty and relocation to reserve lands. In addressing the House of Commons, Macdonald stressed that he was keeping the hungry from dying, but that food would be refused "until the Indians were on the verge of starvation" (cited in Daschuk, 2013, p. 134). And, as Daschuk states, "as hunger spread across the plains, so did disease" (2013, p. 120). The total number of Indigenous lives lost during this time is unclear, but an estimate of the Qu'Appelle reserves indicates that death rates rose from 4% to nearly 13% in only five years.

The Rhetoric of Reconciliation

A portion of the 'Canada 150' material titled "First Nations in Canada" invites the reader to learn about the history of Indigenous Peoples and Reconciliation (http://canada.pch.gc.ca/eng/1446836350664). The information is provided in a six-part anthology that begins by detailing the "Early First Nations." The publication continues by acknowledging the "civilization program" beginning with the 1839 passing of the *Crown Lands Protection Act*, and details several harmful policies that followed, such as the introduction of the *Indian Act* in 1876. It also mentions the use of assimilation in the Indian Residential Schools (IRS), as well as Indigenous acts of resistance such as the Oka standoff in the summer of 1990. However, the anthology ends abruptly with the "Residential Schools Apology," employing discourses of commemoration and reconciliation, which imply an end to colonial harms.

While truth and reconciliation discourses such as these provide the potential for decolonization, many argue that liberal policies of recognition and reconciliation have "come to serve the interests of colonial power" (Coulthard, 2014, p. 25). The state's assertion that colonial injustices are a thing of the past invisibilizes the present state of colonial oppression (Coulthard, 2014).

It follows that a necessary line of reasoning is one that poses the question: What are the implications of implicit assumptions embedded in contemporary discourses of nationalism that imply an end to colonial harms? As Memmi (2013) argues, in order to legitimize the colonial project, and absolve colonizer guilt, history must be rewritten in such a way as to falsify actions as progressive achievements. A second tactic, he states, is to "harp on the [colonized] demerits" (Memmi, 2013, p. 53). By writing these falsehoods into law, embedding them within institutions and internalizing them as memory, these discursive representations become "absolute fact" (Memmi, 2013, p.53). I argue that the 'Canada 150' web-based promotional material demonstrates that the notion of progress persists as a national re-settler narrative. Furthermore, it's (re) telling of history relegates colonial violence to the past and, by omission, justifies present colonial harms such as those experienced by Indigenous children who have been separated from their families and placed in the child welfare system.

Discussion: Colonialism 150[160]

While the majority of residential schools were officially shuttered between 1950 and 1980, critical scholars argue that colonial policies of assimilation were merely shifting and evolving (Bennett, Blackstock and De La Ronde, 2005; Walsh and Aarrestad, 2015). From the mid-1960s to the mid-1980s, it is estimated that approximately 15,000 Indigenous children were removed from their families by provincially run child welfare services, then fostered or adopted into non-Indigenous homes (Bennett, Blackstock and De La Ronde, 2005). It is argued that Indigenous child welfare services in the 1960s had evolved from the Eurocentric set of values and beliefs that had informed the implementation of the residential schooling system (Blackstock, Brown and Bennett, 2007; Libesman, 2004). Thus, similar to the 'civilizing mission' of the missionary-run residential schools, Indigenous child welfare practices, primarily enforced by non-indigenous social workers, was premised on the principle that "the only hope for the salvation of the Indian people lay in the removal of their children" (Sinclair, 2007, p. 67).

The over-representation of Indigenous children in custody continues to plague the child welfare system today and as Walsh and Aarrestad (2015) argue, it is a crisis that is "inextricably bound up with persistent colonialism" (p. 74). Indeed, as Blackstock and Trocme (2005) state, "we estimate that there may be as many as three times more Aboriginal children in the care of child welfare authorities now than were placed in residential schools at the height of those operations in the 1940s" (p. 13). Moreover, it is argued that the majority of Indigenous children removed from their homes come into contact with the child welfare system because of problems associated with the residual effects of settler-colonial dispossession and the residential schooling system, such as poverty, rather than physical or sexual violence (Blackstock and Trocme, 2005; Trocme, Knoke and Blackstock, 2004).

I argue that the justification, rationale, glorification, myth-making and rhetoric of progress, that structurally maintained and reinforced the initial colonial project and assimilationist policies, underpin the practices of contemporary child welfare practices. While the discourses shave shifted and evolved, the structural undergirding remains intact. As evidenced through a critical discourse analysis of the 'Canada 150' web-based promotional material, the notion of progress persists as a national re-settler narrative. It continues to denote a sense of superiority to colonial regulating bodies and justifies their continued intrusion, domination and oppression. Additionally, the rhetoric of reconciliation and its (re)telling of history, relegates colonial violence, if remembered at all, to the past and, by omission, justifies present colonial harms such as those experienced by Indigenous children who have been separated from their families and placed in the child welfare system.

Conclusion

This critical analysis of the Government of Canada's 'Canada 150' web-based promotional material has examined the ways in which national narratives and discourses function to maintain the structural foundations of colonial superiority. In its (re)telling of history, I argue that it falsely represents the true nature of the colonial project in its historical and contemporary form and thereby (re)establishes a rationale of colonial superiority. I argue that the discourses evident in the 'Canada 150' material are used to justify persistent and adaptive eliminative strategies such as the ongoing removal of Indigenous children to child welfare custody. I conclude that that de-colonization requires actively deconstructing colonial and Eurocentric regimes of power; to move beyond symbolic forms of reconciliation by interrogating and exposing colonial assumptions that underpin national narratives and by replacing colonial myth-making with historical accuracy.

References

Alfred, T. (2010). Forward. Unsettling the settler within: Indian residential schools, truth telling, and reconciliation in Canada. UBC Press.

Alfred, T., & Corntassel, J. (2005). Being Indigenous: Resurgences against contemporary colonialism. Government and Opposition, 40(4), 597-614.

Anderson, M. C., & Robertson, C. L. (2011). Seeing red: A history of natives in Canadian newspapers. Univ. of Manitoba Press.

Bennett, M., Blackstock, C., & De La Ronde, R. (2005). A literature review and annotated bibliography on aspects of Aboriginal child welfare in Canada. First Nations Child & Family Caring Society of Canada.

Berkhofer, R. F. (1979). The white man's Indian: Images of the American Indian from Columbus to the present. Vintage.

Blackstock, C. (2011). The Canadian human rights tribunal on First Nations child welfare: Why if Canada wins, equality and justice lose. Children and Youth Services Review, 33(1), 187-194.

Blackstock, C., & Trocmé, N. (2005). Community-based child welfare for Aboriginal children: Supporting resilience through structural change. Social Policy Journal of New Zealand, 24(12), 12-33.

Blaut, J. M. (1993). The colonizer's model of the world: Geographical diffusionism and Eurocentric history. Guilford Press.

Brown, L. A., & Strega, S. (2005). Research as resistance: Critical, indigenous and anti-oppressive approaches. Canadian Scholars' Press.

Coburn E. & LaRocque, E. (2015). More Will Sing Their Way to Freedom: Indigenous Resistance and Resurgence. Fernwood Publishing.

Coulthard, G. S. (2014). Red skin, white masks: Rejecting the colonial politics of recognition (p. 256).

Daschuk, J. (2013). Clearing the plains. Disease, Politics of Starvation, and the Loss of Aboriginal Life.

Dickason, O. P. (1984). The Myth of the Savage: and the Beginnings of French Colonialism in the Americas. University of Alberta Press.

Duchemin, P. (1990). A Parcel of Whelps: Alexander Mackenzie among the Indians. In E.H. New (Ed.), Native Writers and Canadian Writing. Vancouver: UBC Press.

Fairclough, N. (2013). Critical discourse analysis: The critical study of language. Routledge.

Foucault, M. (1990). The history of sexuality. Volume 1: An introduction. Translated by Robert Hurley.

Francis, D. (1992). The imaginary Indian: The image of the Indian in Canadian culture. Arsenal Pulp Press.

Green, J. (1995). Towards a détente with history: Confronting Canada's colonial legacy. International Journal of Canadian Studies, 12, 85-105.

Harding, R. (2006). Historical representations of aboriginal people in the Canadian news media. Discourse & Society, 17(2), 205-235.

Henry, F., & Tator, C. (2002). Discourses of domination: Racial bias in the Canadian English-language press. University of Toronto Press.

Jennings, F. (1975). The invasion of America: Indians, colonialism, and the cant of conquest. University of North Carolina Press.

Jørgensen, M. W., & Phillips, L. J. (2002). Discourse analysis as theory and method. Sage.

LaRocque, E. (2011). When the other is me: Native resistance discourse, 1850-1990. Univ. of Manitoba Press.

Libesman, T. (2004). Child welfare approaches for Indigenous communities: International perspectives.

Mangan, J. A. (1993). Images for Confident Control: Stereotypes in Imperial Discourse. The Imerperial Curriculum: Racial Images and Education in the British Colonial Experience, edited by J. A. Mangan. London, Routledge.

McLeod, J. (2013). Beginning postcolonialism. Oxford University Press.

Milloy, J. S. (1999). A national crime: The Canadian government and the residential school system, 1879 to 1986 (Vol. 11). Univ. of Manitoba Press.

Memmi, A. (2013). The colonizer and the colonized. Routledge.
Regan, P. (2010). Unsettling the settler within: Indian residential schools, truth telling, and reconciliation in Canada. UBC Press.
Sinclair, R. (2007). Identity lost and found: Lessons from the sixties scoop. First Peoples Child & Family Review, 3(1), 65-82.
TRCC. (2012). They Came for the Children: Canada, Aboriginal Peoples, and Residential Schools. The Truth and Reconciliation Commission of Canada. Winnipeg, MB.
TRCC. (2015). Honouring the Truth, Reconciling for the Future: Summary of the Final Report of the Truth and Reconciliation Commission of Canada. Ottawa: Truth and Reconciliation Commission of Canada.
Trocmé, N., Knoke, D., & Blackstock, C. (2004). Pathways to the overrepresentation of Aboriginal children in Canada's child welfare system. Social Service Review, 78(4), 577-600.
Tuck, E., & Yang, K. W. (2012). Decolonization is not a metaphor. Decolonization: Indigeneity, Education & Society, 1(1).
Van Dijk, T. A. (2001). Discourse, ideology and context. Folia Linguistica, 35(1-2), 11-40.
Walker, J. W. S. G. (1971). The Indian in Canadian historical writing. Historical Papers, 6(1).
Walsh, C.A. and Aarrestad, S.A. (2015). Incarceration and Aboriginal Women in Canada: Acts of Resilience and Resistance. In E. Coburn (Ed.), More Will Sing Their Way to Freedom. Winnipeg: Fernwood Publishing.
Woolford, A. (2015). This benevolent experiment: Indigenous boarding schools, genocide, and redress in Canada and the United States. U of Nebraska Press.

notes

[160] Conceptualized by artist Eric Ritskes – see CBC article "What does Canada 150 mean for Indigenous communities?" retrieved from http://www.cbc.ca/radio/thecurrent/the-current-for-march-16-2017-1.4026463/what-does-canada-150-mean-for-indigenous-communities-1.4027484

Chapter Thirty-One

Deconstruction of Barriers in Anti-Racist/Decolonization Discussions Trough the Education of Canadians Vis-à-vis DiAngelo's Theory

"White Fragility"

Belinda (Wandering Spirit) Nicholson

The foundation of North American society is colonialism. A human cultural hierarchical scale, created and reinforced by European "re-settlers" (LaRocque, 7). This has created the dichotomy of civilized/savage (civ/sav) or the colonizer/colonized in Canadian society (LaRocque, Memmi). Sociologically and structurally these colonial maxims are both insidious and pervasive; they create a framework in which all interactions between the colonizer and the colonized are governed. In contemporary society, anti-racism and decolonization have become important discussions, with both non-whites and whites claiming their goal is unified. Yet positive change is slow. When applying DiAngelo's theory of "White Fragility" to the topic of decolonization, it becomes evident why decolonization has been delayed. White Fragility acts as a barrier to appropriate discussions, and until this concept is better understood and dealt with – progress towards decolonization in North American society will continue to face obstacles.

In North America, as with other nations, colonialism is fundamentally entrenched in society. Struggles with power and oppression, arise on both a macro and micro level every day in Canada and the United States. To first approach a macro level discussion about colonization in North American society, a working definition is imperative in order to frame this discourse. In Oxford University's Dictionary, they define *colonialism* as: "the policy or practice of acquiring full or partial political control over another country, occupying it with settlers, and exploiting it economically" ("colonialism"). This rudimentary definition provides a base from which an exploration of colonization in North America can occur, but can be viewed as overly simplistic and negates many other important components of colonialism. This definition will be expanded upon to create a more valid description to gain a fuller understanding of the impacts of colonialism on North American society and the attempts (or lack thereof) towards decolonization.

Joyce A. Green delves into Canada's colonial origin in her paper "Towards A Détente with History: confronting Canada's Colonial Legacy" by defining her interpretation of colonialism and its interplay with imperialism in North America:

> While the term "colonialism" is used throughout [Green's paper], the author accepts the ontological relation of colonialism to imperialism, grounded in the emergence and expansion of the global phase of capitalism. Arguments are premised on the view...that imperialism and colonialism are economically motivated, but also culturally embedded processes which create and also suppress knowledge. In Said's words, "Both are supported and perhaps even impelled by impressive ideological formations that include notions that certain territories and people require and beseech domination, as well as forms of knowledge affiliated with domination..." (Green 86; as qtd. in Green 86).

Green's definition of colonialism as a financial endeavour mirrors Oxford Dictionary's definition. Yet Green's description is more developed. She includes the cultural impact and suppression of knowledge, along with the pairing of imperialism and capitalism in her definition.

For an even more nuanced definition of colonialism, we can explore "The Colonial Experience" by Peter Puxley. A post-colonial theorist, Puxley comprehensively details the various elements in colonialism. One such element is the activeness of colonialism, that it is a dynamic process, and not a static one. Puxley states that "Colonialism must be seen as an experience, and not simply a structural relationship. As such, it conditions both the colonizers and the colonized" (104). Puxley also discusses the "psychology of colonialism" (104). He theorizes that colonialism breaks the innately human cycle of: "action-reflection-consciousness-choice [...] the essential ingredient[s] of being human" which takes away the capacity for conscious actions and therefore the colonized person's humanity (107-109). He argues,

> The colonial relationship [...] is maintained by replacing human consciousness, which is the awareness of the human vocation of man as subject and creator of his world, with a colonial false-consciousness, with its dehumanized concept of man as object rather than subject of his world, and

with its natural concomitants at the social level: racism and cultural superiority" (Puxley, 109)

Puxley lists a few more categories of colonialism: the inherent structural violence, bureaucracies as a justification to overlook despotic action and the "theft of human history" (112). Overall Puxley sums up colonialism as the elimination of choice from the oppressed, which he calls the removal of humanity. This act of dehumanization acts upon the very basis of human rights, the need for conscious action and autonomy. This in turn, further subjugates the colonized and perpetuates colonialism on a societal level.

When looking at Puxley's definition – he demonstrates how members of North American society may be influenced by colonialism. One must remain mindful, that these 'influences' do not excuse one's ignorance or actions (or absence of action) in challenging their (or societies) harmful behaviours. They merely provide a jump off point in disrupting and redirecting conversations in order to educate the general public on challenging our colonial roots.

The Colonizer, the Colonized and The Civ/Sav Dichotomy

After the invasion and the imposition of colonialism, a dynamic between the Euro-whites and the other Nations occurred: of the colonizer and the colonized. This dichotomy becomes the name of Albert Memmi's groundbreaking book. Born in Tunisia, Memmi states he was a "sort of a half-breed of colonization, understanding everyone because I belonged completely to no one" (xvi). This paradox of his identity meant Memmi had insider information on both sides of colonialism, and as a result, his writing encompasses both viewpoints.

Peter Puxley also weighed in on the colonizer/colonized relationship. "If it can be shown that the product of a colonial relationship is dehumanization, then we must assume that the relationship is opposed to the development of not only the colonized but also the colonizer. If human life entails acting out a uniquely human vocation, then the colonial relationship destroys rather than creates life" (103). Puxley's statement closely echoes Albert Memmi's perspective on the colonial relationship. Memmi states "for if colonization destroys the colonized, it also rots the colonizer" (xvii). Through both these theorists, it is made clear that it is a fundamental truth that colonialism erodes all members of Canadian society.

Dr. Emma LaRocque's book, *When the Other is Me*, is the "inevitable Aboriginal contrapuntal reply to Canada's colonial constructs" (4). In her introduction, LaRocque discusses the interplay between the colonizer and the colonized. She quotes Memmi who states "The distance which colonization places between him and the colonized must be accounted for and, to justify himself, he increases this distance still further by placing the two figures irretrievably in opposition; his glorious position and the despicable one of the civilized" (LaRocque 3,4). LaRocque goes on to explain,

> This distance has been fashioned in terms of civilization confronting savagery (or as we might say, "savagism"), a super-myth that has provided the basis for the colonizer's psychology and institutions. This means that, as Canadian Native and non-Native peoples, we find ourselves, our respective cultures, lives, and experiences, constructed and divided as diametrically opposite to each other (4)

LaRocque builds on her frame of the civ/sav, Native/non-Native dichotomy by explaining, "behind the dichotomy of civilization versus savagery is the long-held belief that humankind evolved from the primitive to the most advanced, from the savage to the civilized" (39). When looking at current society, it can be argued that this belief is still expressed. The idea that the Euro-whites/settlers/re-settlers were the 'advanced' people, the creators of history, the civilized, still occurs. Through textbooks, classrooms and general discussions, these categories and ideas are upheld. Therefore, when we wade through the various explorations of colonialism and the civ/sav or colonizer/colonized dichotomies, we see some of the impactful influences on our current society. Within these theories, we see the perpetual cycle our society has been caught in. The word 'decolonization' is used, often by parties who are not necessarily committed to all that decolonization requires.

Hindrances to Anti-Racism and Decolonization Discussions

In contemporary society, it is increasingly common to hear the term decolonization used in progressive discussions. People say they are committed to positive social change, so why has change been so slow? When you talk to the average Canadian, they often have knee-jerk responses to words such as anti-racist or decolonization, or uncomfortable reactions to the suggestions on how to approach these topics. It can be argued that our history of colonialism and the civ/sav dichotomy acts as a buffer for the possibility of an empathetic response by the colonizer. The colonizer experiences cognitive dissonance; their internal struggle activates a protection mechanism – the Eurocentric worldview or "white fragility" (DiAngelo). It is through this worldview that the colonizer justifies their inherent white privilege, or ignores it, and rationalizes to themselves (or to others) that the colonized has become deserving of their unfortunate fate. The white North American consciously or unconsciously recognizes that some of their gains or opportunities may have come from a non-legitimate place of oppression, so they falsify history. The colonizer begins to employ stereotypes and in doing so further elevates themselves to a place of veneration. From this comes the 'deserving' belief, they work harder, therefore, they deserve more. They look at other Nations and view them through a stereotypical lens, noting the individuals that confirm their bias and overlooking those who do not. This further justifies their Eurocentric belief as they perceive People of Colour (PoC) as living according to their racist interpretations. This cycle continues indefinitely, and often its pervasiveness goes unnoticed by general society; despite the fallaciousness of the theories and the harm caused to PoC.

So! How do we disrupt this cycle then? By looking at White Fragility and how to disrupt it.

White Fragility

In Canada Euro-whites are habitually stubborn in addressing their colonial history, their biases and acknowledging that they are on Indigenous land. Often when discussions of race occur, white Canadians can become distant, removing themselves from the topic, or the opposite can occur, they can become confrontational or angry – or even cry. In her paper, "White Fragility" by Robin DiAngelo, she clarifies the cause of these common reactions:

> White people in North America live in a social environment that protects and insulates them from race-based stress. This insulated environment of racial protection builds white expectations for racial comfort while at the same time lowering the ability to tolerate racial stress, leading to [the concept of] White Fragility (54).

This environment means that white North Americans can feel their whiteness is invisible, and when confronted with discussions on race, can and often will react negatively. DiAngelo explains,

> White Fragility is a state in which even a minimum amount of racial stress becomes intolerable, triggering a range of defensive moves. These moves include the outward display of emotions such as anger, fear, and guilt, and

behaviors such as argumentation, silence, and leaving the stress-inducing situation. These behaviors, in turn, function to reinstate white racial equilibrium." (54)

When White Fragility is activated, the individual may react with emotional/verbal violence or tears. These hyperbolic reactions act two-fold to protect the white person. It quiets any discussions on racism and acts as a protection for their privileged position while power is reasserted. The white person makes it clear that such topics upset them, so the conversation will be stopped. Therefore, the person encouraging the decolonization discussions must obey or be subjected to emotional upheaval or rage. Needless to say this makes discussions of decolonization difficult, if not impossible.

Why do people react in such a fragile manner? There are multiple answers to this question. As whites have not been subjected to a magnifying glass aimed at their whiteness, they are not comfortable with these discussions, and they have a low tolerance to topics based on race. Another cause of these fragile reactions is the idea of privilege translating to: 'I have achieved what I have achieved not due to my own hard work and dedication, but that my privilege got it for me.' That overly simplistic viewpoint is not only incorrect, it makes race-based or decolonial discussions more difficult and creates internal tensions, as well as external debates (or sometimes stonewalling). Lastly, our social 'default' has been coded to white. When listening to a news story, this is clearly displayed. When an individual commits a crime, their race is only mentioned if they are a Person of Colour. Headlines declaring: "Local Man Commits Crime" versus "Local Aboriginal Man Commits Crime" are a day to day occurrence in North American media, constantly othering and classifying only non-white people. Commonly it seems to be forgotten that white is indeed a race and whiteness in our society often remains unlabeled. Despite the reasons for North American white people's fragility, White Fragility continues to act as a derailment to positive discussions. In order for change to occur, these thoughts need to be challenged.

How to disrupt white fragility and allow anti-racist and decolonization discussions to occur more openly?

Firstly, we need to challenge ourselves. We need to be open to participate in racial and decolonial discussions. We should be willing to learn and listen to People of Color when they are teaching. It is imperative that we learn to find a supportive space without overstepping or co-opting others struggles, to engage respectfully, and in a manner needed by the community that we are allied with. We have to remain understanding, patient and be willing to be guided if we have not yet found that 'sweet spot' of support. More importantly, we need to challenge our defensiveness. Defensiveness shuts down conversations and learning. It is a quick and unproductive reaction. When encountering the internal pull of defensiveness, that is the moment to pause. Stop talking, stop defending, and pause with your thoughts. This is the moment to understand why; Why do I feel uncomfortable. Sit with that feeling. Unpack it. That is where the most personal growth comes from, challenging oneself when going into defensive mode. Without white people challenging themselves on their defensiveness or White Fragility, the negative cycle will continue, and social progress will remain stalled.

How do white people help encourage conversations about racism/decolonization with people who may not be on the path of solidarity or allyship? As white people that is our job, to encourage healthy discussions with other white people. As we gain more education and knowledge in the field of anti-racism and understand the topics being deliberated, our job is to teach other whites and to help other white people to understand the discussion. Everyone has a different method to engage and teach. Some choose to remain gentle, attempting to teach fellow whites before fragility is activated, especially when interacting with whites who may not truly be on a path to decolonization or realizing their internal biases. Some follow a 'call-out' culture – where whites are immediately (and sometimes publicly via social media) called out and addressed on their prejudicial statements. Different people have different strengths and approaches. But what is vital is consistently addressing harmful white people and informing them that their racist opinions will not be overlooked, that it is not a social 'faux pas' but racism. That our society is not becoming full of 'snowflakes' or becoming too 'politically correct' but more tolerant and less racist, or at least that is the goal. At the end of the day, the most important component to these positive changes is education. Educating ourselves, educating others. Continued education is the key to a less racist society. And with this education comes more discussions and more dedication to applying the steps needed to further the ultimate goal of decolonization and living in a racism-free society.

References

DiAngelo, Robin. "White Fragility." *International Journal of Critical Pedagogy*, vol. 3, no. 3, Mar. 2011.
Green, Joyce. "Towards A Detente With History: Confronting Canada's Colonial Legacy." *International Journal of Canadian Studies*, vol. 12, 1995, pp. 85–105.

LaRocque, Emma. *When the Other Is Me Native Resistance Discourse, 1850-1990*. University of Manitoba Press, 2014.

Memmi, Albert. *The Colonizer and the Colonized: a Destructive Relationship*. Citizens International, 2005.

Watkins, Mel, editor. "The Colonial Experience" *Dene Nation - A Colony Within*, by Peter Puxley, U Of T Press, 1977.

Chapter Thirty-Two

Reframing Catholicism

Agency and Resistance in Mi'kmaw Stories

Micheline Hughes

In this chapter, I argue that Mi'kmaq Peoples used stories to negotiate and contextualize Catholicism. There are those who contend that Christianity cannot be meaningful in Indigenous contexts; Vine Deloria Jr. argues that Christianity makes sense in its original setting but to remove this religious tradition from that context renders it incoherent. "What has been the manifestation of deity in a particular local situation is mistaken for a truth applicable to all times and places, a truth so powerful that it must be impressed upon peoples who have no connection to the event or to the cultural complex in which it originally made sense."[161] I argue for an alternative view regarding the religions that were brought to, what is now known as, North America by colonizers. As noted by Bradford and Horton, "many Indigenous people continue to interpret and live Christianity in ways meaningful to them, just as others, and sometimes the same people, persist in the practice of specifically Indigenous forms of spirituality."[162] The relevance and appropriateness of any version of Christianity for Indigenous Peoples is a matter that must be complicated. What follows is an examination of Mi'kmaw Catholicism and an exploration of how stories helped to contextualize this tradition, making it meaningful in a Mi'kma'ki context.[163]

This chapter explores my research interests and is based on the proposal for my Ph.D. dissertation. At this time, I have not begun my independent research so the ideas that I present are simply my framing and exploration of the available readings. What I offer is a thinking-through of what this research might look like, some important contextual factors, and a discussion of some inklings that I have about the power of story. Thus, this chapter is a collection of pieces of knowledge, story, and history, and a discussion of how Indigenous Peoples might make meaning from Catholicism.

Before getting into ideas about how Catholicism might have been contextualized to be meaningful to Mi'kmaq nation, there are two broad elements that must be detailed. As indicated above, my work will focus on two elements of the Mi'kmaq nation: stories and religion. These two elements are expansive, and so this chapter offers a cursory discussion on each topic. First stories are addressed and then the context that is relevant for a discussion of Mi'kmaw Catholicism is provided, I conclude with an example of a Mi'kmaw story that contains Catholic elements and discuss what this story, and others like it, might be capable of doing.

The Power of Stories

Before addressing the power that stories have, stories must be defined. According to Kovach, many Indigenous epistemologies include stories from two large categories: stories that have mythical elements, such as creation stories, and stories which are personal and can include narratives of experiences, events, and places.[164]

The character of stories must also be addressed. Stories are not just a collection of words or images that share a theme; they are much more than this. "Indeed, stories often make connections between ordinary and exceptional, render comprehensible the norms and departures from them. A story is, on this account, much more than a description of events in a real or imagined world. It is a modelling of how to understand and interpret them—what to make of them."[165] Stories teach us. As stated in the preceding quote, they are more than a description of related events; stories allow people to create something of the world and can be transformational in nature. Warren Cariou discusses orality and qualities associated with these types of stories. Transformation and, not necessarily unrelated, the ability to forget are inherently linked to oral stories. Cariou states,

> [k]eeping and transforming is what oral stories do best, I think, even though we worry about their fragility [ability to be forgotten]. They remain themselves in some way, even when official recognition of that identity washes away and they remain so because they are open to new possibilities, new contexts. Perhaps their transforming *is* their keeping, even though that may seem like a loss from some perspectives.[166]

Thus, oral stories' ability to transform is what allows them to be kept in our memories and to remain relevant. Because stories hold great power, this study wonders how this power might be used to render a religion not innocuous, but advantageous.

Mi'kmaw Stories

Mi'kmaq Peoples have a rich tradition of telling stories. Stories helped, and likely continue to help, Mi'kmaq Peoples understand their lived experience. They were also educational, teaching the listeners about Mi'kmaw values and philosophies.[167] Some Mi'kmaw stories have an inherently liminal quality. In Mi'kmaw stories, there are six worlds, and transport between worlds is possible.[168] A buoin, or a spiritual leader who has power or someone with magic, can accomplish travel between worlds. However, sometimes in Mi'kmaw stories, a non-buoin person travels between worlds, often without the knowledge of what has transpired. This travel happens in a space that is undefined.[169] Liminal, transformative, spaces then, such as passing by a wigwam post, when one is neither in the wigwam nor out of the wigwam, facilitate a transformation in the individual's reality.

Mi'kmaw stories have other values. As argued by Ruth Whitehead, other modes of investigations, like archaeology, can tell us how the Mi'kmaq lived, but these methods cannot

> tell us much about what the People thought or felt, the conversations they had while they cooked and ate their moose and groundnuts. Archaeology cannot show us their hearts, and neither can recorded history. It is mostly through our stories and legends that one can come to understand how we see the world and how we understand it. Long before their world began to be described in writing, and their history set down in books, the People described it, remembered it, and by word of mouth passed it on to the generations which were to come after them.[170]

Therefore, in addition to transforming reality, stories can teach us epistemologies and ontologies; how people made meaning from the lives they lived. They tell us of the spirit and intent of a people. The character of stories and knowledge that they hold means that it is important to consider them in a study of how religion is negotiated.

Mi'kmaw Catholicism

Before discussing Mi'kmaw Catholicism, the term 'religion' must be defined. Western models of religion need to be questioned because they may not be relevant in Indigenous contexts.[171] Religion has been considered the "exclusive property of Westerners, and the explanatory categories used in studying religious phenomena have been derived from the doctrines of the Christian religion."[172] Because Mi'kmaq believed, and continue to believe, that the sacred is a part of everyday life,[173] Western concepts of institutionalized religion are not appropriate. Therefore, religion must be redefined. "Religion is the mode by which, as individuals and community...sustain the sense of our own significance...It is...the way in which we define what it means to be a human being within any given context of time and place."[174] Religion, for this work, encompasses any interaction with what is considered to be sacred and how people come to understand themselves as human beings. This interaction occurs in all spaces regardless of constructed boundaries of the sacred and the profane. My work will consider Mi'kmaw Catholicism, though it is important to note that this is not the only religion practiced by the Mi'kmaq.[175]

The Mi'kmaw nation began to practice Catholicism in 1610 when Sagamore Membertou was baptized by Jessé Fléché.[176] By the mid-1600s, most Mi'kmaq had converted to Catholicism.[177] Many Mi'kmaq continue to practice Catholicism and consider it a traditional religion.[178] Mi'kmaw Catholicism is a distinct religious tradition that does not exist elsewhere. It incorporates elements of Mi'kmaw tradition with Catholicism and has been negotiated to serve the needs of the Mi'kmaq Peoples. The creation of this tradition allowed, and continues to allow, Mi'kmaq Peoples to maintain their own identity, agency, and permits them to define the world for themselves. Just because the Mi'kmaq are baptized and practice Catholicism does not mean that they abandoned their pre-contact beliefs. Rather, they are combined, "[w]hile our Elders are Catholic, the old traditions and customs associated with our traditional spirituality are now blended."[179] Part of this adaptation involved the Mi'kmaq challenging the carriers of Catholic tradition, the missionaries, and integrating Catholic figures into Mi'kmaq kin-relationships.[180]

Even though this religious tradition was negotiated to become a relevant and meaningful expression of humanity, my work cannot neglect the harms that were carried out in the name of Catholicism. Post-European contact, Catholicism was used to justify the land theft and assignment of subhuman status to Indigenous Peoples thereby upholding colonialism. Several papal bulls were issued to validate the violence and overarching colonial narrative that accompanied the colonization of the Americas by European nations. Missionaries whose task it was to proselytize, convert, and undermine pre-contact Indigenous religions and beliefs were sent all over the Americas.[181] A nuanced examination of this religious tradition cannot be completed without acknowledging the role that Catholicism, as defined by Europeans, had in aiding and promoting the colonial project.

The overarching narratives that underlie the colonial project are that Indigenous Peoples are worth less than Canadians whose ancestors were European settlers; that Indigenous Peoples somehow deserve the stereotyping, racism, and poor treatment they receive; that Indigenous Peoples had no social structure, religion or knowledge and that any culture they currently practice they have received from Europeans. The belief that Indigenous Peoples were passive recipients of culture continues to persist.[182] As Linda Tuhiwai Smith argues, history, or the dominant narrative, is about power.[183] Colonial narratives serve to keep colonizers in power while silencing and erasing Indigenous Peoples.

The dominant narrative characterizes Canada's history as a "celebratory settler story," which contends that colonialism was not a violent process.[184] The dominant narrative blames Indigenous Peoples for their own colonization and colonial stories argue that Indigenous Peoples are not able or willing to help themselves and therefore require saving.[185]

These racist stereotypes are supported by a binary which is informed by a Eurocentric perspective. This binary distinguishes Europeans, who consider themselves civilized, from Indigenous Peoples, who are considered savages. LaRocque terms this the civ/sav dichotomy.[186] Regan states "settler history...characterizes Indigenous people as victims of progress who must be saved from their own cultural and economic backwardness by superior, wise, and benevolent fathers."[187] Such 'superior, wise, and benevolent fathers' include the Church.[188]

Thus, the dominant narrative argues that colonizers must 'civilize' Indigenous Peoples for their own good, through assimilatory means such as conversion to Christianity. Because of this narrative and because many Mi'kmaq have identified as Catholic for hundreds of years, Western scholarship sometimes, mistakenly, argues that the Mi'kmaq have all been assimilated or that they all wish to be assimilated (Wallis & Wallis 1955).[189] Such claims are colonial and imply that there are no 'authentic' Mi'kmaq Peoples left. There are several points in these claims that must be refuted.

Firstly, change does not equal inauthenticity. As Emma LaRocque so eloquently argues, neocolonial thinking which characterizes Indigenous Peoples and cultures as stagnant

> translates to intellectual genocide because it demands that Indigenous peoples remain "traditional," that is, fixed and frozen in time; and when they change, they are charged with "assimilation" (even when assimilation is forced) - one way or another we are consigned to irrelevance, a modern version for the Vanishing Indian!...Meanwhile, the western world, which has more than liberally taken from the Indigenous (both materially and conceptually), acts as if it has neither been acculturated, indigenized, hybridized nor colonized by its own colonial globe-trotting.[190]

There is a clear double standard occurring in these modes of thought. An example will easily illustrate one way that Indigenous Peoples are required to remain frozen in time while others are not. For instance, people with European heritage are not accused of being inauthentic because they dress in jeans and t-shirts, rather than Victorian garb. However, how many Indigenous people have been charged with not actually being Indigenous because we similarly wear jeans and t-shirts, live in cities, do not 'look' Indigenous, or any other number of reasons.

Next, the idea that Indigenous Peoples were passive recipients of Christianity must be challenged and disproved. Since the beginning of the relationship between the Mi'kmaq and the Catholic church, missionaries have noted that Mi'kmaq Peoples have not easily accepted their claims. Pierre Biard, a Jesuit missionary who lived in the early 1600s, recounts "[a]ll your arguments, and you can bring on a thousand of them if you wish, are annihilated by this single shaft which they always have at hand....'This is the Indian way of doing it. You can have your way, and we will have ours; every one values his own wares.'"[191] This questioning continues today. Robinson notes that priests who work in Eskasoni, a Mi'kmaw First Nation in Unama'kik,[192] who adjust their ministration to fit with Mi'kmaw ways of practicing Catholicism get along very well with the community, but priests who go in with rigid ideas about how Catholicism should be practiced do not share the synergistic and communal experiences of their colleagues. Fr. Ryan recounts, "[m]any of the people in Eskasoni are proud of their Mi'kmaw heritage. When I first arrived there, a male elder said, 'Do you want to be happy here Father?...if you want to be happy you have to change. Eskasoni has four thousand people who will not change, and it's easier for you to change than everyone else.' That was one of the soundest pieces of advice I ever received."[193] Thus, more than simply not passively accepting Catholicism, Mi'kmaq Peoples require the clergy to change.

In addition to the agency displayed by requiring missionaries and priests to change and questioning their teachings, Mi'kmaq Peoples, even in the face of rigorous 'campaigns of decatholization' by the English in 1749, remained staunchly Catholic.[194] Why would the Mi'kmaq choose to remain Catholic in the face of such destructive, colonial forces? I hope that my research can begin to answer such questions, but it should be clear that the Mi'kmaq's version of Catholicism meant something to them. This religious tradition suited their needs and, potentially, was a location where resistance and autonomy could be couched.

Proposed Research

Now that important contextual factors have been reviewed, I will discuss my plans for research. My topic looks at Mi'kmaw Catholicism through the lens of Mi'kmaw stories. I want to use Mi'kmaw stories which have been recorded, as well as stories I will record, and look for instances of the negotiation of Catholicism. As noted above, I dispute the dominant narrative, which might argue that there can be no Mi'kmaw Catholicism since it views all Mi'kmaq Peoples as being assimilated and Catholicism as a tool of the colonizers. I maintain that Mi'kmaw Catholicism was negotiated by the Mi'kmaq and their stories. And insist that because stories are such transformative, liminal, spaces, Mi'kmaw stories must be considered when studying how religion can be adapted.

Liminality is the idea of ambiguous, undefined space. Although Victor Turner argues that liminality is created in ceremony, I believe his definition of liminality captures the liminal quality that transformative stories must have. He defines liminality as, "necessarily ambiguous since this condition and these persons elude or slip through the network of classifications that normally locate states and positions in cultural space. Liminal entities are neither here nor there; they are betwixt and between the positions assigned and arrayed by law, custom, convention, and ceremon[y]."[195] Liminality is an important concept for this work because undefined spaces, such as stories, are imbued with possibility. Such possibilities are particularly necessary when autonomy and agency are at stake. When paternalistic colonial powers have control, creating a space where colonial powers can be put at bay and where anything can happen is crucial. Imagination and transformation are necessarily liminal, and these tools are found in narrative. As J. Edward Chamberlin notes, "This...is...the place of stories, the place where things happen that don't and things are that are not."[196]

And so, because stories can create spaces that are not defined, where anything is possible, some stories exist which allow Indigenous figures to interact with Christian figures. An example is found in a story recorded by Frank Speck. This story places Christ in conversation with Kluskap, the Mi'kmaq primordial man.[197] The story is as follows,

> One time Gluskap had become the [Mi'kmaq's] god, Christ wanted to see if he was fit: so he took Gluskap to the ocean, and told him to close his eyes. Then Christ moved close to the shore an island which lay far out to sea. When Gluskap opened his eyes he saw it. Christ asked him if he could do as much as that. Then Gluskap told Christ to close his eyes a while. When Christ opened his eyes, he found that Gluskap had moved it back to its place again.[198]

Some important context for this story is that Mi'kmaw narratives understand that Kluskap had shaped the geography of Mi'kma'ki. There is a story about how Kluskap begins a journey in Unama'kik and ends up creating the Bay of Fundy.[199] So not only does this story suggest that Kluskap is on equal footing as Christ, but it shows Christ having the same abilities as Kluskap. This story contextualizes a prominent Catholic figure and gives him abilities that are appropriate in a Mi'kmaw context. I believe that the transformational and liminal power of narrative is what allows such stories to exist.

There is also a religious element present in this story, even beyond the two figures who are conversing. While this story may not relate directly to the practice of Catholicism, it does relate to the Mi'kmaq's place in a new colonial reality and shows that they have not been found wanting. As noted at the beginning of this chapter, religion is the way that we, as human beings, make sense of who we are and affirm our own significance. Although there are longer stories which contain more elements of Catholicism being negotiated by the Mi'kmaq, this short story shows that something interesting is happening in Mi'kmaw narratives. Not only is a Catholic figure being rendered more relevant for a Mi'kmaw context, but there is a clear message about power and worthiness. Stories such as these are not taken into account in dominant narratives, but they are important to consider if we wish to understand our shared history. Colonialism was not (and is not) something that Indigenous Peoples accept, ways to resist and validate identity continue to be found.

I began this chapter by arguing that Christianity can be made relevant in a Mi'kma'ki context. The Mi'kmaq have imbued Catholicism with their own ways of making meaning and have created a pertinent religious tradition, Mi'kmaw Catholicism. Mi'kmaq Peoples have created a way to practice this tradition while remaining Mi'kmaq; their practice of this tradition is not an indication of assimilation, rather it shows autonomy in the face of colonizers. The Mi'kmaq nation changed Catholicism from a tool of the colonizer to a way to validate their own identity and take agency for themselves, and it is quite possible that stories played a crucial role in this transformation.

References

Axtell, James. The Invasion Within: The Contest of Cultures in Colonial North America. New York: Oxford UP, 1985.
Bradford, Tolly and Chelsea Horton, editors. Mixed Blessings: Indigenous Encounters with Christianity in Canada. Vancouver: UBC Press, 2016.
Cardinal, Harold. The Unjust Society. Vancouver: Douglas & McIntyre, 1969.
Cariou, Warren. "Who is the Text in this Class?: Story, Archive, and Pedagogy in Indigenous Contexts" in Learn, Teach, Challenge: Approaching Indigenous Literatures, edited by Deanna Reder and Linda Morra. Waterloo: Wilfred Laurier UP, 2016.
Chamberlin, J. Edward. If this is your Land, Where are your Stories? Finding Common Ground. Toronto: Vintage Canada, 2003.
Deloria Jr., Vine. God is Red: A Native View of Religion. 3rd ed. Colorado: Fulcrum Publishing, 2003.
Gespe'gewa'gi Mi'gmawei Mawiomi. Nta'tugwaqanminen: Our Story The Evolution of the Gespe'gewa'gi Mi'gmaq. Halifax: Fernwood Publishing, 2016.
Greer, Allan. Mohawk Saint: Catherine Tekakwitha and the Jesuits. New York: Oxford UP, 2005.
Henderson, James (Sakej) Youngblood. The Mikmaw Concordat. Halifax: Fernwood Publishing, 1997.
Hornborg, Anne-Christine. Mi'kmaq Landscapes: From Animism to Sacred Ecology. England: Ashcroft, 2008.
Kovach, Margaret. Indigenous Methodologies: Characteristics, Conversations, and Contexts. Toronto: University of Toronto Press, 2009.
LaRocque, Emma. When the Other is Me: Native Resistance Discourse 1850-1990. Winnipeg: University of Manitoba Press, 2010.
—. Foreword to More Will Sing Their Way to Freedom: Indigenous Resistance and Resurgence, edited by Elaine Coburn, 5-23. Halifax: Fernwood Publishing, 2015.
Lessard, Hester, Rebecca Johnson, and Jeremy Webber (eds). Storied Communities: Narratives of Contact and Arrival in Constituting Political Community. Vancouver: UBC Press, 2011.
Marshall, Murdena. "Values, Customs and Traditions of the Mi'kmaq Nation" in The Mi'kmaq Anthology, edited by Rita Joe and Lesley Choyce, 51-63. East Lawrencetown, NS: Pottersfield Press, 1997.
Paul, Daniel N. We Were Not the Savages: Collision between European and Native American Civilization, 3rd edition. Halifax: Fernwood Publishing, 2006.
Regan, Paulette. Unsettling the Settler Within: Indian Residential Schools, Truth Telling, and Reconciliation in Canada. Vancouver: UBC Press, 2010.
Reid, Jennifer. Myth, Symbol, and Colonial Encounter: British and Mi'kmaq in Acadia, 1700-1867. Ottawa: University of Ottawa Press, 1995.
—. Finding Kluskap: A Journey into Mi'kmaw Myth. University Park, PA: Pennsylvania State University Press, 2013.
Robinson, Angela. Ta'n Teli-ktlamsitasit (Ways of Believing): Mi'kmaw Religion in Eskasoni, Nova Scotia. Toronto: Pearson Education Canada Inc., 2005.
Sable, Trudy and Bernie Francis. The Language of this Land, Mi'kma'ki. Sydney: Cape Breton University Press, 2012.
Smith, Linda Tuhiwai. Decolonizing Methodologies: Research and Indigenous Peoples, 2nd ed. Dundedin: Otago University Press, 2012.

Speck, Frank G. "Some Micmac Tales from Cape Breton Island." Journal of American Folklore, 28 (1915): 59-69.

Turner, Victor. The Ritual Process: Structure and Anti-Structure. Ithica: Cornell UP, 1969.

Upton, L.F.S. Micmacs and Colonists: Indian-White Relations in the Maritimes, 1713-1867. Vancouver: University of British Colombia Press, 1979.

Wallis, Wilson D., and Wallis, Ruth Sawtell. The Micmac Indians of Eastern Canada. Minneapolis: University of Minnesota Press, 1955.

Whitehead, Ruth Holmes. Stories from the Six Worlds: Micmac Legends. Halifax: Nimbus Publishing Limited, 1988.

notes

[161] Vine Deloria Jr., *God is Red: A Native View of Religion* (Colorado: Fulcrum Publishing, 2003), 65.

[162] Tolly Bradford and Chelsea Horton, editors, *Mixed Blessings: Indigenous Encounters with Christianity in Canada* (Vancouver: UBC Press, 2016),

[163] Mi'kma'ki is the land of the Mi'kmaq and includes what is now known as Nova Scotia, Prince Edward Island, New Brunswick, parts of Newfoundland, Quebec, and Maine. See Sable and Francis, *The Language of this Land, Mi'kma'ki*, (Sydney: Cape Breton University Press, 2012), 21-22.

[164] Margaret Kovach, *Indigenous Methodologies: Characteristics, Conversations, and Contexts* (Toronto: University of Toronto Press, 2009), 95.

[165] Hester Lessard, Rebecca Johnson, and Jeremy Webber, editors *Storied Communities: Narratives of Contact and Arrival in Constituting Political Community* (Vancouver: UBC Press, 2011), 8.

[166] Warren Cariou, "Who is the Text in this Class?: Story, Archive, and Pedagogy," in Indigenous Contexts" in *Learn, Teach, Challenge: Approaching Indigenous Literatures*, ed. Deanna Reder and Linda Morra, (Waterloo: Wilfred Laurier UP, 2016), 475.

[167] Angela Robinson, *Ta'n Teli-ktlamsitasit (Ways of Believing): Mi'kmaw Religion in Eskasoni, Nova Scotia*, (Toronto: Pearson Education Canada Inc., 2005), 37.

[168] The six worlds are the world beneath the earth, the world beneath the water, the earth world, the world above the earth, the world above the sky, and the ghost world. See Ruth Whitehead, Ruth Whitehead, *Stories from the Six Worlds. Micmac Legends*, (Halifax: Nimbus Publishing, 1988).

[169] Anne-Christine Hornborg, *Mi'kmaq Landscapes: From Animism to Sacred Ecology*, (England: Ashcroft, 2008), 32-35.

[170] Whitehead, *Stories from the Six Worlds*, 1.

[171] Robinson, *Ta'n Teli-ktlamsitasit (Ways of Believing)*, 5.

[172] Deloria, *God is Red*, 288.

[173] Robinson, *Ta'n Teli-ktlamsitasit (Ways of Believing)*, 58.

[174] Jennifer Reid, *Myth, Symbol, and Colonial Encounter: British and Mi'kmaq in Acadia, 1700-1867*, (Ottawa: University of Ottawa Press, 1995), 14.

[175] See Robinson, *Ta'n Teli-ktlamsitasit (Ways of Believing)*.

[176] Jennifer Reid, *Finding Kluskap: A Journey Into Mi'kmaw Myth*, (University Park, PA: Pennsylvania State University Press, 2013), 1.

[177] I struggle with the term 'convert' as it means to change from one state to another. This term must be problematized as ways of knowing, existing beliefs, and values, are not washed away with the water of baptism. Many expressions of Catholicism exist, adopting and adapting Catholicism cannot be equated with assimilation. For a discussion on Christianities see Bradford Horton, *Mixed Blessings*, 4.

[178] Robinson, *Ta'n Teli-ktlamsitasit (Ways of Believing)*, 110-111.

[179] Murdena Marshall, "Values, Customs and Traditions of the Mi'kmaq Nation" in *The Mi'kmaq Anthology*, eds. Rita Joe and Lesley Choyce, (East Lawrencetown, NS: Pottersfield Press, 1997), 56.

[180] See Axtell 1985; Robinson 2005; Upton 1979.

[181] James (Sakej) Youngblood Henderson, *The Mikmaw Concordat*, (Halifax: Fernwood Publishing, 1997), 37-44.

[182] Allan Greer, *Mohawk Saint: Catherine Tekakwitha and the Jesuits*, (New York: Oxford UP, 2005), 111; Reid, *Myth and Symbol*, 5; Linda Tuhiwai Smith, *Decolonizing Methodologies: Research and Indigenous Peoples*, 2nd ed., (Dundedin: Otago University Press, 2012), 44-45; Daniel Paul, *We Were Not the Savages: Collision between European and Native American Civilization*, 3rd ed., (Halifax: Fernwood Publishing, 2006), 38.

[183] Smith, *Decolonizing Methodologies*, 35

[184] Paulette Regan, *Unsettling the Settler Within: Indian Residential Schools, Truth Telling, and Reconciliation in Canada*, (Vancouver: UBC Press, 2010), 74.

[185] Ibid., 83-86; Harold Cardinal, *The Unjust Society*, (Vancouver: Douglas & McIntyre, 1969), 82.

[186] Emma LaRocque, *When the Other is Me: Native Resistance Discourse 1850-1990*, (Winnipeg: University of Manitoba Press, 2010), 38.

[187] Regan, *Unsettling the Settler*, 86.

[188] See Henderson, The Mi'kmaw Concordat.

[189] See Wilson D. Wallis and Ruth Sawtell Wallis, *The Micmac Indians of Eastern Canada*, (Minneapolis: University of Minnesota Press, 1955).

[190] Emma LaRocque, foreword to *More Will Sing Their Way to Freedom: Indigenous Resistance and Resurgence*, ed. Elaine Coburn, (Halifax: Fernwood Publishing, 2015), 17.

[191] As cited in James Axtell, *The Invasion Within: The Contest of Cultures in Colonial North America*, (New York: Oxford UP, 1985), 38.

[192] Cape Breton, NS

[193] Robinson, *Ta'n Teli-ktlamsitasit (Ways of Believing)*, 60.

[194] Axtell, *The Invasion Within*, 277.

[195] Victor Turner, *The Ritual Process: Structure and Anti-Structure*, (Ithica: Cornell UP, 1969), 95.

[196] Edward Chamberlin, *If this is your Land, Where are your Stories? Finding Common Ground*, (Toronto: Vintage Canada, 2003), 75.

[197] Kluskap is spelled differently depending on which orthography is being employed. Other spellings include Gluskap and Glooscap.

[198] Frank Speck, "Some Micmac Tales from Cape Breton Island," *Journal of American Folklore*, 28 (1915): 60-61.

[199] Frank Speck, *Some Micmac Tales*, 59-60.

Chapter Thirty-Three

A Colonial Institution with Colonial Voices and Values

Exposing Daniels v. Canada's Tribute to the Colonizers

Karine Martel

Indigenous peoples across Canada are now very familiar with having to assert and defend their rights through the Canadian legal system. Recently, the Métis have achieved significant declarations from the Supreme Court either reaffirming their rights or acknowledging past government wrongdoings. Most notably, the 2003 *Powley* decision (*R. v. Powley*) reaffirmed the Métis' section 35 Aboriginal rights which had been denied for so long, despite the Métis being clearly included in section 35 of the Constitution Act, 1982. More recently in 2014 Manitoba Métis Federation decision (*MMF v. Canada*) acknowledged that the Métis were never delivered the 1.4 million acres they were promised under section 31 of the Manitoba Act in 1870, which ushered Manitoba into confederacy. Though these were pivotal court victories for the Métis, these decisions have yet to deliver concrete benefits as Métis individuals are still persecuted for exercising their section 35 rights (see *R. v. Beer*) and the Manitoba Métis have not seen their *MMF* court victory come to full fruition yet. The main culprit for such inaction has been the federal government's continued denial of its jurisdiction over the Métis. Section 91(24) of the Constitution Act of 1867 states that Canada has the exclusive jurisdiction over "Indians and lands reserved for the Indians," but the federal government has long denied that the Métis are "Indians" for the purposes of section 91(24) (*Daniels* FC 501). As such, the Métis have been thrown around like a "political football" from the provincial to federal governments who have both denied having jurisdiction over the Métis (*Daniels* FC 86).

Frustrated with being in constant jurisdictional limbo, the late Métis leader Harry Daniels brought an action forward on behalf of the Congress of Aboriginal Peoples, which sought a clarification from the Supreme Court on whether the Métis fall under the federal government's jurisdiction as "Indians" under section 91(24) (*Daniels* FC). On April 14, 2016, the Supreme Court ruled in favour of Harry Daniels, meaning the Métis are a federal responsibility along with First Nations and Inuit people (*Daniels* SC). Though *Daniels* was quickly portrayed as a victory for the Métis, many legal scholars are beginning to unpack the Court's decision and are realizing that it may not usher in as much change as it appears to promise (Vowel and Leroux 33, Chartrand 182, Macdougall 1). However, even before thinking about the future implications from the Daniels ruling, it is important to unpack the decision itself.

Joyce Green, a scholar of politics of decolonization, has argued that "through scholarship, law, politics, policy, and culture, the dominant narrative reproduces itself while legitimizing and reifying its origins" (par. 16). This chapter will show that in *Daniels v. Canada,* the courts have reproduced the common colonial narrative surrounding early Canadian history and have created law that is based and achieved through relying on the goals and values of early Canadian colonialists and government officials. This paper will then question whether it is possible for the Métis to utilize a decision produced within a colonial institution and fraught with colonial influences as a platform from which to decolonize.

The Fork in the Road of Legal Interpretation: The Living Tree or Originalism?

As this case was brought forth in the western legal system, those deciding *Daniels* had to operate within the system's rigidness. The Supreme Court had two different options of interpretation that were available to them: The Living Tree approach and the Originalist interpretation. First, the Originalist interpretation demands a conservative and rigid interpretation of the words of the Constitution. It requires viewing the Constitution as somewhat "frozen" from the time it was created (Miller 331). As its name specifies, under the Originalist approach the Constitution must be interpreted to maintain the original text, the original intentions, original understandings, and original values of the provision (Richard 336-339). In other words, the Court must operate from the framers' perspectives regarding the provision in question. An Originalist interpretation may also include a purposive approach, where the Court asks themselves what were the intentions of the framers when they created the provision at hand (Miller 342-348).

This method of interpretation is at odds with the more modern Living Tree approach, which allows for a broader, more liberal and flexible interpretation of the Constitution. It views the Constitution as a Living Tree, which "accommodates and addresses the realities of modern life" (*Reference re. Same-sex Marriage* 22). Chief Justice Beverly McLaughlin rejected an Originalist interpretation of the Constitution in the Same-Sex case, saying that "the 'frozen concepts' reasoning runs contrary to one of the most fundamental principles of Canadian Constitutional interpretation," namely that the Constitution should be allowed to change as society progresses (*Reference re. Same-Sex Marriage* 22). While the Originalist approach focuses on the provision's purpose at the time of enactment, a Living Tree approach focuses on a living, organic purpose that does not necessarily coincide with the original purpose of the provision (Miller 339-340).

The courts could interpret the *Daniels* question from a modern perspective, in line with present-day realities, or from the perspectives of the framers of the Constitution, pertaining to the goals of a newly formed Confederacy. They chose the latter despite the circumstances surrounding this case requiring a Living Tree approach.

Choosing an Originalist Interpretation: The Colonial Agenda Prevails and Survives

Early in its *Daniels* opinion, the lower courts demonstrated that they would try to uncover what the framers of the Constitution would have intended while drafting the word "Indian" (*Daniels* FC 24). However, as there were no records of what the framers meant by "Indian" in 1867, the Federal Court said it would "rely on how Canadian government officials interpreted this provision just before and for some period after Confederation to give context and meaning to the words of s. 91(24)", thus giving a clear indication of its choice to implement the Originalist approach (*Daniels* FC 24). Furthermore, the Supreme Court stated it would work with the original purposes behind section 91(24) and the overall Constitution in order to determine the *Daniels* question when it opined that "the purpose of s. 91(24) was closely related to the expansionist goals of Confederation" such as "expanding the country across the west" and "building a national railway" (*Daniels* SCC 4), and "to eventually civilize and assimilate Native peoples" (*Daniels* SCC 5).

The courts should have realized that times had changed since 1867 regarding Crown-Aboriginal relations, and Canada no longer uses its jurisdiction over "Indians" to assimilate and control Indigenous people. Rather, in the modern-day Canada should be using its jurisdiction to engage with Indigenous peoples on a nation-to-nation basis, to promote Indigenous peoples' rights, and to work towards reconciliation. Métis legal scholar Larry Chartrand has found that the proper approach in *Daniels* would have been to interpret this question from a Living Tree approach, to "be consistent with contemporary human rights values and principles" (185). However, by choosing the Originalist method, the Court has demonstrated its loyalty to the framers of the Constitution.

Colonial Voices and Colonial Perspectives

Edward Said has asked "Who writes? For whom is the writing being done? In what circumstances?" (Said 7). Linda Tuhiwai Smith in her groundbreaking work "Indigenous Methodologies" provides some answers to this question, as she describes that "history is also about power. In fact, history is mostly about power. It is the story of the powerful and how they became powerful, and then how they use their power to keep them in positions in which they can continue to dominate others" (Smith 34). By presenting the voices of early Euro-Canadian officials, the history presented and relied on in *Daniels* is exactly this.

With its originalist approach, the Court placed an overwhelming amount of weight on Euro-Canadians' perspectives of history and of the Métis during colonial times. This is evidenced by the *Daniels* trial relying on 800 pieces of evidence contained within 15,000 documents (*Daniels* FC 70), most of which were speeches or archival records made by government officials, fathers of the Confederation, priests and missionaries, as well as legal statutes, treaties, acts of legislation, and Supreme Court rulings[200]. These types of sources do not present the voice of the Métis, but rather the voice and interpretation of white Euro-Canadian colonialists.

Some of the only Métis voices and perspectives presented in the *Daniels* hearing are found within archival evidence. However, these exhibits typically represent Métis voices from the past which have been reinterpreted by Europeans and Canadian officials. For example, the trial judge quoted a speech by Sir John A. MacDonald made in the House of Commons in July of 1885, who said "The half breeds did not allow themselves to be Indians" (*Daniels* FC 413). While this seems to be a clear indication of what the Métis thought of themselves, this is simply a representation of the Métis' voice and thought through a government official. It also disregards some of the realities the Métis needed to consider in making such statements, like the fact that being considered Indian at this time would likely mean facing many discriminations by government and peers. An expert witness in the *Daniels* trial testified that many Métis chose to distinguish themselves from the Indians because, according to government thought of the era, "the closer you were to being considered white, the higher you were on the social scale" (*Daniels* FC 377). By highlighting these colonists' perspectives, the courts further perpetuate a history that chooses to be blind to colonial oppression, which would have influenced such assertions from the Métis. With so few Métis voices presented throughout the *Daniels* trial, the Métis simply become what Jennings calls, "participants in the white man's history" that is being told in the *Daniels* case (29).

In choosing to retell a Euro-Canadian history, it is clear whose perspectives the courts idolized. James Blaut in his manuscript *"The Colonizer's Model of the World"* writes about our presumed preference and un-censoring of all western knowledge as he describes eurocentrism as "a set of beliefs that are statements about empirical reality, statements educated and usually unprejudiced Europeans accept as true, as propositions supported by 'the facts'" (Blaut 9). In regurgitating and not questioning such a colonial history, the Court has made us aware of its own Eurocentric beliefs, and therefore, it has put forth a "colonizer's model of the world," or more precisely, a colonial model of Canada (Blaut 10).

Colonial Values and Colonial Goals

As the Supreme Court chose to implement an Originalist interpretation, the Court had to rule in line with the original intentions of the framers when they created section 91(24). Namely, the court had to place themselves in an 1867 mindset and wonder whether having the Métis included as section 91(24) Indians would have assisted the newly formed confederacy's goals of assimilating the "Indians" (*Daniels* SC 5) and in expanding the confederacy out west (*Daniels* SC 4). Thus, the Supreme Court found evidence to show that the federal government would have wanted to include the Métis as "Indians" as the Métis had already blocked government surveyors from entering their lands in the process of opening them up for settlement, and therefore, could have presented an obstacle to Canadian westward expansion (*Daniels* SC 25). Moreover, the Court found that "with jurisdiction over Aboriginal peoples, the new federal government could 'protect the railway from attack'" from the Métis (*Daniels* SC 24).

Contained within this historical evidence used by the Supreme Court are two problematic assumptions often told in Canadian history. First is the idea of the savage Indian needing to be tamed and controlled by a colonial entity who will, in turn, enlighten the "Indians" by bringing them "the gift of civilization" (Blaut 6). However, what the Court has failed to mention while recounting such history is that if the Métis chose to prevent the construction of a railway, such protests would have been calculated demonstrations by the Métis to protect their land from encroachment by the colonial state. Hence, the Court has engaged in what Green describes as the "repetition of historical accounts that are partial and exclusionary; in the carefully maintained incomprehension at Indigenous nations' resistance to assimilation and struggle for self-determination" (par. 20).

The next problematic assumption often told in Canada's popular history and contained within this piece of evidence is the assumed inevitability of Canadian expansion out west. LaRocque calls this "peopling the West," which the colonizers saw as an inevitable and benevolent gesture on their part (LaRocque 44). This reiteration of colonial history is in line with the colonial theory of the "myth of emptiness" articulated by Blaut, which he describes as viewing a non-European region as barren land, which may include inhabitants, though they are nomadic and therefore not utilizing the resources properly (Blaut 15). However, this idea forgets the fact that Indigenous people already inhabited these lands and did use the resources available to them in a highly sophisticated way and that many Indigenous peoples were displaced in the name of colonialism[201]. While it is true that expansion out west would have been a goal of the Confederacy in 1867, we now know that such motivations were problematic and section 91(24) has very contradicting goals today. Thus, the court has paid homage to the colonizers by choosing to base a modern-day court decision on such outdated values.

Furthermore, the Court opined that the framers would have also utilized their section 91(24) powers to assimilate the Métis (*Daniels* FC 151, 278, 353, 567; *Daniels* SC 5). For example, the Court highlighted that the federal government exercised its jurisdiction over the Métis as section 91(24) "Indians" in order to control the sales of "intoxicating liquors" to the Métis who were causing problems in their inebriated state (*Daniels* SC 27). This piece of evidence evokes the image of the "savage Indian" which plays upon the "civ/sav" dichotomy, a term coined by LaRocque which she describes as "an ideological container for the systematic construction of self-confirming 'evidence' that Natives were savages who 'inevitably' had to yield to the superior powers of civilization as carried forward by Euro-Canadian civilizers" (LaRocque 37-38). In fact, the Federal Court proved that it interpreted Indian identity along a civ/sav dichotomy when it said "the dichotomy between Indian/Half-breed and Whites, between civilized and uncivilized/savage was further complicated by the varying degrees of civilized behaviors or ways of life practiced by the Indian/Half-breeds". The court then goes on to list evidence of the Métis's not-quite "civilized", yet not-entirely "savage" behavior (*Daniels* FC 380). Commenting on the *Daniels* decision, Larry Chartrand has also suggested that "the objective of 'civilization' is no longer acceptable in a society that realizes that Indigenous societies were far from uncivilized" (185) and should therefore not form the basis on lawmaking. Moreover, as Francis Jennings has explained, the "civilized/uncivilized distinction is a moral sanction, not a set of traits" (8), and such a determination was never an objective "standard of measurement" (8) which relied on "empirical data" (10), but was rather a political and self-serving distinction. Therefore, if the distinction of civilized/savage was never made on facts but rather on whatever served the government's interest, then such distinctions should not serve as the foundation from which to build a modern court decision.

While section 91(24) may have been drafted to give the government the power to expand the new Confederation out west and assimilate and control the "Indians" in 1867, these are no longer goals pertaining to Indian policy today and such values should have no place in our legal institutions. In telling history, Green says the way forward is by "facing up to the colonial past, in taking responsibility for it" which she says, "means owning all of our history, rather than perpetuating the myth of white settlers creating civilization in uncharted wilderness" (par. 62). Perhaps there is a place and time to bring up this colonial understanding of history, but only if we wish to learn from it and not simply perpetuate its myths. We certainly should not use such history as the basis of modern-day legal analysis.

As Glen Coulthard remarks,

> "Over the last forty years Indigenous peoples have become incredibly skilled at participating in the Canadian legal and political practices…however, our efforts to engage these discursive and institutional spaces to secure recognition of our rights have not only failed, but have instead served to subtly reproduce the forms of racist, sexist, economic, and political configurations of power that we initially sought, through our engagements and negotiations with the state" (179).

Unfortunately, this seems to be the case for the Métis in regards to the *Daniels* decision. While the Métis were engaging with the Canadian legal system to better themselves, along the way archaic colonial values, goals, and understandings of Indigeneity have been upheld and given standing in modern legal analysis.

How to Use a Decision Full of Colonial Influences to Decolonize?

This brings us to one last question: Is it truly possible to use a Supreme Court decision achieved through a colonial institution, which values and upholds colonial perspectives, from which to decolonize? Some scholars have argued that you can operate within the existing western legal system, though the system needs some serious revamping. Anishinabek legal scholar John Borrows argues that effective constitutionalism in Canada must acknowledge Indigenous peoples' legal traditions and therefore incorporate Indigenous concepts and perspectives in the law. He worries that the current system is ineffective, as the courts test Indigenous history and law against their own western norms, which leads to the courts having a large control over Indigenous peoples in the past but also in the present (Borrows 170). He finds that a more supportive environment for Indigenous peoples in the law has the ability to heal Indigenous peoples from past trauma in a way they see fit and promote peace in Canada-Indigenous relations (Borrows 174).

Glen Coulthard has argued for a bit more of an emancipatory process regarding the western legal system. In his text, *Red Skins, White Masks*, he explores how the politics of recognition and reconciliation in Canada are just another masked tool of colonization furthering Indigenous oppression. Coulthard worries that even while working cautiously with a colonial government you cannot get rid of "some of the effects of colonial-capitalist exploitation and domination" without addressing the "generative structures" of colonialism (35). Instead, he argues that we must create "a resurgent politics of recognition that seeks to practice decolonial, gender-emancipatory, and economically nonexploitative alternative structures of law and sovereign authority grounded on a critical refashioning of the best of Indigenous legal and political traditions" (Coulthard 179).

Similarly, Taiaiake Alfred and Jeff Corntassel have argued for decolonization to occur outside any colonial institution, with a focus on the level of the individual and the community. They write that "we will begin to realize decolonization in a real way when we begin to achieve the re-strengthening of our peoples as individuals so that these spaces can be occupied by decolonized people living authentic lives", and that decolonization "lies in our relationships with our land, relatives, language and ceremonial life" (605). However, perhaps even this requires some privilege which the Métis are not afforded. What can the Métis do when they do not have ownership of their homeland and the federal government denies their responsibility to the Métis? Can you blame the Métis for turning to the Canadian legal system in the *MMF* case to achieve reparations for stolen land? Or for turning to the courts in *Daniels* to simply be able to have a seat the table in Ottawa alongside their First-Nations and Inuit brothers and sisters?

Concerning the *Daniels* question, some scholars have argued that it is impossible to ignore the colonial history contained within section 91(24), as the Crown has asserted sovereignty over every aspect of Indigenous peoples lives and Indigenous people's lands under this provision (Stevenson 302-306). As Stevenson points out, section 91(24) has come to characterize much of the Crown-Aboriginal relations today (302-306). It has been used to enact legislation such as the Indian Act, which has a long history of attempting to control and assimilate Indigenous peoples[202]. Many Métis individuals today worry that being included under section 91(24) and thus under federal jurisdiction will translate into Indian Act-like oppression (Adese 18).

Métis legal scholars have also wondered how this section characterizes Indigenous-Crown relationships. Larry Chartrand has suggested that by bringing this action forward, the plaintiffs have stated that they are willing to give up their self-determination to have the federal government exercise its unilateral governance over the Métis (182). He adds that giving the federal government the ability to legislate unilaterally over Indigenous peoples is itself colonial thinking (Chartrand 185).

Similarly, I am skeptical of this decision's emancipatory or decolonizing potential for the Métis, for the simple reason that the Daniels decision pays tribute to the colonizers, further embedding the Métis in a "colonizer's model of the world", to borrow Blaut's words. Green writes that "the denial of Canada's origins in colonial enterprises prevents scholars and legislators from grappling with the consequences of that initial relationship" (par. 19). As I have demonstrated, my concerns with this decision even before I can begin to look at its potential, are that it does not grapple with or fully acknowledge the consequences of colonialism in Canada, and instead, uses this colonial history as a foundation from which to build a modern court decision that will surely shape the future of the Métis relations with Canada. Smith writes that "history is not important for Indigenous peoples because a thousand accounts of the 'truth' will not alter the 'fact' that Indigenous peoples are still marginal and do not possess the power to transform history into justice" (34). I wonder when our legal system will begin to tell better histories and whether this will aide in providing true redress and justice for Indigenous nations seeking to better themselves, such as the Métis nation.

References

Adese, Jennifer. "A Tale of Two Constitutions: Métis Nationhood and Section 35's Impact on Interpretations of Daniels." *TOPIA: Canadian Journal of Cultural Studies*, vol. 36, 2016, pp. 7–19. topia.journals.yorku.ca/index.php/topia/article/view/40395/36495.
Alfred, Taiaiake and Corntassel, Jeff. "Being Indigenous: Resurgences against Contemporary Colonialism." *Government and Opposition*, vol. 40, Issue 4, 2005, pp. 597-614. www.corntassel.net/being_indigenous.pdf
Blaut, J.M. *The Colonizer's Model of the World: Geographical Diffusionism and Eurocentric History*. The Guilford Press, 1993.
Borrows, John. *Canada's Indigenous Constitution*. University of Toronto Press, 2010.
Chartrand, Larry. "The Failure of the Daniels Case: Blindly Entrenching a Colonial Legacy." *Alberta Law Review*, vol. 51, 2013, pp. 181–189.
www.albertalawreview.com/index.php/ALR/article/viewFile/63/63.
Coulthard, Glen Sean. *Red Skins, White Masks*. University of Minnesota Press, 2014.
The Constitution Act, 1867, 30 & 31 Vict, c 3, 12. The Canadian Legal Information Institute, www.canlii.ca/t/ldsw
Daniels v. Canada, 2013 FC 6, [2013]. The Canadian Legal Information Institute, www.canlii.org/en/ca/fct/doc/2013/2013fc6/2013fc6.html
Daniels v. Canada, 2014 FCA 101, [2014]. The Canadian Legal Information Institute, www.canlii.org/en/ca/fca/doc/2014/2014fca101/2014fca101.html
Daniels v. Canada, 2016 SC 12, [2016]. Lexum, https://scc-csc.lexum.com/scc-csc/scc-csc/en/item/15858/index.do
Gaudry, Adam, and Chris Andersen. "Daniels v. Canada: Racialized Legacies, Settler Self-Indigenization and the Denial of Indigenous Peoplehood." *TOPIA: Canadian Journal of Cultural Studies*, vol. 36, 2016, pp. 19–30. topia.journals.yorku.ca/index.php/topia/article/download/40396/36496.
Green, Joyce A. "Towards a Détente with History: Confronting Canada's Colonial Legacy." Reprinted with permission of the author from International Journal of Canadian Studies 12, Fall 1995. sisis.nativeweb.org/clark/detente.html
Indian Act, R.S.C. 1985, c.1-6. The Canadian Legal Information Institute, www.canlii.ca/t/7vhk
Jennings, Francis. *The Invasion of America: Indians, Colonialism, and the Cant of Conquest*. University of North Carolina Press, 1976.
LaRocque, Emma. *When the Other Is Me: Native Resistance Discourse 1850-1990*. University of Manitoba Press, 2010.
Macdougall, Brenda. "The Power of Legal and Historical Fiction(s): The Daniels Decision and the Enduring Influence of Colonial Ideology." *International Indigenous Policy Journal*, vol. 7, no. 3, July 2016, pp. 1–6. ir.lib.uwo.ca/cgi/viewcontent.cgi?article=1323&context=iipj
The Manitoba Act, c. 3, 20-27. Library and Archives Canada, www.collectionscanada.gc.ca/confederation/023001-7118-e.html
Manitoba Métis Federation Inc. v. Canada, 2013 SC 14, [2014]. Lexum. scc-csc.lexum.com/scc-csc/scc-csc/en/item/12888/index.do
Miller, Bradley W. "Beguiled By Metaphors: The Living Tree and Originalist Constitutional Interpretation in Canada." *The Canadian Journal of Law and Jurisprudence*, vol. 22, no. 02, 2009, pp. 331–354. papers.ssrn.com/sol3/papers.cfm?abstract_id=1272042
Reference re Same-Sex Marriage, [2004] 3 SCR 698, 2004 SCC 79. Lexum. scc-csc.lexum.com/scc-csc/scc-csc/en/item/2196/index.do

Richard, Kay S. "'Originalist' Values and Constitutional Interpretation." *Harvard Journal of Law and Public Policy*, vol. 19, no. 2, 1995, pp. 335–341. opencommons.uconn.edu/law_papers/93/

"The Indian Act." *Report of the Royal Commission on Aboriginal Peoples*, vol. 1, chap 9, 1996. pp. 234-308. data2.archives.ca/e/e448/e011188230-01.pdf

R. v. Powley, [2003] 2 S.C.R. 207, 2003 SCC 43. Lexum. scc-csc.lexum.com/scc-csc/scc-csc/en/item/2076/index.do

Said, Edward. "Opponents, Audiences, Constituencies and Community" The Politics of Interpretation, edited by W. J. T. Mitchell. University of Chicago Press, 1983.

Smith, Linda Tuhiwai. *Decolonizing Methodologies: Research and Indigenous Peoples.* Zed Publishing, 1999.

Stevenson, Mark L. "Métis Aboriginal Rights and the 'Core of Indianess.'" *Saskatchewan Law Review*, vol. 67, 2004, pp. 301–313.

Vowel, Chelsea, and Darryl Leroux. "White Settler Antipathy and the Daniels Decision." *TOPIA: Canadian Journal of Cultural Studies*, vol. 36, 2016, pp. 30–42. topia.journals.yorku.ca/index.php/topia/article/view/40397.

notes

[200] see *Daniels* FC 92, 208, 291, 297-301, 310, 413 for example.

[201] See Francis Jennings' Chapter 5 where Jennings destroys the myth that "Indians" were savage and therefore, unable to properly use the land; a myth invented by the colonizer for its own benefit.

[202] see Chapter 9 of the Royal Commission on Aboriginal Peoples Report titled "The Indian Act" for a detailed history of Indigenous peoples' experiences with the Indian Act.

Chapter Thirty-Four

Indigenous Schools in Brazil and Canada

A Call to Action for Sovereignty

Eduardo Vergolino

Introduction

There are more similarities between Brazil and Canada than some people would believe. First Nations have in Brazil and Canada the same opportunity to develop their own schools and manage most of them by the community and for the community. However, the government has a crucial role in this play of the schooling process in First Nations communities in Brazil and Canada. The present paper is a call to action to let the schools in First Nations community be free to develop their own schooling process. The idea of submitting all the children in the same structure of schooling based on western pedagogies and curriculum does not represent the holistic perspective of First Nations knowledge and pedagogy. The holistic perspective that embraces the First Nations knowledge is attached to land, family, mother nature and many other aspects that do not fit inside a western schooling process and it is substantial to believe that we need an alternative schooling process to congregate the two ways of seeing the world. Let us be free is a call to action to change the schooling process inside the First Nations schools in Brazil and Canada, which follow the same western-capitalistic-pedagogy based in results more than looking to the individual as an individual full of subjectivity. The school should be the centre of recognition of differences and not a government instrument of unification and universalization of subjects' individualities. We do believe it is time to create and think a First Nation Schooling Process autonomous and independent.

Is it possible to do it another way?

This paper views two realities that may be different in many aspects, but at the same time when approaching the Indigenous issues, it looks very similar regarding the Educational challenges that both countries must deal with and create ways to respect and give opportunities to the Indigenous people. Brazil and Canada, regarding the educational process, have a lot in common and a lot of differences in the educational process that Indigenous people must undergo in their communities. Although there is visible progress in the educational system, Indigenous people are still working hard to get their schools indigenized for themselves. Kerr (2014) points out that epistemic dominance is an important determinant to limit the Indigenous perspectives in the Eurocentric educational spaces. Schools are the reproduction of the mainstream society inside the community because, in many ways, the school reproduces the aspects of education that Indigenous people fight against. What I would like to discuss and call the attention to, in this paper, is the idea of letting the Indigenous people be free to develop their own educational system which will look on behalf of the traditional knowledge and specific pedagogies in a way that will correspond better to their wishes. "Recognizing and affirming that the Canadian Indigenous experience embodies emotive, cultural, spiritual, traditional, and language-based dimensions may be a crucial step for school and classroom leaders in the provision of such learning opportunities" (Deer, 2015, p. 39). We must think a school system based on Indigenous Perspectives of Knowledge where it will be based on the specificity of each community and, not in a universal framework forced by non-Indigenous governments. First, we must agree that Indigenous people have an Educational System, which for hundreds of years, millenniums, from immemorial times, their knowledge has been passed on by individuals in a way which until today still is being taught in various places and communities, even in schools.

Second, we must agree that the pedagogy used by Indigenous people for centuries was not based on placing the knowledge in a framework divided by age, time, grades, or any other subdivision used by school systems today. As Goulet (2014) points out, "A compassionate and respectful approach is a prerequisite to teaching students who have direct experience with the demoralizing and destructive effects of racism and colonization" (p. 86). Traditional knowledge was taught in life, based on the life experience. This is how it use to be and how it is still being taught, however, inside the schools, this way to approach knowledge is becoming more difficult to see nowadays. Brazil and Canada have the same challenge: How to create an Educational System that respects and acknowledges the Traditional Knowledge of Indigenous people inside schools? In my opinion, it is time to think in another way. Condensing the Traditional Knowledge to fit inside the classroom, inside the books, inside 45 (forty-five) minutes, units, grades, assignments and so on, it is not the proper way to teach contents based in life experience, land-based knowledge which brings with itself the land-based education as a contrast of the mainstream educational process.

Schooling Process in Brazil and Canada

The schooling process in Brazil and Canada are very similar. Schools in both countries follow the same Western framework of education where knowledge is compressed in "boxes" to be taught inside the classroom by teachers. Freire (1998) points out, "It's my good sense in the first place that leads me to suspect that the school, which is the space in which both teachers and students are the subjects of education, cannot abstract itself from the sociocultural and economic conditions of its students, their families, and their communities" (p. 42). Both countries struggle in regarding the participation of Elders, community, and family inside the school because the idea of teachers as the holders of knowledge are the same. "In Aboriginal communities and educational contexts, we share the value of taking guidance and learning from elders who are Aboriginal knowledge holders." (Newhouse, 2011, p. 161) There are many difficulties to insert the Elders in the schools because there is no recognition by the government of their wisdom and knowledge.

> Elders have a special value within the discipline of Native Studies, as keepers or holders of the traditional, indigenous, and local knowledges that concern us. Elders are highly respected Aboriginal individuals, usually of an advanced age, who may have knowledge of life on the land, of ancient stories, of aspects of society such as law, decision making, and clan systems; they may also be respected for their knowledge of how to maintain the core values of their people in contemporary times (Kulchyski, 2000, p. 19)

Indigenous people when approaching the schooling process suffer similar problems like racism, prejudice, and negligence. Governments do not accept the Traditional Knowledge of communities, and without this recognition, it is almost impossible to indigenize the schools and to break the process of teaching. To teach using Indingenous pedagogies it is necessary to recognize the Traditional Knowledge as valid and worthy to be taught inside the school system. Brazil and Canada without accepting the TK as a key point of the educational system, lack the possibility of indigenizing schools and creating a safe and recognizable space in the community, with teachers, and students. Although the Indigenous schools have the right to be increasing the TK participation in the curriculum, schools are still struggling to change this reality inside the classroom. To think critically to create a space where TK will be part of the content inside the school is a challenge for teachers, principals, and the government to open space for knowledge that for a long time has been excluded and oppressed by the westernized idea of the rational logic of knowledge.

Thinking Critically

There is a necessity to think critically regarding the Indigenous schools and the prospects that those schools must change their curriculum, and their system to become spaces that reflect their cultural specificities and knowledge inside the classrooms. To think about Indigenous schools critically is necessary to understand that there is an urgent call[203] to respect the traditional ways of knowing and Indigenous pedagogy as in opposition to Eurocentric perspectives.

Eurocentric approaches inside the schools usually force teachers and students to think based on rational logic which incorporates the European epistemology and rejects the Indigenous knowledge as a less important content to be taught inside the classroom.

> State sovereignty depends on the fabrication of falsehoods that exclude the indigenous voice. Ignorance and racism are the founding principles of the colonial state, and concepts of indigenous sovereignty that don't challenge these principles, in fact, serve to perpetuate them (Alfred, 2009, p. 83)

States do not recognize the sovereignty of Indigenous people regarding their own education, which can be seen in legislation and the school's curriculum across Canada and Brazil. Nevertheless, there is a necessity to incorporate Indigenous content in a manner that increases the participation of Traditional Knowledge inside the schools to create spaces of recognition. Even though self-government has come to the Indigenous schools, it doesn't reflect sovereignty to create new standards of education because there are several rules imposed by the government to maintain indigenous schools tied up to a colonial mentality.

Self-Government or Colonization

One of the various issues and challenges that draw upon my attention in both countries, and I believe is worthy to mention here, is the Government relationship with Indigenous people regarding the manner that Indigenous schools are managed. According to Alfred, "There is a fine line to walk between playing the system and being played, and leaders must be concerned with achieving balance in their political lives" (2009, p. 103). Indigenous people obtained, after years of struggle, the opportunity to be able to develop their own schools, however, up till now there are various aspects of the Educational Legislation that tie schools to a model of education that does not correspond to what Indigenous people are looking for in various aspects. To mention just one specific challenge, the pedagogy and ways of teaching that Indigenous people are looking for respects the individuality and the life experience in a perspective that pedagogies deriving from Eurocentric models are most of the times ignoring, which is the Indigenous perspectives. Indigenous pedagogy is intrinsically related to land and community to the extent that goes beyond the classroom and its encapsulated contents. It is important to note that even though the schools are managed by Indigenous people there are in most cases no space for schools to change their realities and change the curriculum framework forced by governments which follow the Eurocentric model of education. The government creates a false image that is impossible for Indigenous schools to apply to their specific customs of knowing, teaching, and learning, however, the laws which those schools are obligated to follow is based and created by non-Indigenous people who are in power. On this point, I do agree with Paulo Freire when he believes that, at this point there is no education, but only domestication (1998, p. 37). What the government is looking for is the domestication of Indigenous knowledge in a Eurocentric framework giving the management of schools to indigenous people as a false image of letting the community run their schools but at the same time not opening spaces and opportunities for real change in the schools' systems. The curriculum, funding, legislation, and instruction planning still being forced by the government which has the power to impose the rules in every school.

Pedagogies

First Nations have different pedagogies to teach their knowledge to younger generations. One of the most important aspects of pedagogies utilized by First Nations in both countries is the intrinsic connection to the land. Land plays a significant role in several Indigenous communities around the world and it is not different in Brazil and Canada. The connection to the land is more than only a place to live, this connection is the history, the identity embedded in the land where our ancestors walked and lived for immemorial times. As Basso (1996) points out regarding the Apaches, "The people's sense of place, their sense of their tribal past, and their vibrant sense of themselves are inseparably intertwined" (p. 35). Indigenous perspectives of pedagogies and ways of teaching are the contraposition of western pedagogy based on teachers and the curriculum.

> Children are taught about self-confidence, risk-taking, innovation, and experience so that the community continues to grow in effectiveness and efficiency. Growth for its own sake is not valued. From an early age, children are taught to "think for yourself and act for others." This approach creates respect for others that western society has interpreted as non-competitiveness. (Wuttunee, 2004, p. 23)

In Brazil, Indigenous teachers keep teaching in westernized methods not because they like them, but because the government does not tolerate and accept the Indigenous idea of teaching while you live the experience in your own life. It is not acceptable for a western model of education the pedagogy where the child is the focal agent, the one who will build his or her own knowledge from the living experience. When Briggs (1998) talks about Chubby Maata, a three-year-old girl, the idea of a pedagogy that contradicts the westernized idea is presented.

> As far as she can see, she is free to make her own decisions and many of her own discoveries, weighing the far-from-simple variables – the benefits and the costs – as well as she can. Her mother and uncle have modelled for her a "responsible" mode of thinking, and the correlations that they suggest will probably rattle her baby complacency a little. In these interactions, as in many others, that is their contribution to her growth (Briggs, 1998, p. 86)

In Brazil and Canada, there is no space at First Nations schools for pedagogies that focus on children life experience. The westernized (scientific) pedagogies are closed to the idea of bringing life experience as knowledge and letting the children be free to learn. "Thus, a strong element of the socialization of children is built around family and extended family relationships, and around sharing and respect" (Battiste & Henderson, 2000, p. 50). To be free to learn goes against the whole logic of school systems in both countries and it is not different when approaching First Nations schools, even though they have the right to increase and use their traditional ways of teaching and learning.[204]

Perspectives

It is important to recognize that Indigenous perspectives on education open spaces to increase the participation of the families, community, and environment in the process of creating schools safe to children. "The exploration of Aboriginal perspectives may provide a complete picture of Aboriginal culture and the peoples and histories that these perspectives represent" (Deer, 2014). The perspective in focus belongs to an idea of education that surpasses the closed mindset of the Eurocentric model. Education goes beyond the relationship of contents between teacher-student and approximates the entire world of the individual's subjectivity to an environment where the subjects are seen in their totality. "Traditional Native education reflected 'all of life', that is, every element of their cultural lifestyle was incorporated into the teaching and learning process" (Friesen & Friesen, 2002, p. 77) Indigenous perspectives of education do not comprehend an exclusive way of teaching or of separating the knowledge from the subject as a matter of fragmenting the knowledge to distribute inside a framework which deviates the indigenous students from their own culture. A consequence of creating gaps of recognition, the different perspectives play a crucial role in the educational system when approaching Indigenous students. Battiste (2000) points out that, "For most Aboriginal students, the realization of their invisibility is similar to looking into a still lake and not seeing their images. They become alien in their own eyes, unable to recognize themselves in the reflections and shadows of the world" (p. 59). It is a crucial point the emergence of Traditional Knowledge inside the schools in a respectful way to recognize and include the perspectives and pedagogies associated with their specific way of understanding the world without taking away their possibility to comprehend the differences. "Further, they need to be able to think and act critically, anti-colonially and honourably from an Indigenous perspective. They are the ones that will carry on our responsibility in building resurgence" (Simpson, 2011, p. 127). There is a strong effort from Indigenous communities to increase or adopt their perspectives in the Educational process in Brazil and Canada, even though the legislation in both countries still are the main barrier for the change.

Conclusion

What we can conclude from the schooling process in Brazil and Canada regarding Indigenous communities is that there is enormous work to be done. A call to action for sovereignty of the Indigenous people to create and develop their own schooling system is vital to endeavour for recognition and stop the universalism of knowledge that western perspective forces on everyone.

> A key component of nationhood is a people's idea of themselves, their imaginings of who they are. The ongoing expression of a tribal voice, through imagination, language and literature, contributes to keeping sovereignty alive in the citizens of a nation and gives sovereignty a meaning that is defined within the tribe rather than by external sources. (Eigenbrod, 2005, p. 36)

What I mean when I say that we must do another way, is that we must open our minds to an epistemology, a knowledge, and a culture that claims to have their own ways of knowing, being recognized and approached inside the classrooms around Brazil and Canada. We must stop thinking that incorporating stories into kindergarten books is enough. We must decide to push the government away and create an original school based on Indigenous ways of knowing and recognizing all the cultural values, epistemologies, and methodologies of teaching and learning incorporated in Traditional Knowledge. We must agree that Indigenous people are sovereign people and they have the right to decide how the schools should be, and what contents the children should learn. This, in the end, is a call to action for sovereignty for the Indigenous people to run their own schools in the way they decide they should be run.

References

Alfred, T. (2009). *Peace, Power, Righteousness: An Indigenous Manifesto*. Don Mills: Oxford University Press.
Basso, K. H. (1996). *Wisdom Sits in Places: Landscape and Language Among the Western Apache*. Albuquerque: university of New Mexico Press.
Battiste, M. (2000). *Reclaiming Indigenous Voice and Vision*. Vancouver: UBC Press.
Battiste, M., & Henderson, J. Y. (2000). *Protecting Indigenous Knowledge and Heritage: A Global Challenge*. Saskatoon: Purich Publishing Ltd.
Briggs, J. L. (1998). *Inuit Morality Play: the emotional education of a three-year-old*. New Haven: Yale University Press.
Deer, F. (2014). The Institutional and Community Capacity for Aboriginal Education: A Case Study. *In Education*, 3-16.
Deer, F. (2015). Indigenous Rights in Canada: Implications for Leadership in Education. *Antistasis*, 37-40.
Eigenbrod, R. (2005). *Travelling Knowledges: Positioning the Im/Migrant reader of Aboriginal Literatures in Canada*. Winnipeg: University of Manitoba Press.
Freire, P. (1998). *Pedagogy of freedom: ethics, democracy, and courge*. Lanham: Rowman & Littlefield.
Friesen, J. W., & Friesen, V. L. (2002). *Aboriginal Education in Canada: A Plea for Integration*. Calgary: Detselig Enterprises Ltd.
Goulet, L. &. (2014). *Teaching each other: nehinuw concepts and indigenous pedagogies*. Vancouver: UBC Press.

Kerr, J. (2014). Western Epistemic Dominance and Colonial Structures: Considerations for Thought and Practice in Programs of Teacher Education. *Decolonization: Indigeneity, Education & Society*, 83-104.

Kulchyski, P. (2000). *Expressions in Canadian Native Studies.* Saskatchewan: Unversity of Saskatchewan Extension Press.

Markides, J., & Forsythe, L. (2018). *Looking Back and Living Forward: Indigenous Research Rising Up.* Boston: Brill Sense.

Newhouse, D. R. (2011). *Hidden in Plain Sight: Contributions of Aboriginal Peoples to Canadian Identity and Culture.* London: University of Toronto Press. Vol. 2.

Simpson, L. (2011). *Dancing on Our Turtle's Back: Stories of Nishnaabeg Re-creation, Resurgence and a New Emergence.* Winnipeg: ARP Books.

Wuttunee, W. (2004). *Living Rhythms: lessons in aboriginal economic resilience and vision.* London: McGill-Queen's University Press.

notes

[203] See more in the Truth and Reconciliation Commission Report: Call to Action.

[204] In Brazil, the National Education Law (Lei de Diretrizes e Bases da Educação, 1996) asserts that Indigenous Schools have the right to be different and create their own curriculum based on their own knowledge and tradition. In Canada, the Truth and Reconciliation Commission Report: Call to Action, asserts that Education is a priority on Indigenous education and the Traditional Knowledge should be incorporated in schools across Canada.

Chapter Thirty-Five

Indigenous Self-government, Land Management and Taxation Powers

Esteban Vallejo-Toledo*

Most literature on Indigenous self-government presents this concept as a means to: (1) protect distinctive institutions and collective identities;[205] (2) maintain customary ways of life;[206] or (3) dismantle colonial control;[207]. Considering in a social context: (1) the median income of 81% of Indigenous reserves is below $22,133;[208] (2) the deficit for housing and infrastructure is higher than $8.2 billion;[209] and (3) the deficit for water and wastewater systems exceeds $1 billion;[210], the literature has missed the main goal of Indigenous self-government: contributing to Indigenous development and self-sufficiency, which provide the means to maintain, support and enhance Indigenous cultures, governments and identities.

By examining Indigenous self-government from this alternative perspective, to see it as an opportunity for social well-being is possible. Presenting socio-economic development and self-sufficiency as essential objectives of Indigenous self-government could be another argument to suggest that Canadian law recognizes it as an Aboriginal right, to some extent. In this context, some questions arise. First: what do Indigenous peoples need to achieve development and self-sufficiency by exercising this right? A tentative answer is: they need to be able to manage their territories and revenues. Second: to what extent does Canadian law allow Indigenous peoples to make decisions that could lead to development and self-sufficiency? A possible answer is: Canadian law grants them the possibility to control their territories, resources and revenues to some degree. Third: could that degree of control be sufficient to achieve development and self-sufficiency? No. Institutional factors impede Indigenous peoples from making decisions to benefit from their territories, resources and revenues.

This paper explores in more depth these questions. Before providing some answers, note that the term "Indigenous development" – as used in this paper – not only considers the common socio-economic meaning but also acknowledges a definition proposed in the Seventh Annual World Indigenous Business Forum:

> Indigenous development is the organized effort by Indigenous Peoples to honor, enhance, and restore their well-being while retaining a distinctiveness that is consistent with their ancestral values, aspirations, ways of working, and priorities on behalf of all Future Generations. Their efforts also strive to share a holistic model of livelihood that respects the Creator, the Earth and promotes sustainability now and for the generations to come. [211]

1. Right to Self-Government

To begin, I will analyze why Indigenous development and self-sufficiency are the main aspects of the right to self-government. By virtue of a broad right to self-government, Indigenous communities would have complete authority to: (1) decide their form of government and enact laws; (2) administer justice; (3) define conditions for membership; (4) manage their territories and resources; (5) regulate property use; (6) implement taxes.[212] If Section (35) of the *Constitution Act*, 1982 provides for the recognition of Indigenous peoples' right to self-government, as the Royal Commission on Aboriginal Peoples-RCAP and the Special Committee on Indian Self-Government-SCISG have argued,[213] does it mean that Indigenous communities exercise all these faculties?

Ideally, they would exercise all these faculties; however, Canadian law has not developed an adequate institutional framework to exercise them. Does it mean that the right to self-government is not recognized by Canadian law? No. Canadian law permits, to some extent, exercising authority over such faculties as (3),[214] (4),[215] and (6).[216] Therefore, Canadian law somehow provides for the recognition of the right to self-government. Nevertheless, if the most important objective of the right to self-government is to promote Indigenous development and self-sufficiency, then mere recognition of a collective right is not enough. Recognizing this right must be accompanied by an adequate institutional framework that contributes to achieving Indigenous development and self-sufficiency.

An adequate institutional framework, which is based on rules that lay the groundwork for socio-economic development and self-sufficiency, supports constructive exercise of Indigenous self-government. Thus, the right to self-government cannot be exclusively determined by the capacity to control and exploit resources.[217] This right is determined by an institutional framework that can boost the constructive management of

Indigenous lands and resources. In this context, exercising this right implies changing socio-economic arrangements that prevent Indigenous communities from benefitting from these assets.

2. Right to Self-Government: Structural Disadvantages

To promote Indigenous development and self-sufficiency, the right to self-government should amend the structural disadvantages that limit Indigenous communities' opportunities. These structural disadvantages relate to three aspects of Canada's institutional framework, specifically: inconvenient location of Indigenous reserves, problematic regulations, and dependency on unclear funding mechanisms.

First, most reserves are located in areas that prevent them from integrating into regional economic networks. This situation has resulted in small populations[218] and small-scale business initiatives. Second, due to a problematic set of rules, Indigenous people struggle to make a living on reserves because: (1) there is lack of certainty about the scope of Indigenous people's customary property rights;[219] (2) access to capital is limited because reserve lands cannot support loans;[220] (3) communities cannot completely manage their territories and resources because the Crown holds title to reserve lands; (4) intricate regulations force them to obtain a variety of permits, making economic activities more complex than elsewhere in Canada. Third, Indigenous communities depend on a centralized, unclear and insufficient system of transfer payments operated by Indian and Northern Affairs Canada-INAC. This system's purpose is to ensure that Indigenous communities can provide public services. This funding system is unclear because it does not operate according to homogenous criteria and formulae.[221] It is insufficient because the resources allocated do not provide coverage for services that match the standards of services provided to non-Indigenous people.[222]

An adequate institutional framework can contribute to supporting the right to self-government to correct structural disadvantages that affect Indigenous communities. Through bolstering Indigenous development and self-sufficiency, this institutional framework would benefit communities that lack access to abundant natural resources or privileged locations. The next section explores both objectives of the right to self-government.

3. Indigenous Development and Self-Sufficiency

If Indigenous development and self-sufficiency are the right to self-government's objectives, it is necessary to provide details about these objectives. Both objectives have traditionally been proposed from an economic perspective highlighting three aspects: (1) control of land and natural resources, (2) free exploitation of those assets, (3) regulation of economic activities related to them. This traditional understanding of development and self-sufficiency has largely remained uncontested, even by authors who advocate for institutions compatible with Indigenous traditions, like Alfred.[223] Defining Indigenous development and self-sufficiency from this perspective means accepting notions incompatible with Indigenous views. The three aspects that sustain this understanding are not only associated with the traditional notion of sovereignty, but also with with "the ideas of capitalistic profit and environmental degradation, which are criticized by Indigenous communities.

Is there another alternative to explain Indigenous development and self-sufficiency? These two objectives of the right to self-government can be explained in a way that reconciles Indigenous communities' needs for material progress and collective well-being. Hence, Indigenous development and self-sufficiency imply a balance between economic progress, cultural preservation, social equality, and environmental protection. Indigenous development and self-sufficiency combine the possibility of preserving traditional means of subsistence, using new ways of production, and exploring alternative economic activities. Consequently, the ultimate goal for Indigenous communities would be to become self-sustaining by preserving their distinctive heritage and taking care of the land.

With this in mind, what are the characteristics of an adequate institutional framework that allows Indigenous communities to exercise their right to self-government to achieve socio-economic development and self-sufficiency? An adequate institutional framework is essential for the right to self-government because it creates wealth and is supported by the wealth it creates.[224] An adequate institutional framework is a set of rules that: (1) promotes social structures that favour Indigenous communities' right to self-government; (2) contributes to integration of reserves in regional and national systems of development; (3) implements policies that amend social and structural disadvantages created by inadequate policies; (4) guarantees individual and collective property rights; (5) enables Indigenous people to manage their lands and resources; (6) supports them in making decisions according to their values; and (7) facilitates and respects their decision-making processes. From these aspects, it is possible to assert that the mere recognition of the right to self-government is not constructive enough because self-government must be institutionally created and structurally supported. Therefore, if an institutional framework promotes the right to self-government according to these criteria, it can lead to Indigenous development and self-sufficiency.

In the context of this institutional framework, it is possible to determine how Indigenous communities can constructively exercise their right to self-government to achieve development and self-sufficiency by: (1) making decisions about their internal and external affairs; (2) adopting rules to solve the challenges of self-government; (3) opting for specific development policies that respect their culture.[225] As a consequence, a constructive exercise of the right to self-government would lead Indigenous communities to make decisions to ameliorate their situations at local, regional and national scales.

If we understand Indigenous development as the outcome of the right to self-government within an adequate institutional framework, then we cannot support the view that development emerges from policies tailored to local conditions without considering a national plan.[226] It is true that Indigenous communities must rely on their own capacities and assets; however, they cannot develop by exercising self-governance without taking into account the context in which they operate.[227] Indigenous communities are not only political entities; they are economic actors who, unfortunately, have been deprived of development opportunities by an inadequate institutional framework. Suggesting that reserves should not participate in a regional and national system of governance and economic interaction could displace them even more. In contrast, the exercise of the right to self-government within an adequate institutional framework can contribute to building local productive capacity to reduce Indigenous communities' economic dependence.

Before continuing to the next section, what is the connection between Indigenous development and self-sufficiency with land and resources? Land and resources are two of the most valuable assets Indigenous communities have. Both are the main focus for production because they provide the means for economic and cultural practices. The greater the possibilities to manage their lands and resources, the more development opportunities Indigenous communities will have. To reduce Indigenous dependence on government transfers, they must be able to manage their land in ways that promote production, generate revenue and facilitate access to funding. Access and ownership of land and resources are an indispensable first step to Indigenous development and self-sufficiency; however, this step alone is not enough. To achieve socio-economic development and become self-sufficient, Indigenous communities need to be allowed to make relevant decisions about their lands and resources. Consequently, Indigenous development and self-sufficiency do not depend on land and natural resources, for both objectives depend on an adequate institutional framework that contributes to a constructive exercise of the right to self-government.

The case of modern treaties illustrates how a better institutional framework can create conditions for an effective right to self-government that facilitates development. Modern treaties define the territories that belong to Indigenous communities. Besides, modern treaties recognize Indigenous governments and detail their territorial jurisdiction, including land-management and taxation. Furthermore, modern treaties promote land and resource-management according to the needs and values of Indigenous communities. Therefore, they provide Indigenous communities with instruments for development and self-sufficiency. Similarly, modern treaties can set the conditions for the regional and national economic integration of Indigenous communities. In brief, modern treaties illustrate why institutions matter for socio-economic development and self-sufficiency.

These sections have proposed a different view of the right to self-government that is grounded in two main objectives: Indigenous development and self-sufficiency. The next sections explain how an appropriate institutional framework contributes to exercising the right to self-government in land-management and taxation.

4. Indigenous Self-Government and Land-Management

Ownership of land and natural resources does not secure development and self-sufficiency by itself. Indigenous development and self-sufficiency are consequences of managing and making significant decisions on both assets. Nowadays, the amount of productive land base available to reserves is still small (3,554,836 ha in 2014),[228] which means that land base available is not enough for housing and production initiatives. Therefore, expanding this land base is imperative for Indigenous governance and land-management.

Until Canada adopts an institutional framework to allow all First-Nations to expand their territories, they will have to administer their 3,554,836 ha (35,548.36 km²) land base by using land-management instruments granted to them: *Indian Act, Framework Agreement on First-Nation Land Management*[229] and *First-Nations Land Management Act*-FNLMA. The *Indian Act* describes in general terms the powers and responsibilities of federal and Indigenous authorities regarding reserve administration. The *Indian* Act does not prescribe a real land-management system for Indigenous communities in Canada because this Act does not deal with the faculties that real land-management requires. Nevertheless, this limitation of the *Indian Act* has been covered by the *Framework Agreement*, FNLMA, and land codes of Indigenous communities.

The First-Nations-land-management was institutionalized by the *Framework Agreement* and the FNLMA. This system recognizes Indigenous governance on aspects like: (1) enactment of land laws and codes; (2) land register; (3) use of on-reserve lands; (4) accountability and responsibilities for land management; (5) matrimonial land regulations; (6) transfer of lands; (7) revenue regulation; (8) resolution of land conflicts; (9) interests in land for community purposes; (10) lease and license regulation; and (11) community consultation.

According to FNLMA, to exercise land-management, Indigenous communities must prepare land codes that are certified by federal authorities, approved by each community, and sanctioned by Indigenous governments and the Minister of Indigenous and Northern Affairs. Until now, 78 First-Nations have ratified their land codes.[230] Land codes present important advantages, for example, the possibility to implement mechanisms to protect customary property rights that are not supported by certificates of possession.[231] This important feature fills gaps created by the lack of recognition to customary rights in the *Indian Act.*[232] In addition, land codes allow communities to reduce the participation of federal authorities in reserve land administration.[233]

Land codes cannot contradict the restriction on any attachment, charge, distress, execution, levy, mortgage, and pledge mentioned in Section 89 (1) of the *Indian Act*. Therefore, Indigenous communities do not have enough access to capital yet; however, the advances made in securing property rights could promote investment and employment.[234]

The land-management system is a positive step towards Indigenous self-government. This system implements an adequate institutional framework that secures property rights, attracts investment, promotes land-management according to each community's values, and amends inefficiencies of the *Indian Act*. Therefore, this land-management system contributes to Indigenous development and self-sufficiency.

5. Indigenous Self-Government and Taxation Powers

Indigenous taxation powers are an alternative to reduce dependency on government funding. The *Indian Act*, the *First-Nations Fiscal Management Act-*FNFMA and the *First-Nations Goods and Services Tax Act-*FNGSTA establish a taxation system that allows Indigenous communities to create local taxes. Sections 83 and 87 of the *Indian Act* contain rules on taxation issues related to Indigenous governments and individuals. While Section 83 grants Indigenous governments authority to apply taxes on land and interests, Section 87 exempts from other taxes (like income taxes) property and interests of Indigenous people and governments, located on reserve or surrendered lands.

In addition, Section 5 (1) (a) of FNFMA authorizes Indigenous governments to enact tax laws on lands, interests in reserve lands, and rights to occupy, possess or use reserve lands. These laws require First-Nations Tax Commission approval. From 2008 to 2018, 1,382 local-revenue laws have been approved.[235]

The FNGSTA completes the Indigenous taxation system. It divides Indigenous communities into two schedules. According to Section 4, Indigenous communities listed in Schedule 1 can impose the First-Nations Goods and Services Tax-FNGST on: (1) taxable supply made on-reserve; (2) personal property brought to reserve lands from a place in Canada; (3) imported taxable supply made on the lands of First-Nations. Since FNGST is administered by the Canada Revenue Agency for Indigenous communities, laws approved under Section 4 require tax agreements. According to Section 23, Indigenous communities listed in Schedule 2 (located in Manitoba, Saskatchewan and Quebec) can enact laws that impose sales taxes within their reserves. These laws cannot be enacted unless parallel provincial laws exist.

Four points summarize the taxation system created by these three Acts: (1) Indigenous communities can create local taxes and impose goods and sales taxes within their reserves; (2) Indigenous' interests and personal property located on reserve lands are exempt; (3) income earned off-reserve is not exempted; (4) corporations' income is not exempted.

There are three main reasons for this taxation system, with the first two mentioned in paragraphs 18, 43 and 70 of *Canadian Pacific Ltd. v. Matsqui Indian Band*.[236] (1) to promote the inherent right to self-government; (2) to contribute to socio-economic development; (3) to reduce dependency on government funding. These reasons suggest that this taxation system could contribute to Indigenous development and self-sufficiency; however, this system is insufficient to support all public services provided by Indigenous governments. For example, in 2016-2017, Indigenous communities that operate under *Indian Act* rules levied just $36 million, and communities that operate under FNFMA rules levied only $50.26 million.[237]

Five structural disadvantages do not allow this system to operate adequately. First, reserves do not have sufficient land bases; therefore, property taxes do not generate sufficient revenue. Second, not enough taxpayers live within reserve lands[238] which means that transactions charging with Indigenous sales taxes are limited and report low revenue. Third, the *Indian Act* and FNFMA do not allow Indigenous governments to levy income taxes and other direct taxes on reserves; however, if that were the case, the amount of revenue would not be significant since the median income of 81% of reserves is below $22,133 per person.[239] Fourth, according to RCAP, some Indigenous people alleged that the exemptions created by Section 87 of the *Indian Act* were less-than-inclusive because they did not benefit corporations.[240] However, the problem is not the lack of exemption; the real problem is that the income tax regulations do not allow taxes paid by corporations to stay within reserves.

What solutions could be implemented? First, creating conditions to allow Indigenous communities to expand land bases and gain access to more productive lands. This would increase local tax bases. Second, as Sanderson suggests, allowing Indigenous people who earn income off reserve to direct their income taxes to their home communities.[241] Third, allowing Indigenous governments to implement different direct, indirect, local and environmental taxes. Fourth allowing income taxes paid by corporations that reside within reserves to stay on reserves.

In brief, the Indigenous taxation system is not a bad one; nevertheless, it has been designed for local governments without the complex problems that Indigenous reserves face every day. Due to structural disadvantages, local and sale taxes implemented do not generate sufficient revenue.

Conclusion

This paper has explored the concept of Indigenous self-government from an alternative perspective that maintains that the notions of Indigenous development and self-sufficiency are essential objectives of this concept. To explain this concept, I have analyzed two main aspects of self-governance: land-management and taxation powers. Doing this has allowed me present information that leads to the conclusion that Canadian law recognizes, to some extent, the right to self-government.

I presented three questions that might not have definite answers in the ongoing national debate; however, I would like to present some succinct answers to conclude:

1. What do Indigenous peoples need to achieve development and self-sufficiency by exercising their right to self-government? They not only need to be able to decide and manage their territories and revenues within an institutional framework that reduces structural disadvantages.

2. To what extent has Canadian law allowed Indigenous people to make decisions that could lead to development and self-sufficiency? Canadian law has granted Indigenous peoples the possibility to manage their territories, resources and revenues to some degree. However, structural disadvantages maintain Indigenous communities as dependent communities.

3. Could the degree of control that has been granted be sufficient to achieve development and self-sufficiency? No. Institutional and structural factors impede Indigenous communities from making decisions to govern over their territories, resources and revenues to achieve Indigenous development and self-sufficiency.

notes

* LL.M candidate, University of Toronto.
** Many thanks to Professor Kerry Wilkins and Glenn Merritt for their feedback.
[205] Menno Boldt & J. Anthony Long, "Tribal Traditions and European-Western Political Ideologies: The Dilemma of Canada's Native Indians" in Menno Boldt & J. Anthony Long eds, *The Quest for Justice: Aboriginal Peoples and Aboriginal Rights* (Toronto: U of T Press, 1985) 333, at 333.
[206] Lorie Graham & Siegried Wiessner, "Indigenous sovereignty, culture, and international human rights" in Eric Cheyfitz, N. Bruce Duthu & Shari M. Huhndorf, Sovereignty, Indigeneity, and the Law (Durham: Duke University Press, 2011) 403, at 410.
[207] Darlene Johnston, *The Quest of the Six Nations Confederacy for Self-Determination* (1986) 44 U.T.Fac. L. Rev. 1, at 32.
[208] Statistics Canada, 2016 Census Profiles Files, online: <http://dc.chass.utoronto.ca.myaccess.library.utoronto.ca/ grid1/2016/main/download_status.cgi?jobid=hKi7w2UfOu>.
[209] Aboriginal Affairs and Northern Development Canada(2013), quoted by: Standing Senate Committee on Aboriginal Peoples, *On-Reserve Housing and Infrastructure: Recommendations for Change* (2015), online: <https://sencanada.ca/content/sen/Committee/412/appa/rep/rep12jun15-e.pdf>, at 8.
[210] Aboriginal Affairs and Northern Development Canada (2011), quoted by: *Ibid*.

[211] World Indigenous Business Forum (2016) *WIBF Resolution: Change of the Definition of Indigenous Development*, online: <http://wibf.ca/>.
[212] See: Kirke Kickingbird, "Indian Sovereignty: The American Experience" in Leroy Little Bear, Menno Bold & J. Anthony Long, Pathways to self-Determination: Canadian Indians and the Canadian State (Toronto: U of T Press, 1984), 46 at 49.
[213] Royal Commission on Aboriginal Peoples, Report of the Royal Commission on Aboriginal Peoples, 2:1 (Ottawa: Minister of Supply and Services, 1996), at 212-2013; Special Committee on Indian Self-Government, Indian Self-Government in Canada. (Ottawa: House of Commons, 1983), at 43-44.
[214] Indian Act RSC 2015, c3, s.118, Section 6 [Indian Act].
[215] Indian Act, Section 53; First-Nations Land Management Act SOR 2017-46, Section 6 (1) [FNLMA].
[216] Indian Act, Section 83; FNFMA, Section 5.
[217] See: Jane Hofbauer, Sovereignty in the exercise of the right to self-determination, (Leiden: Brill Nijhoff, 2016), at 78.
[218] 44.2% of First-Nations people lived on reserve in 2016. Statistics Canada, Aboriginal Peoples in Canada: Key Results from the 2016 Census, online (2017) <http://www.statcan.gc.ca/daily-quotidien/171025/dq171025a-eng.htm>
[219] See: Christopher Alcántara, "Privatize reserve lands? No. Improve economic development conditions on Canadian Indian reserves? Yes" (2008) 28: 2 Canadian Journal of Native Studies 421, at 424 [Alcántara, Privatize]; Christopher Alcántara, "Reduce transaction costs? Yes. Strengthen property rights? Maybe: The First-Nations Land Management Act and economic development on Canadian Indian reserves" (2007) 132:3-4 Public Choice 421, at 424. [Alcántara, Reduce]
[220] For specific details on this topic, see Alcántara, Privatize, at 424.
[221] Douglas Sanderson, "Overlapping Consensus, Legislative Reform and the Indian Act" (2014) 39:2 Queen's LJ 511, at 526-527.
[222] Emmanuel Brunet-Jailly, "The Governance and Fiscal Environment of First Nations' Fiscal Intergovernmental Relations in Compartaive Perspectives" (2008), at 7.
[223] See: Taiaiake Alfred, *Peace, Power, Righteousness. An Indigenous Manifesto*, (Don Mills: Oxford University Press, 2009), at 172.
[224] See: Michael Trebilcock & Mariana Prado, *What Makes Poor Countries Poor? Institutional Determinants of Development*, (Cheltenham: Edward Elgar, 2011), at 32-33.
[225] See: Stephen Cornell & Joseph P. Kalt, "Reloading the Dice: Improving the Chances for Economic Development on American Indian Reservations", at 56 and 57, online (2003): <https://www.innovations.harvard.edu/sites/default/files/2003_CORNELL.kalt_JOPNA_reloading.dice_.pdf>.
[226] Dennis Ickes, "Tribal Economic Independence-The Means to Achieve True Self-Determination" (1981) 26 SDL Rev 494 at 527.
[227] See: Cornell & Kalt, *supra* note 21, at 8-10.
[228] Indigenous and Northern Affairs Canada, *Land Base Statistics*, online (2017) <https://www.aadnc-aandc.gc.ca/eng/1359993855530/1359993914323##ft3b>.
[229] Framework Agreement on First-Nation Land Management, online (1996) < http://www.labrc.com/wp-content/uploads/2014/03/Framework-Agreement-Amendment-5.pdf> [Framework Agreement].
[230] First-Nations Lands Advisory Board, *Member Communities*, online (2018) <https://labrc.com/member-communities/>
[231] See: Alcántara, Reduce, *supra* note 15, at 425-427.
[232] *Ibid*.
[233] *Ibid*., at 422.
[234] See: Joseph Quesnel, "A decade of Nisga'a self-government: a positive impact, but no silver bullet" (2012) 31 Inroads: A Journal of Opinion 47 at 48; Fernando M. Aragón, "Do better property rights improve local income?" Evidence from First Nations' treaties" (2015) 116 J Development Ec 43, at 44-46.

[235] First-Nations Tax Commission, e-mail message to author, February 22, 2018.
[236] *Canadian Pacific Ltd. v. Matsqui Indian Band*, [1995] 1 S.C.R. 3.
[237] Canada, First-Nations Tax Commission, *Annual Report 2016/2017*, at 9. Online: <http://sp.fng.ca/fntc/fntcweb/FNTC-AnnualReport-2016_17-ENG-WEB.pdf >.
[238] Cfr. *supra* note 14.
[239] Cfr. *supra* note 4.
[240] Royal Commission on Aboriginal Peoples, Report of the Royal Commission on Aboriginal Peoples, 2:2 (Ottawa: Minister of Supply and Services, 1996), at 810.
[241] Sanderson, *supra* note 17, at 543.

Chapter Thirty-Six

Reconciling Diversity

Acknowledging the Challenges

Paul D. Hansen

More than 250 years after the *Royal Proclamation* pledged to protect "...the several Nations or Tribes of Indians with whom We are connected ...",[242] Indigenous peoples throughout Canada remain burdened by legal orders that negatively affect their culture and personal outcomes. Despite ongoing efforts to redress past wrongs, there is little evidence of tangible progress being made towards reconciling Canada's complex Crown-Indigenous relationship. Differences between Canada's dominant legal order and Indigenous legal traditions, and the lack of viable international laws to protect Indigenous rights exacerbate the problem. The *United Nations Declaration on the Rights of Indigenous Peoples* (UNDRIP), particularly its call for the free prior and informed consent (FPIC) of Indigenous peoples in matters of legislation, resource management, and use of their traditional lands is a conspicuously problematic element of the reconciliation project.

Diversity in Legal Traditions

When exploring Indigenous and non-Indigenous legal traditions one immediately discovers differences that may affect the administration of justice and hence, disadvantage Indigenous litigants. Broadly speaking, Canada's state-centric legal order embraces the principles of legal positivism. Conversely, Indigenous perspectives often echo the much different tenets of natural law. Admittedly, these are generalizations because within every community there exists a wide range of political, and ideological perspectives.[243] Hence, it would be inappropriate to characterize all Canadian jurists as positivists, and equally incorrect to characterize all Indigenous people as adherents of natural law. Nevertheless, common law's reliance on statutes, precedents, and formal procedures and the civil system's focus on statutes and the *Code Civile*, suggests a positivistic orientation, whereas the literature on Indigenous legal traditions more frequently reflects connections to spirituality, moral propositions, and the role of individuals in society.[244]

To some, these philosophical differences may represent impediments to reconciliation. John Borrows, however, disputes that perspective, arguing "...Indigenous laws can be recognized and affirmed in the Canadian context...and justified through Western legal argumentation".[245] In that regard, Borrows believes that different traditions can be reconciled in an environment of legal pluralism that accommodates the cultures of all participants. However, one may reasonably ask how many unique traditions can exist in a single legal order or, in the alternative, how many legal orders can exist in a single country without risking inequality between peoples and regions? Is it reasonable, for example, to believe that the legal traditions of the Anishinabek, Haudenosaunee, and Inuit could be amalgamated a single, legal order, or as proposed by the 1996 Royal Commission on Aboriginal Peoples (RCAP), should self-determination be organized along the lines of 60 leading nations? Finally, how might one reconcile Canada's 'punishment-focused' legal tradition with the Indigenous 'restorative justice' paradigm?

Accommodating diverse legal traditions test courts' ability to balance Indigenous and Western perspectives in arriving at judgments. They must, for example, decide if Indigenous customary norms qualify as laws that can be administered on a consistent basis. They must also determine if laws must be "clothed with legal sanction" to be acknowledged as enforceable.[246] Moreover, they must ask if the legitimacy of a legal system requires the endorsement of a sovereign authority, or the tenets of positivism.[247] Critically, courts must avoid falling into a 'homogeneity trap' that assumes legal or cultural traditions are uniform across Indigenous nations. It would be patently unreasonable to assume congruence of legal orders or governance systems among the hundreds of First Nation, Inuit, and Métis communities located throughout Canada. Borrows makes a compelling case that all legal traditions (Common, Civil, Indigenous) influence one another: none being fully autonomous: each reflecting the history and culture of its proponents.[248] It is through the interaction of Canada's legal orders that Indigenous traditions are able to sustain their influence, notwithstanding the significant power imbalances that permeate the system.[249]

To further complicate equitable adjudication of Indigenous cases, the Supreme Court of Canada in *Mitchell v MNR*, reiterated three colonial-era conditions under which Indigenous customary law may be disregarded altogether.[250] Consequently, although Canada's dominant legal order is anathema to some Indigenous beliefs, it persists as the paradigm most frequently invoked by courts, arguably to the detriment of Indigenous peoples.

International Law

International law provides a framework for interstate relations and, to a lesser extent regulates the relationship between states and their citizenry. Where international law exists, it is universally binding, and may in the case of formal treaties ratified by domestic legislation supersede domestic laws.[251] In that regard, it is important to acknowledge the difference between treaties and declarations, each of which has different effects in law - a distinction that is particularly relevant in the context of the *United Nations Declaration on the Rights of Indigenous Peoples* (UNDRIP) and the dilemma it creates in Canadian political and legal arenas.

International law is universally binding on otherwise independent sovereign states. Its ultimate manifestation is located in the *jus cogens* 'compelling' law concept that forbids states from ignoring or 'contracting out of' fundamental values such as the prohibition of slavery, war-making, or genocide.[252] International treaty law is normally expressed in formal treaties and conventions such as the *United Nations Convention on the Law of the Sea* (UNCLOS) that *inter alia* governs maritime boundaries, rights of access to international and territorial waters, and resource extraction, but is silent on the rights of Indigenous peoples. Less binding than formal treaties (conventions) are declarations, which may be universally endorsed but are not necessarily adopted into law by UN member states. Declarations, even important ones like the *Universal Declaration of Human Rights* (UDHR) are essentially 'aspirational statements' that have little or no force of law despite their political popularity and public support. Such is the case with UNDRIP in the Canadian context.

The *International Court of Justice* (ICJ), also known as the World Court, whose mandate is defined in the *Statute of the International Court of Justice*[253] is the United Nations' principal judicial mechanism. Its remit includes settling legal disputes between states on a wide range of matters, and providing advisory opinions to United Nations departments and agencies. The IJC's decisions are binding and may be enforced through mechanisms including monetary fines, trade restrictions, or formal sanctions.

Importantly, the ICJ is only available to states wishing to bring claims against other states. Consequently, individuals or groups, such as First Nations, Métis, and the Inuit cannot bring their concerns to the ICJ for adjudication. Their issues, unless characterized as crimes against humanity, must be settled by domestic courts or tribunals. One of the best known Canadian examples of the futility of Indigenous appeals to international bodies is described in *The Last Speech of Des-Ka-Heh*, which recounts repeated attempts to prevent the imposition of Dominion and Provincial laws on the Six Nations Haudenosaunee people – attempts that were rebuffed by Ottawa, London, and finally, the League of Nations (Geneva) where despite a year of waiting, literally on its doorstep, no hearing was ever granted.[254]

It can be reasonably argued that international law provides limited protection for the rights of Indigenous peoples, particularly those under Canadian jurisdiction. Moreover, it is apparent that international institutions offer little support for those seeking justice unavailable from domestic legal orders. In that regard, international law can be characterized as caught between the doctrines of Westphalian-style state sovereignty and the cosmopolitan global governance ideal. It seeks to influence inter-state behaviour while being constrained by historic independence principles that are increasingly difficult to rationalize, but nevertheless prevail.[255] As observed by Currie et al, "...international law is not always universal law".[256]

The UNDRIP Dilemma

At first glance, UNDRIP is *prima facie* one of the United Nations' most significant and progressive achievements – arguably equal to the *Universal Declaration of Human Rights* (UDHR) in scope and potential. In part, it affirms Indigenous rights of self-determination, cultural preservation, collective and personal freedom, dignity, land title, and religious practice. The Declaration was adopted by the United Nations General Assembly in December 2007 after a twenty-five-year period of crafting and debate. Canada, along with Australia, New Zealand, and the United States initially objected to the Declaration, arguing, in Canada's case, that its principal requirements were already in place and that some articles might conflict with the adopted *Constitution Act, 1867*.

In 2010, Canadian Prime Minister Stephen Harper removed Canada's objection and pledged to adopt UNDRIP, albeit within Canada's laws and

Constitution. However, no formal process or timeframe was established for its adoption. Consequently, beyond political rhetoric, little tangible progress was made towards implementation. Following his election in 2015, Prime Minister Justin Trudeau directed Indigenous and Northern Affairs Minister Carolyn Bennett to begin the process of implementing UNDRIP as a precursor to Crown-Indigenous reconciliation.[257] However, as with the Harper government, no commitment was made to adopt UNDRIP into Canadian law as written. Rather, in July 2016, Justice Minister Wilson-Raybould, a former Indigenous Chief, declared Canada's intention to implement UNDRIP "meaningfully" in the spirit of reconciliation.[258] Thus, at the time of this writing, UNDRIP remains an aspirational document that has no legal force in Canada and is unlikely to become law in the foreseeable future.

Canada's hesitation to implement the Declaration can be linked to political ideology, constitutionally-defined division of powers between the Federal government and the Provinces, and possible conflicts with section 35 of *Constitution Act, 1982*. Issues relating to a third (Indigenous) order of government, free prior and informed consent (FPIC), and compensation for lands historically taken by Crown agencies or others are particularly sensitive.

The FPIC Challenge

Of UNDRIP's various problematic factors, free, prior, and informed consent (FPIC) which is embodied in six articles (10, 11, 19, 28, 29 and 32), presents the greatest challenge to Canada's extant constitutional and legal orders. FPIC promotes the inherent right of Indigenous people to make decisions, or at least participate in the decision-making process whenever their traditional lands or cultural interests are involved. Hence, FPIC is a cornerstone of the self-determination principle to which Canada has committed and UN Special Rapporteur James Anaya has described as the universal right of people to define and control their own destinies.[259] However, as with the term 'reconciliation', there is debate over FPIC's meaning, limitations, and parameters. For example, would implementation of FPIC into Canadian law give Indigenous groups veto power over proposed legislation, budgetary measures, or major projects like inter-provincial pipelines or national infrastructure projects?

In 2015, the Boreal Leadership Council addressed the FPIC issue as it relates to Canada, and offered the following interpretive guidelines: *'free'* eliminates any opportunity or form of coercion, including any attempts to intimidate, manipulate or otherwise apply force; *'prior'* establishes a timeframe that permits participants sufficient time to appropriately consider any proposed measures and the right to be engaged throughout the evaluation process; and *'informed'* assumes an appropriate understanding of the issues involved and the impact they may have on current and future circumstances.[260] The outstanding issue – the colloquial 'elephant in the room' concerns the definition of 'consent'.

The meaning of 'consent' is clear to most observers, but perhaps less certain in the context of law and politics. Black's Law Dictionary defines 'consent' as "...agreement, approval, or permission as to some act or purpose, esp. given voluntarily by a competent person".[261] Few would disagree with that definition. However, one should not assume that consent, which implies agreement (consensus) between parties, is a reasonable expectation when societies are not homogeneous, or lack shared values and comparable power. As previously observed, there are fundamentally different legal and cultural understandings between Indigenous and non-Indigenous peoples that are underscored by an historical power imbalance that *inter alia* affects achievement of consent.

From the Crown's perspective, UNDRIP's implementation concerns center on the prospect of an Indigenous veto over government decisions made in the national interest. Particularly controversial areas include resource development, environmental protection, and economic growth responsibilities which are allocated to Parliament and provincial legislatures in the *Constitution Act, 1867* sections 91, 92, 92A, 93 and 94.

There are, however, differences of opinion concerning the creation and consequences of an Indigenous veto. Assembly of First Nations (AFN) National Chief Perry Bellegarde argues that the term 'veto' is not included in UNDRIP, and it should not be assumed that the absolute right to reject an law or development proposal would arise through UNDRIP's adoption into Canadian law.[262] UN Special Rapporteur Anaya similarly rejects the assumption that UNDRIP gives Indigenous peoples a veto, arguing instead that the objective is to create a consultative mechanism through which consensus and consent can be achieved.[263] Moreover, in *Haida Nation v British Columbia*, the SCC ruled unequivocally that the legal doctrine of consultation and accommodation "...does not give Aboriginal groups a veto [and] Aboriginal consent is appropriate only in cases of established rights, and then by no means in every case".[264]

Regarding the consequences of an Indigenous veto, Martin Papillon and Thierry Rodon, argue "...the current focus on the veto question obscures...the debate on FPIC [and] the fear of veto [power] ... is simply not borne out by reality".[265] They dismiss arguments that FPIC is a "unilateral, negative, and decontextualized principle" that pits parties against each other in an adversarial rather than cooperative relationship.[266] Rather than adversarial proceedings, they recommend a five point program based on mutual respect and equal standing during the negotiation process.[267] In the Canadian context, they observe that the consultation and consent provisions currently embodied in Canadian law contrast with the UNDRIP FPIC interpretation, leading to costly ambiguity, delayed development of resource-based projects, and increased Indigenous activism.

Indigenous Institutions

UNDRIP Article 32, which declares the right of Indigenous peoples to develop strategies and priorities for development or use of their lands and resources, reinforces the FPIC principle by adding the requirement for state consultation with Indigenous peoples through their own institutions. The principle argument against this requirement cites the absence of a formal Indigenous institution, *i.e.* a third order of government in Canada, with authority to speak on behalf of all Indigenous nations and peoples. The Assembly of First Nations (AFN) purports to speak for all First Nations, but there is no compelling evidence that its decisions reflect broad consensus among First Nations, some of which are politically sophisticated and extremely wealthy while others live in poverty with no effective voice or cohesive governance structure. Moreover, the AFN does not represent Métis or Inuit peoples; thus despite its power and sophistication it cannot claim legitimacy as a national voice for Indigenous peoples located throughout Canada. Norway addressed the challenge of creating a common voice and venue for Indigenous people through creation of a nationally funded Sámi Parliament to represent Indigenous people and negotiate with the Norwegian National Parliament on their behalf. No comparable structure or procedural model exists in Canada, which, it can be argued, features a more complex Indigenous environment than exists in Norway or elsewhere in the World.

It is unlikely that these legally complex, emotive issues will be resolved through negotiations, and equally unlikely that the government will embark on the politically 'explosive' and complex constitutional amendment process to achieve full UNDRIP implementation. This suggests that Canada will, following its traditional dualist approach to international treaties, adopt UNDRIP except for articles that conflict with the constitution or longstanding conventions or are so vaguely crafted as to create confusion and ongoing dissensus. That approach, particularly as it relates to Article 19 and 32, will be an ongoing point of contention with

Indigenous activists and political leaders, further impeding the reconciliation process.

The Path Forward

To some it may appear that Canadian governments have historically tended to treat reconciliation as a project rather than a process -- something that can be done once ... ticked off a political 'to do' list and forgotten. The transactional mindset that underlies that approach reflects a fundamental misunderstanding of Indigenous beliefs and traditional methods, and will not likely be successful. Reconciliation involves more than clearing a task list with inquiries, apologies, and cash. Although those things may be elements of the reconciliation process, they are not, either individually or collectively, complete solutions to the challenges at hand.

As stated by Senator Murray Sinclair (then Chairman of the Indian Residential Schools Truth and Reconciliation Commission (TRC)), reconciliation is a process of healing relationships that requires public truth sharing, apology, and commemoration intended to acknowledge and redress past harms...[268] It is widely acknowledged that reconciliation is an ongoing process that will take years if not generations to ultimately achieve.

The TRC report's ten principles and ninety-four 'calls to action' identify the key steps it associates with achieving reconciliation. Chief among them is implementation of UNDRIP as the framework upon which reconciliation can be built. As previously discussed, however, the prospect of full UNDRIP implementation in Canada is unlikely, despite political promises and passage of a Senate Bill calling for its adoption.

In addition to clearing the government 'reconciliation' check list, which includes implementation of the TRC calls to action, a wholesale revision of the Crown-Indigenous relationship is an essential first step. Canada must move from its colonial mindset, political and legal orders, towards a contemporary version of the nation-to-nation environment that existed at the time of first contact. In current terms, that relationship is referred to as self-determination and governance.

Self-determination is a particularly challenging matter when one considers the geographic distribution, comparative wealth, political sophistication, and cultural diversity of Canada's First Nations, Métis, and Inuit peoples. As noted, to some, that diversity may raise a question of who will speak for the approximately 1.7 million Indigenous peoples located throughout Canada? One might argue that even asking that question is a reflection of colonial thinking, *i.e.* that First Nations must conform to a Eurocentric hierarchical governance model, and that all nations should be treated equally.[269]

On first glance, moving to an environment of Indigenous self-determination and governance may appear to be an insurmountable challenge. However, there is evidence to suggest that self-determination, even if functionally limited at the outset, is possible. For example, the 'Anishinabek Nation', a political organization of forty Ontario First Nations, recently obtained the agreement of twenty-three members to ratify an agreement giving full educational authority to its Indigenous communities. A similar agreement concerning policing powers is in place for the Nishnawbe-Aski Nation – a forty-nine First Nation political organization spread across northern Ontario. Ten other First Nations policing agencies, work cooperatively with the Ontario Provincial Police (OPP) under similar agreements to serve First Nations throughout Ontario. Through these and similar agreements, longstanding jurisdictional debates are replaced with authority being transferred to those closest to and best able to manage the issues – a clear retreat from the paternalism that has characterized the Crown-Indigenous relationship to this point.

There are, however, complex issues still to be resolved. For example, who will have authority to make laws that extend beyond local issues, and how will resources and economies be managed? Critically, how can we assure that everyone enjoys the protections guaranteed by the Canadian Charter of Rights and Freedoms? Or should those even be issues if we recognize First Nations as truly self-governing states? How do we reconcile our punishment-based legal tradition with the Indigenous restorative justice paradigm? Is the maintenance of law and order the exclusive domain of states, or should it be shared with families and communities?

These are not easy questions to resolve, which may contribute to governments favouring a transactional rather than relational approach to Indigenous affairs. It's far easier to show voters the items that have been checked off a 'reconciliation to do list' than it is to conduct the complex, time-consuming work of relationship building. Power sharing or transfer agreements like *Nunavet* and *Algonquin* can take decades to produce – far longer than the tenure of most Provincial or Federal governments.

Conclusion

The principal conclusions arising from this analysis are twofold. First instruments such as UNDRIP, as reviewed in this paper do not necessarily reduce the legal or cultural disadvantages experienced by Indigenous peoples in any material sense: and second, greater accommodation of Indigenous knowledge and traditions in the operation of courts and governmental agencies at all levels has the potential to materially improve the circumstances of Indigenous peoples throughout Canada, with immediate effect. Resolving the reconciliation challenge, however, requires more than legislative and structural adjustments. First and arguably foremost, it requires the courage and political will of all parties to move forward towards an environment based on equality, dignity, and respect for the culture and traditions of the Indigenous and settler peoples of Canada and the potential it holds for all.

notes

[242] The Royal Proclamation of October 7, 1763 RSC 1985. App II, No 1. Although this quote fragment concerns land rights, the Proclamation can also be interpreted to include other protections, including those provided by British laws.

[243] I acknowledge the diversity of First Nations, Inuit, and Métis legal traditions, and mean no disrespect by generalizing their core principles for the purposes of this paper.

[244] John Borrows, Canada's Indigenous Constitution (Toronto: University of Toronto Press, 2011) at 28. [Borrows Constitution]

[245] John Borrows, Drawing Out Law: A Spirit's Guide, (Toronto: University of Toronto Press 2010) at Preface xiv. [Borrows Law]

[246] Borrows Constitution, at 12.

[247] Borrows Constitution, at 12.

[248] Borrows Constitution, at 113.

[249] Borrows Constitution, at 114.

[250] *Mitchell v MNR* 2001 SCC33, [2001] SCR 911, at para 10. "...Aboriginal interests and customary laws were presumed to survive the (British) assertion of sovereignty...unless (1) they were incompatible with the Crown's assertion of sovereignty; (2) they were 'surrendered' voluntarily... or (3) the government extinguished them."

[251] International law may not apply in cases where: parties willingly enter a treaty whose terms are inconsistent with international customary law; where established regional practices (law) contradict international customary law; or if a nation is deemed to be a 'persistent objector' to a specific customary law or convention.

[252] Vienna Convention on the Law of Treaties, 23 May 1969, 1155 UNTS 331, Can TS 1980 No 37, in force 27 January 1980. Article 53 prohibits the enactment of treaties that violate jus cogens norms. Article 64 addresses the application of emerging jus cogens rules on existing treaties. Online: https://treaties.un.org/doc/publication/unts/volume%201155/volume-1155-i-18232-english.pdf.

[253] Charter of the United Nations, 26 June 1945, Can TS 1945 No 7, Articles 92-96, Statute of the International Court of Justice.

[254] Des-Ka-Heh, "The Last Speech of Des-Ka-Heh" in John Borrows *Aboriginal Legal Issues – Cases, Materials and Comments* (Toronto: LexisNexis Canada Inc, 2012) at 43.

[255] Economic globalization and supranational entities such as the United Nations and European Union are increasingly superseding 'unfettered' Westphalian sovereignty and diminishing the traditional concept of 'absolute power'. See: Neil Walker, Essays in European Law (Portland: Hart Publishing, 2006).

[256] John Currie et al, *International Law – Doctrine, Practice, and Theory* 2nd ed (Toronto: Irwin Law Inc, 2014) at 47.

[257] Canada, Office of the Prime Minister, "Minister of Indigenous and Northern Affairs Mandate Letter", Justin Trudeau, (Ottawa: Office of the Prime Minister, 13 November 2015). Online: http://pm.gc.ca.

[258] James Munson, "Ottawa won't adopt UNDRIP directly into Canadian law: Wilson-Raybould", (12 July 2016), *iPolitics* (blog), online: http://ipolitics.ca.

[259] James Anaya, *Indigenous Peoples in International Law* (Oxford: Oxford University Press, 1996) at 81. [Anaya]

[260] Boreal Leadership Council, *Understanding Successful Approaches to Free, Prior and Informed Consent in Canada,* "Part 1: Recent Development and Effective Roles for Government, Industry, and Indigenous Communities", Ginger MacDonald and Gaby Zezulka (Ottawa: Boreal Leadership Council, September 2015) at 8.

[261] *Black's Law Dictionary,* 4th Pocket ed, *sub verbo* "consent".

[262] Gloria Galloway, "Trudeau's promises to aboriginal peoples feared to be unachievable". *The Globe and Mail (22 October 2015.* Online: www.theglobeandmail.com.

[263] Anaya, *supra* note 259, at 16.

[264] *Haida Nation v British Columbia (Minister of Forests)* 2004 SCC 73, [2004] 3 SCR 511 at para 48.

[265] Martin Papillon & Thierry Rodon, "Indigenous Consent and Natural Resource Extraction: Foundations for a Made-in-Canada Approach" (2017) 16 IRPP Insight; Montreal, (Proquest) at 3.

[266] Ibid at 4.

[267] Ibid at 4-5.

[268] Canada, Truth and Reconciliation Commission of Canada, Final Report of the Truth and Reconciliation Commission of Canada, Vol 1: Summary (Toronto: Lorimer Publishers, 2015) at 16.

[269] There are many examples of First Nations working together to maintain peace and promote their interests and well-being. For example, the Mohawk, Oneida, Onondaga, Cayuga, Seneca, and Tuscarora Haudenosaunee Nations, located throughout Ontario and the upper United States, formed the sophisticated Iroquois Confederacy in the 16th century – a political organization that currently represents the interests of more than 25,000 members.

CPSIA information can be obtained
at www.ICGtesting.com
Printed in the USA
BVHW082342210821
614436BV00003B/19